God's Daughters

God's Daughters

Evangelical Women and the Power of Submission

R. MARIE GRIFFITH

UNIVERSITY OF CALIFORNIA PRESS

Berkeley   Los Angeles   London

University of California Press
Berkeley and Los Angeles, California

University of California Press, Ltd.
London, England

©1997 by
The Regents of the University of California

Library of Congress Cataloging-in-Publication Data

Griffith, R. Marie (Ruth Marie), 1967–
    God's Daughters : Evangelical women and the
power of submission / R. Marie Griffith
        p. cm.
    Includes bibliographical references and index.
    ISBN 0-520-20764-5 (cloth : alk. paper)
    1. Women's Aglow Fellowship (Lynnwood,
Wash.) 2. Pentecostal women—United States—
History—20th century. 3. Women's prayer
groups—Christianity—History—20th century.
4. Evangelicalism—United States—History—20th
century I. Title.
BR1644.5.U6G75 1997
267'.43—DC21   97-4931
                                                     CIP

Printed in the United States of America
9 8 7 6 5 4 3 2 1

The paper used in this publication meets the mini-
mum requirements of American National Standard
for Information Sciences—Permanence of Paper for
Printed Library Materials, ANSI Z39.48-1984.

For my parents
Ruth Nannelle Stevenson Griffith
and Charles Russell Griffith, Jr.

Contents

Acknowledgments

This is a study of a female world of religious devotion and the ways in which its participants, charismatic evangelical women in twentieth-century America, talk about prayer and pray together. More precisely, I have examined an interdenominational organization of charismatic Christian worshipers, Women's Aglow Fellowship International, through the group's published literature and through extensive fieldwork, as a case study of broader developments among female participants in contemporary American evangelicalism. Because of the personal nature of many of the narratives recorded here, I have changed the names of all the women I interviewed and altered many identifying details; only in cases of published material do I give full attribution. I am indebted to the numerous Aglow women who graciously welcomed me into their local meetings and their homes, taking time to tell me their stories and answer endless questions to help me understand the role of this network in their lives. I am also grateful to everyone at Aglow headquarters, past and present, who supported my study, granted me access to the archives, and agreed to be interviewed. I must particularly single out Jane Hansen, Maria Lyon, and Kay Rogers for special thanks, and also Rita Bennett, Katie Fortune, and Ruth Gothenquist. Although they will not agree with all aspects of my interpretation, I hope the women of Aglow will sense the respect and care with which I have listened to their stories and attempted to retell them to a wider audience.

This book has benefited from the support of numerous individuals and institutions. I am indebted to the Institute for the Study of American Evangelicals and the Whiting Foundation for funding my research at an early stage. Many friends and colleagues at Harvard University commented on various sections of the project, and I especially want to thank the members of the American Colloquium for their instructive suggestions. William R. Hutchison's warm humor and editorial candor saved me from many textual errors, and I am grateful to him also for urging me to follow my instincts about this project rather than be led by the vagaries of the field. I trust that the vital influence of my mentor, David D. Hall, will be evident not only in the following pages but in future endeavors as well.

A postdoctoral fellowship grant from the Center for the Study of American Religion at Princeton University enabled me to pursue further research in this and related undertakings and to revise the original project. The year I spent there is particularly memorable for the collegiality of the Religion and Culture Workshop and the forging of several new friendships. Many thanks go to Robert Wuthnow for his support of my work and his accessibility during my time at Princeton. I am also grateful to Anita Kline, Al Raboteau, and John Wilson, and to workshop participants for their insightful and challenging comments on a chapter I presented to them. A subsequent Mellon fellowship at Northwestern University allowed me to put the finishing touches on my manuscript, while gaining new colleagues in the Department of Religion and elsewhere.

Others who have reviewed chapters or who have offered useful instruction include Clarissa Atkinson, Rob Baird, Courtney Bender, Courtney Bickel, Edith Blumhofer, Ann Braude, Virginia Brereton, Sarah Coakley, Harvey Cox, Caroline Ford, Rebecca Gould, Philip Joseph, Catherine Kroeger, Alexis McCrossen, Michael McNally, Margaret Poloma, Susan Rose, Vinson Synan, Grant Wacker, R. Stephen Warner, Beth Wenger, and Catherine Wessinger. Margaret Lamberts Bendroth, Lynn Davidman, Cynthia Eller, Pamela Klassen, Robert Orsi, David Watt, and Robert Wuthnow read the entire manuscript and offered valuable critiques. Susan Setta encouraged me at a very early stage and generously shared with me some of her own source materials on Women's Aglow Fellowship. Jim Zeigler, archivist at the Holy Spirit Research Center at Oral Roberts University, has been gracious with his resources, while June McEwen and Charles Lippy gave me the opportunity to present some of this material at the University of Tennessee at Chattanooga. Doug Abrams Arava, my editor at the University of California Press, has offered incisive counsel throughout the revision process, and his assistance, along with that of Gail Hapke, has significantly improved the clarity of the final work.

My husband, Leigh Schmidt, has read and responded to an excessive number of chapter drafts without losing patience, and he has consistently made splendid suggestions for focusing my inquiry and sharpening my prose. Our partnership, enabling vocation and marriage to overlap and energize one another with what I imagine to be rare accord, is an extraordinary gift. Thanks go also to my in-laws, Ann and Roger Schmidt, for their enthusiastic interest in this project and care for its author.

Finally, this work is dedicated to my father and my mother, whose role in shaping my academic and educational pursuits is surely apparent to them. Only I can fully appreciate, however, the extent to which their examples and encouragement have nourished and influenced other areas of my life as well. This project has occasioned fresh realizations of my fortune in having been born to people of such love, generosity, and integrity, and I am profoundly grateful to them both.

Introduction

Prayer is a powerful medium of expression, alliance, and desire.
It invites self-reflection and demands wakefulness. It quickens hope,
rouses individual and collective memory, and implores understanding
from all witnesses, seen and unseen. Family members may pray for the
healing of sick loved ones; children may pray for relief from punishment of misdeeds; religious congregants may pray together for the dead
as well as for the living. Whether they make their petitions in public or
private, those who pray seek comfort, assurance, and courage in the
face of adversity and circumstances seemingly beyond their control.

Countless signs indicate the enduring popularity of prayer in America,
with some commentators noting a renewed interest in prayer even
among those not considered religious in a conventional sense. Recent
Gallup polls report that 90 percent of Americans say they pray to God at
least occasionally, and nearly 60 percent say they consider prayer very effective in situations such as war. While these claims can be neither vali-
dated nor disproven, the commercial success of books about prayer and
related spiritual exercises like meditation gives evidence, if not of devotional constancy, at least of the *will* to pray. Even many medical professionals attest to the usefulness of prayer for human healing. Prayer is indeed popular in late twentieth-century America.

As a tool for communicating the aspirations of hopeful petitioners,
this time-honored act of devotion opens a fascinating gateway into
themes, beliefs, and concerns that have helped shape modern American

culture. Persuaded of the importance of prayer as both an individual and a cultural practice, I began searching some years ago for a way to understand it more thoroughly. At the time, I was attending an Episcopal women's prayer group, not simply as a student researcher or an observer but as an ordinary member. One evening each week, for approximately two hours, between two and ten women from a local parish in eastern Massachusetts met in a basement room to share recent events in our lives and the lives of those near us, read a brief passage of scripture, and pray—sometimes silently, sometimes aloud—for the needs and requests that had been raised within the group. I participated in this prayer group from its first meeting in the summer of 1992 until the late spring of 1993. It was not merely a relief from the stresses of graduate school but one of the most pleasant activities of my week. We were an oddly mixed bunch, composed primarily of theologically liberal feminists but including some very conservative participants as well—a mix that reflected the composition of the church to which we belonged. I was unsure about my own belief in the efficacy of prayer beyond its psychological benefits and was also rather uncomfortable about praying aloud; still, I appreciated the amiability of the group and enjoyed meeting other women in an easygoing religious setting.

One evening, in February of 1993, I half-seriously presented what I assumed to be a fairly minor concern for the group to hear: my search for a new research topic. Trained as a historian of American religion, I told the others I wanted a project that would explore forms of women's prayer. These women were intrigued by such a project and delved zestfully into its possibilities for some time before concluding this lively discussion by praying on my behalf, requesting that I be guided toward the "right" project and blessed with renewed knowledge, understanding, and faith.

"Have you ever heard of Women's Aglow Fellowship?" Deborah, one of the more faithful participants, asked me immediately after the meeting.[1] I responded affirmatively. During my studies of Pentecostalism, I had heard about this group of charismatic ("spirit-filled") women, but I did not know much about it. With obvious enthusiasm, Deborah described the fellowship's origins as a female prayer and mission association and its global outreach, then informed me that she had been actively involved in a local Aglow chapter for several years. Intrigued by her account of the group as an evangelical organization devoted to women in the United States and around the world, I asked her many questions. As it happened, the annual retreat of several regional area fellowships was soon to be held at a nearby hotel. Deborah urged me to attend so that I could assess the fellowship's research potential. She herself would be there and could introduce me to some of the local leaders and members—would I go?

My curiosity piqued, I accepted her invitation. Arriving at the large hotel on a gray day during a bitter cold spell, I scurried into the main entryway and encountered there a bustling, colorful gathering of women in luxurious conference center surroundings. Taken aback at the grandiosity of this event, I surveyed the scene. Elaborate hand-crafted banners, all proclaiming lofty scriptural messages and distinctive slogans from area Aglow chapters, hung throughout the plush lobby as a witness to the many local fellowships in attendance. Glossy promotional posters for recently published books and Bible studies offered by Aglow Publications stood atop long display tables, where these and other items were available for browsing and for purchase. Sign-up sheets and inspirational videos publicizing the upcoming "March for Jesus" were readily at hand, along with coffee mugs, bumper stickers, and sundry trinkets sporting the Aglow logo, "A Network of Caring Women."

Middle-aged women, many attired in floral print dresses and adorned with jewelry, makeup, and vivid nail polish, milled energetically around this ample space, scanning the table exhibits for potential purchases and searching for friends amidst the streaming crowd. Some were black, fewer were Hispanic, most were white. Several women stood out as official greeters, smiling broadly and wearing special Aglow aprons emblazoned with Bible verses as they efficiently ushered newcomers toward the registration desk and oriented the bewildered to their surroundings. Laughter rang out across the lobby, punctuating the contemporary Christian music in the background and elevating the already high level of excitement. When I found Deborah, she introduced me to some of her friends, informing them that I was writing a book on prayer and wanted to see how women in Aglow pray together. They responded enthusiastically, greeting me with warm embraces and joyous outbursts of "Well, praise the Lord!"

The opening worship service started at seven o'clock and went past midnight. Nearly five hundred women were packed into the large conference hall, creating a drama that seemed to mix the ecstatic rhythms of contemporary charismatic worship with the therapeutic language of popular culture. Belting out lively praise songs to Jesus, the women originally appeared rapturous: many danced up and down the aisles, most waved their arms elatedly, and nearly all intoned the name of Jesus or shouted out their love toward heaven. Two hours later, however, more than half of these same women were sobbing heartbrokenly and seemed racked with agony as the evening speaker called them to focus on the pain in their lives and to pray for healing. Finally, the tears gave way to renewed joy, as participants found themselves miraculously released from their sorrow, many testifying aloud to experiences of restoration. I sat near the back of the room, raptly scribbling detailed notes on these successive waves of emotion. I felt as if I had ventured unwittingly into a numinous world, one in which miracles were still believed to take place, prayers answered, and healings divinely enacted. My mind spun with questions: Who were these women and what did they think they were doing? What impact did their prayers and embraces have on one another? What would happen to them after they left this place and returned home?

This Aglow meeting, my first of many, left me astonished. Here I heard for the first time a Christian charismatic speak publicly and in graphic terms about her own sexual abuse; here I first witnessed hundreds of women mourn aloud their lost childhood and beseech prayer from others who claimed similarly wrenching experiences. My pretense to scholarly detachment was shaken by the suffering I observed, and I listened with awe as two elderly women sitting near me at the back of the room told one another about their own experiences of sexual abuse, then held each other like mothers cradling their children. I thought of the cultural stereotypes commonly depicting conservative Christian women as meek followers of the men who run their churches, puppets duped by the leaders of the religious right, or, more threateningly, militant antifeminists in the tradition of Phyllis Schlafly and Beverly LaHaye. In this context, such images seemed ludicrous.[2] Rather, it appeared far truer to think of these women as survivors, in the therapeutic sense, as women who love and nurture one another and, in the phrase of noted feminist theologian Nelle Morton, "hear each other to speech."[3] Although my initial perceptions would evolve and shift over time, the poignancy of these prayers, their sorrow and their power, moved me profoundly and drew me in.

Over the next few weeks I began my field research in earnest, traveling frequently to Aglow chapters in the northeastern United States and making contact with numerous women in those chapters. Early on, I observed that these primarily middle-aged women had apparently rejected feminism in favor of a theology enjoining female submission to male authority, yet at the same time they denounced the abuses of male power and professed to experience what they variously called deliverance, liberation, and empowerment through prayer. Such a pattern for female devotion has manifold historical precedents, yet its complex juxtapositions have remained largely invisible in accounts of American evangelicals in the latter decades of the twentieth century.[4] Historical treatments of women's piety have tended to present a flattened version of modern religious nonfeminists, as if choosing to believe in "absolutes" of morality, theology, and gender roles in today's world renders them unworthy of the careful analysis ordinarily accorded women from the past who professed similar religious certainty. It seemed to me that by fully scrutinizing the meanings of gender, identity, and power within the Aglow organization, I could help to bring the broader mainstream evangelical culture in America, especially its female participants, into clearer focus.[5]

As my exploration progressed, other questions emerged. Because the research method was open-ended, I let the themes emphasized by the women themselves expand my inquiry. Thus the theme of female submission, though still significant, receded somewhat in importance as motifs more often evoked in women's narratives—intimacy, healing, and transformation, for instance—moved to the center. As I gradually abandoned the stereotypes with which I had initially approached the organization, I became better able to hear the women's stories and prayers on multiple levels and to understand the power of these accounts to rework female religious identities. The intricate blending of the themes from these religious stories into what initially seemed to me to be a tangled web of conflicting messages recalled the messiness of lived experience, the plasticity of storytelling, and the creativity entailed in arranging the pieces of one's life into a coherent narrative form.

My fieldwork spanned a two-year period, during which I participated in close to a hundred Aglow meetings at several chapters in and around New England (as well as a few others scattered elsewhere). I twice traveled to Aglow headquarters in the Seattle suburb of Edmonds, Washington, to explore the organization's archives and interview a number of past and present leaders of the organization, and I attended two major organizational conferences, one international and one national. While my initial impression of Aglow as a mostly white, middle-class organization was not statistically far off the mark, I discovered a broader ethnic and racial mix of women, as well as a greater range of ages and class backgrounds, than I had expected. I also observed a diligent commitment among the women to increase the diversity within the organization and to help compensate for America's racist past and present, thereby joining the chorus of contemporary evangelical Christians now accenting white repentance and promoting racial reconciliation. Although I was often aware of the differences, religious and otherwise, that separated me from most of the women I met in Aglow, those differences did not keep me from empathizing with them. Their stories of frustrating and painful relationships saddened me and made me reflect upon the torment inflicted on family members, male and female, by impossible domestic ideals. Sometimes affronted or dismayed by beliefs or assumptions held by the women, I was just as often impressed by their courage and the love they showed one another. I regularly found myself hoping, amidst doubts, that the healings recited and manifested in public would not prove ephemeral. My fieldnotes provide evidence for this mix of responses, filled as they are with personal expressions of incredulity, bewilderment, admiration, gratitude, and hope.

My encounters with the women I visited, interviewed, and spoke with informally were frequently pleasurable, although also sometimes perceptibly awkward as we simultaneously negotiated our involvement with each other. From the beginning I informed local leaders and many participants of my project, identifying myself as a Christian (though noncharismatic) and a Harvard doctoral student writing on prayer in Women's Aglow. A few seemed wary or alarmed—distrustful, perhaps, of my liberal Episcopal and/or Harvard affiliations—but most appeared enthusiastic about the project and were willing to speak with me, several graciously inviting me into their homes. It took time to build some of this trust. Caroline, for example, a leader who appeared deeply suspicious of my motives, sometimes purposefully sat behind me in order, I assumed, to read my notes. After some months had passed, she informed me that she had prayed to God about me and that God had assured her "he" was in charge of my investigation and had in fact sent me to Aglow, whether I knew it or not. I interpreted her remark to mean that she no longer felt threatened by my presence. Once I had notified the women of my study, I did not continue to emphasize it at subsequent meetings, although my constant note-taking and occasional tape-recording were obvious reminders. As might be expected, most of the women seemed far more interested in me—and in recruiting me as a new member—than in my thesis. Whatever prompted their curiosity or concern, however, the women were nearly always eager to share with me the role of prayer in their lives.

I was somewhat conspicuous at Aglow meetings for other reasons as well. I began the research when I was twenty-five years old, whereas the median age for Aglow members is about fifty. Occasionally other women in their twenties would appear at meetings, and often they would be introduced to me by members eager to expand the age range of their membership. Mostly, however, I sat alone or among older women who genially invited me to join them. Age played a critical role in determining the kinds of information I could receive from these women and in establishing the typically maternal way they approached me. For instance, Nancy, a woman with whom I shared many pleasant lunches, recounted stories about her dangerously alcoholic and often-depressed daughter, who was almost exactly my age. As Nancy spoke of her terrible fears that her daughter Christine would be killed in a drunk-driving accident or be infected with AIDS by men she picked up in bars, I gave her advice and comfort as well as I could, assuring her (as I sensed she wanted me to) that Christine would eventually pull her life together. Other women too described their problems with adolescent or adult sons and daughters, many expressing guilt about being bad, even abusive, mothers. In these ways, I sometimes filled the combined roles of pseudo-therapist, substitute daughter, and friend.

Occupying a daughterly role meant that I was not always privy to certain kinds of stories, at least not instantly, and I had to probe beyond the mother-daughter issues that seemed to arise so frequently in my conversations with Aglow women.[6] Because I was unmarried at the time, for example, the women often seemed hesitant to discuss their marriages with me, even those who freely commented upon their husbands in public meetings. Yet I felt that hearing about their marriages was important for understanding their attraction to and experiences in Aglow, and I tried to elicit their stories by sharing aspects of my own life. As I ventured to describe my own feelings about men and marriage or commented upon incidents in my own relationships or that of my parents, some women responded with stories from their own marriages, whether to affirm, counter, or moderate the views I had expressed. Telling my own stories seemed to move these discussions to more intimate levels and to bridge certain gaps between the women and me, so that both they and I felt more comfortable in our encounters.

Narrating my own life to the women with whom I spoke also helped me to move beyond the safe, daughterly role so often attributed to me and into more complex territory. There I sought to avoid the dilemma of the ethnographer who does not fully belong to the community he or she is studying yet wants in good faith to be trusted by members of that community.[7] While my own piety and politics at times seemed worlds apart from some of the women in Aglow, I emphasized the common ground between us so they would feel at ease talking about their lives with me rather than stamping me negatively as a feminist. Although I sometimes avoided spelling out the differences in our religious or political positions, I more often felt free, when asked, to acknowledge my own more liberal opinions and affiliations. Moreover, like most ethnographers, my sense of otherness subsided over time as I participated more fully in communities of Aglow women and formed real and affectionate bonds with several participants. Karen McCarthy Brown's observation that, "ethnographic research is, whatever else it is, a form of human relationship," rang true, as I found my own work thrive where relationships were most fully and authentically developed.[8]

Partly because I am a sociable person and enjoy talking to women about their lives, partly because these women were interested in knowing more about my life and asked me numerous questions, my ethnographic approach was based on open-ended questions and conversations. Just as I was sometimes asked for my own opinions about how to solve a particular relational problem or for my prayers, I asked others in turn for advice and prayers as well. An aunt of mine in Texas was dying of breast cancer during the course of my research, and I suspect she may well have received more numerous and sustained prayers from Aglow women in New England who had never met her than from her fellow Presbyterian congregants and friends in Houston. Inquiries were repeatedly made to me, meanwhile, by women who had felt a "special burden" to pray for my aunt and her grieving family, demonstrating a constancy of attention and care that were poorly repaid by my own weak efforts to do the same.

There were, of course, more than a few discomfiting moments during my field research, when I found the balance I sought between observer and participant difficult to preserve. The pressure on me to become a dues-paying member of Women's Aglow Fellowship, for instance, often seemed great. Yet because I could not agree to Aglow's statement of faith and because I needed to retain a certain degree of "outsiderhood" in my research, I could not in good conscience take that step. Misconstruing my inaction and thinking that perhaps I could not afford the $25 annual membership fee, one woman told me eagerly that she had prayed for me and felt led to pay the cost of my membership as a special gift, leaving me to explain rather shamefacedly why I could not accept her generous offer. A couple of times, when leaders would send those gathered at meetings into small groups or have us pick a "prayer partner," I found myself in the uneasy position of having to pray aloud for other women, knowing that they wanted and expected me to offer spirited vocal prayers that were not my habit; in such cases I tried my best to comply and, seeing the needs of those awaiting my words, hoped profusely that my prayers could somehow be efficacious. A more awkward incident occurred once after a particularly emotion-filled service, as one woman shouted out to me, "Have you received the baptism in the Holy Spirit yet?" When, oddly embarrassed and a bit irked, I shook my head "no," she laughed and shouted more loudly, "Well, you will!"

Another time, after the conclusion of a weekly morning prayer meeting that I had attended for some months, two women began to press me more directly about this same spirit baptism. I was beginning to realize that my seeming failure to undergo the baptism was causing them more dismay than I had anticipated and that my continued presence in their midst was generating increasing anxiety. Trying politely to end the conversation while already seated in my car to leave, I was taken aback when one of the women, Doreen, stretched her hand through the open window, clasped my head, and began to pray that I would be filled then and there with the Holy Spirit. The second woman, Helen, immediately joined Doreen, and the two of them prayed, in English and in tongues, for perhaps fifteen minutes. I felt a peculiar mix of emotions as I sat there, longing to escape and yet not wanting to discourage them or to appear hostile in refusing what they considered to be a gift. As an ethnographer, I also did not want to shake their faith in the experience that I knew was so important in their lives, however unlikely this concern seems in retrospect, as if my mere failure to speak in tongues could have had such an impact. Yet I could not give them what I felt they wanted, could not "pretend" to be who I was not, no matter how much my apparent obstinacy bothered them. Eventually, seemingly disappointed, they stopped praying and Doreen gave me a tract on spirit baptism, urging me to pray at home.

My interpretation of this incident shifted, however, when Helen approached me the following week and referred apologetically to Doreen, telling me she "is not our usual Aglow lady." In fact, I had noticed Doreen preaching on public street corners in the Boston area, where

she carried an enormous wooden cross and wore t-shirts warning view-
ers—mostly smirking adolescents who booed and taunted her—about
the fires of hell, and I assumed Helen also knew of Doreen's notoriety
in that area. As Helen talked to me, trying to give me reassurance about
Aglow without criticizing Doreen, I realized that she—and likely others
who attended this meeting—felt distinctly uneasy about Doreen and
perhaps ambivalent about her participation in the group. Though an
active and enthusiastic participant, well schooled in the intricacies of
charismatic theology, Doreen hardly personified what seemed to be the
prevailing model in Aglow of evangelical femininity—self-effacing, tender, and charmingly solicitous—and yet the women who were most
heedful of this standard possessed neither an explicit rationale nor a
definite procedure for refining her more zealous behavior. It occurred to
me then that Helen had possibly joined Doreen in praying for me not,
as I had thought, to increase the pressure of my situation but just the
reverse: to protect me from Doreen's emphatically "unladylike" coer-
civeness. Helen's careful words illuminated the importance of both
defining and maintaining boundaries for Aglow participation in a context where group membership is extremely fluid and restrictions on attendance few.

Other ethnographers have recounted their own embarrassment in incidents far outside their own cultural and linguistic contexts as well as
in groups closer to home. These kinds of emotional reactions and mis-
understandings work as a kind of index of the ethnographer's engagement, bringing cultural assumptions and differences to the fore and
opening space for new insights and understandings to emerge.[9] My
own feelings of anxiety and occasional irritation with the expectations
placed on me in Aglow settings became the occasion not simply for
self–reflection—though that was one result—but also for increased
attention to the tenuous position of any newcomer in such a religious
setting and the rapidity with which she may be expected to undergo
conversion to charismatic Christianity. I was also able to observe the
delicacy with which regular participants tried to deal with newcomers
and outsiders, including the social awkwardness of explaining their intense religious experiences to those not immediately disposed to accept
them. Most of all, my emotional reactions illuminated the cultural assumptions underlying my perspective and so warned me of interpretive gaps that, if ignored, would seriously impede my analysis.
Remaining disengaged from the proceedings that I witnessed or denying my responses to them would have blinded me from that risk.

The difficult moments in my research were accompanied and, indeed, surpassed by many enjoyable and pleasant ones. Most women with whom I discussed my project were eager to talk with me about their own experiences and beliefs about prayer, and their enthusiasm helped ease some of the anxiety I often felt as an ethnographer intruding into their lives. The interviews were almost invariably delightful experiences, as the women relaxed with me and seemed truly to enjoy our time together. My lunches with Nancy were a particular highlight, as were my continuing contacts and growing friendship with my fellow Episcopal churchwoman, Deborah. One of the most gratifying moments of all occurred late in 1993, when one woman called me on the telephone and exclaimed, "I've been learning so much about prayer lately, and I just keep thinking, 'I gotta tell Marie!'"

From the beginning of my fieldwork, then, I found that I truly liked the women with whom I talked and relished the time we spent together. Not only did I consider their lives interesting and their stories worth telling, but I felt many of them to be admirable women, working diligently to love their families and their friends and to bring healing to a broken, afflicted world. Again and again, I watched women rally around one another to bring "encouragement"—an oft-used word—to the anxious and fearful in their midst, and I respected their manifest commitment to one another's survival and development. While the transformations to which participants attested often seemed fragile and in many cases temporary, the women's tenacious determination to conquer despair, and their refusal to give in to the easy cynicism of our time commanded my increasing admiration and affection. It will cause me immeasurable regret if those who read this book do not perceive this fond regard amidst my more critical interpretive perspectives.

In speaking or writing for outside audiences, I have tried to communicate as accurately as I can the views of Aglow participants rather than to dismiss, condemn, or carelessly distort them. One of the impulses behind this study, and one that I often articulated in my conversations with the women in Aglow, has been a desire to redress current depictions of evangelical women, to render such women with the depth and complexity that their lives warrant and thereby dispute the flat, stereotypical terms to which so many journalists, political scientists, and various hostile bystanders still cling. The heated responses that I have occasionally received in progressive academic settings—responses bidding me to censure evangelical notions of Christian womanhood and, by necessary extension, the masses of women who claim such patterns for their lives—suggest the hazards of this endeavor, including the ease with which it may be mistakenly construed as antifeminist. Still, I remain convinced of the need to bridge disparate worlds, to translate the lives of evangelical women in terms nonevangelicals can understand, insofar as such an enterprise is possible. If properly executed, such translation ought to contribute to what I take to be a central feminist goal: a heightened understanding of "other"—read "nonfeminist"—women, who challenge particular assumptions and contradictions within feminist thought and thereby help both to expand and to refine feminism's possibilities.

While I have attempted to listen to Aglow women on their own terms—appropriating the task of "hearing to speech" as integral to my research—I have not simply taken their own words as the whole truth about their lives but have applied broader analytical perspectives as well. The lived worlds of human experience, after all, are not identical to people's descriptions of these worlds.[10] I have sought out a variety of critical voices both within and outside the Aglow organization, not because such voices are necessarily "truer" than others but because they supplement the public face of Aglow and thus provide a fuller portrait of the communities that make up the larger organization. Scattered examples of dissent and alienation, from former as well as current members, suggest that Aglow women experience more tension among themselves and anxiety regarding their participation in this group than is commonly acknowledged, yet such stories also reveal the prodigious loyalty often felt by participants to the association. By bringing some critical voices to light, I have not meant to imply ominous problems within the organization but rather to acknowledge conflicts of a kind that exist in all closely knit groups and explore Aglow women's ways of trying to solve or attenuate them.

In my research and writing, I have remained conscious of my anomalous position in relation to the women of Aglow and have carefully reflected upon the limits of my own vision. This reflexive stance has been shaped by current critiques of ethnographers working in earlier periods who, in seeking to appear objective, tried to erase any evidence of their own restricted perception from their texts and so failed to acknowledge the inequitable power relations between researcher and informants.[11] As a strategy for managing this dilemma, for owning up to my own restricted vision while resisting undue self-preoccupation, I have chosen to confine most of my personal remarks to this introduction, focusing the following chapters on Aglow history, practice, literature, and devotion and relying on textual materials as much as ethnographic observations in my analyses. I do not pretend to present my arguments from a transcendent, omniscient perspective, as if my text were an actual mirror of the culture it purports to survey instead of the interpretation that it is. Rather than trying to erase my own perspective, my aim is to focus on the women themselves, whose narratives finally are far more important to this enterprise than are my own stories.

Emerging from both field research and close analysis of printed texts, the present study elaborates the workings of religious narrative and prayer in Aglow, focusing on two central themes: the potentially radical renegotiations of power in these networks of praying women and the reshaping of personal identity that results from such shifts. Both themes participate in larger conversations about the dynamics of culture, conversations pursued among historians and other humanistic scholars as well as social scientists in a variety of fields. So that readers may understand what is at stake here, I want to highlight briefly some of the crucial issues embedded in these themes of power and identity.

For at least the past thirty years, social theorists have attempted to reintroduce the study of individual agency and practice into analyses formerly preoccupied with broader sociopolitical power structures. From the Marxist approaches of Antonio Gramsci and Raymond Williams on "hegemony," to the somewhat different approach taken by Michel de Certeau in his theory of "tactics," to the highly influential formulations of Pierre Bourdieu's "habitus" and Anthony Giddens's "rules" and "resources," analysts have sought to describe human action in a way that captures the complicated workings of power and resistance in both private and public arenas.[12] While earlier studies tended to focus on peasant insurgency and large social revolutions, more recent studies have examined "unlikely forms of resistance, subversions rather than large-scale collective insurrections, small or local resistances not tied to the overthrow of systems or even to ideologies of emancipation."[13] The term "practice," as Sherry Ortner observed in her 1984 overview of this body of literature, has emerged as a "key symbol" in debates about resistance and the mediating term between structure and agency. "Practice" aims at overcoming the problematic dichotomy between structure and agency without ignoring the shaping power of the former on the latter altogether.[14] This interdisciplinary enterprise has influenced work in the humanities as well as the social sciences. For instance, theorists in religious studies and history have developed a great interest in the dynamics of power and practice.

Developments in feminist theory have led to increasingly sophisticated analysis of the role of gender in this power-practice nexus,
displacing older models of subjugation versus liberation with subtler
formulations of individual and collective dissent. The work of distinguished feminist historians such as Natalie Zemon Davis and Caroline
Walker Bynum has reminded those who interpret gender relations
solely in terms of male "patriarchy" and female "oppression" that the
realities are far more muddled, that women have always carved out
spaces for themselves within the social, historical, cultural, and religious structures that constrain them and have resisted those structures
in subtle and unexpected ways.[15] Closer to my own topic, ethnographers such as Judith Stacey and Elizabeth Brusco have persuasively
argued for the subversion of gender roles in the framework of evangelical Christianity; Brusco has even ventured to suggest that Colombian
evangelicalism serves as a strategic women's movement aimed, "like
Western feminism," at reforming traditional sex role hierarchies.[16]
Gradually, older models that analyze conservative forms of religion as
intractable bastions of male privilege and female subordination are
being supplanted with richer and more complicated frameworks for interpreting female religious activity and women's power within organizational bounds.

Women's Aglow Fellowship provides a fascinating window into
these important questions, as the largest interdenominational women's
mission organization in the United States—indeed, the largest in the
world—and one burdened with the task of recasting the traditionally
Christian doctrine of female submission to male authority into formulations appealing to women. Amidst the current academic ferment
around issues of practice and power, such emphasis on female submission, particularly when promulgated by women who sometimes claim
to have once been feminists, demands thorough analysis and investigation. In my research on this organization I have attempted to discover
the meaning of women's continued adherence to the doctrine of submission and authority, in theory and in practice, when men not only
occupy positions of leadership as pastors and as husbands but also
hold leadership roles as "advisors" to Aglow itself; not surprisingly, I
have discovered a high degree of innovation, not to mention historical development, in Aglow women's interpretation of female submission. Equally significant are the dynamics of power and resistance that
occur among the women within the Aglow organization, between participants and leaders—comparable in some cases to the lay-clerical

tensions evident in congregations—as well as within and among participants themselves.

A significant dimension of these themes of power and dissent pertains to the many tacit restrictions put in place to safeguard the system. Various incidents that I witnessed during the course of my research alerted me to the pressures within the organization toward conformity in both experience and narrative, pressures that oppose the freedom participants claim to find in Aglow. For example, I observed that Aglow did not deal comfortably with conflict, criticism, or disagreement. Women often spontaneously shared with me their concerns about the organization—that it had become too focused on the spiritual gifts instead of evangelism, that so-and-so had become too authoritative as a leader, that too much emphasis was being placed on "appearance" rather than "substance," and so on—but such concerns were never treated thoroughly in the monthly meetings I attended, presumably because "complaining" was perceived as disloyal and divisive. As my research continued, I became increasingly aware of a set of unarticulated but nevertheless powerful rules, codes, and disciplines that restrict dissent within Aglow by framing it as a kind of betrayal.

At the same time, I noted various modes of resistance to these boundaries. One evening I watched as Evelyn, a newcomer to Aglow who did not quite understand the rules yet, resisted as one of the prayer leaders—the evening's guest speaker—pressed her hands down hard upon Evelyn's head, the leader evidently wanting her to fall down as if "slain in the spirit." Not feeling overcome in this way, Evelyn continued standing, even after the leader visibly increased the pressure on her head. A frail woman, Evelyn finally stumbled back into a chair, then vigorously shoved the woman's hands away; silently and without expression, the leader turned her back and began to pray over the next person in line, as a confused and frowning Evelyn returned to her seat and prepared to leave the meeting. When I approached her—the only one there, besides myself, too recalcitrant to be "slain"—she informed me angrily that the other woman had been forcibly pushing her down, concluding in a huff, "This worries me!" Evelyn attended one more Aglow meeting after that night, then never returned.

The resistance Evelyn displayed toward a forceful leader would be inconsequential were it not for its echoes elsewhere, both within the group and in relation to the world outside. Such direct rejection of expected behavior is rare among more devoted participants, who would argue that this leader's forcefulness is equally rare in Aglow.

Nonetheless, Aglow women bend the rules, negotiate the disciplines, and subvert the expectations and requirements of the group in various ways. Perhaps more importantly, the women daily repudiate those metaphorical hands from the outside culture whom they feel, as Evelyn felt, are pushing them down, coercing their obedience to social structures that, in their view, reward greed, dishonesty, and sheer ambition and scorn traditional Christian values along with those who believe in them. Herein lie more expansive, if ambivalent, forms of resistance, and I have tried to write about these shifting patterns and "tactics" in their diversity and complexity, without coming to simplistic conclusions about their ultimate results.[17] The cultural dissidence of Aglow women is by no means total, as they would surely acknowledge; further, these women, like most of us, participate more than they may know in recreating and supporting the very cultural norms they criticize.

Even so, I have witnessed significant instances of what I believe to be real challenges to status quo standards, along with a variety of means through which conservative evangelical women rework the social roles they inhabit. Throughout, I have struggled against the temptation to romanticize resistance, that is, to read all forms of resistance as ultimately liberating rather than simply "a diagnostic of power" that illuminates the ways in which people are caught up in various forms of power, discipline, and control.[18] Thus a major focus of the following chapters will be the analysis of challenges to the ideological norms of Aglow, and of the external social world, along with the means by which contemporary evangelical women continuously redraw and renegotiate the boundaries of power and authority.

American evangelicalism is a tradition saturated in narratives of personal experience, testimonies that echo biblical stories of conversion and rebirth, recounting events that have irrevocably changed one's life. In the women-centered context of Aglow, the sharing of these narratives encourages participants to recount their own life stories in terms permitted and galvanized by the group's protocol, a blueprint that is at once both narrower and wider than the narrative forms of ordinary evangelical culture. When women accept this worldview, their personal identity is reshaped, as previous forms of belief and behavior are apparently replaced by new ideals and practices. At the same time, the women come to feel truly loved by a heavenly father and friend, and their hopes for intimacy are partially fulfilled through this relationship.

This sense of having received a new life, described as healing, transformation, liberation, and deliverance, is intensively cultivated within Aglow and similar religious settings. It is a reshaping of personal identity, grounded in what I have somewhat awkwardly termed a capacity for ritualization: a learned ability to experience healing and transformation through ritual enactments of prayer. By describing these experiences as "learned," I do not mean to suggest that they are fraudulent or contrived but only that they depend on the presence and observation of ritual models, such as other charismatic Christians. I have tried to analyze the intricate formation of this capacity for ritualization along with its broader implications in everyday living.

The theme of new life also relates to wider theoretical discussions in the humanities and social sciences, which are concerned with the construction and endless reconstruction of a particular identity and its placement in wider historical and contextual narratives. Feminist ethnographers have contributed various analytic tools to these discussions of the role of narrative in identity formation. Writing about Pentecostal women preachers, for instance, folklorist Elaine Lawless has described the ways in which her subjects' religious narratives are indebted to "community collaboration on the 'authentic' story, its structure, its components and its performed delivery."[19] Other researchers have similarly theorized about the "supportive comradeship" of other women "who were asking similar questions" in the formation of religious narratives, illuminating again the processes by which narratives are constructed and transmitted in female communities.[20] There is, then, a direct relationship between communally recited narratives of personal experience and the formation of personal and religious identity.[21]

Always working to evangelize the lost and to inspire the disheartened, Aglow women readily share their testimonies, created out of the experiences that give their lives instructive value and structured according to the conventions of the community. In many ways these oral narratives fit the genre of what Lawless has termed "spiritual life stories," flexible rather than perfected entities that contain "a pastiche of stories, many of them based on both personal experience and traditional expectations at the same time."[22] Such stories do not follow a fixed chronological order or give equal weight to all events in one's life; they constitute a series of vignettes constructed with an end in view, that of God's constant guidance and care and the storyteller's realization of her need to surrender to God's loving will.

No less important than these oral narratives in understanding Women's Aglow has been the devotional literature published by the organization since 1969. Twenty-two years of *Aglow* magazines, filled with testimonies and teachings on prayer, and scores of tracts, Bible studies, inspirational pamphlets, and practical advice books have provided the resources necessary for understanding the trajectory of Aglow over time and the meanings constructed around God, Christian womanhood, home and family, intimacy, illness, and prayer. Printed narratives, found in all of these materials, but particularly in the nationally circulated magazines, differ in technique from those that are orally composed. Set down in type, printed chronicles give the illusion of fixity, enclosed in a form that purportedly tells "the whole story" detached from a reader's response. Oral narratives, on the other hand, appear somewhat more flexible, as speakers, who observe and interact with an audience, may play directly to listeners' sympathies and impart finer shades of meaning to their accounts.

Despite such apparent differences, oral and written testimonies are more alike than different, adhering to practically identical rhythms and guidelines that emanate from the same devotional world. If anything, the written testimonies, only published after passing editorial standards of correctness, offer important evidence of a kind of ideal narrative tradition to which oral stories may be expected to conform. Thus, while folklorists would undoubtedly want to investigate in greater detail the differentiation between these two genres, I have been content to find their general affinities and have not analyzed them as separate forms. Like oral testimonies, these printed narratives are "spiritual life stories," constructed from individual experiences but framed in the structuring terms of the community; and these stories also embody the strategic process of "rescripting," the invention of a new set of choices beyond those normally allotted to women in a context where female power is strictly limited.[23]

Yet this new set of choices contains limits of its own. For example, the structures into which Aglow narratives must fit—what sociologists generally refer to as "frames" or "scripts"—are confining in ways that the women themselves may not realize (or admit). Narratives about new life and a new self resurrected from the ashes of the old are not always easily verified, and it stands to reason that many women must struggle to fit their experiences into these ideal structures. Still, most of those who join Aglow apparently *feel* that narrative become theirs, almost effortlessly. They find in this new narrative—just as other persons find in other narratives—their "real" identity, as if it were suddenly revealed to them after a lengthy concealment. Such revelations have a long history in traditional Christianity, whose message seeks to convince people of their utter sinfulness and need for grace; the ways in which these experiences are reworked in this all-female, modern American context, however, surely reflect the contemporary therapeutic culture that this religious message helped create.

What all the Aglow narratives, written and oral, hold in common is a sense of the healing power and transformative potential of prayer. Through prayer, a woman who feels angry, despairing, or powerless in her everyday life may experience a sense of intimacy with God as her loving father, friend, and husband. Through prayer, she can perhaps feel that someone hears her cry and cares about her pain, and that he will not only comfort her but will heal her suffering and fill her with joy. She can also feel herself to be a stronger, more capable person than she was before, imbued with a new "self-esteem"—another buzzword in the Aglow vocabulary—that she never felt before. What the narratives affirm, again and again, is that only through the surrender of prayer can a woman be completely healed, transformed, empowered, and set free.

Aglow tries to provide a refuge in which such prayers can occur, a sympathetic community where women may learn together about all that God will do for them in their lives. Theirs is a vision of abundance but also obedience, of receiving the infinite gifts God has to give them through their own submission to his scriptural and prophetic commands. Repeatedly in the narratives I have examined, oral as well as written, women praise Aglow for having set them free from "bondage," giving them the courage to be the "mighty women" God intended them to be. Again and again Aglow women told me of the ways in which their participation in the organization gave them the opportunity to foster their leadership capabilities, roles that their churches were not allowing them to pursue. Other women emphasize the healing that has occurred in their lives since they joined Aglow: Glenda, a onetime local chapter president, described to me her first Aglow meeting, in which she surprised herself by sobbing uncontrollably but was immediately consoled by a white-haired woman sitting behind her, who gently rocked Glenda in her arms without saying a word. It was an act of kindness that astonished Glenda, who recalled, "I just remember thinking that this woman *cared* about me."[24]

In like terms, other women have described Aglow as "women loving women," as a "safe place" for women, and as a "big support group for middle-aged women."[25] Nora, whose physical and emotional problems had taken her to a variety of medical doctors and therapists, gave a public testimony thanking her fellow Aglow members for praying for her in one woman's kitchen, saying they "took over where the best professionals in the world were stymied."[26] Another woman, also speaking to a public gathering of local Aglow women, thanked them for healing her from her "brokenness" and testified about her first meeting, "I looked around this room and thought, 'Wow! I'm not alone! I'm not alone!'" She went on to tell of her mother dying when she was seven years old, concluding that Aglow "provided me with mothers I never had, and also sisters I never had."[27]

Such statements about the role of Aglow groups in the lives of its participants epitomize the therapeutic role Aglow has increasingly assumed for women. In small, local fellowships, participants have intentionally forged alternative communities that claim to provide not only (or even primarily) theological or doctrinal instruction but loving nurturance, diagnosis of women's particular ills, and guaranteed treatment. Part of what sociologist Robert Wuthnow has called the "small-group movement" in American society, Aglow focuses on deepening participants' levels of spirituality yet does so not simply by means of the historic Christian tradition but by borrowing extensively—if selectively—from the wider culture, thus altering in visible ways some older meanings of "spirituality."[28] Emerging from this powerful mix of Christian piety and popular culture are observably reconfigured personal narratives, as Aglow women learn to tell their life stories in terms of surrender, healing, and transformation while reworking their own perceptions of authority, freedom, and womanhood.

Aglow chapters differ from each other, certainly, and yet even amidst such diversity, a semblance of unity and of common culture persists, maintained through the institutional hierarchies that govern the organization at every level, the literature produced and disseminated throughout Aglow, and the scripted narratives told and retold within Aglow settings. Moreover, Aglow represents a much wider female evangelical culture in twentieth-century America, one that has gained recent media attention as women inspired by the Christian men's group, Promise Keepers, have begun initiating parallel groups such as Women of Faith, Praise Keepers, and Promise Reapers. These and countless other groups of conservative Christian women across the country are more or less newcomers to the institutional landscape that Aglow has occupied for thirty years, yet their beliefs, commitments, and prayers closely correspond with those sanctioned in Aglow. For that reason, analyzing the particular practices of Aglow participants, readers, and writers should further illuminate the outlines of that larger religious culture and its overlapping social worlds. I have omitted analyzing Aglow's increasing growth outside the United States not because that growth is in any way unimportant—indeed, it may be one of the most significant developments in the organization today—but because my focus pertains to the ways in which Aglow groups reflect and refract American culture. By tracing the responses of one small but arguably representative segment of charismatic women to social currents in American middle-class life, this study explores the dynamics between evangelicalism and gender in a context that has implications for a broader understanding of the changing face of religion in contemporary America.[29]

Anyone writing about the multifaceted and overlapping traditions of American evangelicalism encounters difficulties in terminology, owing as much to the elasticity of the words used to describe various constituencies as to the intertwining of the traditions themselves. Labels such as fundamentalist, pentecostal, evangelical, and charismatic have both historically specific meanings pertaining to their origins and diverse contemporary uses spanning an array of often disparate groups.[30] When one studies a transdenominational group such as Aglow, particularly in light of the broader religious culture out of which it has emerged and been sustained, all neat categorizations fail. While no term works perfectly, I have tended to use "charismatic" or "spirit-filled"—their own preferred term—to refer to Aglow participants and their closest religious kin. When speaking more generally, I have used "evangelical" to indicate the larger religious culture in which these women participate and which includes noncharismatic fundamentalists and classical Pentecostals as well as "ordinary" evangelicals: all those who, in historian Randall Balmer's words, "insist on some sort of spiritual rebirth as a criterion for entering the kingdom of heaven, who often impose exacting behavioral standards on the faithful, and whose beliefs, institutions, and folkways comprise the evangelical subculture in America."[31]

The following chapters approach the stories and devotional lives of Aglow women from several vantage points. The first chapter recounts the origins and trajectory of the Aglow organization and situates its unfolding in the midst of broader historical developments in American culture, including pentecostal and charismatic awakenings, the so-called recovery movement and burgeoning therapeutic culture, and prescriptive norms aimed at middle-class women. The next chapter depicts the ethos, including worship spaces, theological idioms, and actual devotional practices, of contemporary Aglow meetings, analyzing the meanings attached to feeling "set free" in those settings. The following three chapters trace particular cultural and religious motifs as they recur in testimonial narratives and prayers, including healing and transformation (Chapter three), secrecy and intimacy (Chapter four), and discipline and sacrifice (Chapter five). Throughout these chapters, I also investigate the elusive (and sometimes not so elusive) dynamics of authority and power within Aglow, attending to the steady reshaping of narrative and identity that occurs in that context. Chapter six explores the conjoining of these themes in ideals of Christian womanhood, ideals that, like the doctrines of submission and surrender that inform them, have shifted substantially over time. Finally, the conclusion connects these discussions to wider contemporary debates pertaining to the interplay between women, religion, and power, and here I clarify my ongoing desire as a feminist to confront and unmask the distortions of bad faith that polarize contemporary women into bitter enemies across the "culture wars" divide.

Throughout, I have tried to focus on the texture of the stories themselves, heightening the elaborate range of feelings they recount in forms that are at once collectively constructed and highly individual in their expression. Taking a domain often viewed by social and cultural theorists, including many feminists, as supremely repressive—religion, and a highly conservative form at that—and focusing on the practices by which female participants improvise, resist, and continually reshape their own roles and relations, my analysis centers on the interplay between the repressive or disciplinary aspects of women's devotionalism and the ecstatic, liberatory potential of particular practices. Lest my personal interests in this subject be mistaken, I remind readers that respectful treatment of a group is not the same as agreement with its convictions. I have learned much from Aglow women about courage, endurance, and kindness; yet I necessarily remain only a bystander to their world.

One question frequently posed to me during my work on this project is whether or not I believe that the intense religious experiences pentecostal and charismatic Christians claim to experience are "real," meaning whether they are of divine origin. The only answer I can give is that my analysis sets aside such questions, neither affirming nor negating the possibility that what happens in prayer is truly "of God" but instead focusing on what is human.[32] My seeming refusal to accept the women's experiences as divinely wrought may cause some unintended disappointment or offense, and many charismatic evangelicals will understandably feel that this account is irrevocably compromised by my silence on the subject. Yet, throughout my reflections on the construction of self and identity in these settings, I have kept in mind the words of one Aglow member, who said to me, "These are regular women, like you and like me, with a *story* to tell."[33] I hope that at the very least I have rendered their stories decently and that the women may recognize something meaningful about themselves in my description of their experiences, understanding that I do not pretend to have revealed the "whole truth" about their lives. Mine is an attempt to construct what one anthropologist has called "new, less false stories" than those usually told about American evangelical women, and I ask that these particular readers accept my analytic perspective not merely as error (though it may well be that in certain cases) nor as hostility to their worldview (which it is not), but finally as an interpretation that strives to be critical as well as empathetic and that consequently leaves certain questions open.[34]

1

For Such a Time as This

Aglow and American Culture

On an ordinary Saturday afternoon two hundred women have gathered inside a small meeting room to attend "Alone in the Pew," a workshop about husbands who refuse to attend church with their wives. Eleanor Jacobs, the workshop coordinator, begins the session by asking how many women present attend church alone; nearly everyone in the room raises her hand as participants smile knowingly, tiredly, at one another. Eleanor informs them that she too has been "unequally yoked" for the fourteen years she has been married to her non-Christian husband, and that only after considerable prayer has she learned to deal with this problem. Just over a year ago, she continues, "God spoke to me in the shower, said to me, 'Alone in the Pew,' and dropped this workshop in my lap." Although her husband and sons sometimes call her a "big wacko" because of her faith, Eleanor says, she keeps on praying for them and knows that the members of her family are slowly "coming into the Kingdom," according to God's well-timed plan.

For the next hour Eleanor teaches her listeners how to live with their common dilemma, exhorting them to "give up your husband as your problem," "begin to praise God for your husband," and "go back and remember what made you fall in love with him." She urges the women to retain hope in their marriages because "if a woman loses hope in the marriage, you might as well count it gone; but if a man loses hope and a woman still has hope, it can be saved!" It becomes clear that what was advertised as a workshop for dealing with irreligious husbands is actually a session on coping with unhappy, even unbearable, marriages and turning them into loving or at least endurable ones.

Even while dispensing advice on marital enrichment, Eleanor assures the women that if they have become the object of mockery and scorn in their own homes, God is their deliverer and rescuer. She chastises them for their own role in creating discord and notes that, despite what the churches teach, "Sometimes you need to stay home on Sunday mornings and lie in bed with your husband! . . . Or stay home from a special [religious] service on Friday night and cook him dinner." After giving tips on how to make husbands happy, including explicit instructions on "trade-offs" within sexual relations, Eleanor concludes with a tearful prayer of repentance, inviting the women to pray with her for the ability to yield fully to their husbands, to stop blaming their husbands for personal failings, and to be cleansed from all sin within the bonds of marriage. The room filled with murmurs of assent, the women spend another hour praying with Eleanor and with each other, embracing and sometimes weeping, as they seek redemptive love and solace from fellow strugglers and from a loving, sympathetic God.[1]

Some three months later, inside the spacious town hall of a wealthy northeastern suburb, Jeannine Gilbert leads a full-day workshop entitled "Will the Real Woman Please Stand Up?" sponsored by women in the community. Jeannine is well known in some evangelical circles for her books on achieving marital success and happiness by submitting to the authority of one's husband, a process codified in what she calls the "marriage principles." On this warm Saturday afternoon about a hundred Aglow women, mostly middle-aged, have come to hear Jeannine teach them about "love, marriage, and intimacy with God."

From her podium at the front of the room, Jeannine exuberantly proclaims to the women her message that God yearns for them to find true fulfillment and joy in their daily relationships, quoting scripture copiously to validate her point. Assuring her listeners that their greatest contentment will always be located in the home, she teaches them to "let go" of anger and to act only in love, to create families full of joy and marriages free from resentment. She delicately acknowledges that all women have felt pain and victimization, from husbands and others, because of the "sin that has been brought into the world"; and she comforts those suffering the effects of abuse by guaranteeing them that even in their "darkest times" God has been with them and borne that torment with them. Many sniffle into crumpled tissues, nodding in agreement as Jeannine concludes her talk by enjoining them to forgive their husbands for their failings.

She invites others to speak, and Nancy, the local Aglow leader in charge of the event, moves swiftly to the front of the room to give her personal testimony, or, rather, a celebration of the blessings Jeannine's message have long brought to her life. Having read Jeannine's first book on marriage principles twelve years before, during a "broken period" in her life when her marriage was rapidly crumbling, Nancy declares that these principles saved her own family by convincing her to give up trying to control her alcoholic husband. She learned, she says, that he was not the one who needed to change to make her happy but rather that she herself needed to change. Tearfully she concludes: *"In my eyes he was transformed! . . . My husband is my favorite person in the world now, and I thank God for doing that."*

As Nancy returns to her seat amidst applause, other women rise in turn to testify to what they have gained from Jeannine's marriage principles, disseminated largely through Nancy herself in local Aglow meetings. One confesses to being a "burden" to her husband, literally spitting at him in anger, before learning to forgive him for his faults; she now tries to be "sweet and adorable," she says, and has noticed that her husband will "do anything" for her because of it. Another woman describes her life in and out of mental hospitals, recovering from memories of incest, alcoholism, and compulsive overeating; she too credits Jeannine's teachings for saving her marriage and filling her with new courage and self-esteem. A third tells of divorcing her husband and then, after learning of the marriage principles through Aglow, remarrying him, their relationship cleansed and restored. "Nothing's too hard for God," she concludes.[2]

The sighs and murmurs of approval released after this final declaration, like those uttered during Eleanor's marriage workshop, reveal a female world of abundant hope in the power of God to reach deep into people's ordinary lives, heal their misery, and fill them with enduring love. This is a domain wherein every form of evil, depression, and fear may ostensibly be surmounted and all physical disorders healed, a world where women believe "nothing's too hard for God." Cutting across distinctions of social class, race, ethnicity, and region, this is a culture representing thousands of American women who call themselves "born again" or spirit-filled Christians and who believe that miracles, divinely wrought by a loving God, occur regularly in everyday life. In its particulars, this is the world of Women's Aglow Fellowship.

Accounts of the group's origins, printed in numerous Aglow publications, declare the group to be the fulfillment of a vision divinely imparted by God to a small coterie of women in 1967. The group emerged from the Full Gospel Business Men's Fellowship International (FGBMFI), an organization of Pentecostal and charismatic men founded in 1952. Four wives of men in this Fellowship prayed together for a corresponding women's devotional association, one where "those coming into the charismatic renewal could meet to pray, fellowship, and listen to the testimonies of other Christian women."[3] In a few months the women had formed the Full Gospel Women's Fellowship, which spread rapidly and incorporated as Women's Aglow Fellowship International in 1972. Expanding across North America and into more than 120 nations, Aglow has developed into the largest interdenominational women's evangelical organization in the world.

Today, annual Aglow retreats occur regularly around the United States, attended by thousands of women every year. Local monthly meetings attract sizable numbers of women as well, many of whom drift in and out of Aglow over time according to their circumstances and current needs. Individual chapters are interdenominational and convene monthly for prayer and worship, often in restaurants, civic centers, or public auditoriums. Each chapter is part of a larger regional group with its own board of officers, who together oversee the meetings and the chapter leaders. In every region some chapters meet during the day, mostly to accommodate homemakers who want or need to be at home in the evenings, and others meet in the evenings or on Saturdays, mostly to accommodate women working outside the home. Chapters also offer a variety of small Bible study and prayer groups, which tend to meet in members' homes, Sunday school classrooms, or other meeting places.

Regular chapter meetings follow a generally uniform schedule, opening with music led by an appointed musician in a time called "praise and worship," followed by announcements, testimonies, an offering, and a talk by a special speaker, and concluding with more music and a time for receiving prayers from specially trained prayer counselors or coordinators. While these elements of the services have to some extent become highly formalized, the women continue to value and emphasize "spontaneity" over "ritual," believing the former to maintain openness to the spirit of God while the latter effectively hinders or even closes off such a possibility. Leaders believe that the various components of the monthly meetings will enable the participants to experience the presence of God more intensely than in the ordinary time and space of their daily lives, and that, having once experienced God in this way, the women may return to their everyday routines with a fresh awareness of that presence and renewed conviction as to how to live as Christian women.

This female world of ardent devotion and earnest faith extends far beyond the scope of the Aglow organization. The historical and cultural contexts from which Aglow has emerged include, first, the Pentecostal and charismatic movements in twentieth-century America. These movements comprise prominent strands of evangelical Protestantism (and, since the 1960s, Roman Catholicism) in which women's organizations have been perennially active. Second is the so-called recovery movement within twentieth-century America, an integral part of what has been called "therapeutic culture." The third context is the recent social history of American middle-class women, a history rife with tensions over gender roles and filled with both antifeminist and feminist prescriptions for coping with conflicting notions of women's proper "place." These three contexts are in fact deeply interconnected. Separating them, however, provides three distinct lenses for viewing Aglow's formation and development, allowing us to observe, from a multilayered historical perspective, the beliefs and practices steadily recycled and reworked within the organization. The chronicle of Women's Aglow Fellowship then emerges in full, a familiar yet distinctive story of women assembling an all-female association out of the cultural and religious fragments at hand and struggling to maintain its stability in the midst of what feels like a rapidly changing world.

Living in the Days of Pentecost

As early as 1900, various groups of evangelical Protestants in both the Wesleyan and Reformed holiness movements began modifying some of their earlier teachings on the Holy Spirit and sanctification, insisting that baptism in the Holy Spirit must be accompanied by the experience of speaking in tongues with the "enduement of power for service." The many adherents of this new view came gradually to be known as Pentecostals, referring to the New Testament account of the day of Pentecost, in which the Holy Spirit filled Jesus' apostles and enabled them to speak in tongues—that is, foreign or spiritual languages that they had not previously known.[4] During the early decades of the twentieth century, Pentecostalism spread rapidly among black and white believers around the country, as its prophetic message and experiential, ecstatic style of worship attracted converts from diverse sectors of urban and rural society.[5]

Like earlier renewal movements in American Christianity, Pentecostalism thrived on revivals and spawned hundreds of revivalist preachers. The most successful of these set themselves apart from the conventional church order and roamed the nation as itinerants, setting up large tents or renting out huge auditoriums for services that typically lasted several hours or even spanned several days. These Pentecostal evangelists, most famously William Branham, Oral Roberts, Gordon Lindsay, Jack Coe, Tommy Osborn, and Asa Allen, focused their energies less on preaching the gospel and calling people to salvation than on bringing down the power of the Holy Spirit to enact miraculous healings. Utilizing the gifts of the spirit, these preachers prayed and shouted for hours at a time to get the lame to walk, the blind to see, the deaf to hear, the sick to heal. Attracting thousands of people in search of well-being, they led what the historian David Edwin Harrell has termed the American "healing revival" of the late 1940s and 1950s.[6]

While the revivalists preached their message, the ordinary women and men who made up their audiences created formal "prayer bands" as well as informal networks that financed and spread that message. The successful money-raising campaign of the 1955 "Billion Souls Crusade" revealed the breadth of support among denominational Pentecostals and independent, nondenominational worshipers alike, who, like so many other Americans during the 1940s and 1950s, hoped fervently for a revival to sweep across the country. Just as Pentecostal ministers had hoped, miracles of healing drew in thousands of people from a wide spectrum of social and religious backgrounds to tents and auditoriums everywhere. As the historian Edith Blumhofer notes, the people's willingness to contribute financially to the revivalists' campaigns both made the healing revival possible and took needed support away from denominational church programs.[7]

In addition to local religious communities, then, vast numbers of women and men who had little access to stable church life also participated in the Pentecostal and healing movements. Denominational magazines and newspapers published in the first half of the twentieth century provided weekly forums for readers in need to ask for prayers as well as spaces wherein believers testified with exuberance to prayers divinely answered, sufferings alleviated, and lives restored.[8] These sensational and often minutely detailed accounts required responsive action from Pentecostal readers, who were urged by writers as well as editors not merely to skim through the prayer requests sympathetically but to "tarry before the Lord" in diligent and prayerful supplication for all requests. The prayer practices described in such accounts—praying for one another's needs, sending anointed handkerchiefs or other objects as signs of grace, and continually assuring one another of the ardent prayers sent out on their behalf—enabled the formation of Pentecostal communities that transcended the ordinary bounds of geography and social position, imparting comfort, benevolence, and recognition to the suffering hopeful across the land.[9]

Out of the healing revival emerged what has come to be known as the "charismatic movement," as members of the older churches, more affluent and often younger than their Pentecostal predecessors, began accepting the doctrines of speaking in tongues and healing.[10] Still preaching a prophetic message of healing and immediate experience of God's power, those most successful in attracting this new constituency were people who, like Oral Roberts, managed to appear more middle-class and respectable than their evangelistic competitors and to appeal more consistently to mainline churchgoers. One of the largest and most powerful arms of the charismatic movement was the Full Gospel Business Men's Fellowship International, the parent group of Women's Aglow.

The FGBMFI originated in 1952, led by a wealthy Armenian dairy farmer in California, Demos Shakarian, at the urging of Oral Roberts. Shakarian had observed with some dismay that at most revival meetings women outnumbered men by what appeared to be a margin of ten to one. He lamented what he described as "a resistance of men to religion," most particularly among successful businessmen. In 1951 Shakarian organized the first FGBMFI meeting at a Los Angeles cafeteria. More meetings followed, often held in fine hotels, and they increasingly attracted men from mainline Protestant churches, men who might never have attended an Oral Roberts revival.[11] The fellowship's magazine, *Full Gospel Voice,* began publication in 1953, and by 1972 the organization claimed 300,000 members and an annual operating budget of over $1 million.[12] What had begun as an organization of businessmen from Pentecostal churches had quickly expanded into the mainline, to reach successful middle-class non-Pentecostal men as well.[13] For many men, the fellowship was a point of entry into the charismatic movement and the beginning of a new or revitalized religious life.

The FGBMFI was the single most important parachurch organization (meaning a Christian group that disregards ordinary denominational boundaries) to give some order to the charismatic revival during the 1950s and 1960s, continuing to fund independent revivalists and to provide a way for many of them to avoid financial dependence upon ecclesiastical structures. Within the churches, however, changes were also taking place, though on a much smaller scale. The first event to receive wide publicity involved Dennis Bennett, rector of the wealthy St. Mark's Episcopal Church in Van Nuys, California, which had at the time 2,600 parishioners. In 1959, after talking to some lay Episcopalians and a fellow priest who claimed to have been baptized in the Holy Spirit, Bennett himself underwent this experience and began studying the Bible to learn about other gifts, or "charisms," as well. Testifying to his experiences during an ordinary worship service led to Bennett's resignation, but he was later assigned to St. Luke's parish in Seattle, Washington, where he became a sort of folk hero and remained a major leader in the charismatic movement, including acting as an advisor to Women's Aglow Fellowship, until his death in 1991.

Like other renewal movements in American religious history, the twentieth-century charismatic movement became routinized in ways that its early adherents did not foresee. Failing to revitalize the mainline denominations, the renewal impulse was most successful when it seeped outside the churches to create parachurch organizations and other so-called "special purpose groups." Joining forces with other biblical literalists, including certain fundamentalist and Pentecostal groups, as well as some conservative evangelicals, charismatics expanded their activities to encompass the political realm, thereby exemplifying the process that the sociologist Robert Wuthnow has described as the "restructuring of American religion" along liberal and conservative lines in the postwar period.[14] The impulse to revitalize religious faith and practice, deeply interwoven with a yearning to return to the imagined purity of the New Testament church, became yoked to political conservatism and fantasies of a once and future Christian America.

The loose configuration of groups that Wuthnow and others have placed on the conservative side of the religious spectrum have come to be described, rather vaguely, as the "religious right," somewhat more descriptively as the "New Christian Right," or rather more usefully, as "cultural fundamentalism."[15] According to the historians Donald

G. Mathews and Jane Sherron De Hart, cultural fundamentalism—as distinguished from biblical fundamentalism—involves absolute commitment to particular "traditional" social and cultural forms as "sacred templates of reality," fixed patterns that transcend ordinary historical change. Not necessarily limited to participants in traditional religious institutions, such a conservative commitment to received forms is readily observable in ideas pertaining to the gender and family roles presumed necessary for the maintenance of social order, ideals of masculinity and femininity that are believed to comprise universal and constant sets of behavioral rules and scripts. Just as adherence to such ideals helped defeat the Equal Rights Amendment, so too has cultural fundamentalism grounded the arguments of activists in contemporary pro-life, school prayer, and antigay movements, whose perceptions of an increasingly chaotic and licentious culture are decidedly apocalyptic.[16]

Part of the broader "new right" agenda consolidated through a generally conservative swing in American politics, versions of cultural fundamentalism have been propounded by political as well as explicitly religious organizations to fortify traditional gender roles and sexual rules.[17] Women's organizations have spanned the spectrum from Phyllis Schlafly's Eagle Forum on the political side through Beverly LaHaye's Concerned Women for America (founded in 1979) as a group both political and religious, to Women's Aglow Fellowship on the wholly religious side. For the religious, commitments to these and related beliefs have been invigorated by charismatic emphases on prophecy, apocalypticism, and powerful forms of prayer. Like spirit-oriented Christians in earlier eras, many of these modern enthusiasts have fervently sought spiritual gifts as proof of their own holiness and righteousness; perhaps even more than in the past, they have hoped to harness this power for concrete political ends, in what has often amounted to a rejection of the "otherworldliness" embraced by so many of their spiritual ancestors. Seeing themselves as "in but not of" the world, adherents utilize the power of the spirit to fight against the "principalities and powers" of the world, which encompass most of what is defined as "liberal" across the current political landscape.[18]

Aglow's relationship to the political mobilization of the religious right, however much the theological beliefs of Aglow women may resemble those of conservative religious activists, is oblique. Exempt from federal income taxes, the organization differs from explicitly political groups such as the Christian Coalition, founded by Pat Robertson and now headed by Ralph Reed, or Beverly LaHaye's Conservative Women for America, and it is not supposed to influence legislation or be involved in politics. However, a printed statement on "Aglow and Political Issues" suggests underlying political currents: "Although we've agreed under the law not to 'influence legislation or political campaigns,' we're mighty influencers through the power of prayer and through our personal touch in the hearts and lives of women in our communities."[19] The statement, which concludes by urging participants to pray for their political leaders, leaves room for indirect persuasion, of course, and it is not uncommon to hear aspersions against "liberals" in Aglow meetings or to hear participants casually mention to one another the latest briefing from LaHaye or Reed. General assumptions in Aglow literature and at meetings, as with much conservative evangelicalism, hold that true Christians oppose any laws protecting or endorsing homosexual life styles and abortion and that they vote as conservative Republicans. Yet Aglow leaders are careful to disavow all ties, formal and informal, with the Christian Coalition, Concerned Women for America, and like groups, focusing on Aglow's primary role as a "network of praying women" working to evangelize the world.[20]

The Recovery Movement and Therapeutic Culture

A second context for understanding Women's Aglow Fellowship is that of the twentieth-century healing movement known variously as "twelve-step," "self-help," or "recovery." Current participants trace its origins to 1935, when Bill Wilson and Robert Holbrook Smith formed Alcoholics Anonymous. Wilson, hospitalized numerous times for severe alcoholism and apparently on the verge of irreversible physical damage due to years of heavy drinking, had recently undergone a kind of spiritual conversion in which he felt God's presence as immediate and "electric": "There was a sense of victory, followed by such a peace and serenity as I had never known. There was utter confidence. I felt lifted up, as though the great clean wind of a mountain top blew through and through. God comes to most men gradually, but His impact on me was sudden and profound."[21] Wilson's conversion occurred through the influence of the independent evangelical Oxford Group, a movement formed in 1908 that emphasized individual conversion, acceptance of strict moral standards, mutual confession among group members, and submission to God. Professing belief in direct and immediate access to God, Oxford Group adherents claimed to be returning to the pure truth of Christianity that had been corrupted by the church through the centuries. While not always noted in the literature, the teachings of Alcoholics Anonymous have obvious links to the theological doctrines of the Oxford Group.[22]

As Wilson and Smith's initial small group rapidly grew, its teachings were codified into the "twelve steps." Emphasizing individual powerlessness over alcohol (expanded later to include drugs, food, and other apparent sources of addiction), the prescribed cure begins with acknowledging "a Power greater than ourselves" and surrendering to that Power ("God *as we understood him,*" italics in original) for restoration to health. In language evocative of Christian confession, the steps require the addicted to admit their "wrongs" to God, to themselves, and to others, by taking a "fearless moral inventory" of themselves. They are then enjoined to make amends to all whom they have injured and to remain alert to further wrongdoing in the future. The final step advocates spreading this message to other addicts and continuing to live out this transformation in all areas of life.[23]

As of January 1995 Alcoholics Anonymous estimated its membership at over a million in 50,685 groups in the United States and another million in 40,000 more groups throughout the world.[24] Even more significant, however, has been the growth of the wider movement spawned by this organization in recent decades, including Al-Anon, Overeaters Anonymous, Narcotics Anonymous, Adult Children of Alcoholics, and Sex and Love Addicts Anonymous, as well as a host of related therapeutic groups. Elaborating the concept of "addiction" and following the treatment model of the "twelve steps" formulated by Alcoholics Anonymous, these groups claim to offer support and recovery for a wide range of dysfunctions, from compulsive overeating to a corrupted form of love described as "codependency."[25]

The boom of twelve-step groups or recovery groups has often been treated as marking a kind of spiritual shift in American life, in which the boundaries between the public and the private have been repeatedly challenged and redrawn. Little of a personal nature is felt to be off limits for discussion, and whatever remains hidden is a potential source of "shame." These shifting boundaries have also been linked to a near obsession with self-analysis and psychological health, in what has been described as the "therapeutic culture" in twentieth-century America. In his 1966 book, *The Triumph of the Therapeutic,* Philip Rieff predicted the demise of traditional "Christian culture" and its replacement by "the therapeutic" in terms that cultural critics have echoed ever since:

"Religious man was born to be saved; psychological man is born to be pleased. The difference was established long ago, when 'I believe,' the cry of the ascetic, lost precedence to 'one feels,' the caveat of the therapeutic. And if the therapeutic is to win out, then surely the psychotherapist will be his secular spiritual guide."[26] Not wanting to be left behind in this burgeoning therapeutic culture, "churchmen," Rieff suggested, had rapidly learned to become therapists themselves, "administrating a therapeutic institution—under the justificatory mandate that Jesus himself was the first therapeutic."[27]

This therapeutic culture was shaped in part by American preoccupations with so-called modern psychology, a slippery term that includes a wide array of diagnostic models rooted in the psychoanalytic theories of Freud and his successors. The relationship of psychology to American religion has been a story of endless change and near-constant tension, among Protestant liberals adapting theology to modern science as much as among conservatives seeking to preserve traditional doctrine.[28] All sought, whether keenly or cautiously, to appropriate the most helpful insights from theories and therapies produced by psychologists while speaking out against the fetishization of such techniques. Most joined in a common wariness toward the narcissism that the "talking cure" and its later incarnations might be hiding within its trojan horse.

Evangelicals in particular held mixed attitudes toward modern psychology. Fearful that psychology would displace religion, fundamentalists long maintained a hostile stand against it, denouncing psychology in no uncertain terms as "the foe of truth," its outlook sinful for being purely "materialistic."[29] As the historian David Watt has shown, fundamentalists of the 1920s and 1930s assessed psychology as "a satanic view of the world that was radically at odds with the gospel" and cautioned Christians that acceptance of even the most innocent-seeming psychological concepts would result in loss of faith.[30] At the same time, however, other evangelicals were in the process of developing what amounted to Christian versions of modern psychology, referring to God as the Great Psychiatrist and to the Bible as a therapeutic guide to life. In 1952 the Christian Association for Psychological Studies was formed, and in 1954 the first annual Calvinistic Conference on Psychology and Psychiatry convened. Fuller Theological Seminary started a graduate school of psychology in 1965, as Christian counseling centers and psychiatric clinics, providing mental health services "from a biblical perspective," surged.[31] By the 1970s, as Watt concludes, "the evangelical subculture was less a bulwark against than a variant of the therapeutic culture."[32]

As evangelicals gradually ceased denouncing psychology outright, they shifted the battle lines, accepting the psychologists' diagnosis of modern dilemmas while asserting that the cure for emotional sickness was religious faith rather than secular therapies.[33] Popular evangelical writers increasingly began to discuss problems in terms of "anxiety" and "inferiority complexes" and advised readers on heightening "self-esteem" and fulfilling emotional "needs," however, and the boundary between religious and secular prescriptions steadily blurred. Religious writers quoted enthusiastically from psychotherapists and other "positive thinkers" such as Dale Carnegie and Joshua Loth Liebman.[34] Continuing to denounce liberal Protestants for accommodating and selling out to "secular humanism," evangelical authors devised an updated theology of their own, in which sin was often reconceptualized as sickness and concerns over salvation were replaced by concerns for earthly happiness, comfort, and health. Those who packaged their message most successfully, such as the well-known Christian pediatrician and psychologist James Dobson, tended to address a largely female audience and directed their concerns to marriage and family life, sex, and depression.

The historian Donald Meyer, whose 1965 study of "religion as pop psychology" was published just prior to *The Triumph of the Therapeutic,* shared Rieff's argument and gave it a historical frame of reference, looking back to Mary Baker Eddy and the theology of mind cure for precedents of current therapeutic religion.[35] Having failed to recognize evangelicals as participants in the phenomenon he described, fifteen years later Meyer added a chapter attributing the recent upsurge of conservative evangelicalism to that group's appropriation of positive thinking and practices of healing therapy. Tracing the career of Oral Roberts, who ceased his tent meeting healing services in favor of building a colossal modern hospital, Meyer noted the urge among evangelicals to make healing "obtainable as a predictable and rational expectation."[36] Not only in the Christian counseling centers and medical centers but also in the charismatics' and other evangelicals' continuing emphasis on divine healing, the mixing of the therapeutic with popular religion became highly visible. It seemed irrefutable that a deep cultural shift "from salvation to self-realization" had taken place, as two historians independently noted not long after Meyer's postscript.[37]

Middle-class Americans, straining against the "iron cage" of cultural rationalization, have long looked for release and authenticity in therapies of physical and psychic health and personal growth.[38] In the early years of the twentieth century, the shift from moderation and prudence toward abundance and intensity helped shape the emergent consumer culture and has continued to mold popular attitudes toward community and church, as both have been transformed into consumer products. These changing attitudes have led to a surge in the so-called "small-group movement" where, according to Wuthnow, "the sacred becomes more personal, but, in the process, also becomes more manageable, more serviceable in meeting individual needs, and more a feature of group processes themselves."[39] This increase in small groups, filled with people seeking the authentic, intense experience that they fail to find elsewhere, is rooted in the cultural shift toward the therapeutic both decried and appropriated by evangelicals.

In his recent study of the small-group movement in contemporary America, Wuthnow estimates that 40 percent of all American adults (as well as a significant percentage of children and adolescents) are involved in small groups—some 75 million people. His calculations suggest that there are around three million small groups in the United States today. Under the "small group" heading Wuthnow includes discussion groups, support groups, special interest groups, prayer fellowships, Bible study groups, Sunday school classes, women's groups, self-help groups, youth groups, men's groups, couples' groups, house churches, therapy groups, singles' groups, anonymous groups, and covenant groups. According to his survey results, members of small groups most often say they feel "the need for friends who value the same things in life that they do and . . . the need for people who can give them deep emotional support"; 83 percent cite "the need for people who are never critical of them." In short, Wuthnow argues, the small-group movement is based in part upon a widespread "desire for intimacy, support, sharing, and other community involvement." While noting that small groups have long been a feature of the American religious landscape, he maintains that their current popularity among people searching for spirituality, as well as religious leaders aspiring for new forms of ministry, is unprecedented and points to a "new quest for community" in contemporary American culture.[40]

People join a support or recovery group for a variety of reasons and felt needs, many of which overlap and may remain undisclosed, diffuse, or even unconscious. Such groups then reorient the needs and desires of

their adherents in ways that change people's sense of self and push them
to conform more fully to group discipline. Critics of the movement lam-
baste the tendency among members to describe themselves as victims of
abuse, "laying claim to the crown of thorns," in Wendy Kaminer's acer-
bic words. Kaminer and others criticize the movement for its "failure
to acknowledge that there are hierarchies of human suffering," pointing to the alleged tendency to exaggerate personal pain as evidence of
the "selfism" and "narcissism" of recovery discourse.[41] Such denunci-
ations notwithstanding, recovery discourse is grounded in notions of
surrendering control over one's life, learning to be vulnerable with others and with God in order to cultivate relationships of deeper intimacy.
The paradox is that the therapeutic process supposedly also involves
learning to take charge of one's life, accepting responsibility, and cultivating discipline. It is a process involving very specific notions of illness,
disease, and healing, which have come to play an immense role in modern American culture.[42]

These themes of recovery and healing have held particular attraction
for women, as those marketing them for profit have long known. While
AA continues to count more men than women among its ranks, the per-
centages have shifted dramatically in recent years, particularly for
younger participants.[43] Other small groups, such as Codependents
Anonymous and Overeaters Anonymous, have consistently drawn
more women than men for a variety of interrelated reasons.[44]
According to Wuthnow's data, women are rather more likely overall to
get involved in a small group than are men (44 percent versus 36 percent, respectively).[45] In attracting an observably higher proportion of
women, therapeutically oriented groups resemble most organized religious communities.

Women's Aglow Fellowship is steeped in these therapeutic currents,
although adherents are not wholly comfortable with that appraisal; in
fact, perhaps to refute such a charge, one of the original founders of the
organization declared, "This was not a 'Bless Me Club' meeting once a
month: this was a group of women whose hearts were committed to in-
troducing other women to Christ."[46] Yet as Aglow has become ever
more entwined with the recovery or small-group movement over its
thirty-year history, its particular forms of shared testimonies and prayer
for healing have fostered a growing therapeutic orientation. The two
movements share emphases on surrender and discipline, rooted in their
linked evangelical history, while in recent years Aglow has appropriated
such familiar recovery concepts as codependence and knowing the

inner child. Its publications in the 1970s and 1980s increasingly made reference to the twelve steps and seemed to sanction members' participation in such groups with little or no hesitation.

An important innovation in this area occurred in 1989, when Aglow support groups were first introduced. Marking an awareness of Aglow women's desire to talk about the pain in their lives and seek healing from one another, these groups profess to offer women safe spaces for discussion, empathic listening, and prayer. Aglow support groups are less formally organized than monthly meetings or Bible studies and are inspired in large part by the recovery group model. Support group leaders receive training and certification by answering a series of questions in Aglow's *Support Group Leader's Guide,* published in 1993. According to Aglow's support group resource person, Jennie Newbrough, 239 Aglow women had been certified by May of 1996, with "probably three times that number" in the process of completion.[47]

Like the broader evangelical populace, however, Aglow leaders have remained wary of "secular" therapy and insist that God offers more than a twelve-step group possibly could. These tensions emerge in the careful words of one speaker: "Many women are helped by twelve-step groups, and that's good! But . . . don't misunderstand me here, but those groups can only carry you so far. . . . The real healer is Jesus."[48]

Curing Women's "Eerie Restlessness"

In 1881 the neurologist George Beard of New York City published his second book on a puzzling illness that was coming to be known as "nervous exhaustion," or "neurasthenia." Convinced of the peculiarly American quality of this illness, Beard pointedly entitled his book *American Nervousness.* For Beard and other observers, this term did not refer to the kind of agitated state it would later denote but instead suggested a condition of inexplicable malaise, related to what would later be loosely termed "depression."[49] "Nervousness is nervelessness—a lack of nerve force," Beard wrote, listing a wide range of symptoms that included insomnia, unreasonable fears, exhaustion, and actual physical pains. Beard anticipated new ways of understanding and treating this perplexing sickness that would be worked out more fully by psychiatrists such as Freud.[50]

Leisured women in late Victorian America seemed especially prone to nervousness, frequently complaining of mysterious fatigue or anxiety and seeking relief from a variety of curative methods. Magazines such as *Harper's Bazaar* and *Ladies' Home Journal* published myriad self-help articles advising "nervous women" to eat properly, exercise moderately, and rest well in order to still their nerves and control their emotions. Other researchers attributed female nervousness to sexual frustration. Havelock Ellis, for instance, called attention to the 55 percent of women in his study who said they had high sexual desire but only rare orgasms and lamented that their husbands were "undersexed."[51] Freud also noted women's sexual dissatisfaction as a clinical problem and, deploring the "social factors" that forced women to live thwarted lives, argued for healthier sexual mores and practices.[52] By the 1920s, with birth control practices on the upswing, the gynecologist Robert Latou Dickinson and the psychologist G. Stanley Hall were praising the apparent trend toward viewing sex as "wholesome, pleasurable, and essential for health," not only for men but for women too.[53] In what seems a reversal of Victorian concepts of health and morality, sex was now being touted as a kind of miracle cure for women's nervousness.

Even as it sought to liberate women from illness, however, this cure advanced repressive ideologies of its own, steeped in persistent Victorian notions of gender. In a fascinating discussion of sex and female psychology in the twentieth century, the historian Mary Ryan has noted that the increased acceptance and celebration of women's sexuality beginning in the 1920s worked less to free women from the constraints of Victorian morality and to heal them from nervous prostration than to bind them more tightly into the cult of femininity and plunge them headlong into such newly discovered maladies as "frigidity." Intrigued by biological sexual differences, thinkers such as Ellis and Hall concluded that women's supreme fulfillment was to be found in reproduction, which was seen as the zenith of sexual pleasure. Those women who chose not to bear children, and those who became feminists, were labeled as deviant in a variety of ways. As one psychological expert wrote of feminists: "A certain proportion of at least the most militant suffragists are neurotics who in some instances are compensating for masculine trends, in others, are more or less successfully sublimating sadistic and homosexual ones."[54]

By the 1940s, Ryan notes, this form of female psychology, a kind of vulgarized, antifeminist Freudianism, was formulated and popularized by American theorists, many of whom were women themselves. They wrote books aiming to explain the persistence of female nervousness, now described as "neurosis" and frequently attributed to hysteria, sadomasochism, narcissism, and homosexuality. Urging women to seek happiness in home and family life, fulfilling their roles as mothers, the literature on female psychology reinforced ideals of domesticity and reflected a growing anxiety over the changes in gender roles that accompanied women's increasing participation in the labor force during World War II.[55]

Not unlike bourgeois Victorian women some years earlier, middleclass and working-class American women in the 1920s, 1930s, and 1940s appeared to be afflicted with a vague sense of dissatisfaction, often construed as stemming from sexual dysfunction but just as often as the result of role confusion. Throughout women's magazines, popular psychology, and romance novels, writers stoked anxiety over female restlessness and offered their own prescriptions for it, amounting to what Elaine Tyler May has described as "a pervasive endorsement of female subordination and domesticity" that extended throughout the 1950s. Images of family life, especially those of the "happy housewife"—"the smiling, pretty, suburban matron, devoted mother of three, loyal wife, good housekeeper, excellent cook"—were extolled as the cure-all for women's unhappiness.[56]

Beneath the images of happy domesticity, however, sinister problems continued to lurk. Popular books of the postwar era decried changing gender roles, focusing not only on women's problems but also on the perceived problem of "emasculation," articulated most famously as "Momism" by Philip Wylie in his 1942 best-seller, *Generation of Vipers,* and by Edward Strecker in his 1946 examination, *Their Mothers' Sons.*[57] Underscoring this anxiety was the great success of Ferdinand Lundberg and Marynia Farnham's *Modern Woman: The Lost Sex* (1947)—Farnham was described in one contemporary study as "possibly the most frequently quoted writer on the modern woman."[58] Lundberg and Farnham claimed that "being a woman today is in many ways more of an ordeal than ever." They argued that, as a result of deep "physiological and psychological" differences between the sexes, women trying to succeed in "the male spheres of action" were paying a terrible price: the "sacrifice of [their] most fundamental instinctual strivings." Lundberg and Farnham's solution for "rehabilitating women" involved "public recognition . . . of the powerful role and special importance of mothers as transmitting agents, good or bad, of feelings, personality, and character." Reconstructing the home and elevating women's place within it was at the heart of their proposed cure.[59]

Similarly, in 1949, when *Life* magazine described the perplexing "eerie restlessness" of American women, the authors made particular reference to the home and motherhood. Seven years later a special issue of *Life* focused on problems of American women and suggested that the solution lay in thinking less about "rights" and more in terms of "privileges," defined as femininity, childrearing, and devotion to beauty.[60] The apparently immense dissatisfaction among American women, at least among middle- and upper-class white suburbanites, was to be cured through renewed attention to domesticity.

In *Blue-Collar Marriage*, first published in 1962, sociologist Mirra Komarovsky attributed the problem of women's dissatisfaction to confusion over boundaries between the masculine and feminine spheres, which, suddenly seeming to overlap in startling and unforeseen ways, left many young women with conflicting images and expectations about their proper roles in the world. In one of the earliest and most thorough studies to explore the dissonance between ideals of domestic life and the more complicated reality masked by them, Komarovsky analyzed marital satisfaction among white working-class Americans, employing case studies based on extensive one-on-one interviews with husbands and wives to determine patterns of communication and behavior and levels of happiness. Komarovsky concluded that while the majority of these families were relatively stable, about one-third were not even "moderately happy." In fact, a full 14 percent of her data sample ranked as "very unhappy," and all but one of the wives in the latter category voiced "strong regrets about their marriages." Slightly over one-third of the marriages were rated as "moderately happy," while less than one-third ranked as "happy" or "very happy."[61]

Most couples in Komarovsky's study married young and expected marriage to provide a kind of "liberation" from the constraints of the parental home. Many felt, however, that, as one woman put it, "I got married to get away from it all, but I got out of the frying pan into the fire." Komarovsky discovered numerous cases in which wives felt neglected by their husbands, whose time and interests were often absorbed by unions, friends, and church activities. Conflicts were also caused by wives' outside club activities, particularly among those who were high-school graduates.[62]

Two factors that often led to marital dissatisfaction, according to Komarovsky, were "the sharp separation of masculine and feminine tasks" and "the absence of the expectation of friendship in marriage." In women whose domestic routine was unrelieved by companionship with husbands, she observed frequent signs of dissatisfaction, including "irritability," "apathy," and "desire for a job outside the home." As Komarovsky noted, "Some situations create frustrations even when they do not violate any norms. The young wife who has no expectation of friendship in marriage can still feel lonely. The young husband who never expected a wife to share his interests can still experience boredom with her conversation." The basic problem was that traditional patterns of marriage were inadequate for "adjustment in the modern world." Arguing that "the need for psychological intimacy" was not being met within marriage, Komarovsky concluded that such marriages were only deemed "happy" if each spouse had a strong network of relatives and close friends.[63]

The crisis of female "restlessness," defined and repeatedly explored by observers in the postwar era, was reformulated yet again in 1963, when Betty Friedan gave voice to the "problem with no name" in her best-seller *The Feminine Mystique*. Wife and mother of three small children, Friedan surveyed her Smith College classmates fifteen years after their graduation, trying to ascertain whether they felt dissatisfactions and inadequacies similar to what she experienced as a woman in America. She concluded that there was "a strange discrepancy between the reality of our lives as women and the image to which we were trying to conform," that is, the image of "the feminine mystique."[64] Straining to live up to the impossible ideal of the blissful housewife, American suburban women were insultingly bombarded with vapid advice on a variety of domestic matters: "how to catch a man and keep him, how to breastfeed children and handle their toilet training, how to cope with sibling rivalry and adolescent rebellion; how to buy a dishwasher, bake bread, cook gourmet snails, and build a swimming pool with their own hands; how to dress, look, and act more feminine and make marriage more exciting; how to keep their husbands from dying young and their sons from growing into delinquents."[65] Friedan's solution, described as "A New Life Plan for Women," was to stop "conforming to the conventional picture of femininity" and actually begin to enjoy being a woman.[66]

Others viewed the crisis of American womanhood in very different terms. Like Lundberg and Farnham some twenty years earlier, various psychologists, physicians, and other clinical "experts" of the 1960s continued to view the real problem as women's rejection of their biological roles as wives and mothers, roles seen as crucial to the upholding of American democracy. Now that the so-called second wave of

American feminism was gaining ground, however, the experts had a more tangible enemy to fight. As these writers increasingly aimed their attacks at the Women's Liberation Movement, they were joined by a number of women who rejected the feminist label and fought for a return to the traditional home and family values. Many of these women were conservative evangelical Christians.

A vast literature emerged from this traditionalist perspective, much of it written by women, and most of it insisting that total fulfillment for women was to be found in marriage and motherhood. Acknowledging that under certain circumstances women might still choose to work outside the home, the writers hastened to admonish women who spent the greater part of their energies on their jobs rather than their families. Ever insistent about the seriousness of American women's "plight," Christian writers such as Anita Bryant, Marabel Morgan, and Beverly LaHaye advocated returning to the Bible and restoring one's relationship with God in order to find true freedom, self-esteem, and love.[67]

The writers of these prescriptive texts carefully utilized and reappropriated the language of women's liberation to argue that true liberation for women is found only through conforming to the will of God. Numerous Christian writers argued that God mandates a "return to the home" for those women who have misguidedly sought fulfillment outside of it. In 1971 Ruth Stafford Peale wrote a book centered on her joy at being the wife of positive thinker Norman Vincent Peale, noting that "too many people go around downgrading marriage these days. It has become a favorite indoor sport. The result is that wherever I go young married women come up to me and bewail their fate. They've been brainwashed into thinking that they're caught in an unrewarding, unstimulating, unchallenging, drab existence." The solution offered by Mrs. Peale and illustrated in various stories throughout the book was the cultivation of femininity, along with "the art of wifely persuasion." Through these methods of conforming to their own true nature and learning how to please their husbands, women would find the love and fulfillment that had thus far eluded them.[68]

Likewise, in *Let Me Be a Woman* (1976), Elisabeth Elliot, ostensibly writing to her soon-to-be-married daughter Valerie, delineated her own critique of feminism by describing the necessary restraint and discipline involved in attaining "true freedom." Noting that "equality is not a Christian ideal" (and asserting that "there is great relief in not having to be equal"), Elliot emphasized the joy to be found in subordination to the God-given authority of husbands. Counseling her readers on wifely submission, Elliot assured them that they were not to become "doormats," but rather that they should find their true selves, lovingly created by God, liberated through submission. Echoing the sentiments of a wide range of conservative evangelical women writers dismayed by feminism, Elliot urged domesticity and a renewed emphasis on femininity as the divine cure for women's persistent restlessness.[69]

Women's Aglow Fellowship, founded during the infancy of the Women's Liberation Movement, drew its early constituency from Christian housewives, appealing implicitly to their felt dissatisfaction—the "nervousness" of an earlier era—and seeking to cure it through a renewed relationship with God. Like Anita Bryant, Marabel Morgan, Beverly LaHaye, and other popular spokeswomen for evangelical Christianity, early Aglow leaders celebrated what they considered the God-ordained roles of wife and mother as the source of true liberation for women who properly pursued and fulfilled them. Women who participated in Aglow during its early years were drawn to its feminized version of Christianity, seeking a community in which to share the frustrations of their daily lives and, through prayer and encouragement, to feel these burdens transformed into privileges worthy of gratitude and joy.

As Aglow has grown and matured, and as its constituency has broadened, its prescriptions for women's problems have shifted perceptibly, reflecting a growing recognition among both leaders and participants that millions of American women, whether out of choice or of necessity, work outside the home, live as single women, or otherwise do not fit the traditional model of the ever-happy homemaker. Particularly since the 1980s, then, Aglow norms for Christian womanhood have expanded in ways unthinkable to founders and members in the fellowship's early years, a shift more thoroughly explored in Chapter 6. Even the doctrine of wifely submission to male authority, so precious to Aglow writers of the 1970s, has undergone such significant transformations that by 1995, Aglow International President Jane Hansen could repudiate the doctrine as a distortion of Biblical truth long perpetuated by men and women alike and call for displacing it with the "authentic" God-given message of mutual submission and intimacy between women and men.[70] An expansive vision of liberation for Christian women, one closer to that of some feminist thinkers than either evangelicals or feminists might like to believe, has been gathering steam among Aglow leaders; and while its eventual impact remains to be seen, its appearance may well presage a new era in evangelical thinking about gender.

This Is Home!

Aglow's history is spun out of fragments from the three contexts outlined here—the Pentecostal/charismatic tradition, the recovery movement and therapeutic culture, and the annals of middle-class women's "eerie restlessness." Aglow leaders, concerned with the religious dynamics of the group's origins, include in their formal accounts of its emergence only the first of these strands. Four Seattle-area women, wives of FGBMFI leaders, attended that group's 1967 international convention in Portland, Oregon. There, they are said to have felt a "hunger . . . for an opportunity to share their testimonies about the Lord Jesus Christ as Saviour, Baptizer, Healer, and Deliverer."[1] On the last night of that May conference, according to most accounts, these four women gathered to pray "that the Lord would raise up a Full Gospel Women's Fellowship if it be His will," a devotional group for charismatic Christian women.[72] Inspired by a sense that God was calling them to organize such a group and that their efforts would be blessed, these women returned to Seattle after the FGBMFI convention and soon arranged a Saturday morning meeting in a downtown Seattle hotel.

This first meeting took place in August and was held in a location chosen for its proximity to "the Baptist, Presbyterian, Lutheran, Catholic, and Congregational Churches in the [University] District," from which those in charge hoped to draw many mainline Protestant women. An estimated audience of 125 women attended that first meeting, which featured as its main speaker Rita Bennett, wife of the charismatic rector of St. Luke's Episcopal Church in Seattle and, with him, a leading figure in charismatic circles. Monthly meetings followed, and after several chapters formed throughout the Seattle area the organization spread rapidly across North America and eventually much of the world as Women's Aglow Fellowship International.

Ruth Gothenquist, one of the original "praying women" and a leader of the first meeting in August 1967, later recalled that the women who attended this and subsequent luncheons were "Old-Line Church members," and explained: "These women were hungry when they heard that there was more of God to be realized and experienced than had been preached in their own churches." Having been warned against or turned off by old-style Pentecostals, those attending were apparently able to feel comfortable among women of a similar lifestyle and social class and "responded freely to God" in that atmosphere, praying, worshiping, and sharing testimonies. As Gothenquist viewed it, this dynamic was "an instant formula for exponential growth."[73]

Monthly luncheon meetings multiplied rapidly, and over the next two years several women's groups formed in the Seattle area. Reminiscing about the early days of the organization, Gothenquist later described the first participants: "They faithfully invited and brought women to the meetings with the goal of seeing changed lives. They prayed for their guests, shared their own personal testimonies with them while driving to and from the hotel and were rewarded as they witnessed God's continuing blessing on our meetings."[74] Later that year one of the chapters began meeting in a furniture store, with up to two hundred women in attendance. As Katie Fortune, the soon-to-be founding editor of *Aglow* magazine, later recalled of her first meeting (in 1968), "There was absolutely no leadership, except women who felt led to do things. There was a speaker, but the meeting was pretty spontaneous. There was such an *anointing,* and I just thought to myself, 'This is home!'"[75]

The fast gains in membership and participation during this time suggest that the group began to feel like "home" for great numbers of women. They in turn were enjoined to evangelize their friends and neighbors, bringing their message of salvation to those who were not already Christians as well as urging those who were only "nominal" or "backslidden" Christians to experience a richer religious life through the empowerment of the Holy Spirit. Between 1967 and 1969 participants brought other women not yet baptized in the Holy Spirit to the meetings with them, in hopes that they would perceive their spiritual emptiness and seek spiritual gifts.

As the numbers expanded, some of the leaders began to look for ways of developing a more structured environment. In October of 1969, some of the women met to pray about forming a newsletter for participants. A few of them had some experience in writing or publishing and wanted to get the testimonies into print, to be used as a mission tool for reaching women outside of their fellowships. They gathered at the home of one of the leaders to "pray the magazine into existence," and several heard God tell them to call it "Aglow," from the scriptural verse: "Be aglow and burning with the Spirit."[76] At the same meeting, several other women received the message to print seven thousand copies of the first issue, a number reportedly far greater than the women had expected. As for financing the magazine, the women donated "as much [time and money] as they could." The first issue came out in November of 1969, filled with testimonies and notices of charismatic prayer meetings in the greater Seattle area, and according to those who worked on it, all seven thousand copies "disappeared quickly," many of them mailed to friends and relatives around the country. In fact, as Fortune later noted, "The magazine grew really before the organization grew. . . . Because the Lord knew that once we got these testimonies out, more women would want to be a part of [it]."[77]

Fortune and her loyal staff of unpaid workers (who would not receive salaries until some years later) deserve credit for advancing a successful formula for their magazine and so immeasurably aiding the organization's expansion. That formula, long used in similar forms of devotional literature, was simple, informal, and affable, forging a sense of caring identification between writers and readers. From the beginning, the digest-sized magazines included author photos with every testimony, along with a short informational blurb describing the writer's family, religious background, church affiliation, and Aglow participation. Author photos often included husbands and children in cozy scenes of family togetherness. There were no advertisements for any products other than materials published by Aglow authors. Readers were invited to become magazine distributors and to start their own monthly fellowships, providing a sense of participation in a vital, growing ministry.

Originally printed in black and white, by 1972 the magazine used glossy, colored graphics and photographs and managed to look professional without being suspiciously sleek, maintaining the warmth that appealed to the thousands of women who read it and contributed personal testimonies. In an interview with me, Fortune insisted that under her leadership stories were not edited for content but only for spelling and grammar, so that authors could give their testimonies in their own words. She also acknowledged rejecting testimonies that seemed "suspect" or inappropriately "glorified the person rather than God." By the time Fortune resigned as editor in 1977, the yearly subscription price remained only two dollars (four issues at fifty cents per issue), a price insisted upon by Fortune in order to keep the magazine affordable and accessible to all women. Her successor, former managing editor Ann Thomas, changed the magazine from a quarterly to a bimonthly publication and raised the total cost to $2.50 per year (a reduction in cost of single issues), where it remained steady through the tenure of another editor until a whole new group of editors, declaring that the Aglow organization no longer wished to subsidize the cost of the magazine, raised the price to six dollars in 1983.[78]

The same year that the magazine was founded, 1969, the group received status as a nonprofit religious group called the "Full Gospel Women's Fellowship." In 1970 the official "Purpose" and "Doctrinal Statement" were codified, although both evolved somewhat in later years.[79] The organization became more structured in 1971, when the first national officers were elected and a constitution was written, establishing five male pastors as "advisors" to the women leading the group. The group continued to expand its staff, naming an international outreach director and six national directors to oversee the rapid growth across the continent.[80]

In 1972, with more than sixty fellowships operating in the United States, the organization was incorporated as Women's Aglow Fellowship International. Subscriptions to *Aglow* magazine reached fifteen thousand that year and the first Aglow Bible study, *Creation,* was published. During the next two years new fellowships formed in Canada, New Zealand, and the Netherlands, and the first international conference was held in October of 1974 at the Seattle Center, with "up to one thousand people" in attendance from twenty-five states, the Netherlands, Mexico, Canada, and Nigeria. By that year 197 fellowships were in existence. *Aglow* magazine had a volunteer staff of twenty women and a subscription rate of over seventy-five thousand, with issues "going to America, Canada and fifty foreign countries." Aglow Publications had also begun to produce books, audiotapes, and Bible studies "designed especially for charismatic women."[81] Three years later, in 1977, eight hundred fellowships were thriving worldwide throughout the Americas, Africa, Europe, and Asia.

The year 1980 was a significant one for Aglow, a kind of turning point in the organization's history. The group sponsored its first international conference outside North America, and more than seven hundred women and men convened in Jerusalem for that event. Also, Margaret Moody, elected as Aglow's second president in 1975, was ousted from office after an internal squabble in which her competence as a leader was challenged and found wanting. At this point, control changed hands and Jane Hansen was elected the third international president of Aglow, an office she continues to hold in 1997. This shift in leadership had enormous implications for the shape taken by Aglow since that time. Jane Hansen has proved to be a powerful and occasionally controversial leader. A dynamic woman with ties to powerful evangelical organizations around the world, Hansen has been at the helm of what some earlier leaders have perceived as a major shift toward world (as opposed to local) evangelization.[82]

In 1982 *Aglow* magazine dramatically changed format, leaving behind its modest digest-sized issues for a "new" and larger version. An opening editorial in this fall issue noted these and other changes, citing the need to compete in the market of Christian women's magazines. The editor also informed her readers that the new magazine would now have more "teaching articles" along with extensive information about all Aglow publications and statistics on the global growth and mission work of Aglow. These changes would come at an increased price of one dollar per issue, double the previous cost. The cozy familiarity of the early magazine, and its enthusiasm for ordinary testimonies, had apparently passed along with the small format: now, rather than encouraging readers to send in their testimonies, photos, and personal information to be "prayerfully considered" by the editors, a tiny blurb tersely advised that articles and testimonies would be "considered," adding, "No poetry please."

Even that somewhat half-hearted statement was amended in 1988 to read: "Articles and testimonies that encourage, instruct, inform, and entertain Christian women and relate to the work and gifts of the Holy Spirit will be considered after the submission of a written query. These should deal with issues relevant to women today." Meanwhile, as the number of such testimonies printed in the magazine declined, the space allotted to articles written by Aglow's international leaders, advisors, and *Aglow* editors substantially increased. Now, instead of being filled with testimonies sent in by subscribers around the country, the magazine's pages were devoted primarily to educational articles from famous male ministers such as John Wimber, Jack Hayford, and Larry Christenson; female public figures like Dee Jepson, former special assistant to President Ronald Reagan; and established Christian writers and "regular contributors," such as Elizabeth Sherrill, Marie Sontag, and Kathy Collard Miller.[83]

Other changes, many unacknowledged, were also evident. Those testimonies from subscribers that were printed seemed to be more heavily edited than before; consistently, for example, an author's name would be followed by "as told to," indicating substantial revisions in the story (with the presumed effect of standardizing them more thoroughly).

Also, though in 1984 the editors had proudly asserted their refusal to accept paid advertising, in 1987 editor Gwen Weising announced as "exciting" the reversal of this anti-advertising policy and noted that subscribers would now receive "the opportunity to read about products and services that will benefit you and your family" (though adding a disclaimer absolving Aglow from responsibility for the merchandise or claims of advertisers). Immediately, subscribers could learn not only about Aglow products and conferences but those sponsored by other religious publishers, along with curricula for home-schooling parents, audiotapes on Christian financial planning, bank checks inscribed with Bible verses, seminary programs, greeting cards, rhinestone "Jesus" pins, rehabilitation clinics, weight-loss products, and Christian exercise videos. That same year, the system for numbering issues changed from "number so-and-so" to "volume 18 number 1" and so forth, perhaps to sound more professional. By now hardly distinguishable from other glossy evangelical magazines like *Today's Christian Woman*, *Aglow* lasted less than five more years and folded in 1991.[84]

By 1987 the Aglow organization counted 1,827 fellowships in the United States, and members paid ten dollars in annual dues.[85] That same year, however, the number of fellowships in the United States began to decline, even as the numbers abroad continued to grow. Though *Aglow* magazine was discontinued in 1991, apparently because of financial strain, the organization continued to publish books and a newsletter for members entitled *Aglow's Connection* (which became simply *Connection* in 1996), later published both in hard text and on-line at Aglow's Web site on the Internet.[86] Also in 1991 Aglow raised its yearly dues to twenty-five dollars and lost more than sixteen hundred members. In September 1993 Aglow claimed a membership of 19,717 women in the United States and an estimated twenty thousand more throughout the world, from Pentecostal, Roman Catholic, Eastern Orthodox, and mainline Protestant affiliations.[87] In 1995, down to 18,828 American members, Aglow initiated "candlelight groups" (internationally) and "field fellowships" (nationally), signifying groups working toward full affiliation but "not yet able to meet the requirements of a local fellowship." Consequently, in March of 1996 Aglow could count 1,454 active fellowships in the United States and 41 field fellowships and touted a renewed growth in its numerical strength.[88]

For an organization whose magazine alone once worked with a budget of $1 million and had sixty-five thousand subscribers, the current numbers indicate that the organization's membership has declined.

While still the world's largest interdenominational evangelical women's organization, Aglow's growth—particularly in North America—has not measured up to many members' numerical expectations, although outwardly the women appear optimistic about Aglow's future and refer expectantly to an imminent global "revival" in which Aglow is expected to play a major role. Such references are mixed with statements of disapproval at the current "worldliness" of the United States, a belief that may help leaders as well as participants explain the declining numbers in Aglow membership. In interviews with me, a few early Aglow members who no longer actively participate in the organization expressed some reservations about the direction Aglow has taken over the last ten to fifteen years, viewing the organization as not only shrinking in numbers but also declining in purpose. The thousands of women who continue to participate in Aglow of course think differently.

Another recent development in Aglow is the attempt to foster racial reconciliation, both within the organization itself and in American society at large. The impressive ethnic diversity of audiences gathered from around the world for international conferences has undoubtedly contributed to this development, as has the growing participation of women of color in U.S. fellowships. African American, Native American, and Hispanic women have spoken to Aglow audiences on numerous occasions about the enduring ills of racism in America, urging their mostly white audiences to take it upon themselves to work for healing between and among various racial and ethnic groups in their neighborhoods, towns, and churches. The 1994 national conference, held in Nashville, Tennessee, was largely devoted to acknowledging and ameliorating the bitter racial divides in America, a task that, as Hansen noted in her opening remarks, "starts and stops at the cross." One of the main workshops the following day, entitled "Racial Reconciliation," was facilitated by a Haida Indian woman who is a member of Aglow's International Board of Directors and an African American woman who is a former board member. The main thrust of their message to workshop participants was that "racial reconciliation needs to begin with women."[89]

At another session during the same conference, a male speaker discussed a "stronghold of death over our cities" that he described as rooted in white racism toward "people of color, especially African Americans and Native Americans." Giving a fervent message on the absolute need to humble oneself before those whom one has injured before one approaches God, he forcefully enjoined the white members of the audience to summon the courage to speak words of confession to people of other races and to "turn from your evil ways." Then the speaker asked everyone from African American and Native American backgrounds to stand, and as perhaps 150 women of the 500 participants stood, he talked about the cross of Jesus and of their obligation as Christians somehow to forgive whites for their wickedness. Reminding the white members of the audience of the immensity of their task and responsibility, he asked them to stand with the women of color, move toward them, and offer them prayers of sincere repentance and promise. In a scene that was at once profoundly moving and relentlessly uncomfortable, women of all races wept aloud, embraced one another, and pronounced a desire to break through the barriers that had long separated them.[90]

The theme of reconciliation extended into the closing session of the conference, when several Native American Aglow members representing different tribes presented a Star Quilt as a symbol of racial unity and "God's wisdom and love." With a red star in the center, "represent[ing] the blood of Christ" and other colors of the star "represent[ing] different races of people," the quilt became for conference leaders and attendees "a symbol of Aglow's reconciliation into oneness in Jesus, the body of Christ."[91] The conference illuminated what appears to be a major theme within Aglow in the mid-1990s, one that echoes similar attempts at white repentance and interracial cooperation made by evangelical groups such as the Southern Baptist Convention, Promise Keepers, and the Christian Coalition.[92] Aware of stereotypes that incorrectly portray Aglow as wholly white, leaders are devoting much effort to reaching out to women of color and making Aglow a more thoroughly diverse organization at all levels. Whether that effort will ultimately succeed remains to be seen.

In recent years Aglow has produced astonishing success in international expansion—there will soon be more Aglow chapters in Africa, Asia, Australia, New Zealand, and Europe than in the United States—and has forged strong connections to large evangelical networks and powerful leaders, both in the United States and around the world.[93] Yet in many ways what happens at the top levels of Aglow has little immediate bearing at the local level, where chapters serve "smaller" purposes, bringing women together to pray for one another and share stories about their relationships and daily anxieties more than to pray unceasingly for the conversion of the world. In this sense one participant's characterization of Aglow as a "big support group for hurting women" captures a significant measure of truth. Whatever differences or tensions may exist between the global aspirations of the international leaders and the rather more limited concerns of local participants, Aglow ultimately serves both purposes, aiming to establish an intimate network of caring, praying women that can evangelize and heal their sisters across all parts of the earth.

2

Released, Restored, Set Free

Spirituality in Practice

On a frosty winter evening, ten o'clock, five hundred women sit in long rows of chairs in a high-ceilinged, windowless conference area, facing a wide stage. Behind their backs, stretching wall to wall, are tables holding coffee machines, plastic pitchers filled with ice water, and paper cups. The room, decorated in soft peach and green hues, is dimly lit and very warm, and many of the women have removed their sweaters and sit in short sleeves. A spotlight shines on the central podium, where all eyes appear to be fixed, and a concentrated silence marks spectators' rapt attention to the program.

Gwen, the main speaker for the New England Women's Aglow Winter Retreat, concludes her hour-long talk here by inviting all women present to come forward and receive prayers for healing. As the music swells amidst murmured supplications, she speaks the following prayer: "Lord I know you came to deliver us, to cleanse us, to make us holy. . . . Father, we choose in the name of Jesus to release those who have shamed us. . . . Father, I thank you that your word said, 'You will not be ashamed.' . . . I pray now in the name of Jesus for women here tonight who have been shamed, maybe by rape or by something else. . . . Father, right now in the name of Jesus, I thank you that we are being set free from shame. Help us to realize tonight that we're bone of your bone, flesh of your flesh, that you've made us holy, and we are your bride." Looking out at her audience, Gwen asks the women to remain seated a moment longer while she tells about her own "shame."

The events she describes in excruciating detail include being raped by her babysitter at the age of five and later molested repeatedly by her brother, being obese as an adolescent and overwhelmed by mocking in school, and being neglected and "pushed around" by her husband during the early years of their marriage. She insists that God has healed her from the shame of these events but admits that she continues to have difficulty loving and accepting herself. She paces rapidly back and forth as she talks, gripping the microphone close to her lips and reaching out her free hand with upturned palm as if to embrace or caress the women listening to her.

Gwen's voice shakes as if she is recalling her own pain and feeling the suffering of other women like her; suddenly, she stops and shouts out for anyone who has experienced shame of whatever kind to hand her burden over to Jesus, to let God cleanse her and heal her. The background music intensifies as Gwen begins to cry and moan while continuing to urge her audience to come and receive healing, her pleas growing louder and increasingly fervent. Her prayers are interspersed with cries of resistance against Satan: "Devil, we come against you, we *rebuke* you, in the name of Jesus!" The women, most of whom have hardly taken their eyes off Gwen except to close them in supplication, respond actively, yearningly, to her call. Many weep in their seats, some calling out, "Father!" or "Oh Jesus!" Others, in varying states of emotional need or distress, rise and move down the aisles to the stage to receive prayers from Gwen and her crew of prayer counselors. Abruptly Gwen puts down her microphone, motions to the musicians to keep playing, and descends the stairs to the floor. For over two hours she stands at the front, praying over individual women by laying hands on their heads and shouting for the spirits of shame to come out, then murmuring more softly, "Thank you, Father," "Thank you, Jesus." Meanwhile, those seated in the audience sing, hold one another, and pray together, stopping occasionally to watch the gripping events at the front of the room.

Now a poised, slender woman with tinted blonde hair, stylishly attired, Gwen shows little trace of the traumas that apparently colored her early life. She travels throughout the country sharing her testimony and urging other women who have suffered the pain of abuse to fight against the satanic powers of darkness and surrender to Jesus, who will free them from their anger and give them peace. While Gwen appears rather more affluent than many members of this particular audience, both her story and her tears seem to bridge the gaps between herself and those listening to her. On this particular night the laying on of hands following her impassioned talk and prayer lasts for two hours, as more than three hundred women go forward to pray for release from the shame that continues to bind them.

The effects on the women present seem immense. Throughout the room women are sobbing, embracing each other, praying over one another, shouting out in the name of Jesus for the demons of shame to leave the bodies of those they inhabit and defile. Some women fall to the floor, "slain in the spirit," as if entranced or temporarily unconscious; others wail with anguish, as helpers and friends gather round to guide them through a torturous process of remembrance, exorcism, and forgiveness. After receiving prayers, women walk slowly back to their seats, wiping their eyes with matted tissues and soothing each other with promises of Jesus' healing power and the eternal love of their heavenly father. Some quietly share stories with those sitting near them about violence and shame they experienced as little girls or adolescents, still struggling with feelings of guilt and anger and seeking reassurance and comfort from each other.

Midnight. The last women to receive prayers at the front return to their seats. Gwen ascends the stage and stands at the podium once again, this time to close the evening service. The music ceases as she raises her arms and tells the audience to stand. Following Gwen's lead, the women lift their arms and repeat after her, invoking the four winds of God to blow upon them and release them from any remnants of shame and fear. Standing upright, many swaying slowly, the women face Gwen as she delivers the closing prayer, thanking God for sending his Holy Spirit down to chase the demons of shame from the souls and bodies of everyone present tonight and for restoring them to wholeness, victory, and freedom. The room buzzes as women tearfully murmur "Thank you, Jesus," "We praise you, Lord," "Yes, Father." The four-hour session is concluded, and five hundred women leave the room to face the world outside.[1]

For charismatic Christian women, this kind of scene is less extraordinary than ordinary, replayed in seemingly endless permutations and settings throughout the country. No matter how often it recurs, however, the event retains for participants its sense of miracle and mystery, as the women come to feel healed, inwardly transformed, and outwardly set free through the power of the Holy Spirit. Having endured painful events that left them angry, disappointed, despairing, fearful, ashamed, self-hating, and perhaps even suicidal, participants come to experience God's loving presence in sessions such as this one, discerning heavenly embraces to be almost as tangible as those of the women with whom they pray. Enveloped in what they feel to be Jesus' loving forgiveness and affirmation, the women publicly experience joyous release from bondage and deliverance from shame, again and again.

The capacity for feeling healed, transformed, and liberated in these settings is animated by shared theological beliefs as well as by culturally informed assumptions about the dynamics of suffering and restoration. However natural and authentic these experiences and emotions may feel, they are patterned after narrative accounts told by other women and so are generated out of a social context that defines what have been called "emotion rules." To analyze the emotions that accompany charismatic healing is not to deny their power or reality, but simply to interpret these emotions as cultural and social codes and to ascertain the values—crystallized, in this case, as religious or theological—that help create and frame them in specific narrative forms.[2] Those women who choose to participate in the emotional experiences cultivated in charismatic meetings must reconstruct their life stories and refashion themselves according to these available forms, forms flexible enough to allow variant meanings yet sufficiently restricted to sustain the authority of the narrative itself, elicit correct attitudes and feelings, and produce disciplined religious selves. This chapter explores these transformations by examining the theology, ritual spaces, and religious practices of prayer in Aglow settings, analyzing the formation of a ritual sense by which these women construct and assimilate newly transformed identities not previously imagined.

Into the Heart of Jesus

In the first chapter I described the theological background of Women's Aglow as composed largely of evangelical, Pentecostal, and fundamentalist strands, intertwined in the healing and charismatic movements of the mid-twentieth century. The original founders of Aglow were mainline Protestants, and many of the early members were connected to Dennis Bennett's charismatic Episcopal church in Seattle. The women who organized and led the early meetings aimed at attracting women from all Christian denominations, including the Roman Catholic Church, as well as the previously "unchurched" and those who were "backslidden." This theological diversity has remained

strong in Aglow over the years; indeed, Aglow has been highly successful at attracting women from a wide range of theological affiliations.
Although Aglow headquarters does not keep precise statistics on members' denominational preferences, a 1992 survey of Aglow members
produced the following results: 47.4 percent of respondents said they
attend a Pentecostal or charismatic church; 22.7 percent said
"Protestant"; 17.9 percent said "nondenominational"; 9.2 percent said
"Catholic"; and 2.8 percent specified "Baptist."[3]

Since Aglow is a transdenominational organization, discussions of
theological distinctions between denominations—indeed, of systematic
theology in general—have been discouraged in favor of the "simple"
theology that they claim all true Christians hold. This de-emphasizing
of theological intricacies is expressed in part as a desire to return to the
purity of the early church and also as a challenge to the supposed
"deadness" of the churches. In 1972 a Baptist woman writing in *Aglow*
magazine told of her distress over the "indifference, lukewarmness and
even coldness" of the churches and of her own "emptiness and spiritual
hunger" within her denomination: "I had accepted, without reserva-
tion, what my denomination believed and taught. But now there was
such a stirring deep down in my soul that I wanted instruction and direction from God alone."[4] Moving beyond church structures and theological doctrines to the simplicity of "God alone" was, for her as for
other Aglow women, a necessary step along the Christian path to salvation. One of the purposes for the founding of Aglow, as I noted in the
previous chapter, was to provide a meeting ground for women who
wanted to share this orientation toward "God alone" with each other,
a move that could effectively work to undercut the message of the
churches.

Aglow leaders, long aware of this potential of parachurch organizations to subvert the churches, have sought to retain the approval of
church leaders by encouraging members to find and participate actively
in a "church home." Sometimes lamenting the division of Christianity
into multiple denominations, they have also described Aglow as a tool
for unity within and among the different churches. In the second issue
of *Aglow* magazine, for instance, a Dominican sister voiced her longing
for a new "sisterhood that would reach beyond denomination into the
heart of Jesus" and requested prayers that this new fellowship would
be "a means of unity rather than division."[5] Fourteen years later, an as-
sociate editor of the magazine found it necessary to chide her readers
for concentrating all their energy on Aglow at the expense of local church

congregations, insisting, "Aglow is not competing with local churches or in any way replacing them. In fact, Aglow is a loyal ally of the church, a friend who encourages women to become vital members of their respective congregations."[6]

As much as Aglow leaders may insist upon their essential harmony with the churches, however, tensions persist, stemming in part from the common assumption among religious leaders that parachurch growth can drain energy away from the churches (and vice versa). In 1993 one of the international coordinators for Aglow informed me in an interview that the major reason Aglow had been going through "rocky times" in the United States was that "the church is fulfilling a role that it wasn't when Aglow first began." In contrast, she continued, the church is "still way behind" Aglow's progress in most other parts of the world, so that Aglow fellowships are able to flourish in foreign nations.[7] Another time, one of the national leaders of Aglow in Australia told me that "twenty-five years ago, when Aglow began," there were "very few openings for women's ministry in the churches," but now "there are so many more opportunities" that women are getting more involved in their churches today than ever before. This woman also emphasized, however, that the credit for women's expanded role in church ministry is largely Aglow's, so that, ironically, Aglow's growth and influence has furthered its own decline.[8]

Other tensions, less explicitly addressed in the Aglow literature, came to the fore during the "Alone in the Pew" workshop described in the previous chapter. As I noted there, Eleanor, the leader of that workshop, urged participants (all of whom were assumed to have non-Christian husbands) to stay home from church on occasional Sunday mornings and "lie in bed" with their husbands. Even as she noted that this advice to skip church "flies in the face of everything the church teaches," she stood her ground, resolved that church obligations should in this case be temporarily shelved for the sake of the marriage. Eleanor strengthened her point by reminding the women that men's jealousy could easily be incurred by their wives' religious practice, noting, "Your husband may see Jesus or the Church as your *lover* that takes you away from him."[9] These words highlight not only the peculiar competition that Aglow women sometimes feel to exist between their husbands and their own piety, but also the recognition among religious women that sometimes, to maintain harmony at home, they must disobey their pastors. Eleanor's defense of that practice undercuts the claims of church authority in bounded but certain terms.

Other tensions result from the attempt to minimize differences in denominations, as well as in theology, to bring unity within the organization. Theological and denominational differences persist, particularly between Protestants and Catholics, and may erupt as conflict in unexpected places. A story published in *Aglow* magazine about a family who tried to "convert" Catalina, a seventeen-year old Spanish Roman Catholic exchange student living with them, drew an angry rejoinder from a Catholic reader: "As a Christian who is of the Catholic persuasion, I find the whole idea that Catalina 'needed' to be converted disgusting. If the family was more interested in a loving exchange of ideas rather than 'converting a student' they could have alternated attending different churches—Spanish mass one week, the author's church the next, a Spanish evangelical congregation the third week. I think the result would have been an appreciation of how God's power works through the different churches." In response the magazine editor printed a carefully worded apology "for our insensitivity to our Catholic friends" and asked forgiveness for "our blind spot."[10] Strains between Protestants and Catholics have endured—there are few Roman Catholic women at the highest levels of the organization—but have been generally muted, since numerous members and local leaders are Catholic.

What the women of Aglow have shared throughout the organization's history, regardless of denominational affiliation, is an emphasis on the power of the Holy Spirit to effect healing and transformation in and through them, power administered through the bestowal of the spiritual gifts.[11] Calling themselves "spirit-filled Christian women," their only requirement for regular membership, other than yearly dues, has been an "openness to the spiritual gifts" described in the New Testament: wisdom, knowledge, faith, healing, miracles, prophecy, discernment of spirits, speaking in tongues, and the interpretation of tongues.[12] The Holy Spirit is believed actually to enter their physical bodies and fill them to overflowing with joy and power. The initial sign of this experience, described as the "baptism in the Holy Spirit," is glossolalia, or "speaking in tongues," interpreted as a spiritual language known only to God. Once baptized in the spirit, the tongue speaker may thereafter will to pray aloud in this spiritual "prayer language," accessing it like a secret code. Tongue speaking then becomes a language of worship, a way of expressing that love for God which is so profound as to be inexpressible in ordinary human speech.[13]

Aglow women share a conception of God as male, omniscient, and omnipotent. As creator and master of the universe, God rules over a divinely ordered hierarchy that extends down through men, then women, and finally children. Traditionally, Aglow has affirmed the conservative evangelical teaching that just as children are to obey their parents—or, to switch metaphors, just as the Church is to obey Christ—women are to be in submission to men as their leaders. As Eadie V. Goodboy, author of an early Aglow Bible study on this topic, writes: "The laws of God are immutable. When we 'break' them we are in reality only breaking ourselves against them. We must learn to obey our husbands, and obey other members of the Body [the church] who have authority as God's delegates. In the honoring of and submission to these leaders, we are honoring and being in submission to Jesus."[14] Obedience to God, from this perspective, requires from women obedience to those believed to be his earthly representatives: husbands, ministers, and other male authorities. At the same time, however, Aglow writers have long been careful to remind their readers that God does not favor men over women but loves and treats them in equal and balanced fashion. Although by the 1990s some modifications of this gender hierarchy had begun to take place among Aglow leaders, the older model, dominant for most of the group's history, has exerted considerably greater influence over all aspects of the organization since the beginning.

Not simply an authoritarian taskmaster, God is believed to be a loving father, ever concerned for his children's welfare and available to them in times of suffering. He is thought to have implanted a "need" in the hearts of people everywhere, described often as a "God-shaped void" or vacuum that only he can fill. In testimonies of conversion, Aglow women describe searching anxiously for happiness in all the wrong places, desperate and dissatisfied until finally they recognize God as the source of love and peace, surrendering to him and feeling as if they have "come home" at last. Only God can fulfill the deep needs for comfort, acceptance, and intimacy felt by all people, the women contend, and they continually remind one another to seek joy in obedience to him. Like devout Christians in other times and places, these women's search for power ends "in the arms of the Lord."[15]

Additionally, the women of Aglow hold in common a sense of Jesus as a personal companion, easily accessible via conversational prayer and always ready to intercede on their behalf to God. As "the One who will never leave you or forsake you," Jesus is both Savior and Baptizer, having given up his life and shed his blood to bring salvation to those who believe in him and to empower them to live in a fallen world.[16] Metaphors describing Jesus range widely, from friend, to lover or husband, and even to a child who needs the protection of a mother. Even more than God, Jesus is envisioned as longing desperately for human beings to turn to him with love and gratitude, and Aglow women often pray to Jesus in a nurturing, maternal way.

The three persons of God—Father, Son, and Holy Spirit—are distinct in evangelical theology; yet these women often mix them as if they were interchangeable, in prayer as well as narrative accounts of God's working in their lives. This theological blurriness is part of the tendency to emphasize intimacy over conceptual intricacy and so rank "the heart" higher than "the head." This is a frequent theme in Aglow stories, as in Claire's admission of the manner in which her intelligence interfered with her spiritual growth: "As an intellectual, having studied toward a Ph.D., I acknowledged Jesus as the Son of God but never conceded to Him as my Savior and my Lord." Only when she surrendered her intellect and accepted God into her heart was she made "whole."[17] Another woman, Judith, described resisting the Holy Spirit after going to graduate school: " 'After all,' I'd rationalized, 'speaking in tongues doesn't really fit comfortably in the world of intellectual theology and psychology.' " Like Claire, Judith had to learn to ignore the "textbooks" in order to "pour out [her] heart" and walk with God.[18] Not simply professing a detached acceptance of Christian dogma, Aglow women have sought to experience God through a personal relationship.

Not surprisingly, then, the doctrinal statements codified in Aglow have provided a kind of broad theological reference point for Aglow women, yet have played little role in the everyday workings of the organization. In its early days Aglow adopted a statement that generally followed the Nicene Creed, adding points about the Bible as the inspired word of God, the gifts of the Holy Spirit, and divine healing.[19] That statement was revised several times through the years but remained essentially the same.[20] Rather than being printed in every issue of *Aglow*, however, the statement was condensed to this brief affirmation, inscribed on the magazine's masthead from 1988 to 1991:

> Women's Aglow Fellowship provides support, education, training, and ministry opportunities to help women worldwide discover their true identity in Jesus Christ through the power of the Holy Spirit. We believe that:

- All women and men are created equal in the image of God, each with dignity and value
- God has a unique purpose for each of us and equips us for that purpose
- We can reach our full potential only after finding identity and restoration in Jesus Christ.[21]

Downplaying theological specifics, the statement emphasizes equality, personal growth, self-esteem, and emotional closeness with Jesus over orthodox belief, revealing its resonance with the broader culture of American evangelicalism.[22]

Aglow theology receives its fullest expression in the stories the women tell each other about their lives. Describing the ways in which they have felt the presence of God or the movement of the Holy Spirit, the women teach each other to identify divine intervention in their everyday lives, sometimes by shattering previous assumptions but more often by reinforcing existing beliefs or verifying faith that has been shaken. Theologically, what emerges from Aglow narratives is not one but many ideas about how God works in the world, filling countless roles but always working for the good of his children. Worshiping God in various manifestations—father, son, spirit, husband, lover, friend, and so on, all of which are continually reimagined and reworked—the women celebrate a God of continual surprises whose one unfailingly predictable quality is love.

One of the best ways to understand a particular religious tradition or community is to examine its eschatology, that is, its vision of the end of history and of ultimate human destiny. Like some strands of the broader charismatic and healing movements from which it emerged, Aglow has vividly conceptualized an imminent apocalypse and described the late twentieth century as the "end times."[23] Along with many of their evangelical and fundamentalist cousins, charismatics believe that Jesus will soon return to earth in order to rescue—or "rapture"—all true believers from the tribulation, or hell on earth, to come. Signs of the end times include evils ranging from increasing abortion rates and relaxed social policies toward homosexuals to the global AIDS crisis and political wars in Europe, Africa, and the Middle East. Aglow women thus endorse a sustained crisis mentality, urging continued vigilance, warfare against the devil and other enemy forces, and, most importantly, unceasing prayer.

Like other Pentecostal and charismatic offspring, Aglow combines theological elements from various sources outside the received orthodoxy of their revivalistic traditions, including the positive thinking made famous by Norman Vincent Peale; the message of prosperity offered in different ways by Oral Roberts, Kenneth Hagin, and Pat Robertson; and the forms of healing taught by John Wimber. In line with the Pentecostal emphasis of religious experience over or prior to doctrine, Aglow has intentionally remained open to the stirrings of the spirit manifested in these distinctive teachings and tolerant of a challenging variety of Christian interpretation, thereby avoiding the dryness of strict theological formalism. Like the "soft Pentecostalism" noted by Randall Balmer and Jesse Todd in their description of the California megachurch Calvary Chapel, Aglow has successfully amalgamated conservative theology with elements more in accord with popular middle-class tastes and concerns.[24] Ever aware of the need to strike a middle ground between extreme responses to secular culture—accommodation versus condemnation—leaders skillfully appropriate modern influences and reframe them to religious ends. The result, a zesty potpourri of moral austerity, cheerful pragmatism, and apocalyptic urgency, is a classic example of the eclecticism and adaptability of the evangelical tradition in America.

The shifting nature of Aglow theology is richly demonstrated by the oscillations between traditional views of personal sin and culturally influenced ideas about victimization at the hands of others. Aglow, along with American Christianity more broadly, has gradually but perceptibly adapted the therapeutic discourse of "shame" and recovery to its own ends, focusing on the prevalence of emotional, physical, and sexual abuse in the lives of participants and on various divinely ordained measures for healing and "deliverance" from such suffering. While not doing away entirely with more orthodox formulations of sin and guilt, the modern approach to conversion has appeared to be more occupied with healing shame than urging repentance. In this way divine images are softened, and, as one sociologist writes, "God becomes an instrument for the alleviation of the psychological burdens of men and women."[25] To suggest that the emphasis on shame has replaced sin altogether would be exaggerated, but clearly the more traditional script of repenting sorrowfully before a stern and majestic God has been modified and reframed, making way for a somewhat domesticated version of divinity to emerge.

Although conservative in many respects, Aglow doctrine does not constitute "fundamentalism" strictly defined. Pentecostals and charismatics have long been mistakenly equated with fundamentalists in popular as well as scholarly accounts, despite the fact that Pentecostalism and fundamentalism have distinct historical origins and were for some time separated into enemy camps. According to the New Testament scholar and Pentecostal historian Russell Spittler, Pentecostalism in North America "sustains the fundamentalist urge" that coalesced in the early decades of the twentieth century and was retooled by Jerry Falwell in the 1980s. Still, fundamentalism is too narrow a term to encompass the diversity of theological styles and biblical interpretation of latter-day Pentecostals and charismatics. Spittler describes the category of Pentecostalism into which Aglow may be placed: "On balance, the Pentecostals turn out to be more restorationist, less aware of the course of Christian tradition, less polemic, collectively less antimodernist, more oriented toward personal charismatic experience, less politically involved, as much or more socially involved . . ., more ecumenical and less separatist, considerably less rationalistic and more inclined toward religious emotion, increasingly less dispensational, and perennially less theologically sophisticated."[26] Aglow women may well "think and act like fundamentalists" in some cases—interpreting the Bible as inerrant, for instance—yet the theological elasticity of the organization and its emphasis on the "heart of Jesus" rather than the intellectual refinement of believers clearly differentiate them from classical fundamentalists.

Aglow theology, then, is a fluid mix of ideas gleaned from widely diverging cultural, social, and religious milieux. At the same time that it is bounded by an emphasis on ordered hierarchy and a supposedly simple biblical orientation, this theology is strikingly mutable, continually reshaped by details of individual experience and cultural influence. Emphasizing both discipline and deliverance, this theology aims at revitalizing the drier theology of most conventional churches and hinges on the oft expressed desire, believed to be fulfilled in Jesus, "just to be free."[27] That desire receives concrete expression in the settings where Aglow ritual activity occurs and where theology is performed, taught, and variously experienced.

Sanctified Spaces

Aglow women believe that all space is holy space, since God is everywhere active and accessible and cannot be limited by human will or imagination. Nonetheless there is a difference between ordinary spaces—a car, for instance, which may be a site of private prayer—and intentionally created places of sacred worship, such as the rooms in which monthly Aglow meetings occur and the hotel conference centers reserved for regional or national retreats. There are also places set apart for less formal gatherings such as Bible study meetings and support groups, which usually take place at someone's home. Because women meet in these places to pray, they are all potential locations for healing and transformation.

Monthly Aglow meetings usually take place in nonreligious public buildings rented by local chapters. Hotels, restaurants, city halls, and civic auditoriums are far more common meeting places than churches, although occasionally meetings do occur in church sanctuaries or basements. (In at least one case, monthly meetings are held in a Reform Jewish synagogue.) Aglow officially claims to avoid church settings so as to reach women who are alienated from these institutions (the "unchurched") as well as to refrain from appearing to show preference toward one Christian denomination over another. I have wondered whether this avoidance also reflects tensions between Protestants and Catholics or between various Protestant groups, although participants and leaders have repeatedly denied this.

It may seem incongruous for Aglow to hold meetings in so-called secular spaces such as these, spaces that may be just as easily used for Rotary Club meetings, high school graduations, or wedding receptions. Yet American evangelical worshipers have long situated themselves outside of church settings. From the frontier camp meetings of the Baptists and Methodists in the eighteenth and nineteenth centuries to the football stadium revivals led by Oral Roberts, Billy Graham, and the Promise Keepers in the twentieth, evangelical Christians have taken their gospel into the most ordinary or "profane" of spaces, in part to suggest that God exists and should be worshiped everywhere and anywhere, not just inside traditional church buildings. Urging each other to pray in all the mundane spaces of their daily lives, including supermarkets, beauty salons, subways, automobiles, and bathtubs, Aglow women welcome the chance to bring God's love and power into the restaurants, auditoriums, and gymnasiums where they hold their meetings.[28]

Yet, as the social theorist Émile Durkheim long ago observed, communities that perceive a sharp distinction between sacred and profane powers generally require sacred space to be ritually separated from the profane world.[29] While not requiring participants to undergo purification rites of the sort Durkheim was imagining, Aglow groups sanctify ordinary spaces in specific ways, using layout and decor that in many cases replicate the arrangement of traditional churches while adding a kind of homey, feminine touch. The chairs are arranged in rows facing the front of the room, where there is a podium for those leading the meeting and an area for musicians to play the piano or guitar and lead songs. Between the chairs and the podium is usually an overhead projector, which displays song lyrics on the front wall. Nearby, either to the side or in the back, are tables displaying books published by Aglow Publications (along with some from other evangelical publishers) as well as tapes from previous meetings. Other tables may display a variety of religious consumer goods: jewelry such as Aglow pins or dove-shaped earrings, bumper stickers inscribed with scripture verses, inspirational bookmarks, and mugs decorated with hearts and the Aglow motto, "a network of caring women." In this area is also a table laden with coffee and snacks, usually cookies or other baked goods. Around holidays such as Christmas, Thanksgiving, St. Patrick's Day, and the Fourth of July, the displays are festively decorated in celebration of the occasion. Flower arrangements may be placed around the room, and there is always a display of the local chapter's Aglow banner, colorfully decorated by proud members. All of these decorative elements work together to give the otherwise blank room a cheerful, cozy feel.

That this cheerful coziness may be shaken during the course of the meeting is made clear by boxes of facial tissues placed in accessible spots around the room. The tissues suggest that there will be tears, as there always are at Aglow meetings; the easy availability of tissues may well encourage weeping, as an important sign of authentic feeling. This is one example of how spatial and decorative elements play an important role in the construction of emotion, as particular items become cues for proper feeling and expressive behavior. Far from contradicting each other, the tissues and the cheery decorative elements work together to create a dramatic emotional journey that participants are expected to make during the meeting, a journey meant to take them into their deepest suffering ("the darkness") and, as they surrender their burdens by confessing them to Jesus, bring them out into newly felt freedom and joy ("the light").

Local Aglow officers are responsible for setting up the meeting and greeting all who attend, particularly newcomers. As they enter the room, the women are welcomed with big smiles, hugs, quick pecks on the cheek, and exclamations such as "Praise the Lord!" Everyone receives a handmade paper nametag inscribed with a Bible verse, and all are invited to jot down prayer requests on small pieces of paper and place them in a basket. The "social time" commences as the women chat and express their happiness to be at the meeting. Often the talk includes the story of one who almost did not come to the meeting because of family or other obligations but was blessed at the last minute with the opportunity to attend. After thirty minutes or so, the musicians move to the front and begin to play and sing songs as a kind of "call to worship." Other women respond to this cue by finding a seat and joining the singing, marking the shift from profane time and space to sacred. At this time, someone discreetly shuts all the doors to the outside, enclosing those within the room in an atmosphere of privacy, safety, and anticipation.

Thus is a kind of holy space constituted, its decorative and musical elements consistent across boundaries of location and time throughout the United States. The women attending the meeting mark its specialness in their brightly colored attire and cheerful smiles. They knowingly follow the lead of musicians and officers concerning when to sing or speak and when to maintain silence, what gestures to perform, how to express emotion correctly and at the proper time, and so on. What occurs at the meetings, therefore, happens inside a very specifically ordered and regulated space, one that involves a full sensory experience and a heightened attention to the details of movement, speech, and behavior. It is a space that has become a "place" in the sense described by ritual theorist Jonathan Z. Smith: a "controlled environment" in which the ordinary is made extraordinary and the mundane blends with the mysterious, a performative setting where purposeful activities may be experienced as meaningful and powerful and transformation and healing may occur.[30]

Every local meeting space is distinct and can be invested with very different meanings for those who attend. Some rooms have windows, others do not; some rooms are carpeted, others have hardwood floors; sometimes the chairs are hard and sometimes they are soft; one room might be shabby while another is newly refurbished; and so on. Moreover, women experience these spaces differently according to personal history, memory, and imagination.[31] What to some may appear a garish or tackily decorated space may seem luxurious to others; some will find a certain space too plain while others find it wonderfully suggestive of the simplicity of faith. There is no single Aglow aesthetic or space but rather a range of tastes and possibilities, bound together in the conviction that divine activity can occur anywhere and everywhere.

Less frequent but equally formalized are the regional retreats, which generally take place once a year for a weekend. Like the meeting described at the beginning of this chapter, these gatherings are open to Aglow women from an entire state or other broad region. Some may travel many hours to attend the retreat and must spend money on hotel rooms, registration fees, meals, and so on. There is a heightened sense of excitement and anticipation at these events, marking an expectation that God is going to "make something happen."

Regional weekend retreats attract upwards of five hundred women and are generally held in conference rooms, at a hotel where participants lodge during the retreat. Decoration is far more elaborate than at monthly meetings, as local chapter officers combine their efforts to bring a degree of intimacy to the otherwise impersonal enclosures. Helium-filled balloons, vividly decorated banners, flags from many places, and elaborate flower arrangements may decorate the main auditorium, while tables for inspirational books, audiotapes, videotapes, and Aglow sweatshirts, aprons, and other paraphernalia may be placed in the abutting lobby. A special "prayer room," softly lit and filled with chairs placed a discreet distance from one another, is often available down the hall, meant to be a tranquil place for those who wish to pray quietly alone. Often set up as a "nature scene," complete with ersatz waterfall (a drizzling cascade down synthetic rock), artificial plants, and plastic trees, the prayer room also holds numerous tissue boxes, again heightening the expectation of strong emotion. Here religious space is created out of conference rooms, usually experienced as impersonal, by objects suggesting the safety of the surroundings and the immediate presence of God.

Annual and international conferences, held yearly in locations around the United States and in other parts of the world, have been attended by as many as eight thousand women. Large convention centers are rented for the occasion, with blocks of rooms reserved for participants' lodging. Conference halls feature booths representing Aglow's mission work in foreign countries and selling goods produced there, such as European dolls, Japanese fans, African figurines, Russian jewelry, and Mexican blankets, alongside tables featuring books and audiotapes by conference speakers. The main auditorium is generally laid out like the smaller meeting rooms, with one additional feature: large television screens are placed throughout the audience for those not fortunate enough to find seats close to the front of the room. Aisles are spacious, allowing room for ecstatic dancing to the music.

While the enormous size of the room may seem to work against the kind of intimacy that is so important a feature at smaller meetings, the ever-present greeters welcoming the women into the auditorium, as well as the expectation that even strangers are "sisters" here and should talk with and embrace one another at will, are intended to foster a sense of familiarity and comfort among all the women present. Additionally, the fact that women from the same local chapter make a practice of reserving rows of seats so that they may sit together helps those women to replicate in some degree the intimate experience of a local meeting. At the same time that the size of the crowd helps confirm participants' commitment to their common spiritual mission, it reinforces their sense of evangelical sisterhood and the support available from sympathetic women across the nation and the world.

The spaces described so far are in an important sense theatrical spaces, carefully chosen and designed to enhance the performance aspect of the worship taking place there.[32] Worshipers gather as an audience of spectators, a role highlighted by the placement of chairs facing the front stage. When combined at larger gatherings with elaborate sound and light systems and larger-than-life video screens, the replication of an entertainment arena is nearly complete. Yet the women also act as performers within the larger drama, evidenced in their freedom to stand and dance in the aisles, shout praises to God during most parts of the service, and speak their testimonies publicly at the front of the room. In following the cues that indicate when simply to watch, listen, or pray in silence and when to move, speak, or sing loudly as active contributors to the theatrical performance, participants express recognition of the dual roles assigned by these idioms and communicate their willingness to enact them.

As well as being theatrical spaces, these are commercial spaces, where religious artifacts are for sale in a colorful variety of forms. Like the wider evangelical culture, where, since the early 1990s, annual sales of Christian products in bookstores alone have reached upward of $3 billion, Aglow administrators are well schooled in modern merchandising techniques.[33] Thousands of attractively packaged Aglow products are sold every month at local meetings around the country, while national and international conventions set aside enormous areas on the outskirts of the main auditorium for this same purpose, engaging row upon row of busy cashiers behind computer screens to serve long lines of eager customers. Costly meals and snacks are everywhere available in these conference halls, produced by food service companies accustomed to the business conventions that ordinarily take place there. Though the repeated offerings taken at worship meetings, analyzed in Chapter 5, identify sacrificial giving as a sacred devotional practice, money retains its this-worldly exchange value just outside those bounds in spaces where Christianity blends easily with consumer culture.

The ritualized spaces of religious meetings are not the only settings where Aglow women meet. The bonds forged in civic halls, auditoriums, and conference centers are nurtured and maintained through social and devotional activity that often takes place in the home. The historian Colleen McDannell has described the importance of the home in nineteenth- and twentieth-century American Christianity as a place for creating an "alternative Christian culture" aimed at both inculcating and protecting particular religious values and practices, tasks considered primarily women's work.[34] Aglow participants strongly emphasize the importance of the home and believe women are the primary makers and keepers of it, a job that includes the hospitality involved in sharing that domestic space with others. As Eadie Goodboy noted in 1974, hospitality is a crucial female ministry: "One of the highest privileges we have, as Christian women, is the practice of hospitality. Whether we reside in spacious surroundings or in a small apartment, we all live somewhere, and that 'somewhere' is the special place God put each of us! As we yield ourselves to Him and seek His will for our lives, our homes become sanctified places—set apart, consecrated to the Lord. . . . Because we, as women, are the homemakers, we have the blessing of opening our homes to God's people." Although the reference to "homemakers" was removed in 1985—the revised sentence reads, "We, women, have the blessing of opening our homes to God's people"—the emphasis on female hospitality as a ministry has remained strong.[35]

The women frequently host each other for Bible study groups and healing prayer sessions, as well as for more ordinary conversation and companionship. Aglow literature contains numerous stories of the most intense religious experiences taking place in a domestic setting, from baptism in the Holy Spirit to healings from various illnesses. The religious significance of the home is further illustrated through magazine and pamphlet covers that feature photographs of cheerful kitchen scenes, depicting smiling women sitting around a table laden with Bibles, coffee, and cookies. In one local Aglow chapter whose meetings I attended, the chapter president's retirement after six years of leadership was celebrated with tearful stories recounting her generosity in opening her home to women in need and hosting diverse events, from

typical prayer and Bible study meetings to "emergency" healing sessions for the abused and afflicted who crossed her path. She had turned
her home, the women agreed, into a "refuge."[36]

As such illustrations suggest, the kind of piety embodied by Aglow
women expands or even transforms the home, traditional site of women's
labor, into a holy place of intimacy and prayer. As much as the
women may use the telephone as a means of communication, practices
of hosting and visiting each other in the home establish it as a place of
serenity and happiness and also a domain where God is both actively
present and accessible. Here, God is always ready to listen to a
woman's prayers and perhaps to break into the moment with ecstatic
power, transforming the home into a space as highly ritualized as the
space of the larger formal meetings. While also a site of family conflict
and perhaps great suffering, the home is felt by Aglow women to be a
sanctified haven against the world, a place wherein healing and deliverance may occur. Yet the home is also an arena of potential distraction,
as evidenced in one Aglow woman's remark: "The hardest thing you'll
ever do is pray at home."[37]

Set Free in Prayer

Within these ritualized spaces, Aglow women attend their
monthly worship meetings. After two or three lively songs that signal
the beginning of the meeting, involving hand clapping in time with the
music, tambourine playing, and other forms of "joyful noise," one of
the leaders approaches the podium and invites the women to join her
in prayer. She thanks God for allowing the women present to attend the
meeting and requests guidance and blessings for the group. When the
prayer is finished, she or another leader welcomes everyone there and
reads a prepared statement describing the Aglow organization and its
purpose, a description serving both to remind members of their mission
and to give information to newcomers. She tells those present for the
first time what to expect from the meeting, noting that they will see others raising their hands during songs, perhaps kneeling, and speaking in
tongues, and she encourages them to worship in the way that is most
comfortable for them. More music then follows, accompanied by piano
or guitar, and lasts for as long as half an hour, moving away from the
livelier "praise songs" into a slower, softer, more prayerful mode.
Interspersed between songs may be occasional "prophetic words," as
women give utterances—in English or in tongues—they feel that God

has "put on their heart" for the comfort or edification of the larger group.

When the music has faded into silence, one of the chapter officers walks to the podium and prays aloud in gratitude for God's presence, while other women may echo her words or respond, "Yes, Jesus," "Yes, Lord." At the conclusion of the prayer she invites the group to be seated and moves into the "business" part of the service. Guests are formally welcomed and are asked to raise their hands, as appointed members hand out brochures describing Aglow and giving information on membership. Prayer requests may then be voiced, along with grateful accounts of prayers answered. Upcoming religious events are announced and various opportunities for ministry are described. This section of the meeting is often interspersed with humor and may include skits or other exercises designed to put participants at ease. It is a time when women are allowed and encouraged to stand and speak their testimony, recounting an event in which God's presence was particularly evident during the recent past.[38] After the treasurer reads some scriptural verses on stewardship and the blessings of giving one's resources back to God, an offering is taken, baskets being passed from row to row and collected by ushers at the back. Together, these activities may take half an hour or so, after which the president enthusiastically introduces the evening's speaker, usually a woman (though sometimes a man) involved in Christian mission work who is believed to have a particularly inspiring testimony to share with the audience.

The speaker may talk for an hour or more, recounting her sufferings and her journey from sin and sickness into wholeness through a personal relationship with Jesus. Most speakers are adept at getting their audiences to identify with them through the use of humor and self-deprecating anecdotes. The lesson is clear: surrender your burdens to God, along with any desire to control your own life, and, healed and transformed, you will receive abundant gifts of peace and joy in return. Like Gwen, described at the beginning of this chapter, speakers detail the trajectory of their lives from despair to joy through finding Jesus, and they offer listeners the chance to turn their own lives around as well. The speech concludes with the invitation to pray, the speaker generally offering to work directly with anyone who feels some particular need for intercession. Much time, even a whole hour, may be spent in this way, as individual women receive prayers from the speaker and other Aglow members. Some may fall down, "slain in the spirit," while others weep with sorrow or joy and tell each other intimate details about their lives.

Long after the official prayer time has ended, many women remain to talk about specific crises in their lives, such as illnesses or marital problems, or to give advice to those sharing such stories. Here, intimations of suffering continue to issue forth, as prayer requests made earlier are elaborated in greater detail. The women smile encouragingly at one another, promising their daily prayers and offering comforting words of hope. Still talking, basking in the intimacy that is such an important element of the meetings, they leave the room to reenter the ordinary world outside, for many apparently a world of pain, isolation, and fear. But with the strength given them by their Aglow sisters and the assurance that Jesus accompanies them in their troubles, the women move forward in an effort to face that world with confidence and tranquility.

The devotional core holding these worship meetings together and the pivotal religious act for participants is unmistakably prayer, enacted in myriad ways in countless settings. Transitions between different parts of the service are marked by prayers, including songs that work as prayers, and it is through prayer that the women begin to articulate the narratives that they share with one another. Additionally, prayer is the chief and most tangible practice wherein participants' social and religious identities are constituted, as it provides a medium through which contradictory idioms are mediated and the tensions between them resolved.[39] For example, the psychological orientation of the group toward victimhood is reconciled by the liberating power of the Holy Spirit, turning heartache into joy and martyrs into victors. Examining the social and spiritual uses of prayer as well as its mediating effects should reveal some of the significant religious and social dynamics within Aglow, including how hierarchies of power are both created and subverted through ritualization.[40]

The anthropologist Carol Greenhouse has distinguished between four forms or "contexts" of prayer: private prayer, prayer with a third party, collective prayer, and prayer narratives.[41] All these forms are evident in Aglow settings, with both collective prayer and narratives about prayer working as especially vital elements that connect the women to one another and suggest to them that they are in the presence of God. As they pray together for healing, forgiveness, and mercy, for husbands, children, parents, and friends, Aglow women feel they are sharing their most deeply felt needs and giving each other courage and assurance that these will be fulfilled. Yet it is also clear that these forms of prayer negotiate and shape the women's religious identities, as their capacity for turning the ordinary into the extraordinary is enlarged and refined and as their sense of their own lives is transformed. Prayer makes painful events that once seemed incomprehensible appear full of meaning as potential lessons about the love of God.

Thus prayer in the Aglow context serves as both a religious and a social practice, communicating with God and with the corporate body of worshipers. Most studies of prayer have taken the second, social function as the focus for analysis, but the first function deserves equal examination, for, as Greenhouse observes, "Prayer mobilizes and actualizes an individuality that would otherwise be ambivalent."[42] In other words, a person's sense that God listens to her, cares about her sufferings, and delivers her from pain gives birth to a distinct sense of self-awareness, the feeling of discovering a self that was lost or receiving a new self in place of one that was "dead." Aglow women believe that God hears their prayers and answers them whether they are spoken aloud or articulated silently, and they also believe that praying together in a group holds particular power because of the increased intensity of many hearts and voices coming together in supplication and praise. Together in the body of Christ, the women endeavor to free each other from the constraints ordinarily felt in everyday life so that they may delight in feeling reborn and rejoice in the glory of God.

When Aglow meetings are over, participants return to the spaces of their daily lives, making a difficult transition into a context that often appears emotionally frustrating and unhappy. Many Aglow women live with husbands who are either non-Christians or are less fervent in their faith than their wives, situations that cause varying degrees of dismay and turmoil for the women. Some live with men who beat them or treat them badly in other ways, while others simply live in a more common state of generalized marital dissatisfaction. Of course, many appear happy in their marriages and testify to the miraculous ways Jesus has helped them through hard times. At the least, many of these women share a common financial dependence on their husbands, potentially replicated in other forms of dependence and submission in their everyday lives. As they exit the place where healing and deliverance were felt to take place, they may trust that their friends will pray for them and that God will continue to hear their own prayers, yet ultimately they will have to confront their domestic trials in some sense alone.

Within Aglow spaces, prayers are both descriptive and prescriptive: they simultaneously describe proper social roles and spiritual attitudes and call listeners to use these as their models. Such prayers translate the problems and dilemmas of everyday life—conflicts in marriage, the death of a loved one, financial anxiety, and so forth—into religious lessons about faith in a loving God and surrender to God's plan for one's life. The persuasive rhetoric by which this translation is enacted succeeds when it convinces readers and listeners to see their own lives in a new way and to reinterpret the conditions of their daily existence in terms of this spiritual framework. Likewise, the rhetoric fails when those it addresses cannot or will not accede to this new way of looking at the world. Perhaps it fails more often than that, when women tied to Aglow for whatever reason do not feel themselves transformed by prayer in the ways that they are supposed to; yet in such cases, the pressure to conform may be great enough to prevent them from admitting failure (which would probably be thought to reflect the obstinacy of the person praying anyway). Such instances can be recounted only as past failures now resolved and as embodying a lesson about surrender and faith.

In the accounts recorded by Aglow women, every prayer becomes an opportunity for a kind of conversion, or reconversion. In prayer the woman surrenders her sense of boundaries, discards the false shell that protects and hides her authentic self from outside gazes, and feels herself transformed. Interior and exterior merge, as layers of stale experience and interpretation are peeled away to reveal the purity of the newly cleansed soul. New possibilities for identity emerge within old constraints, possibilities that have been created out of particular narrative strategies and that are also informed by the circumstances in which the woman lives.

In this moment of rebirth through prayer, old forms are discarded and new criteria for "the real" formulated, creating possibilities for both healing and transformation. While other religious practices—church attendance, Bible study, testimony, and so on—may become dull from overuse, prayer, in the form of direct and immediate experience of God, is thought to retain its spontaneous character. Viewed as an antiritual, prayer is not meant to be about intentional self-fashioning or refashioning but rather represents the surrender of such attempts at self-control and discipline, which are thought to create inauthentic selves. Whether done in secret with only God as witness or before a human audience, prayer is the place where "the real" is articulated, displayed, healed, transformed, and set free. As one prayer leader informed her Aglow audience, "When you pray for someone, you're tearing off the death strips that hold people down, like Jesus did for Lazarus: God will take those death clothes off and you will be set free!"[43]

As time passes, the self becomes re-encrusted with layers of sin, sickness, and falsehood, sinking into "darkness" as before; and once more, the cycle of transformation is initiated. Prayer, then, operates as the climactic moment in an endlessly repeatable pattern of spiraling downward and ascending to victory yet again. Setting the ascent into motion, prayer provides a woman with the courage to look within herself and request a change, whether a return to the purer selfhood of a younger age or the abolition of all former pretenses in favor of a new authenticity. Though always in danger of backsliding, the transformed woman invariably affirms the permanence of her joyous condition and declares her commitment to remaining steadfast in faith so that she will stay pure and whole. Such are some of the crucial narrative conventions around which accounts of prayer and transformation are constructed.

Prayer is thus scripted in the Aglow context, utilizing formulaic, historically patterned language that conforms to particular interpretations of the Christian scriptures and theological tradition and incorporates themes of sin/redemption, sickness/healing, and repentance/grace. Yet these scripts are not acted out in stilted, rigid, or inflexible modes of speech; rather, they provide a kind of foundational structure within which practitioners are able to move creatively, innovating and ad-libbing as their own lives, circumstances, and immediate desires move them. In practice, prayer is meant to restore a sense of wholeness, honor, and goodness to those whose identities have been threatened by suffering or fragmented by conflicting expectations, to those who were "lost" and wish to be "found." Prayer is the most important practice of a spiritual journey forged within the bounds of a community that meets to transform the identities of all who surrender themselves to the power of the spirit.

Aglow narratives resist crystallization into static, petrified forms because every woman has her own story, rife with its own secret shames and its unique capacity to shock its hearers. Mirroring one another's experiences again and again through accounts of prayer, healing, and transformation, Aglow women just as readily add unique bits of their own life histories. Even as a woman's story recycles scripted motifs and participates in the repertory of Christian plot structures, it remains elastic, colored by its peculiar context and its distinct emotions. An Aglow woman's religious identity is configured and reconfigured, then, not by sacrificing but by celebrating the particulars of her own story. What joins these stories together is that they all hinge on moments of personal rebirth, which can in turn enable change to take place at other levels, social and domestic. In such stories, explored in the following chapters, every space or setting in which they live is potentially transformed.

What impact, then, does ritual activity such as prayer have on the women's everyday lives? Does this capacity for ritualization or transformation do anything more for Aglow women than to make them feel momentarily changed? Does it enable them to reenter their daily lives renewed and healed, or does it merely soothe temporarily their anxieties while binding them more tightly into the structures of authority and discipline that gave rise to their suffering in the first place? Such crucial questions do not occasion easy answers, in large part because, to put it plainly, people experience ritual activity in individual and uneven ways, sometimes evident to the outside observer but more often not. What can be said is this: The ritual sense that these women share, forged in a symbolic world that allows them to redefine themselves as healed, delivered, and set free, produces and reinforces power relationships in crucial ways, as the following chapters show. Yet this sense also opens up possibilities for new worlds to be imagined and lived and thus may open the way for vital transformations of another, more concrete and potentially more radical, order.

3

Into Light and Life

Healing and Transformation

Vivian, diagnosed with multiple sclerosis, opens her narrative with a stark description of her decaying body and grieving spirit: "I don't believe there is anyone who can understand what I suffered—except someone whose speech has been garbled, who has had double and triple vision, whose bladder has been uncontrollable and whose husband has asked for a divorce. Such a person would know how I felt, before Jesus healed me." Before she was healed, Vivian writes, she prayed for God to let her die; yet "God didn't answer my prayer." Hardly able to move her body because of the excruciating pain, she relied on cortisone, vitamin B12 shots, muscle relaxants, pain pills, and alcohol. "Sometimes I drank with my husband, but most often I drank alone," she later noted. Once, "in the depths of my misery," she pleaded, "God, do something in my life." Again, nothing happened. After her husband finally left her, she says, she sat utterly alone in her empty house, "completely defeated, distraught, and diseased."

Once more, Vivian cried out to God: "Please, Lord, do something, help me. I'll do anything You want. I can't do anything without You." As she spoke, Jesus miraculously appeared to her, "in his glorified state." Robed in white, with so bright a face that she was nearly blinded, he placed a comforting hand on her right shoulder and said to her in a "rich, beautiful voice," "Everything will be all right." Vivian recalls, "I felt encompassed in the glory and love of God. He had come to me when I needed Him most."

Soon, she writes, God began bringing people into her life to lead her closer to him. A friend from church brought Vivian to her first Bible study, where she prayed "an audible prayer to God, my first prayer in public, asking God to take away my bitterness and resentment over my disease and divorce." That same day, she felt God showing her how miserable her life would be if she failed to let go of her petulant rebelliousness. Shaken up by such a warning, she became ready to "hand it over to Him and let Him heal me."

The same friend soon took Vivian to a prayer meeting, where others prayed over her "in a heavenly language, with the laying on of hands" for healing. To God, Vivian confessed, "I don't really know what they meant, but I trust You completely." Ten days later she was baptized in the Holy Spirit and, feeling extreme heat surging through her body "from the inside out," knew that she was completely healed. Her eyes, speech, bladder, and limbs all became astonishingly "normal," so much of a miracle that she found it too difficult to believe and began to doubt her healing. More healing prayers from members of a prayer group resulted in a feeling of "something like electricity coursing through my body." At this, Vivian's doubts were totally allayed: "I was filled with an indescribable love for Jesus and the friends around me. I knew that now my healing was complete."

Five and a half years later, she writes, she has no symptoms of multiple sclerosis and has used no medications or other stimulants. "My perfect health and strength cause me to praise the Lord continuously." Now remarried to a Christian man, Vivian feels completely healed emotionally, spiritually, and physically, and joyfully concludes: "I *know* that God hears and answers every prayer. My prayer for Him to 'do something in my life' He has honored more abundantly than I could ever have imagined." From being "completely defeated, distraught, and diseased," Vivian says, she has passed "into light and life."[1]

During the praise and worship section of a monthly evening Aglow meeting, as participants hum and pray along with a strumming guitar, a member of the audience leaves her seat and approaches the microphone to speak. Soon it will become clear that this woman, Frances, feels that God has given her a message for the fifty women present tonight, a prophetic revelation of physical restoration. Speaking with calm assurance, her prophecy begins: "Someone here is being healed of neck pain, suffered from the burdens of her life!" Some in the audience gasp audibly, and others continue to hum, but all take notice. Frances speaks with specific examples about the kind of loads that can debilitate the neck, then affirms her prophecy and asks anyone whose neck is being healed to raise her hands. Six women around the room, praying fervently, lift their arms high into the air, as others shout "Praise the Lord!" and the excitement mounts throughout the room.

Frances, still at the microphone, asks these six women to come forward to the front of the room so that she and several local leaders can pray for them. As the women move forward, other members of the audience rise from their seats to join in, still praying aloud. After some minutes pass this way, Frances returns to the microphone and announces that someone with "bad feet" in the audience has just been healed by God as well. Again, several women stand; this time they begin shouting that their feet have been healed and dance about the room to give evidence. Then they too approach the front of the room for further healing. "Just take the healing now!" Frances cries, and then she continues to prophesy about further healings: God is working on people with ear trouble, perhaps two or three women here. . . .There is someone here "with burning in the center of her chest," but God is healing her right away—and on and on. By now, almost everyone in the room is either laying hands on another woman in supplication and thanksgiving or receiving prayers herself. Only five people remain in the audience, including myself and at least one woman who is a first-time visitor to the group.

When the session ends and the regular meeting resumes, the women healed briefly testify to their healing and to the astonishment they felt when Frances spoke about them. At the meeting's close, others embrace them lovingly and marvel at God's goodness. Not all ailments that the women here suffer have been healed, but at this moment no one seems to have the faintest doubt that those healings too will come.[2]

Accounts of miraculous healings have long been prominent within the Protestant evangelical tradition, as well as among diverse religious cousins such as spiritualists, Mormons, Christian Scientists, and Roman Catholics. The growth of the Pentecostal and charismatic movements was largely owing to their theological and practical emphasis on healing and their insistence that divine experiences occur even in this modern, supposedly secular age. Millions have thrilled to hear the dramatic, saved-from-death testimonials of evangelists like Oral Roberts and Kathryn Kuhlman, whose ministries have derived from their apparent gifts for healing other people through their prayers. Public scandals involving the sexual and financial escapades of televangelists have done little to stem the hopes of the afflicted, as hundreds of thousands of women and men continue to flock to prayer meetings of all sizes, held in such disparate settings as storefront churches, suburban living rooms, civic auditoriums, and football arenas, to be restored to health and happiness. Registering occasional disappointment and frustration even while proclaiming ultimate success, their stories follow time-honored patterns and aim at assuring all hearers, skeptical as well as hopeful, that they too may be divinely healed.

Charismatic women like Vivian and Frances who relate such stories in devotional magazines or worship meetings join their voices to this enduring narrative tradition, replaying the familiar drama in which the suffering sinner is eventually made whole by surrendering all to Jesus. But however familiar the contours of that drama, the specific meanings of wholeness and healing in any story are heavily endowed with larger cultural themes as well, giving the narrative the flavor of a particular historical moment and place. While they speak the same Bible-based language of healing, urban and suburban spirit-filled women in the late twentieth century have markedly greater access to modern medicine and psychology than their rural Pentecostal foremothers and so conceptualize illness, disease, and health in distinctly modern ways. In fact, as the sociologist Meredith McGuire has determined, contemporary charismatics have as much in common with the culture of "alternative healing" as with early Pentecostalism. This shift suggests that the Pentecostal tradition has become "modern" to an extent unthinkable to many earlier adherents.[3] This chapter explores the themes of healing and transformation in printed and oral Aglow narratives to scrutinize prevailing evangelical uses of these themes and investigate the ways in which they are enacted in women's ordinary lives.

God Had His Reasons

The testimonies that appear in *Aglow* magazine frequently emphasize miraculous physical healings, either of the author herself or of someone close to her. One woman voiced a typical sentiment when she testified, "The Lord has healed me every time I have asked Him to, from small cuts to a sprained right ankle and severe cramps in my body."[4] Other narratives describe wondrous healings from conditions as diverse as cancer, lupus, autism, multiple sclerosis, meningitis, cystic fibrosis, epilepsy, and heroin addiction. Several writers mention receiving prayers from famous Pentecostal healers, while many more describe the prayers of friends, family, and church members as contributing to the success of their healing. In many of these cases, healing is construed as not simply the restoration of a diseased body to health but a purification of a profounder sort, a kind of exorcism or "deliverance" in which a demonic entity is forcibly eradicated through the power of prayer. At times such a demon is thought actually to cause the illness, whereas in other situations a devil merely implants doubts that prevent the sick person from being totally healed. Either way, purification from this demonic force and the resultant "claiming" of one's healing by faith (even when symptoms of illness persist) are crucial components of the healing process.

Healing as purification is made explicit in stories such as that of Sandra, diagnosed with incurable cystic fibrosis as a baby and given only eighteen years to live. At the age of seventeen she began learning about faith healing and says she heard God speak to her, "I am going to heal you." In just a couple of weeks Sandra experienced a "divine warmth" moving through her pancreas and lungs, clearing them out and purifying them completely. After a few days, however, her symptoms returned, including a collapsed lung. As she later wrote, "The devil tried to steal what God had given me. It was my choice to hang on to God and confess God's Word or to say I was not healed. . . . So I began confessing God's Word continually that 'by Jesus' stripes I am healed.' " Very shortly afterward, "the battle ended" with Jesus as victor. Sandra's body was completely healed of her deadly disease. Now happily married and living "in perfect health," she writes, "God healed and restored every area that had been affected by the disease."[5]

Instances such as this, in which prayers are initially uttered without faith, are common in charismatic women's testimonies. Such "desperate" prayers seem to mark the initial turn to faith seen as necessary for healing. Anne, nearly paralyzed with spinal injuries and excruciating pain and confined to a wheelchair, decided to commit suicide. Although she perceived God as remote and knew "very little about prayer," she felt she ought to pray. Just before drinking the sedative to end her life, she said, *"God, if You are really God, You know why I'm doing this. I can't stand it any longer,"* and was shocked to feel "a wave of love" from God after uttering this prayer. She still wanted to kill herself, yet she prayed again: *"Please let me die. But Lord, if it's not Your will that I should die, then I'll abide by it."* Some hours later, Anne awoke in

the hospital, her attempt at suicide having failed. Over the next few
months, as she read the Book of Job and prayed more earnestly, her
body began to heal and purify until at last she was able to live "a perfectly normal, active life" as a wife and mother. Her initial desperate attempt to speak to God, as feeble and doubting as it may have been,
turned out to be the crucial step on the road to perfect health and
wholeness.[6]

That God will also perform less serious bodily healings is demonstrated in "The Lord Has a Sense of Humor," an amusing story of one
woman who wished to pray for the shrinking of her awkwardly large
breasts. Feeling rather "sheepish" about her seemingly trivial problem,
Kathleen confided her dilemma to her pastor's wife, complaining that
she had to wear expensive custom-made bras, was too ashamed to wear
a bathing suit, and could hardly find properly fitting clothes. Her friend
sympathetically encouraged her to pray about her quandary, and so
Kathleen brought up a need for healing (without being too specific) at
her next prayer group meeting. After the others prayed for her, one of
the members urged her to recite the twenty-third psalm; remembering
the phrase "My cup runneth over" made Kathleen laugh, but the phrase
"and mercy shall follow" gave her hope that God had heard her presumably insignificant prayer. Kathleen concludes: "Mercy was granted
me when, overnight, I went down five cup sizes! Praise the Lord!"[7]

Such a story may be humorous, to the writer as well as to readers,
but it points to a significant lesson promoted among charismatic
Christians about healing: God cares about even the slightest concerns
of his daughters and will heal them not only of major health problems
but of mere annoyances as well. Anyone who thinks that God is too
busy dealing with momentous issues to worry about one woman's embarrassment is wrong, for God is a loving parent who wishes all to be
well with his children everywhere. Yet, by constantly emphasizing their
modest reservations about praying for their own healings, the writers
seem to say it is good to be cautious and unassuming when in need of
God's assistance. The etiquette appears to require meekness, if not
downright self-effacement, so that God will take pity on his daughters
like helpless children. Again and again, these stories emphasize God's
parental benevolence and willingness to ease all difficulties, yet they
also suggest that God demands humility and respect. Even the most dif-
fident prayer suggests enough faith to set the healing process in motion.

Stories about healing have a variety of other messages and functions
as well. Ann writes of having been raised an Orthodox Jew and later

becoming an atheist and left-wing political activist. While a leftist, she suffered from acute allergies and lung problems that eventually forced her to live in a bare room with only a cot and a tank of oxygen. Along the way, she met many evangelical Christians who prayed for and with her, despite her scoffing at their efforts; finally, landing once again in the hospital, she became desperate enough to ask a Christian man for healing prayer. Her companion demanded that she say the sinner's prayer first ("Have mercy on me, a sinner") to indicate her faith, as well as her confession of sinfulness and need for forgiveness; since she had long considered Christianity to be anti-Semitic, she agreed only reluctantly. "I mouthed the prayer, but didn't really believe in what I was saying," she later wrote, but as she finished and the man prayed for her, she felt an old back injury heal. A seed of faith had been planted in her heart, Ann explains, and her body slowly began to mend. Soon her lungs were being completely restored, so that she was finally able to walk and even run with abandon. Believing that Jesus had healed her, she accepted him as "the Lord of my life" and came to understand herself to be a "completed" Jew.[8]

For an audience of charismatic Christian women such a story obviously has plentiful uses, far exceeding an ordinary instance of divine healing. The trajectory from Orthodox Jew to left-wing atheist to charismatic Christian witnessing to her healed body is highly meaningful to readers, reinforcing not only their faith in healing but also, and just as importantly, their belief in the incomparability of their own religious system. This narrative also hints at the link presumed to exist between atheism and left-wing political causes and may even suggest that Jews have a particular leaning in that direction. While not stated explicitly, these connections are easily derived from Ann's narrative, which may leave readers all the more anxious to convert more Jews to Christianity. The conversion of the Jews also has apocalyptic significance for many evangelicals, who believe it to signal Jesus' imminent return.

The general intent of these healing stories is to instill renewed faith, particularly among those more likely to believe in modern medicine than faith healing. One means of persuasion is to seek the validating authority of science, a strategy that has long been practiced by groups as far ranging as spiritualists, phrenologists, Christian Scientists, and others whose supernatural or quasi-scientific cosmologies and biologies have been derided by skeptics. In charismatic stories, confirmations of healings are often established by stories of awestruck medical doctors.

Vivian, for example, recalls her doctor telling her after she was healed from multiple sclerosis, "This looks like a miracle to me."[9] A younger woman, dramatically healed of an embarrassing tongue deformity just before undergoing a complicated operation, proudly recalls the confirmation of her dentist: "Janice, . . . if I had to stand before the medical board today, the only thing I could tell them would be that God healed you."[10] Beneath one woman's printed description of her daughter's near-death experience during emergency surgery was a copy of a doctor's note substantiating her account and thanking God for being present during the operation.[11] Like the medical doctors repeatedly summoned to corroborate the healings performed at large revival meetings, the physicians quoted in these stories are used to lend authenticity to what many people would consider implausible accounts. By describing healings in terms of miraculous occurrences that withstand the meticulous scrutiny of the medical profession, authors attempt to force even the most incredulous readers to acknowledge the power of God to heal and answer prayer.

Not all such prayers for healing work, of course; sometimes sickness lingers or worsens, and sometimes a person who has been prayed for dies. The writers of these stories interpret such events not as "failures" but as lessons rich in meaning, summoning opportunities for renewed faith. Linda, writing of her young daughter's death from cancer, notes that although at first she felt peace when Nanci died, she later wrestled with "pain and anger" toward God for taking her daughter away. God's response, Linda remembers, was rather stern: "I did not call you to understand My will, but to accept it. I move in love and do what is best for everyone. I created all emotions, even the ones that hurt. I want My children to experience them all and know victory through Me and My power in you. Nanci was ready to come to Me. She had fulfilled everything I wanted her to accomplish and I received her with joy. Will you accept her death as My will, and My best?" Linda replies that with God's grace, she will indeed accept her daughter's death. Yielding to God's will, even when it conflicts with her own, allows Linda to experience "victory and wholeness," not once but "time and time again."[12]

Another mother, Ginny, writes of discovering that her two-year-old son Scottie had a brain tumor, and although "God had never been real to me" before that time, in her utter helplessness she cried out, "Oh God, if there is a God, please let Scottie live! Even if it is just for a few more years." In fact Scottie did live a few more years, during which both he and Ginny came to accept Jesus as their Savior and learned to accept Scottie's illness. At the moment of Scottie's death, Ginny writes, she could feel him being lifted from his bed by the arms of Jesus and felt herself to be surrounded by God's immense glory. She was given "a picture of Scottie and Jesus," in which Scottie "was absolutely aglow as he ran his hands through his Savior's beard." Ginny concluded, "Scottie had never asked for healing, but he had sought Jesus face-to-face, and his prayers had now been answered." Ginny never questions her faith, instead claiming to have received a deep peace from this sad event—"the peace only Jesus can give"—in the simple knowledge that "God had His reasons."[13]

Similar stories frequently emerged during my fieldwork in Aglow chapters, where women sought to make sense of tragic deaths in their own families. Martha, a regional Aglow leader who spoke at a local meeting, reported watching the health of her thirty-two-year-old son decline because of AIDS. Though she anointed him with oil for healing countless times, Philip grew more and more ill; worse, in Martha's view, he refused to accept that his "way of life" (Philip was gay) was "sin" but insisted that he had been born that way. Besides anointing him with oil and taking care of him, his mother "ministered to him," prayed for his salvation, and fasted for him, terrified above all that he would die unrepentant and unsaved and so would go to hell for all eternity. Finally, toward the end of his life, Martha says that Philip had a divine revelation and accepted his sin of homosexual acts, spending an entire day immersed in confession and prayer. According to his mother's testimony, Philip became "a new creation" in Christ before he finally died a peaceful death and was assured by God of his own salvation. Martha concluded by saying how comforted she had been since Philip's death by imagining God telling her, "I have your son, and you have Mine." Though tears were flowing around the room by the time Martha finished this story, she repeatedly emphasized the joy of knowing that her son was safe with God and no longer in pain. Interestingly, she also prayed against the self-righteousness of the religious "who click their tongues at people who live this [gay] lifestyle" and enjoined her audience against such an attitude.[14]

Saturated as they are with the pain of loss and unfulfilled desire, these stories instruct readers and listeners to recognize blessings where others perceive only suffering and tragedy. Like the mother who comforts herself after the deaths of two young sons with the thought that "our sons couldn't be with the Father in heaven if they hadn't been born" and that she and the rest of the family will someday join the boys "in the presence of our Savior," these other mothers trust that their children are gifts bestowed by God, to be enjoyed once again after earthly life ends and heavenly life begins.[15] The accounts affirm that God will protect and love each child as deeply and intensely as a devoted mother would, that God will fulfill the promise made to one mother to "come and [put] her in My arms, and all she'll have to do is turn her head from your love to Mine."[16] Mothers left behind to grieve their losses can find solace in imagining that their children may be incorporated into this heavenly world and that the best thing they can now do is willingly relinquish them into the loving care of God.

Such stories echo with the resilience that this kind of faith is expected to bring, involving a determination to yield one's own desires to the will of God and to rely on that will as the path to true healing. Suffering should not ultimately lessen the faith of God's faithful; instead, by forcing people to realize their utter helplessness and dependence upon God, as well as the fragility of their taken-for-granted daily lives, suffering should work to increase and sustain such faith, delivering hope of rewards and greater love to be found in the arms of God after death. As mourning is transfigured into joy, intimacy with God is replenished and fortified, bringing comfort and healing to the bereaved and eternal life and happiness to the dead.

What to outsiders may appear as failed healings, then, are reinterpreted by these women as opportunities for spiritual growth, gifts of serenity bestowed by a loving, omnipotent God to replace the heavy burdens of grief and remorse. Invariably the writers describe going through periods of confusion and doubt as they wonder why God has apparently refused to honor their prayers for healing. As they begin to feel immersed in God's love—Linda hearing God speak comforting words to her, Ginny receiving a vision from God picturing her son with Jesus, and so forth—these mothers come to decipher their own suffering as a lesson in their profound need for God and their complete dependence on him. Brought low by suffering, with their own emotional resources withered if not utterly depleted, the women turn in desperation and faint hope to a new source of love and strength, reimagining their pain to mean victory, wholeness, and healing of a truer kind. All prayers are answered, the writers claim, even if not always in the way one might have wished.

An analogous lesson surfaces in the story of a young woman, wife and mother of two young children, who is diagnosed with terminal cancer. Joyce recalls her dismay and terror upon learning of her diagnosis, when she begged God to heal her ailing body: "I've never asked for a lot out of life, just a happy family, to watch my kids grow up, that's all. Please, God . . ." For many months those around her advised her to "claim her healing" as a way of guarding against the cancer's progression; still, she was not healed. As she grew sicker and more despairing, she found that the prayers of her husband and friends seemed to help the pain subside, and she clung to the hope that God was with her in her suffering. Slowly, as Joyce began to accept the fact that she was going to die, she learned to appreciate every day as a "precious gift" from God. "The difference is," she writes, "I'm living again. I'm watching the flowers bloom. I'm hearing the birds sing. I'm cuddling [my children]." Joyce concludes, "I know that God is quite capable of healing me. But if the seasons of my life end, and the time comes for me to leave, I also know that God will be faithful to change the desire of my heart and I will desire to see only Him."[17]

Here again, the lesson to be learned about faith is not about the fulfillment of physical healing but about accepting death and appreciating everyday pleasures in the meantime. Her wistful closing words about her husband and children, "And they will remember me when they laugh," are poignantly suggestive of the heartache entailed in forsaking her family for the promise of heaven, a task that Joyce suggests is ongoing and perhaps never wholly finished until death. Having given up her hope in physical healing, yet apparently not yet ready to die, Joyce now rests her faith in simple enjoyments and wills to believe that God will "change [her] heart" so that it conforms more closely to the fact of her impending death. It is her attitude, rather than her body, that she now presumes is being healed.[18]

Just as these stories emphasize a kind of grace that may accompany serious illness, as the writers learn to appreciate and experience their lives in fresh and unexpected ways, so other narratives focus on the redemptive power of suffering and pain. One woman, whose seventeen-year-old son died of cancer, describes the importance of sharing her pain and being vulnerable with others so that she can willingly suffer with them and even for them, just as Jesus suffers for the faithful: "To not only sympathize, but to *share* the hurt of those women God put in my life, I had to retreat from my own point of healing. I had to open my wound far enough to let them see the vulnerability and yet not so much that I got caught in its snare again."[19] Other women similarly describe how pain and loneliness help them be compassionate toward those in need.[20] In most cases, such stories affirm both that suffering enables one to help others and that helping others may bring further healing to oneself as well. In this and other ways suffering may be discerned as a gift rather than a punishment from God.

The failure of prayer to produce healing can also cause alarm and doubt, however, as in the story of Judy, whose constant prayers for a dying neighbor's healing ended in confusion and humiliation when the neighbor died. Another writer reports feeling frustrated by her lack of control over her child's continual illnesses and by God's seeming indifference, crying out, "I'm Your child, Lord, but it seems the more I pray the worse things get. . . . I'm trying to believe that You are there, but I doubt that You hear me."[21] Recounting such doubts, authors seek to encourage skeptical or discouraged readers that they too once questioned God's power to heal before that healing became visible in their own lives. In Judy's narrative her faith in healing prayer was restored only when she realized that the error lay not in God's heartless negligence but rather in her own failure to discern God's greater (and sometimes slower) plan, a lesson for the reader who considers prayer a simple, even magical, panacea.[22] Offering consolation for doubt and explanation for failed healings, these writers teach that while doubt may be understandable, especially in a modern world where faith healing is derided along with all things divine, it is also sinful and demands repentance. After all, as some writers explain, while the "perfect ending, in a worldly sense," is physical healing, death itself may well be the perfect healing, from God's perspective.[23]

Still, spirit-filled women continue to hope for healings of a pleasanter kind and have no qualms about mixing prayer with other, more concrete remedies for illness. Doctors, hospitals, and the techniques of modern scientific medicine, while sometimes reported to be unnecessary or extraneous, are more often readily accepted as complementary instruments in the total healing process. Miracles are believed not to be limited to instantaneous and inexplicable events but to encompass a whole range of more gradual movements toward health as well. While to an outsider the variety of methods and meanings attached to healing may suggest potential interpretive tensions, the writers of these narratives do not appear constrained by the prospect of contradictions between distinct healing systems; rather, they accept healing as a mixed assignment: certain tasks may seem more appropriate to an earthly physician's expertise while others come under the province of God, the "Great Physician." Whatever conflicts there may seem to be between divine and medical healing are explained as simply a lack of wisdom on the part of the patient to discern which method is most appropriate.

Unlike most medical doctors, the Great Physician acts as a kind of holistic healer, working to heal and purify the heart or soul as well as the body. Thus these healing narratives are not stories of bodily purification only but of emotional and spiritual cleansing and transformation as well. In the stories of successful physical healings, this connection is especially clear: as the material body, riddled with sickness, is restored to purity, waves of warmth, light, or cleansing water seem to wash over the person, leaving her filled joyously with love and peace. Healed on the outside, her appearance radiant to all who see her, she is made equally radiant within. Rather than outward beauty serving as a disguise for inner ugliness or pain, here the outer mirrors the inner, body and soul existing in perfect harmony.

In stories of apparent failures, however, the outer, diseased body no longer reflects the inner peace bestowed on the suffering person. Rather, the uplifted, radiant soul seems almost to transcend the decaying or crippled body in all its helplessness, spastic movements, and pungent odors. Still, even the diseased body may display signs of healing, as when a dying person's "countenance" changes from fear to "total peace," for instance, or one "basks in the presence of the Lord" and exhibits an outward glow.[24] In this way physical healings of all kinds are also emotional or spiritual healings, curing harmful attitudes such as fearfulness, resentment, and despair, and replacing them with confident faith in God's purpose. Maria's recollection of her miraculous healing from rheumatoid arthritis is illustrative: "It wasn't the healing that was so marvelous, *it was the love of Jesus.*"[25]

He Is Making Me Real

Charismatic women believe that many illnesses stem primarily from emotional causes and require a different kind of treatment than material diseases. Less visible than physical disabilities, emotional ailments may be ignored or endured more easily, hidden beneath a facade of corporeal well-being that belies the person's "true" condition. Just as there exist multiple sources of depression and other emotional problems—anger, fear, pride, rebellion, low self-esteem—there is a concomitant range of interpretive strategies by which sickness is defined and blame assigned. Stemming in part from unresolved pain and disordered thinking, emotional illnesses are also thought to be produced or worsened by demonic spirits, so that healing requires rigorous and disciplined effort on the part of the patient both to root out unhealthy ideas and to resist all satanic influences. Such an assortment of dispositions, behaviors, childhood experiences, and demonic spirits means that the pursuit of healing these infirmities is a highly contested enterprise, as the boundaries around affliction are constantly challenged and redrawn. In various and sometimes contradictory ways evangelical culture has bestowed wide attention upon the emotions and their maladies, promising relief for the latter in the healing love of God.

As with physical healings, an emotional healing generally occurs only after the woman seeking it comes to a place of desperation and cries out to God for help. Many women write of teetering on the verge of suicide before making one final attempt to seek divine healing. Some might empathize with Mary, who looked in the mirror at the age of thirty-nine and saw "an old woman . . . getting older and fatter and grayer every day." "Sick, tired, frustrated," she writes, "I wished I were dead." Contemplating suicide, enduring long bouts of crying, she heard God gently rebuke her: "Mary, you don't love anybody! There is NO LOVE in your life." Later, at a retreat, Mary came forward during the altar call and prayed forlornly, "God, I've made a mess of my life, but if you want me, you can have me." As she received prayers from several leaders, she describes experiencing the healing love that she'd so desperately craved and then being able to feel new love for her husband and six children. The restoration that Mary's prayers initiated in her life has, she says, buoyed her through trials as diverse as the nervous breakdown of her husband, her sons' drug and alcohol problems, the drowning of one child, and abiding marital troubles. Claiming ongoing sustenance from the love of God, she concludes with stirring hope: "He is making me real."[26]

Another woman recapitulates an earlier period of protracted loneliness and despondency, a time when she disliked her husband and only resisted suicide because of her young son. Her images of that time are of an inner "emptiness" that "gnawed at" her constantly and made her think of death. "I could feel it well up inside of me, until it would encompass my entire being: a sickening sadness that I could not control." Fighting constantly with her husband, who sought "solace in a bottle of booze" while she withdrew into herself, she finally received a letter from her mother-in-law telling her to pray, which she did. That very afternoon she felt an "uncontrollable urge" to read the Bible and began feeling her life to be changed, herself to be healed. God, she later wrote, delivered her completely from her "terrible depression." "Praise God," she concludes. "He took my empty life and filled my soul, my body, my very being, to overflowing with His Spirit."[27]

Some narratives recount more dramatic instances of healing, focusing upon individual traumatic events rather than protracted depression. One memorable illustration is the chilling story of Janice, who was assaulted at gunpoint while in her own kitchen, beaten, and violently raped. "Now I understand more fully the power and strengthening of the Holy Spirit in the inner person," she later wrote. "While the intruder raped me I was strengthened to talk to him. 'Jesus loves you. Jesus died for you. Jesus wants you to give Him your heart,' I told him." After smashing a hammer into her head, the man left her to die. Fortunately, a friend arrived just a few minutes later; she took one look at Janice and began to pray for healing, led by "the Spirit" to ask God to "remove all the horror from my memory and to heal and restore my mind completely." Feeling "completely dissociated with everything except prayer and Helen's presence," Janice says that she herself began unthinkingly praying in the Spirit, although afterward she had no recollection of doing so.

Waking up in the hospital several hours later, Janice recalls that while she "went in and out of consciousness," when her mind cleared at last her first thoughts were of her attacker: "I prayed, 'Dear Jesus, I forgive him. Lord, do not hold this sin against him.' It wasn't something that I had to make myself do or talk myself into; it was the love of God abiding in my heart. I deserve no credit for being 'good.' Forgiveness is the normal reaction for a Spirit-abiding child of God. It was this forgiveness that removed the fear and allowed the complete healing of my mind." Janice concludes her story with a lesson of hope for others who have experienced emotional suffering, urging forgiveness toward everyone who has ever hurt them so that God will heal their hearts and minds. Significantly, an editor's note below this story informs readers that Janice's rapist was arrested that same day and confessed to his crime, acknowledging in his confession that Janice had talked to him about Jesus while he raped her. At the trial, where her attacker was convicted and sentenced to two concurrent prison sentences, Janice supposedly stood in the Oklahoma courtroom and said to him, "Mr. ———, I forgive you for what you did to me and I hope that you can ask God to forgive you." Two photographs of Janice in the *Aglow* issue in which this story appears (one on the cover) eerily show a woman meticulously groomed and beaming at the camera, without a trace of the pain that she must have endured.[28]

While many of these healing stories end on a more cheerful note than their subject matter might warrant, Janice's unwavering compassion for her rapist even in the moment that he raped her and her purported tranquility immediately after this grisly episode may seem especially dubious, whether gauged by psychotherapeutic analyses of anger or by the patterns of other evangelical women's narratives. While some readers would consider Janice's actions saintly, her claim that she felt absolutely no anger and that she forgave easily and immediately could be read more critically as an almost pathological attempt to imitate Christ, loving one's persecutors unconditionally and imploring God to forgive them as well. In professing herself restored and instantaneously healed, Janice's narrative presents an extreme example of the ways in which anger can be evaded and denied within this female evangelical world. Yet, as in the more recent story of Gwen (the Aglow speaker who forgave the men who sexually abused her as a child, recounted in Chapter 2), other charismatic women acknowledge the anger they have felt after such experiences and have more direct ways of dealing with the pain of sexual abuse than short-circuiting (or transcending) it as Janice may have done. While in both stories forgiveness is seen as necessary for full emotional healing, the contrast between Janice and Gwen suggests an important shift that took place during the 1980s, in which women's narratives of healing incorporated "anger" as a more acceptable response to pain and violence, ultimately a predictable and even conventional one.

Earlier signs of this shift in representing anger are evident in accounts that vary somewhat from Janice's. In 1978 JoAnne Sekowsky, onetime assistant editor of *Aglow* magazine, described her distress at realizing that non-Christian counselors offered more fruitful advice about handling bitterness and anger by "getting in touch" with it than did most Christians. Turning to the Bible, Sekowsky says she found that the answers to dealing with anger and other emotions could be found in scriptural texts if Christians would only look for them. Rather than denying anger and presenting a falsely cheerful front, Sekowsky argues that Christians must face their anger and establish "honesty" in relationships with other people, "an honesty that exposes us, our weaknesses, our pride, and our sins." The last word is key, however, for Sekowsky goes on to establish anger as a sin, pure and simple: "If our response to anyone's action is anger, resentment, hate and the like, we,

too, have sinned." The rest of this discussion is devoted to asking forgiveness for one's bitterness no matter what the circumstances. Offering
a more complex account of anger than did Janice, Sekowsky insists that
facing such feelings is a matter of Christian integrity and humble repentance a prerequisite for restoration.[29]

By the mid-eighties, however, spirit-filled writers were beginning to
interpret anger in increasingly therapeutic and sympathetic terms. In
her 1984 book *Healing the Angry Heart,* Aglow author Kathy Collard
Miller contends, "Anger begins with low self-esteem." Much of her
book is devoted to helping Christian women attain a more positive self-
image by resisting perfectionism, avoiding "negative self-talk," dealing
more successfully with stress, and establishing a closer relationship
with God. Urging mothers to stop condemning themselves for their
short tempers, Miller advises them to get at the root of their feelings
and verbalize them appropriately as a way of "healing" from anger.
Significantly, she only indirectly associates anger with sin and only
briefly mentions asking for forgiveness, even for severe child abuse; instead, she accents forgiving oneself for behaving angrily or violently
and assures readers that God will help them restore their relationships
with their children. Here, the notion of anger as a sin requiring full repentance has been transmuted into a softer conception of anger as a
sickness rooted in forces outside one's control, a disorder for which the
antidote is increased self-esteem.[30]

This shift in representing anger is further demonstrated in the number of stories from the later period that both acknowledge feelings of
ire and focus on alleviating these in greater depth than Janice's story allows. In a story printed in 1985, for instance, Iris described how she
was once "a child abuser" who beat her three young daughters violently whenever her uncontrolled rage surfaced. Even after she turned
to God for help, her angry outbursts continued until she eventually
"learned to surrender to the Lord in this area" and "allow[ed] the Holy
Spirit to help me control my emotions." Over time, her intense anger
began to dissipate, and Iris stresses that her struggles have been ongoing and difficult.[31] The same muted optimism is manifest in other, later
stories that identify anger as a natural response to loss and suffering
that requires gradual rather than instant healing. In 1989 one woman's
reproachful commentary on another woman's use of "Christian jar-
gon" to bypass pain exemplifies the criticisms made of accounts like
Janice's that may too easily deny suffering and anger: "No person could
have experienced the constant, joyous victory that woman related. . . .

Her personal experiences should have enabled her to reach out and share in my hurt. Instead, because she did not let me see her vulnerability, it was impossible to identify with her and find hope or comfort in her testimony."[32]

These disputes signal the continuing ambivalence evangelical women feel toward anger, wanting on the one hand to avoid or transcend it altogether yet recognizing on the other its inevitability and power. One obvious source of these fluctuating interpretations is the wide array of possibilities that may engender anger and the various degrees of accountability each entails. Increasing examples and discussions of sexual abuse since the 1980s have helped demolish the notion that Christian women should be always pliant and forgiving, replacing older injunctions to grin and bear it, as it were, with encouragement to stand against the abuse and get out. As I heard one nationally known Aglow leader, coordinating a workshop on praying for family and friends, tell her audience: "You all should *not* put up with abuse from husbands! . . . I don't automatically tell women to divorce, but I do tell them not to put up with abuse!" As she led participants into an intense session of spiritual warfare, all the anger in the room was channeled into fighting against the reported "Enemy," Satan.[33]

Charismatic culture assumes not only the existence of Satan but the reality of untold numbers of lesser malevolent spirits, many of which correspond to base emotions, actions, and states of mind. Narratives attributing affliction to evil spirits were particularly evident in my fieldwork. Women stand and testify to having been tormented by a spirit of bitterness or a spirit of fear; perhaps the latest difficulty is a spirit of addiction, a spirit of control, a spirit of anger, or a spirit of jealous envy.[34] While sometimes these appellations sound purely metaphorical, at other times they require dramatic procedures of "deliverance," in which a person is freed from the bonds of a spirit by deliverance prayer invoking the name of Jesus and various forms of spiritual warfare. Communal prayers may be said for participants who are themselves afflicted by such spirits or for others known to the group who seem to need deliverance. At one meeting, for instance, a woman led dramatic prayers of deliverance for all the husbands and children of the women present who were supposedly bound by spirits of addiction, alcohol, witchcraft, and Masonry; then, calling for the women to forgive their family members for their sins, she shouted for the spirits of unforgiveness afflicting those in the room to depart "in the name of Jesus" and not return.[35]

As with physical illness, there may be apparent failures in emotional illness, although these are less frequently described in printed literature (where joy and triumph always have the last word) than in oral accounts. During my fieldwork, I heard numerous women admit to the failures of their efforts to find complete emotional healing. One very sad story was told by Helen, whose twenty-something nephew, Ryan, committed suicide just a couple of days before Helen was scheduled to teach on "inner healing" to a local Aglow prayer meeting. Obviously exhausted and grief-stricken, Helen nonetheless arrived at the meeting ready to give her prepared lesson. She began by telling the group (who had already learned of the suicide) that she came from a "dysfunctional family" and that her sister had had a nervous breakdown some time ago. Ryan (her sister's son) had been troubled for many years and, according to Helen, "refused to let go of anger, resentment, and fear" so that he could not be truly open to the healing of his "inner wounds." The demonic "voices" that had been telling Ryan to kill himself— Helen called this a "spirit of suicide"—finally succeeded, all because he had not been able to deal with the most painful of his memories or believe in the possibility of healing. Helen's main point to the group was that it is all too easy to get "deliverance" at prayer meetings, again and again and again, but unless one gets to the root of one's pain, Satan will continue to prevent total healing.[36]

As in Helen's story about Ryan, healing is perceived as requiring "openness" to its very possibility, a leap of faith against despair. Often in describing these kinds of emotional or spiritual healings, a woman will write of suddenly realizing she had a choice between remaining in her pain and embracing the life held out to her by Jesus. Making the choice for life, and thus moving out of darkness into the light, is perceived as a simple surrender, a taking hold of something freely offered, an opening up of the heart to its deepest desires and their fulfillment. No one wishes to be in pain, such stories tell us; the pain comes because one is misguided, following the wrong path, led astray by Satan. Coming to see that she has the capacity to choose against her emotional suffering by willingly accepting Jesus is a critical step toward healing.

These stories often recount words of warning from God, advising the woman that her time to choose is running out. Sally describes such a moment, occurring months after she'd first prayed to God for help dealing with her alcoholic husband and mother and her dire financial situation. Things had improved for a time but she had drifted far from

God in the interim, increasingly tempted by thoughts of suicide. One Sunday morning, Sally writes, she "heard an audible voice," described as "firm but loving": "Sally, this is your last chance to serve me." Immediately Sally dashed out the door to church, where she begged Jesus to forgive her and to take over her wretched life. Without such a jolt from God reminding her not to take for granted the opportunity for healing, Sally's narrative suggests, she might not have made the life-changing decision that she did, preferring to remain rebelliously adrift while painfully separated from God. Like errant children in need of firm rules and boundaries, such writers depict themselves as greedy and wayward, requiring discipline and strict ultimatums in order to make the right choice for obedience.[37]

One of the most significant choices in the healing process involves forgiveness. According to many narratives, the first step in emotional healing is the recognition of one's own sinfulness and profound need for mercy and forgiveness. Confessing one's evil thoughts and actions, asking forgiveness for them, and believing such forgiveness to be bestowed upon them enables these women to begin feeling healed. One woman describes the importance of asking forgiveness for such actions as having an abortion and abusing one's children: "You don't have to wait for a special prayer time or for next Sunday in church. You can talk to Jesus right now, sitting under the hair dryer, crammed in a subway, or wherever you are. 'Jesus, I've failed. I haven't put love into action, and that's a sin, because You commanded us to love one another. I'm sorry. Truly sorry. Please forgive me.'" She continues by reassuring her readers, "Whether you feel forgiven or not doesn't matter. You have asked for forgiveness and because the Lord is faithful to His word, you have received it."

Besides receiving the forgiveness of God, it is considered crucial to seek forgiveness from oneself as well as from other people whom one may have injured. In terms reminiscent of recovery or twelve-step language, the same author urges readers to tell themselves, audibly if possible: "Self, I forgive you. I don't hold that failure and that sin against you any longer and I won't accuse you of it again." Finally, she teaches, "Go to the person you have hurt and ask their forgiveness. It's a hard thing to do, but you'll find great relief in the process and so will the other person." Forgiveness, then, is a multifaceted process.[38]

In a narrative that richly evokes the benefits of forgiveness, Margaret describes her need to be pardoned for her anger toward her dead mother, who in her will left all her money and possessions to Margaret's brother. Feeling that she had been unjustly cheated out of her inheritance, Margaret writes, she attended a religious meeting and realized that she had "bitterness, resentment, and unforgiveness toward my mother in my heart." Raising her hand, she told the other women present of her transgression and desire for absolution; as they prayed for her, Margaret experienced great "joy and release" through forgiveness, which felt like "a spiritual bath." She concludes by suggesting the serendipitous material gains that may be reaped by seeking forgiveness: "The sequel to the story is beautiful. God provided an even larger inheritance for me through a totally unknown source." Presumably, in Margaret's view God will bless those who ask forgiveness by satisfying even those desires that drove them initially to sin.[39]

For healing to occur, a person must not only repent of specific sins and ask forgiveness, but must also be willing to forgive those who have hurt her, whether such people request forgiveness or not. Often the ones Aglow women say they most need to forgive are their fathers, many of whom are described as distant, if not absent, and very often abusive. Quin, whose father abandoned her as a child when he divorced her mother, realized as an adult that she needed to "let go" of her hate and forgive him. She prayed: "'Father, make me willing. No, Lord, help me forgive him right now,' I prayed, lifting my open palms ever so slightly as though pushing this burden right into my Heavenly Father's lap. Then, somewhat reluctantly, I added, 'Lord, forgive me for hating him.'"[40]

Other women describe learning to forgive their mothers, their children, their in-laws, their friends, and others who may have hurt them. Many, like Quin, emphasize as well their own need for forgiveness. Again, forgiveness is a decision, a "conscious choice," a letting go of anger and pride in order to be filled with love and peace.[41]

This notion fits well with an increasing sense among spirit-filled women that healing some of the deeper emotional wounds from which they suffer requires intensive, prolonged work to uncover unresolved feelings of injury and rejection. Like the broader evangelical culture that has appropriated many contemporary teachings on "the healing of memories" and "the inner child," Aglow has increasingly accented the need for women to recover the most painful incidents of their lives, from childhood to the present, in order to get at the root of feelings of inadequacy that can supposedly cause trouble in later life. In a book of healing meditations for charismatic women, one author describes what she calls "the most important meditation prayer of all." Asking the reader to imagine herself as a little girl of four or five, the writer tells her to say: "'Little (*your name*), I ask you to forgive me for all the demands that I placed upon you. Forgive me for beating down on you. Forgive me for criticizing you. Forgive me for all the hurts that I have done to you.' Just reach out your arms now and visualize that little girl coming into your arms. . . . Just say to her, 'Little ———, even if the whole world turns against you, even if everyone forsakes you, I will love you and I will be your friend . . . I promise you that I will take time every day to hold you in my arms and to talk to you, and to listen to every thing you have to say to me and I will love you.'"[42] Like the spate of therapeutic literature on the inner child that emerged in the late 1980s, these charismatic forms emphasize total acceptance and forgiveness of oneself as a crucial step along the road to healing.

Charismatic women's narratives of healing, in accord with the evangelical domain from which they emerge, echo larger cultural themes pertaining to therapeutic understandings of the self, displacing earlier religious notions about sin, depravity, and the need for vigilant repentance with more recent and less stern models of a self that is essentially innocent but wounded and so in need of healing. Mixing religion with popular psychology is not a new activity, of course, and thinkers from both camps have long been adept at bringing the two together in some kind of harmonious relation, particularly in terms of techniques for achieving happiness. Today, however, as these narratives suggest, the accommodation has reached such an extraordinary degree that the dividing line between popular psychology and popular evangelicalism seems less stable than ever before.[43]

The obvious commonalities between psychology and evangelicalism notwithstanding, evangelicals insistently regard themselves as offering a substantially different mode of healing to that offered by "the world," a path that is not about self-sufficiency, much less self-absorption (as they would characterize much of secular therapy), but about letting the self feel completely fulfilled by surrendering to her loving Father God. Charismatic women, believing that God literally enters their bodies in order to effect healing, write of Jesus having "taken me over . . . making me real" and describe their "very beings" as "filled to overflowing" with God's Spirit in prayer. Emerging from such ecstatic states, the women feel not only healed, purified, and strengthened, but actually transformed and reborn, as the old self in all its sin and sickness is replaced with a wholly new self that is sinless (at least momentarily), fresh, well, and whole. This notion of transformation is the hinge on which all Aglow narratives turn, as the unending cycles of piety work again and again to explode the mere theatricality of the older, inauthentic self and to enable the formation of a newly felt "real" self along with a reformulated and as yet unsullied life narrative.

Becoming a "New Creature"

Transformation is a central theme in the Christian tradition. Biblical accounts of conversion and teachings imputed to Jesus about a second birth have provided paradigms for the transformative changes that Christians believe God effects in human life. In the early modern period, the stress put on the "new birth" by eminent revivalists and reformers such as George Whitefield and John Wesley pushed the idea to center stage, establishing it as the cardinal sign of authentic piety in eighteenth- and nineteenth-century evangelicalism. Corresponding with the epistemology of John Locke in which experience—in Locke's terms, "sensation"—had become the only path to correct knowledge, now individual religious experience had become the only path to true devotion. Augmented, refined, and in some ways simplified by nineteenth-century revivalists Charles Finney and Dwight Moody and further developed by the born-again preachers of the twentieth-century, the inward experience of an intensely felt rebirth has been pivotal for evangelical multitudes across time and cultures.

Notions of new birth and transformation have, like those of healing, evoked the cultural themes of their time and have been viewed differently in different contexts. Traditionally, conversion and sanctification have involved experiences of shedding an older self and obtaining a new, purified one in return, perhaps accompanied by tangible sensations of God's immediacy and activity through spirit baptism and manifold spiritual gifts. More recently, the notion of receiving a new self discontinuous from the old has been virtually superseded in some evangelical circles by an emphasis on discovering the "real" self that was formerly hidden, denied, or otherwise unknown. Such a discovery, thought to recur frequently as one remembers what has already been learned but forgotten, may be better suited to the modern therapeutic formula of steady growth punctuated by wondrous insights into one's inner goodness and truth than is the solitary born-again experience. By no means do contemporary evangelicals discard the idea of a new birth, which remains the essential condition of salvation, yet their narratives tend to place as much emphasis on a perpetual search for authenticity and for a venue that would let that need be fulfilled as they place on a single shift from old to new. The perpetual stress on the "false" and the "true" that marks evangelical piety currently finds its most widely appealing expression in moments of revelation and wistful appeals to "realness," in which the surrendered soul receives assurance of her essential goodness.[44]

For the spirit-filled women of Aglow, transformation encompasses a broad variety of meanings: victory over sin and sickness, whether physical, emotional, or spiritual; the uncovering and/or restoration of the authentic, hidden self; a surrender of the selfish will in favor of God's plan; finding new love in Jesus, whether as father, lover, or friend; the ecstasy wrought by the infusion of the Holy Spirit, accompanied by feelings of freedom, liberation, and power; and so on. "Suddenly," an old way of viewing the world, of actually being in the world, gives way to a revised perspective and mode of living, as she who is transformed realizes herself to be a "new creature," her former self discarded and her sins forgotten. Newly in love with God, the transformed person interprets the world afresh, reveling blissfully in even the mundane aspects of her life rather than succumbing to despair. Through no power of her own, except the effort necessary to accept this freely offered gift, the woman experiences these changes as miraculous and irreversible. Healed, forgiven, purified, and strengthened by the power of God, she feels reborn.

Transformation is often described as occurring in a particular moment, as in Aubrey's description of a prayer that changed her life. Suddenly, she says, "My empty-shell feeling was gone. Instead I was filled with the joy and peace that passeth all understanding." Feeling "infinitely small and insignificant," still she avers that she had "never been so completely happy and peaceful." Realizing the error of trying to control her own life rather than surrendering it to God, Aubrey explains, she suddenly understood that she had been "spiritually dead" for years. Now, however, "I had been given NEW LIFE. I felt like a newborn fowl, still wet and sticky and trying hard to stand up on shaky, newborn legs. I struggled and wobbled and was weak and helpless but I WAS BORN! Re-born in Him." Her past eradicated, a "new horizon" having gloriously emerged, Aubrey's old self has been emptied, purified by the surging power of the Spirit, transforming her into a new creature.[45]

Another woman describes her transformation as a more gradual deliverance from fear, self-hatred, and depression, occurring as she read the Bible and learned to praise God in all circumstances. Through a long process of praying, alone and with others, for healing from the "forces of darkness" in her life and using scripture verses to ward off fear and worry, Margit became renewed: "As I continued in my walk with the Lord, praying in the Spirit, worshipping Him, and confessing the Word, I started to feel like a new person. Deep joy and peace really became a part of me. When I worshipped the Lord, his presence came over me, and I would start to laugh for joy. . . . I started to feel worth something." Hospitalized repeatedly after suffering "nervous break-downs," Margit says she only began to "feel worth something" after discovering closeness with God; and it is this new sense of self-worth that causes her to "feel like a new person."[46]

Transformation, in these stories, brings with it the expectation that others will be able to see the changes wrought in this new creature and will want to experience the same kind of love and joy. Aglow accounts frequently tell of observers, friends, or even strangers approaching the transformed woman to tell her she is "different" and to ask her why. Donna writes: "One time after telling one dear friend about my personal relationship with Christ she gave me . . . a very great compliment. She told me that she and her husband had noticed Doug and I were *different*. She didn't know whether it was the confidence we seemed to have, or the look in our eyes, or what it was, but *now she knew why we were different*" [emphasis in original]. Donna concludes by affirming that the important difference manifested by a Christian is joy rather than rule-keeping: "How sad it would have been if the only thing we had been able to communicate in our being different was that we didn't smoke or drink or dance."[47]

As outer and inner selves become identical, inner beauty is expected to be reflected on the outside, evidenced by increased energy and enthusiasm as well as more material signs. Thus, for many spirit-filled women, manifestations of external attractiveness—bright clothing, slimness, make-up, neatly combed hair, manicured nails, and an always cheerful mien—are emblems of transformation, providing, in the words of one author, "a good advertisement of God's wonderful care of his children."[48] So certain are many women of the power of beauty to signal and even catalyze regeneration that in 1992 at least one midwestern Aglow board directed a mission trip of "pampering" for women, an outreach entitled "Ladies, It's Your Day": "More than 300 women and children were shown Christ's love as the women received a free hair style, manicure, or make-over. While the mothers were served, free childcare was provided. After each woman received her free beauty service, she was invited to a room where a prayer counselor individually shared the good news of Christ's love for her. At least thirty-two women committed their lives to Christ." This apparently successful outreach was repeated in 1993 for women in inner-city Detroit, where, as the director of this outreach explained, "We wanted to encourage the women in their womanhood, and let them know that they are special, they are beautiful."[49] The aesthetic described here sharply contrasts with the plain style of more traditional Pentecostal and holiness adherents, who would no doubt decry its "worldliness"; yet these modern women argue that beautifying themselves and others is not wrong but is simply a way of conforming their outer presentation with the inner, transformed reality, making them respectable witnesses for God's power.

This attitude may lead to anxiety, however, since it is obviously quite possible to "put on" these exterior niceties as a kind of disguise when one is not truly transformed. Surface beauty may well be deceptive, evangelical stories remind female readers, as the writers recount how they themselves once "masked" their true selves before being transformed or click their tongues at others who care more about semblance than substance: "Poor, poor dear! Dressed to the teeth, coifed and jeweled, all dressed up for life, and nowhere to go!"[50] Notions of beauty are conflicted, then, just as the decorated bodies of other women may provoke suspicion (or envy) more than approval. Still, a woman who has been truly transformed by the power of God will supposedly be known to all, as her inner glory is displayed in her outwardly radiant appearance.

Transformation may be immediate or gradual; most often the narratives illustrate both immediate and gradual dimensions to it, looking back at earlier events to see signs or "seeds" of transformative changes. A long period of dissatisfaction or emptiness, often described as a "vacuum," may end in a low point of desperation, in which the woman realizes her need for God and turns to him for help. Like Sally, considering suicide to escape a life with an alcoholic husband who did not love her, a woman may have an immediate understanding of God's love for her: "I sat in that little church and listened to the singing and the preaching as politely as possible. Slowly I became aware of the reality of God's love. Suddenly I understood that I was loved just as I was. I understood that God looked on me, a woman who tried to hide from Him, a woman with a falling-down marriage, a woman who sinned, and found me lovable. I was overwhelmed with his love." Listening to the minister preach about Jesus, Sally prayed "a simple prayer," asking Jesus to forgive her sins and come into her heart. Slowly, yet suddenly, Sally felt the love of God and felt transformed by it. But then, as Sally drifted away from church, her life once more fell apart, until finally the couple filed for bankruptcy and Sally felt suicidal once again. When she asked Jesus to forgive her and come back into her life once again, the transformation felt more permanent. Nine years later, she writes, she continues to live a transformed life.[51]

Sally's story reminds us of the cycles of regression and renewal that pervade spirit-filled women's accounts of transformation. Although the hope of permanent change remains, the sense of being transformed is inevitably and repeatedly challenged by unexpected and difficult situations that continually emerge in daily life. The newly converted may "backslide"; recovering alcoholics may begin drinking again; "healed" abusers may batter their children; wives recently turned "submissive" may rebel against their husbands. Moments of conversion, of repentance, of ecstatic immersion in the Holy Spirit, fade and dissipate into the mundane routines of everyday existence, the circumstances of which are generally not affected by such peak moments and so may continue to disappoint. Female writers acknowledge this dynamic process, offering readers a variety of mechanisms for surviving the rise and fall of religious feeling and the temptations of old behaviors and urging them to accept such cycles as inevitable.

Still, the narrative convention requires the teller to reassure her readers at the end of her account that she is, *this time,* truly a changed person, a "new creature" in Christ, her life unalterably transformed. As one woman asserts, "I know I will never be sick again. I have been well now since 1975, and I know that as I continue to confess God's Word for myself, I will stay well."[52] Even while acknowledging the inevitability of religious "ups and downs," then, the stories ask the readers to affirm and believe in a kind of fixed transformation, whether or not this coheres with their own cycles of piety. Writers continually encourage readers to hope for this kind of transformation in their own lives, and to describe their lives in similarly affirmative terms. Such stories leave no room for doubt, uncertainty, or anxiety for the future: narrators always firmly assert the permanence and irreversibility of the changes God has wrought in their lives as a kind of unalterable progress toward perfect faith. If a woman has been truly transformed, such stories claim, she need not fear falling back into her old self; as long as she continues to be in relationship with God, she will continue to grow as a new creature in Christ, free from the taints of the past.

Often the desire for transformation appears to stem precisely from the hope of escaping such taints, involving immense feelings of guilt and regret for making a mess of one's life. Sandy, who became pregnant at fifteen, writes of her "nice," "normal" childhood, full of country club parties and fairly regular church attendance, all of it "blown" by her shameful pregnancy. A few years after having the baby and giving it up for adoption, she again found herself pregnant and eloped with her boyfriend. When the baby was stillborn, Sandy considered this her punishment for her sinful life, noting, "From that moment, self-destructive guilt became a driving force that shaped my life for many years." Infidelity, drugs, divorce, and promiscuity followed. She sought help from psychologists who urged her simply to "accept myself," which she could not do. Finally, after turning to God in prayer, she felt God cleanse her completely for all her past guilt: "I cried and cried until exhausted. The burden was gone; the yoke was lifted. The 'dirt' was dissolved in the glory of His righteousness! I was made whole and clean, a new creature, and a child of God! I knew deep inside of me what II Corinthians 5:17 says: 'Therefore if any man be in Christ he is a new creature: old things are passed away; behold, all things become new.'" Even as a "new creature," Sandy realized that God loved her just as she was, for she was the person God made her to be. Now happily married and the mother of two healthy children, Sandy's life has been, she says, forever transformed, all the sin and shame of her past absolved and forgotten.[53]

Transformation, as with Sandy and many others, means the chance to make "a new start" and find true freedom. Having been misled by the thought that freedom represented the ability to follow one's own wishes, the transformed woman discovers that it really means the willingness to surrender one's will, ask for forgiveness, and determine to live a purer life. Various stories, such as "Free Indeed!" and "Just to Be Free," suggest that the longing for freedom from the constraints in one's life is a crucial impetus in these processes of prayer and surrender. Invoking that longing in their readers, the authors of these stories encourage other women suffering in "bondage" to surrender their suffering to God and discover the "new life" awaiting them.

Transformation may also mean a renewed perception of God and self, using not merely the mind but the heart and learning to depend on

feeling to experience divine love. Kathy, whose right eye had to be removed because of a cancerous tumor, writes of crying out to God in
self pity, questioning his love for letting this happen. "I cried to the
point of exhaustion. Then came the stillness, the quiet, and with it a
warmth. I could physically feel it, like liquid love, pour over my head
and down my shoulders until it enveloped me. Love that washed me
with the strength and irresistible force of an ocean wave. 'Kathy,' [God]
spoke to my heart, 'your life is a miracle of my love.'" Hearing these
words, Kathy was able to see herself through "God's eyes," knowing
that God loved her "just as I was." Surrendering to him, she whispered,
"Lord . . . if you can use me like this, I'm yours." That moment, she
later noted, "marked the turning point. Gradually my attitude began to
change." No longer did she see her lost eye as a liability but rather as
a "witnessing tool" for describing to others how her life had been
transformed.[54]

As with healing of physical and emotional or spiritual sicknesses,
transformation is often accompanied by a sensory experience of
warmth, light, water, and so on, such as the "liquid love" Kathy reports. Lee, for instance, recalls her "physical exhaustion and despair,"
in which she felt "as though I were sinking into the miry clay." Finally
crying out to God her desire to relinquish her will permanently in favor
of his, she underwent a dramatic experience: "At that moment, on
bended knees beside my bed, I saw a rushing ball of light. Whirling, it
came faster and faster until it was directly before me and then enveloped my very being. I felt the Spirit as never before and I began sobbing, rejoicing, and praising my wonderful Lord all at once." In this
wondrous instant, Lee asserts, "my life was transformed." Suddenly
gone were the "bitterness and resentfulness in my heart," and "new
strength" emerged within her. Lee concludes, "I was free!"[55]

Ruth, like Ann a convert to Christianity from Orthodox Judaism, recalls the moment of her transformation, when her hands suddenly
"shot up toward heaven" and she shouted, "Thank you, Jesus!"
"When I did this, it seemed as though electricity shot down my arms
and body from my fingers to my toes. My whole being was trembling,
my knees were knocking together, and as I was growing weaker and
weaker I held on to the chair in front of me to keep from falling." The
intense physicality of this experience convinced Ruth of its reality, causing her to "realize" that "it could not be mass psychology; this could
not be hypnotism; this was not an emotion stirred up; this was not a
man-made influence. This was the demonstration of the Almighty

God!" Because the experience was so tangible, Ruth continues, "I KNEW then that God is a living reality!" Ruth's account of apparent physical evidence aims at leaving readers with little room for skepticism.[56]

Like other testimonial stories within evangelical culture, Aglow narratives end not with a fear of failure but with the certainty of success, yet there are hints throughout printed and especially oral narratives that one's sense of transformation may be ephemeral and perhaps even deceptive. The assertion of rebirth means little, both within and outside evangelical theology, without the "fruits" that mark true change, and these can seem all too elusive in time. The steady insistence upon transformation and renewal within these narratives may begin to sound hollow to anyone who has ever experienced the fading of a once loyal commitment or the instability of a change of heart. Evangelical Christians themselves may wonder similarly whether narrative assertions of healing and transformation always suggest the success of faith or whether they may sometimes be the product of wishful thinking, arising from an evangelical ethos in which participants must at least *pretend* to feel transformed.[57]

Whatever the source and whatever the impact, the experience of transformation is repeatedly invoked in Aglow narratives, comprising the primary theme and culmination of the women's stories. Though rife with tensions and anxieties about the fragility and transience of the experience, charismatic women guard the ideal of transformation by narrative conventions and material signs meant to demonstrate its authenticity and permanence. Deeply tied to notions of healing, transformation of the self suggests a renewed capacity to get along in the world and engage in the ordinary activities and relationships of daily life. Even as it is contingent on prayerful self-surrender, then, transformation entails feelings of ecstatic freedom, of victory over all previous afflictions and obstacles, and of invincible strength and unfailing courage in the face of future misfortune. Aglow women believe that all who desire real joy both can and must undergo this experience and that no honest woman could deny her longing for it. As a local Aglow leader told her retreat audience in 1993, "Every woman who doesn't have what we have needs it; and even if she doesn't know it, she wants it."[58]

4

Unveiling the Heart

Secrecy, Openness, and Intimacy

In the early 1970s, Shelley, a young mother of three small children, received the devastating news that her husband Bill was involved in a serious love affair with his nineteen-year-old secretary. Bill confessed his infidelity to Shelley, ending with the worst blow of all: "I don't love you any more." Heartbroken and knowing no one from whom to seek comfort, Shelley later remembered, "I thought I'd die." Having "nothing else to do," she "turned to the Lord completely" and prayed "by the hour" for an end to her misery.

Bill continued to live with his distraught wife for eight months. Even after she told him she loved him "desperately" and wanted him to stay, he moved out of the house. Furious with God, Shelley sobbed: "Lord, what went wrong? . . . Lord, what do I do now? I'm so upset I can't even pray about it." God answered her "very clearly," advising her to "start . . . by praising Me and thanking Me." Although still angry at God's apparent disregard of her prayer, Shelley obeyed, praying "mechanically" for three and a half weeks until "one day I was overwhelmed with the peace and presence of Jesus. I knew with certainty that He loved me and was never going to leave me."

Although Bill had insisted that he would not consider reconciliation—"not in a million years"—Shelley still hoped that he would return soon; but months passed with no word from him. While at first he sent money to pay the bills, soon the payments stopped altogether, leaving Shelley so desperate she resorted to food stamps. Barely able to survive, she learned that God was truly her source of love and "daily bread" and felt increasingly grateful for his plentiful gifts. Finally she took stock of her situation, went to a lawyer, and eventually obtained a divorce.

In all these bleak months, even while praying to God continuously for guidance, Shelley had grown angry, not only at Bill but also—and more heatedly—at Bill's parents, who insistently defended him and refused to help her get financial support from him. Slowly she came to realize that she "had a lot of confessing to do" and sought help from "some mature Christian friends." Realizing the "hidden anger" Shelley was harboring, these friends told her to close her eyes and visualize in her mind exactly what she would like to do to her in-laws. A "vivid scene" of brutal revenge came to Shelley's mind in which she spat upon them and kicked them feverishly.

Next, having helped her face up to her virulent animosity, her friends prayed with Shelley for God to show her "how He saw" her in-laws. "Immediately," she later noted, "a beautiful picture came to mind," with her in-laws dressed "in long, white robes with crowns on their heads." Ashamed, alarmed, and "terribly convicted by the contrast" between her rage and God's love, Shelley begged God to forgive and heal her from rancor. A miraculous process of restoration began at that moment, "because my anger was no longer hidden."

That night, at home, Shelley prayed with her young daughters to help them forgive their father for abandoning them. "The seven-year-old cried as she prayed, 'Dear Lord, I forgive my daddy and I ask You to tell him right now in his heart, that I forgive him and I love him. And thank You, Jesus, for saving him.' The four-year-old just sobbed, 'I forgive you, Daddy.'" All of them apparently cured of their bitter grief, Shelley later wrote, "The Lord blessed us with a closeness as we cried and prayed and held one another tightly."

Since that time, Shelley concludes, she and her children have "come a long way from that night when their daddy left," passing beyond their initial misery into a state of joy and inner peace. They have prayed for everything from rent money to shoes, and, she says, "the Lord has always provided." She ends her story by emphasizing the healing that has taken place in her life through the confession of her anger. When people come to her and ask her how to cope with a husband's leaving, she tells them: "Turn to God and let Him come near to you. Praise Him, for His hand is always upon your life. Let Him heal your resentments. Let Him help solve your financial problems. Then one morning you will wake up and there will be peace in your heart instead of pain, and life will be sweeter than it has ever been before. The deep void left in your life when your husband walked away will have been filled by Jesus Himself."[1]

The theme of bringing to light those things that have been hidden in the darkness of the human heart is an old one in Christian theology and practice, acted out in various rites of confession and contrition. The passage from sin to purity, or from bondage to freedom, traditionally begins with the acknowledgment—indeed, the conviction—of personal wickedness, followed by prayers of repentance and acts of penance that allow forgiveness and healing to occur. Without the initial admission of evil, however differently construed by various Christian communities, there can be no hope for salvation; those who deny their own sin by keeping secret their failures have rejected God's grace and may be subject to eternal damnation.

Shelley's story is patterned after this traditional formula. She marks the turning point of her journey from wretchedness to victory at the juncture of confession and remorse. Importantly, however, what requires confession is not a perverse act against the will of God but a torturous configuration of feelings, an emotional response to other people's hurtful behavior. Shelley's supposed failure consists of harboring resentment and anger against those who abandoned her, both an adulterous husband and some less-than-sensitive in-laws; to be healed and released from bondage, she had to bring these hidden feelings to the surface, confess them humbly to God in prayer in the presence of her friends, and let them go. The result, she assures her readers, is no mere abstract sense of forgiveness but a wholly restored relationship with God, bringing with it the renewed capacity to experience life as a gift of love rather than a bitter trial. Openness leads not only to purification, then, but also to a tangible experience of divine intimacy, as "Jesus Himself" comes in to fill the "deep void" in her life.

The themes of secrecy, openness, and intimacy pervade the stories evangelical women tell about healing and redemption. This chapter explores the recurrent Aglow depictions of feelings kept "hidden in the heart" as well as the measures by which such secrets are apparently revealed in the forging of intimate relationships with God and other people. As with the prayers of healing and transformation, practices involving openness and intimacy are inextricably linked to the quest for a particular kind of freedom and to the shaping of an undivided religious identity, forming an important axis along which ideal Christian womanhood can be prescribed, measured, and accomplished.

The Hiddenness of Pain

Aglow stories are filled with pain. Many record the terrors of sexual and physical abuse, while others evoke the frustrations of domestic strife, spousal neglect, or sheer conjugal enmity. Some tell of the grief of alcoholism and drug addiction, estrangement from parents or children, or death of loved ones, spanning a broad range of suffering in the lives of ordinary American women. A common element in these accounts, despite the different problems they depict, is the secretiveness with which people respond to pain. This "hiddenness" is characterized as a kind of coping mechanism and is seen as ultimately doing far more harm than good. Often linked to feelings of shame and anger, hidden pain is attributed to experiences of rejection and abandonment as well as to confusion over personal responsibility, blame, and guilt.[2]

"Shame" is given the following definition in Aglow's *Support Group Leader's Guide,* published in 1993: "This is the emotion a person feels when he is vulnerable involuntarily, the emotion Adam and Eve felt immediately when they recognized they were naked. It is one of the core emotions that produces perfectionism and other methods employed to deny and cover up one's true state. A person who feels ashamed is inhibited in her ability to love God and to develop healthy relationships." One of the most commonly invoked emotions in Aglow narratives, shame is seen as working to thwart self-disclosure and to encourage denial of one's "true state." Acting as a kind of block against honesty and as an impetus for concealment and deceit, shame makes it impossible to achieve authentic, intimate relationships. Stemming from feeling "naked" and all too vulnerable, shame suggests both sickness and sin and characterizes what this author calls a "wounded soul." Women who suffer from shame, she writes, "desperately need compassionate understanding of where they are and why, and hope for a way out of their pain," concluding, "Without a doubt, this is another way Aglow can fulfill the call to be a 'network of caring women.'"[3] The burgeoning of Aglow support groups since 1989 suggests that healing from shame is a commonly felt need, and in fact "shame" has been invoked throughout Aglow's history as a dominant motif.

A frequently cited cause of shame among Aglow women is the shame of childhood and adolescent sexual abuse. Especially since the late

1970s, when sexual abuse of children and teenagers began receiving wide publicity in the United States, Aglow women have discussed this issue as one that has dramatically affected many of their lives. As one Aglow writer noted in 1988, "Many authorities today say that one out of every four women over the age of sixteen has been or will be sexually abused sometime in her life. At least one expert believes the figure should be one in three."[4] The stories shared in Aglow literature and meetings suggest that many of these women too are coping with feelings of shame ascribed to rape or sexual coercion.

Large retreat and conference meetings frequently become arenas where such stories are told and mourned communally, as in the session led by Gwen, recounted at the beginning of Chapter 2. Gwen told her Aglow audience that she had been the victim of rape and incest from the time she was five years old, highlighting the guilt and anger she had felt for most of her life because of these repeated assaults. When she offered the women present the opportunity to experience healing from their own experiences of sexual or other forms of abuse, more than half the audience of five hundred women went forward for prayer, many more breaking up into small groups weeping and praying for God's love to transform them.[5] This is hardly an isolated event in Aglow; many meetings emphasize the theme of sexual abuse, while stories published in *Aglow* magazines since the early 1980s have increasingly invoked it as well.

At sixty years of age, Aglow leader Fran Lance has been counseling victims of sexual abuse for many years. She was one of four children whose alcoholic mother turned to prostitution after the death of her husband. Fran was first sexually abused at the age of four, the victim of her landlady's son. When she was nine years old, living in a foster home, a man hired by the family began abusing her sexually. After moving in and out of thirteen foster homes, she wound up in a juvenile detention center. When she attended a revival led by Billy Graham, she says, her life was transformed. Seeing a light in the corner of her room, she suddenly "knew that Jesus was in my room with me, and I could sense his love for me." While she had felt emotionally "dead or at least numb" before, she writes, "Now I could feel in a way I never had before."

Years later, happily married and mother of five adopted children, she received the baptism in the Holy Spirit and began the process of healing from "all the loneliness, the pain and fear, the terror—all the garbage I'd inherited along with the sexual abuse. . . . With friends' help, prayer, my Bible, and the Lord personally speaking to me, God gradually healed my memories and injuries. Not only that, he took away the scars, too, just as if I'd never been hurt in the first place. I found the rebellious, wounded child in me fading away and a secure, new Fran replacing her." Telling her story to women in Aglow, Fran began a ministry of praying with other women who had experienced sexual abuse. She prayed with women such as Cheryl, molested by five alcoholic stepfathers from the time she was three until she was seventeen; Rose, sexually assaulted by a stepfather, a friend's father, and her stepgrandfather; and Brenda, whose abuse began in a foster home after her prostitute mother was declared unfit to raise her.

"Everywhere I minister, I find women crying out for help," says Fran. "When you work with hurting women, you find sexual abuse is frequently at the root of their woundedness." Describing how and why sexual abuse continues to be a "hidden crime" in America, she notes that sexual abuse occurs "all around us. . . . Not just in the slums and poor neighborhoods, but in 'respectable' middle- and upper-class homes—even in our church families." Advocating support groups and other means of sharing the terrible secret of sexual abuse, Fran, like Gwen, continues to speak to Aglow groups across the country helping participants recover from their shame and silence and to become whole, healthy women.[6] The collective sharing advocated by Fran and other Aglow leaders and participants parallels the feminist consciousness-raising groups of the 1970s and beyond, where many women articulated male violence in their lives and were reportedly heard for the first time.[7]

Another form of abuse more frequently cited by Aglow women as the cause of shame during childhood is emotional or physical abuse by parents. This topic is often raised in printed narratives and has frequently been broached in my interviews. Many Aglow writers describe parental derision as a devastating experience suffered by some children at the hands of their parents: "When Susan was a child, her abusive mother repeatedly told her she was stupid, ugly and never would succeed. When Susan did something wrong, her mother instructed everyone in the family not to speak to her." What usually happens in this situation, this author teaches, is that the abused child grows up having low self-esteem and often abuses her own children in turn. Giving a series of suggestions for healing from the pain of child abuse, the writer concludes, "If you were abused or neglected as a child, forgive your parent and accept responsibility for your actions. Pledge to pray for your parents every day."[8]

Various forms of shame also haunt women in adulthood. Abandonment by one's husband, as seen in the story of Shelley that opened
this chapter, appears regularly in Aglow narratives and is frequently
cited as a cause of low self-esteem and shame. Rejected for another
woman, Shelley tried to discern what she could have done wrong that
would cause her husband to seek a new lover: "Hadn't I been a good
wife? I had always kept the house straight, remembered to put gas in
the car, and never criticized him in front of others. I had lost that
twenty pounds he wanted me to lose. Why didn't he love me? It
seemed so unfair." Poring over the small details of her own faithfulness and unable to pinpoint the cause of Bill's infidelity, Shelley still felt
ashamed that he would leave her. Humiliated and disgraced at being
abandoned and then forced into a divorce, she was able to overcome
her sense of shame only when she felt herself surrounded by the love
of Jesus and "knew with certainty that He loved me and was never
going to leave me."[9]

Accounts of ongoing physical abuse by husbands are not common
in Aglow narratives, oral or written, and yet regular references suggest its hidden existence. The vehement injunction I heard an Aglow
leader tell her audience—"You all should *not* put up with abuse from
your husbands!"—indicates the encouragement abused women may
well receive from their evangelical sisters to get out of their situation,
whether such advice is given out by pastors or not.[10] Yet the well-
publicized and controversial story of contemporary Christian singer
Susie Luchsinger, whose husband has physically beaten her for years
but who now claims their marriage has been totally healed, typifies
the hope of some religious women that God can change their husbands into loving, nonviolent men.[11] Whereas confessions of childhood or adolescent abuse seem no longer to stigmatize their victims,
the shame of current abuse must be extreme and certainly does not
make for the victorious tone demanded by the testimonial narrative
form. While several women, during our interviews, acknowledged
having marital difficulties, only one mentioned that her husband, a
successful physician at a major research university, occasionally hit
her—"not hard," she quickly added, but enough to humiliate; and she
attempted to weave a happy ending to the story by insisting that God
was healing their marriage, gradually but thoroughly. Accounts like
hers are surely not unique within Aglow or the broader evangelical
culture, but they are are most likely told privately rather than publicly, if they are told at all.[12]

A more commonly disclosed cause of shame in these narratives is the feeling of being a "bad wife," often linked to anger at one's husband for failing to be the kind of man that his wife originally thought or hoped he was. Dee writes about not being able or willing to love her minister husband, from her wedding night forward. She began praying for God to take her husband "out of the picture" so that she could find happiness, and she soon became, she says, "ugly and bitter." Significantly, Dee admits keeping her pain and loneliness hidden for a long time, out of shame: "Everywhere God sent special people to be a blessing to us, to pray for us, to encourage us. But somehow it just wasn't enough. I was the pastor's wife. I couldn't share and I didn't know with whom to share. The burden was so heavy and the pain so great I couldn't hide the tears that would run down my face when I was in a class or meeting where people would talk about marriage and its importance. . . . I felt like the loneliest person in the world." Angry—yet ashamed of that anger—and lonely, Dee kept her pain a secret, hidden inside herself, and was unable to heal until she revealed everything both to God and to her husband.[13]

Another homemaker remembers a time when she was overwhelmed by the demands put on her by her fastidious husband. She recalls his imperious tone and his seemingly endless injunctions: "Remember, honey, after you go to the bank, don't forget to pick up my suit at the cleaners. And you'd better get some more cat litter. I see we're almost out. . . . Don't forget to make an appointment for me with Dr. Johnson." Her response suggests the kind of resentment and shame she felt for failing to be a "joyful wife": "Suddenly, I felt like bawling. I leaned against the door and wished I could catch the flu. Then I could just go to bed for a few days and escape from it all."[14] These accounts are typical in their descriptions of marital discord and the feelings of guilt, anger, and depression that emerge so often in evangelical women's stories.

These narratives recall the survey data of married couples analyzed by Mirra Komarovsky and Elaine Tyler May, showing that although many women feel less satisfaction with their marriages than do their husbands, they try hard to deny any feelings of unhappiness. Aglow narratives and similarly religious stories illustrate what May calls some women's "deep ambivalence toward their husbands." As May notes, these women have such an "enormous stake" in seeing their marriages as successful that they submerge their anger and blame themselves for any disappointments they may feel.[15] Burdened with their perceived need to uphold the popular images of happy domesticity presented to them both by secular media and religious institutions, the stories of Aglow women reflect strategies utilized by many other American women: hiding (or, in May's terms, "submerging") their dissatisfaction and pain for as long as possible, characterizing it in retrospect as shame or guilt.

Another source of guilt for Aglow women involves the supposed inability to be a good mother. Doris writes about feeling very tense one day when her child came across a baby mockingbird and tried to get her to hold it. She scolded him, then suddenly realized her error and turned to God in prayer, begging him for forgiveness and for "another chance" to be a better mother.[16] Another mother, Jessica, recalls her aggravation with her irresponsible seventeen-year-old daughter. When she confided her anger to a friend, the friend advised her to "trust and pray more, and nag less." Grateful for this advice, Jessica prayed for forgiveness and for the patience to "help her without controlling her."[17] Women like Doris and Jessica, ashamed of their impatience with their children, find release in bringing their feelings of guilt to the surface in prayer.

In a more chilling confession, Iris writes of a time in her life when she severely abused her young daughters. Self-hating, addicted to valium, Iris repeatedly "flew into an uncontrollable rage" and beat her girls violently. She cried out to God, begging him to "do something," then finally called a priest for help. This conversation with the priest began Iris's process of healing, as she prayed for God to come into her life: "Deep down inside somewhere I felt Him put His arms around me and hold me close to His heart." Still she beat her children, then repented, crying out, "Lord, I am completely out of control." Gradually, Iris writes, she learned to surrender her anger to God and stopped beating her daughters; yet she continued to feel immense guilt for being a child abuser, until God finally spoke to her: "You *were* a child abuser. . . . It's past tense, under My Son's blood. I forgave you a long time ago." Iris concludes: "My story is a tribute to the restoration power of God. Although I violated His precious gift of motherhood, a gift I didn't deserve, God's grace knew no bounds."[18]

Several mothers ruefully confess their inability to love one or more of their children. Betty remembers trying to cope with her troublesome preschool son, Jamey, and recalls her weary question to herself, "How much longer can I go on with this child?" Constantly angry with the boy, she came to realize that she did not even love him; deeply ashamed of her failure as a mother, she prayed, "Jesus, I surrender this problem of Jamey to You. Please help me love him."[19] Another mother tells of adopting a Korean child but not being able to love her. In her limited patience, Jean found herself wanting "to get even with her for all the misery she'd brought into my life." In despair over her "terrible feelings" toward this little intruder, Jean finally cried out, "God, You'll have to love her for me." Eventually, as she and her husband began to "go through the motions" of loving Kim and to surrender themselves to God, she found God supplied the feelings of love they lacked.[20]

Such stories about being a bad mother surfaced in my field research as well, pointing to the recurrent power of this theme. At one meeting, Charlene, a frequent Aglow speaker, recounted to her audience the tragic death of her preschool daughter on an evening when Charlene had left her three young children at home alone, without a babysitter. Feeling immense guilt for her neglect, Charlene became a born-again Christian only a few months afterward.[21] Nancy, a local Aglow leader, often lamented her failures as a mother and recounted privately to me the ways in which she had physically abused her now alcoholic daughter and her own subsequent chagrin. Brynne, another leader, referred on various public and private occasions to her adolescent daughter Laura's severe anorexia and the humiliation Brynne felt in a culture that essentially blames mothers for children's eating disorders. Sorrowful disclosures of delinquent, dishonest, drug-abusing, and even suicidal children were voiced at various meetings by women whose grief and remorse were etched deeply on their faces. All sought comfort in one another's stories as well as tools for healing their own broken relationships.

These cases of shame, guilt, and anger differ from one another in significant ways: failing to be a perfect wife, for instance, is surely not the same as abusing one's children. Yet whatever the particulars, these stories are linked in that they all involve feeling unable to measure up to some idealized standard of behavior or appearance. Whether the image be of the "happy housewife" of the 1950s, the sexual dynamo of the 1970s, or the do-everything Supermom of the 1980s and 1990s, American women have often experienced enormous shame about their failure to conform to the ideal, and their shame is invariably accompanied by what is broadly termed low self-esteem. For Aglow and other evangelical women, such feelings of shame are heightened by a sense of sin, burdening them with the guilty feeling that they are not fulfilling God's plan for their lives. Even as the women claim to resist the standards and images of "the world," then, their theological framework upholds these in various ways and conflates them with the will of God, doubling their power to constrain the women through shame and guilt.

In the published literature, experiences of shame are always described in the past tense, to convey the message of victory. In stories recounted orally at Aglow meetings, on the other hand, the process of healing is more often seen as incomplete and ongoing, leaving room for admissions of lingering guilt or anger and requests for prayers of healing. In either case, narratives describe overwhelming humiliation or guilt and a sense of God as distant, uncaring, or simply absent. The sensed distance of God is related to the distance felt between oneself and other people: husbands and children, perhaps, or the "fair-weather friends" that often play a role in Aglow narratives. Shame is invariably accompanied by extreme loneliness, as one's own suffering seems beyond description or one feels unworthy to bother anyone else with it. As the recognition of emptiness takes hold, however, the sufferer may finally call out in desperation to God, as one woman did during a period of severe depression: "Finally, I knelt on the kitchen floor and cried, 'Oh God, God, what is the matter with me? Why do you seem so far away? Why am I crying like this? Oh, my God, help me! I can't go on like this. I'm at the end of myself and I need you desperately.'"[22] Such a state, comparable to what is known in therapeutic terms as "hitting bottom," is seen as necessary for healing, for it is only in the recognition of her utter helplessness and dependence on God that a person will ever be able to receive the merciful grace offered as a gift. The frequent references to suicidal thoughts and actual attempts, overturned at the last moment by a final plea to God for help, mark the seriousness of this state.

No Aglow story ends there, however; rather, all narratives end with joyful professions of victory and transformation, in the realization that, as one woman put it, "Jesus was shamed so we wouldn't have to be!"[23] These stories also underline the message that the isolation of shame is what makes it so devastating, so that revealing one's hidden pain is crucial to healing. As in the traditional formula of Christian confession, concealed sins and sicknesses must be confessed and repented, then let go. The process of disclosure in Aglow narratives may follow one of two discernible plots: the first hinges on sharing secrets with a friend, who then advises the woman to turn to God in prayer; while in the second the woman is so bereft of earthly companionship that she initially shares her secrets only with God, then later testifies to others about the healing wrought in her life. Whichever path is taken, intimacy is sought both with God and with other, sympathetic Christian women through avowals of scrupulous honesty, complete sincerity, and total obedience to the will of God.

Sharing Secrets

According to the narrative convention, a crisis eventually occurs, making secret suffering intolerable. The woman finally shares her pain with someone whom she hopes can help, in many cases a friend or pastor, who may help her interpret her pain and advise her to seek God for healing. Generally the storyteller describes this pain, a mix of submerged anger and shame, as so hidden that it remained uninterpretable, even to the woman herself, until it was shared and fully disclosed. This repeated lesson reminds women that their healing depends on the sharing of painful secrets.

In some cases, the sharing process does not begin as the woman's choice but is catalyzed by the actions of an outside observer. Rita writes about receiving a telephone call from a woman who said: "'I was praying this morning and God brought you to my heart and began to speak to me about you.' 'He did?' I gulped. (I thought to myself, I didn't know God still knew I was around.)" The woman invited Rita to a prayer meeting a few days later, during which the leader asked, " 'Rita, would you like us to pray for you?' (I thought, 'How embarrassing to be prayed for in front of eighty or ninety strangers, but then maybe it will do some good. It certainly can't do me any harm.')" Sure enough, Rita was baptized in the Holy Spirit that very night, noting that in one half hour, "My life . . . was absolutely transformed."[24] The felt burden of sin released, Rita was able to experience renewed intimacy with God and with the others in the meeting. In this case, the attention of a woman she barely knew led her to realize how far she had moved away from God and inspired her to share herself with others.

The "embarrassment" recounted by Rita at being revealed to another through the power of God is a theme that resonates widely in Aglow narratives, suggesting both the hiddenness of shame and the desire to uphold an image of propriety and correctness. Narrators frequently emphasize their initial embarrassment both to highlight the depth of sickness or sin at the moment of self-disclosure and to help those who hear these stories identify with this shame and share their own secrets. Thus "embarrassment" performs an important function in Aglow narratives: it becomes the necessary transitional stage between an old life of hidden pain and a new life of intimacy and joy.

In Aglow meetings, intimacy is cultivated and encouraged in very specific, scripted ways. Times set apart for testimonies allow participants to tell stories about their lives, involving elaborate and graphic details of sin and shame. During her talk, the main speaker reveals herself to her audience, emphasizing her ordinariness as a woman even as she renders her own suffering extraordinary. The perceived "openness" displayed by the speaker and other public witnesses encourages other women to reveal their secrets of sin and shame in the prayer time following the talk, as well as in informal conversations and moments of prayer thereafter. Just as the leaders of the meeting appear vulnerable to the participants, so the other women feel encouraged to become vulnerable with each other as well, sharing secrets so that their hidden suffering becomes visible and may be healed.

The obligation to be vulnerable, sincere, and "real" with one another in the Aglow setting suggests a kind of sentimentalism with deep echoes in American history and religion.[25] The fear of fakery, the anxiety that what appears on the surface may mask deeper truths, is evoked in many ways by evangelical women, as they testify to their own sinful methods of deceit and religious hypocrisy before they surrendered to Jesus and work to convince listeners of their earnestness. In disclosing painful secrets of sin and shame, the women attempt to be transparent to one another, to conform surface appearances with inward emotional and spiritual states rather than make the one a mask for the other. Intending to create an atmosphere of loving acceptance of each other's struggles and temptations, leaders encourage those in pain to realize and fulfill their need to divulge what would otherwise remain hidden in the heart. Hugs, kisses, and rapturous exclamations should be unmistakable badges of true joy, while murmurs of affirmation and sympathetic, supportive smiles encourage other women to know that here it is safe to unveil their hearts to God and the group in order to be restored. By shattering the sense of disjunction between the surface and the real, shame and anger may begin to be healed.

Weeping acts as a crucial sign of sincerity, if not its *sine qua non*. In meetings (where Kleenex boxes are made readily available) and in printed narratives, heartfelt feelings of repentance, sorrow, and joy are marked with tears. Tears, of course, have a long history in evangelical piety as "the infallible signs of grace in the religion of the heart," and worshipers have frequently made correspondences between, in the words of one historian, being "bathed in tears and being washed in the blood of Christ."[26] As an emblem of candor, weeping is seen as a natural and unaffected act, the outward expression of an otherwise invisible and unknowable heart. Closely associated as well with notions of traditional femininity, tears elaborate and refine the possibilities of healing and transformation for spirit-filled women, in part by enabling them to enter more fully into a distinctively "female" practice that makes them feel "real."

Dolly's story, published in *Aglow* magazine in 1980, illustrates the process through which sincerity is cultivated in this type of group setting. She recalls the "secret ambition" of her childhood to be just like her "ideal woman," described as "sure of herself, wore the best clothes, the biggest diamonds, had the most beautiful home and belonged to just the right clubs." As an adult, she writes, "I began the practice of putting on masks and building facades." Despite her success, "I *knew* the real me and felt that I was unlovable." For Dolly, feeling unlovable was the source of her deception; because she feared rejection and failure, secrets held what psychologist Harriet Lerner calls "strategic and adaptational value," allowing her to masquerade as the success she knew she was not.[27] Only after Dolly reluctantly attended a women's prayer group and found that the other women's vulnerability allowed her to share some of her own painful secrets with them did she begin to feel contrition for her "deceit," as "all masks suddenly dropped and a silent sob began to form somewhere deep within me." For three months she wept uncontrollably in public and private places, from her church to the parking lot of a shopping mall, until her tears of contrition and longing were transformed into a flood of peace and she received "joy unspeakable and full of glory."[28]

Like Dolly, other Aglow women describe the relief of having their "masks" stripped away and their "true" selves revealed. The author of a popular Aglow book articulates this as a universal desire: "The heart cry in every truly honest person is 'Please understand me. Please help me discover who I am.' We may never say those words to anyone, but the yearning goes on behind our masks. Locked inside us are thousands of secrets, happy and sad, we long to share."[29] The Aglow network is intended to provide opportunities for women to share their secrets with one another and to help each other discover their true identities as Christian women. Testimonies invariably emphasize the immense comfort of feeling understood and fully known at last, persuading other women to shed all pretense and affectation to release their natural selves.

The public confession that is so critical at Aglow meetings resonates with the therapeutic ethos described in Chapter 1. Like the recovery movement, evangelicalism claims to be about surrendering supposed control over one's life, learning to be vulnerable with others and with God in order to cultivate relationships of deeper intimacy. "Intimacy," in both therapeutic and religious contexts, requires the admission of suffering, the choice to be vulnerable in order to be healed. A pamphlet entitled *Intimacy,* published by the Hazelden Foundation, makes this point by arguing, "Secrets can be the greatest barriers to intimacy. . . . While we are all entitled to our privacy, secrets about things that make us feel shameful cut us off from intimacy. . . . Being intimate means exposing our vulnerabilities to others."[30] Increasingly focused on concealed pain and humiliation as much as hidden sin, evangelical groups like Aglow have been so deeply influenced by therapeutic discourse that traditional confession has been redefined in terms of intimacy and love.

Although women are presumably free to reveal their secrets and unmask their true selves in the Aglow setting, boundaries inevitably remain. The lines between the permissible and the forbidden are variously marked. Particularly charged, perhaps not surprisingly, is the boundary between affection and sexuality, a complication that may stem in part from the kind of intense physical contact occurring in the Aglow setting. I have already noted that hugs, kisses, and frequent caresses are all part of the scripted behavior that Aglow women enact, and the dividing line between this behavior and more overtly erotic activity may be unclear. I was twice warned during my research to beware of "spiritual lesbianism" among others in the room and Christian women generally. When asked to explain this term, one woman informed me that because so many women are "awfully lonely" and starved for love, they may unconsciously seek affection of a "sinful" kind from each other, "getting thrills" from the intense physical contact shared at the meetings. Whether or not lesbianism, spiritual or otherwise, is perceptible in Aglow is not the point; it is, however, noteworthy that the boundaries around holy friendship may appear conflicted even to the women themselves.

The scant stories in *Aglow* issues whose authors identify themselves as lesbians—ostensibly "healed"—are published anonymously (as is rarely done otherwise), suggesting that this shame remains too powerful to risk exposure. In one such story, printed in 1976, the author describes herself as obsessed with sex and romance throughout her lonely childhood until she finally found an "aggressive, forceful" girl to fill her needs. Already a born-again Christian, the author became "an acting-out homosexual" and took various partners. She says she miserably attended church but, "I knew I was living a lie, crucifying my Jesus again." Wanting to be a good Christian and yet "enjoying what I was doing," she remembers, "The guilt I carried was almost unbearable!" Eventually she married a "Christian man" in an attempt to be cured but secretly read pornographic literature and masturbated "with increasing frequency" to "sordid fantasies," until she was finally healed and set free at a charismatic Christian conference. Not surprisingly, this anonymously written story does not so much attempt to garner sympathy for the shame of its lesbian author (as stories about other subjects might) as to reinforce the propriety of shame as a response to such perceived perversions, as well as to warn against the ease with which lonely young girls may fall into them. Written for an audience of women who publicly deplore homosexuality, this and related stories fortify readers' presumptions about the sorrow and humiliation felt by gay persons but also inspire hope that they may be healed, arguing that surrendering to Jesus is "a sure cure for the homosexual."[31]

Although the narratives of evangelical women often focus on the search for intimacy with God and with their fellow Christians, then, they also allude to a variety of complications that the search for intimacy may bring. All these involve issues of trust, seen as crucial both when revealing hidden things about oneself and when called to believe another's story. The women long to be known and affirmed by one another just as they want to feel useful in the healing processes of their Aglow sisters. The belief in one's ability to distinguish between truth and falsity, and to discern evil from good, is what makes such trust and intimacy possible.

Yet there are particular rules around disclosure in the evangelical context, perhaps unconscious and largely unarticulated but exerting great power nonetheless. The current secrets that women share at Aglow meetings often involve illness or rather mild instances of sin, such as impatience with a family member or a spat with a friend. Such feelings are ones to which other women present can relate, and which do not carry with them inordinate condemnation, as would, for instance,

confessions of ongoing marital infidelity, recurrent "promiscuity," or lesbian relationships. The presence of such unspoken yet apparent rules
reminds us that many secrets may *not* be revealed within the Aglow
setting and so remain hidden in the heart, undisclosed to others and
perhaps unconscious or unacknowledged even to the women themselves. It may also be that the women's own awareness of such omis-
sions fuels their frequent criticisms of "nominal Christians," implying
a strong suspicion that others may not be as holy or spiritual as they
say they are.

Dolly's story, introduced earlier, addresses this fear of spiritual deception by recalling her former habit of concealing her actual impi-
ety: "I had a special mask I wore when I attended church with my
family. It was attractive, respectable, and well-groomed. . . . Oh yes,
and the mask I donned if I were to lead the opening prayer for any
organization. Those pretty, empty words were always neatly typed
on a three-by-five card, and I made sure to remember that everyone
bowed her head so no one could tell I was reading."[32] Likewise, another woman admits her lack of religious feeling before surrendering
to God: "Just as I appeared blasé when I really wasn't, I also appeared religious and confident in my faith when actually I was nothing more than a restless, dissatisfied, professing Christian."[33] Thus
do these authors warn their readers to watch out for spiritual
hypocrisy in themselves and, no doubt, in others as well. Such anxieties over the sincerity of fellow Christians, including their sisters,
are rife among the women, reflecting in part their own awareness of
the ease with which deception may be practiced successfully. These
suspicions notwithstanding, the script requires the women publicly
to accept one another's claims to piety. It would only be in private,
intimate conversations that they might question the sincerity of one
among them.

Sharing secrets in the Aglow setting is a kind of interchange, in
which storyteller and respondent give and receive in equal measure.
The woman who shares her own stories gives permission to her listeners to be vulnerable and share their own, while those listening give her
the loving affirmation and affection that are so desired by women in
Aglow. The respondents are aware that the teller may never have had
anyone listen to her. The teller, on the other hand, is undoubtedly aware
that her exposed vulnerability allows the other women present to feel
needed. She presents herself to them as a child seeking comfort, her
tears emphasizing this childlike quality, while her listeners present

themselves to her as a community of mothers, murmuring sympathetically, caressing her lovingly, offering advice when and where it seems appropriate.

Prayer too is deeply embedded in such transactions. The women pray over each other knowing that they too will have their turn to receive prayer. Often in Aglow meetings the leader will have participants break up into small groups of two or three, share their current suffering, and pray for one another in turn. Here the rules of exchange are clearly marked out; it would not be acceptable in this situation to refuse to participate in a group, as such a gesture would be interpreted as mean-spirited—indeed, anti-Christian. A prayer is not something that may be refused; the answer to the frequent question, "May I pray for you?" should always be "Yes."

These interchanges continue in a variety of settings outside Aglow meetings and retreats. Many women participate in rounds of visits and telephone conversations structured by unspoken rules of reciprocity and obligation. Often they join together in pairs as "prayer partners" and pray daily over the phone together, a practice frequently recommended in prescriptive literature; as one author writes, "Every Christian needs a special friend who will share her secret problems, needs, and concerns and never divulge them to anyone but the Lord." This same author describes her own prayer partner: "Since Lib was my age, we both had children of similar ages. While they were going through the "terrible teens," we supported each other in prayer over the phone almost every weekday. Believe me, we learned new depths of prayer as we went through several crises with our youngsters—car wrecks, illnesses, hospital emergency-room trips, small brushes with the law, even runaways."[34] Even in less exclusive relationships, Aglow women promise to remember the secrets they have shared and to pray for each other frequently. When they next meet, they will often reassure one another of these prayers, or tell another woman that "God laid it on my heart to pray for you," a gesture meant to deflect credit from herself but one that in fact places her in the position of benefactress.

When an evangelical woman asks for her sisters' prayers for a particular problem, she does so knowing that she has or will have something to offer them in return: she will express her appreciation as well as offer prayers for others when they express need. When her prayers appear to be answered by God, she eagerly tells the others of these victories, thanking them for their prayers on her behalf and thereby assuring them that their efforts were worthwhile. Gratitude is unquestioned—and unquestionable—in this context. The exchange of secrets and prayers, then, is governed by a code of mutual responsibility, incorporating principles of expressive behavior and rules of speech intended to foster immediate trust and nurturance among participants. Such rules, however, are repressed or denied, so that the ideals of sincerity, authenticity, openness, and intimacy are upheld and women who in some cases may not be well acquainted can become instant confidants and dear friends.

As women come to feel closely connected to other Aglow members, they may experience conflicts between their religious lives and their family lives. Many women describe their husbands as jealous and resentful of the time their wives devote to Aglow activities, to God, and to religious practices such as daily Bible reading and prayer. Women teach each other how to deal with such pressures: by attending to one's husband more willingly, for instance, and trying to include him and other family members in daily devotions without "forcing" anything upon them.[35] Predictably, however, tensions in this area are not easily resolved. The traditional doctrine of wifely submission, which applies whether the husband is a spirit-filled Christian or not, may in fact increase these tensions, as already suspicious husbands mistrust the motives behind their wives' new and seemingly inexplicable behavior. As Aglow women share strategies, they address these and related concerns about balancing domestic duties with spiritual responsibilities, committing themselves fully to both as they believe God requires.

Seeking Intimacy with God

According to Aglow narratives, the journey to intimacy with God begins with a recognition of one's utter "emptiness" and wretchedness, leading to a "deep hunger" for God. The crisis having grown too great to bear alone, the woman "cries out" to God in prayer, as Dorothy did: "I really cried out to God when I saw my world falling apart around me and I thought I was losing my mind."[36] Miserable, having no one else to turn to, she surrenders her will, crying out, "Oh, God it is Your way and Your will I want and never again my will."[37] One woman describes the divine origin of this spiritual hunger: "You might say that this was the Lord's own way of dealing with us. He knew that we had to get desperate for more of Him and His empowering before we would be willing to receive what He had for us."[38] Invariably in these stories, God responds with words of love and comfort, assuring the woman of his constant presence. Telling her story later, she describes a sense of immense relief at discovering God's love for her, along with a renewed sense of closeness to God.

This closeness does not occur spontaneously but requires effort on the part of the one seeking it. For all this effort, however, it is described as the "simplest thing in the world," a process of opening up to the natural workings of God. It is felt as a kind of surrender of the will and a pure receptivity, and the resulting feeling is one of being utterly filled with love and peace. Women often talk of this feeling as akin to having God wrap his arms around them, both as an expression of love and as a means of protection from the harsh world. Here they are able to "experience the nurturing side of God's character."[39]

This intimate relationship with God may take a variety of forms. Following an ancient Christian practice of identifying the supreme being as a parent, women often characterize God as Father or even "Daddy," as when a participant told me of visualizing herself sitting on God's lap and feeling like "Daddy's girl."[40] Such images often appear deeply tinged with wistfulness, spawned by regret over an earthly father's absence or neglect. Esther, who grew up fatherless, recalls learning, while praying, to trust God as her father: "His warm, strong, comforting presence became overwhelmingly real. I knew that I was with my real Father. He showed me that He and only He could be the perfect father I had always desired." Completing her depiction of perfect fatherhood, Esther continues, "Furthermore, I recognized that He could, and wanted to, fill all my emotional and physical needs as no earthly father can."[41] Having awakened to this father's perfect love, Esther and many other women experience, perhaps for the first time, the sense that they are unconditionally loved and cared for.

The motif of God as perfect father is filled out in the popular *Daddy, Where Were You?: Healing for the Father-Deprived Daughter*. The author, herself deserted as a child by her abusive and mentally ill father, writes of the pain of being denied a "daddy" and assures her readers that, "It is that little girl inside us that needs to have a relationship with *Abba* Father. Only he can restore what was lost in her childhood." She emphasizes God's fatherly love: "Can you see how God is your father in the most down-to-earth, concrete way? He isn't a far-away God who

makes you feel guilty all the time. He wants to relate to you in every
area of life. He cares that your car died today, that your husband is mad
at you, and that your son forgot about his soccer practice." In his unconditional love, she writes, God is always available to give comfort.
"When you're angry at your mother, he wants to talk it over with you.
When you're lonely, he wants to be with you. When you're weary of the
world, feeling dirty and worthless, he is waiting. You're safe with him.
At home." Becoming "God's daughter," in this view, means having all
of one's needs for affection and companionship fulfilled and one's
"shame" healed.[42]

Another metaphor Aglow women utilize to describe their relationship with God is that of a divine lover or husband, also an image with
a long history in the Christian tradition, which resonates in contemporary descriptions of becoming the "chosen bride" of Jesus.[43] Several
Aglow writers have fruitfully utilized a passage from the book of Isaiah:
"For your Maker is your husband—the Lord Almighty is his name."[44]
Jo Anne, a single mother of two, appeals to her readers' desires for a
perfect husband when she writes, "How would you like to be married
to a husband who is always faithful, ever concerned for your welfare,
who wants only the best for you and who will love you no matter what
you do?" Quoting the verse from Isaiah, she responds to her own question: "Surprise! The Bible says we've already got exactly that kind of
husband. The God of the Universe my Husband! What a mind-blowing
idea." Recounting various stories of learning gratefully to accept this
notion and to submit to God as her husband, Jo Anne offers other unmarried women the "opportunity" to "take [God] seriously" and to receive him as the perfect husband.[45]

Another woman, widowed only three weeks at the time she wrote
her story, tells of receiving a dozen long-stemmed roses, with a card
saying they are from friends. "I hold them in my arms and smell their
sweetness. As I lift my face from them, I know without any hesitation
or doubt that despite the card, these roses have come from Jesus. He
knew I needed such a gift at this precious moment: the type of gift that
a man sends a woman, a husband gives a wife. It is just one more way
that Jesus has become my husband, one more way He is saying, 'I love
you.'"[46] Having God as a husband does not necessarily preclude having an earthly husband as well, however, as another widow writes after
her remarriage: "God said that He would be my husband, revealing
Himself to me as the Lord of Hosts, the powerful present One in the
time of need . . . but on top of that He sent me a flesh-and-blood hus-

band, Andy."[47] Whether his spiritual "wives" are widowed or divorced, married or remarried, God acts as their perfect husband, wisely guiding and protecting them in a perfectly ordered "love relationship."[48]

Like the more traditional notion of God as Father, the theme of God as perfect husband echoes throughout evangelical literature. In her 1976 book, *The Gift of Inner Healing,* well-known evangelist Ruth Carter Stapleton urges a young woman whose marriage to Nick has been "miserable" to let Jesus' affection heal her and her marriage: "Try to spend a little time each day visualizing Jesus coming in the door from work. Then see yourself walking up to him, embracing him. Say to Jesus, 'It's good to have you home, Nick.' If you do this each day, you will condition yourself to respond to Nick as you would respond to Jesus." According to Stapleton's story, the wisdom of this strategy was confirmed when Nick showed up to thank her about a year later, telling Stapleton that he and his wife have "a whole new relationship." Imagining Jesus as a husband, and one's husband as Jesus, has the power to refresh and animate even the most broken marriages.[49]

Characterizations of God as perfect husband closely resemble the heroes of contemporary romance novels analyzed by Janice Radway, a literary scholar who interviewed dozens of women who regularly read this literature. "Strong and masculine" yet "equally capable of unusual tenderness, gentleness, and concern for [the heroine's] pleasure," the ideal hero for the romance readers questioned by Radway is one who recognizes "deep feelings" of love for the heroine and who realizes that "he could not live without her." Like Radway's readers, who want their hero to be both protector of the heroine and dependent on her love, Aglow women desire their divine hero-husband both to lead and look after them and to be nurtured by their mutually gratifying relationship. Following God's commands, doing everything he asks of them and more, flattering him continually by "just telling Him how wonderful He is and how much we love Him," Aglow women fulfill their visions of perfect love relationships, satisfying needs for affection, protection, and self-esteem through a perceived marital relationship with God.[50]

Whether they experience him as husband or as father, Aglow women view God as the ideal man, one who makes them feel respected and valued as women and who will not abuse or take advantage of them the way earthly men may. The complexities of this ideal of masculinity, and its intended contrast to earthly models, are suggested by the following interpretation of intimacy with God, from a book published by Aglow in 1991: "Becoming intimate with God means recognizing that we stand naked before him. Yet he is a perfect gentleman and will not invade our secret selves without permission. It is as if the owner of a house waited to enter each room until the renter said, 'Please come in. You are welcome here.' Only emergencies may require more forceful measures."[51] This author assures her readers that God will keep all their secrets "strictly confidential," never embarrassing or humiliating his daughters by exploiting their confessions. "The real *you*," she writes, "remains hidden to all eyes but God's." Unlike the real men in some of these women's lives, God protects his daughters, keeping them safe from the derision of the world and thereby easing the pain of continuing to live in imperfect domestic situations. Through a relationship with God, the author notes, women's "deepest cravings for intimacy and identity" are satisfied: "Once we believe and embrace who he is, our identity crisis is over." Waiting patiently for human beings to surrender willingly to him, God offers women new identities—as his daughter, wife, and friend—meant to erase and replace the old.

These accounts emphasize images of refuge, an ideal referred to as "home." This same author teaches, "Being in the presence of God is the only perfect getaway. . . . He is our only real home." She later approvingly quotes poet Robert Frost's definition of home, "the place where, when you have to go there, they have to take you in," and comments, "We all need a place where love compels that we be let in. Unfortunately, your home may not be that kind of place. If not, you'll find comfort in knowing that God's house is the supreme welcoming place." Assuming that many of her readers have not felt their homes to be safe, loving environments, she assures them that God will always be with them in the midst of their everyday lives, sheltering them from pain and fulfilling their needs for loving intimacy.[52]

Even as God becomes refashioned as the perfect father or husband for Aglow women, Jesus is figured as the companion and "best friend" with whom they can share everything, from the most shameful details of their lives to their most mundane concerns and desires. After her husband deserted her with three children, one of whom was seriously ill, Nettie May writes that she cried out to God and received an answer from Jesus. "And so," she writes, "I began to learn that day what so many have learned already—that any person who chooses to, can trust Jesus with everything." Afterward, as she began to trust him more, she says, Jesus became "my very best friend."[53] Another woman, formerly suicidal, with only her dog Freddie as her friend, attributed the transformations in her life to her new relationship with Jesus, concluding, "In my little house Jesus became more than an invisible, far away God who was judging me, but a true friend who I know for sure does love me."[54] Desperately lonely, their lives devoid of support or care, these women find loving relationships with Jesus, their intimate friend.

Aglow women experience intimacy with God and Jesus, then, in the three divine roles of father, husband, and friend. Involving hierarchical as well as lateral dimensions, these roles are not strictly bounded or separate but are overlapping and mixed, desired and experienced differently depending on circumstances. Then too, they are inflected with the erotic, sometimes explicitly, as when a woman articulated her vision of Jesus waiting for her, his bride, while lying on a "soft, white, canopy bed."[55] This blurring of roles recalls the problematic nature of intimacy, its own ambiguous meanings and often confusing boundaries. It also suggests that what many Aglow women want from their fathers and husbands is something very different from what they presently have and that, like Radway's romance readers, they may seek their fulfillment elsewhere. Failing to receive unconditional love and affirming support from the flesh-and-blood men in their lives, these women seek to satisfy their needs in relationships with God and Jesus, who then become models for earthbound men.

These intimate relationships are sought through prayer, as in the acts of "asking" Jesus into one's "heart" or surrendering oneself to God. These prayers are perceived to be entirely spontaneous, simple, and sincere, totally unlike the formulaic prayers of church liturgies or the showy prayers of hypocrites. As one woman reports her first prayer, "I didn't pray a long, loud prayer. I merely asked Jesus to come into my heart and life so that God could remove the fear, take away the bitterness, and fill the emptiness and loneliness."[56] Similarly, a nun who was urged by another nun to "open her heart and let the Lord in" evokes this experience: "No formula. No strategic blueprint. No set of rules. It sounded too simple and good to be real. But . . . that evening I prayed the simplest prayer of my whole life. 'Jesus, . . . come into my heart and take over my life.'"[57] An Episcopal woman describes how she "gets through" the (obviously undesirable) "ritual" at church: "Since my hearing isn't the best I have ceased really trying to hear. I simply lose myself in prayer for my friends, my family, the many different churches. . . ."[58]

"I simply . . . , I just . . .": in a moment of surrender and illumination, a woman "loses" herself in prayer or suddenly discovers that she "knows" God and is in God's presence as tangibly as if God were embodied in flesh. The spontaneous simplicity of this moment marks what is often called a "heart prayer," as differentiated from the "lip prayer" of rote recitation. Structured as classic "girl talk" in its self-deprecating tone of passive surrender, this form also establishes the authority of the speaker, who by giving up her active strivings suddenly discovers God's immediate presence.[59] Such constructions are echoed repeatedly in other Aglow narratives, written and oral, suggesting that God is here, available and accessible for conversation and comfort, at all times. All it takes to reach God is a supposedly natural gesture of yearning surrender, for God longs to be invited into his daughters' hearts. Reading the prayerbook or following the liturgy are misguided measures, the formula suggests; all that is really needed to attain intimacy with God is honest simplicity and a willingness to receive.

What this intimacy means, according to Aglow accounts, is that nothing is too small for God's attention and concern. One woman describes being painfully shy but refusing to pray about this, as she felt that "God was too busy running the universe to bother with my little problems." When urged by a friend to pray about her problem, she writes, "For the first time in my life I went into my bedroom and got down on my knees and spoke to God as a friend instead of a too-busy King on a throne." Feeling herself growing closer to God, she noticed her shyness disappearing and began reading her poetry aloud in public: "As small as my problem was, He had not been too busy to give me something beautiful. . . . Now I know that He is not too busy to hear and answer even what I think is the most insignificant kind of prayer."[60]

Another woman tells of her sadness and frustration over her "terrible hair," noting that it seemed too trivial a matter for prayer: "I'd often prayed for serious things like souls and sickness, but I'd always felt like God thought we should have enough sense to handle the everyday things ourselves." She "bore with" the situation until she started to teach a high school Sunday school class, where, "there in that group of pretty, young girls my hair was often on my mind because it looked so tacky." She finally decided to pray, insignificant though the matter seemed: "'Dear Lord, if You care how I look when I get in front of that class tomorrow, take these hands and help me do something with this stringy hair You blessed me with.' I had a strong feeling that He heard me and was smiling at me." She then rolled her hair on bobby pins, and "for the first time in my entire life, I was able to get all my hair up neatly. It was as though I had a new pair of hands." When she took her hair down several hours later, she discovered that it looked "really good," as though she'd been "to the best beauty shop in town." Since then, she concludes, "I no longer feel reluctant to bother God with the nitpicking problems in my life. I know now that He cares about everything . . . even the way a Sunday school teacher wants to look."[61] Intimacy with God allows for these sorts of everyday encounters and makes the prosaic dimensions of personal life alive with divine presence.

Reading and treasuring the Bible is another important means through which spirit-filled women seek intimacy with God. Often a woman describes how she felt God speaking "personally" to her as she was reading scripture, even leading her to specific passages that related to circumstances in her everyday life. Aglow women also speak of the Bible as a "personal love letter from God to His children," the key to understanding his loving wisdom in difficult situations and to feeling his presence and direction in one's life at all times. Because the women believe that the Bible is the inspired word of God, and claim that every passage contains divine revelations that are as applicable today as when they were written, they glean meaning from even the most obscure or otherwise unlikely passages, meditating on them until their divine purpose is made manifest.[62]

One woman, after losing her Bible in a public restroom, writes of the many traumas that the Bible has pulled her through, including a life of alcohol abuse and other degradations. As she read the Bible, she says, "Lovingly, [God's] Spirit began to remind me of the never-ending stream of poison I was pouring into my body. I read about Jesus freeing people from habits they hated." Regretting the loss of her Bible, she prays for whoever finds it: "Could it be, Lord, that the Book is not lost, but found by someone who needs to see life and hope written in the grease, blood, and scum on those pages? Forgive, heal, deliver them. Fill them with Your Spirit, and empower them to serve, dear Lord, as You did for me."[63]

The kind of intimacy these women seek with God is not one-sided: they do not merely receive God's love but endeavor to give love back to God; sharing their secrets with God, they ask that he share his with them. A common phrase in Aglow parlance is "to know the heart of God," referring not to total understanding of God's will in ordinary things but to experiential knowledge of and participation in God's loving compassion for all people, as well as his pain and suffering when his people suffer. As one Aglow leader writes, "The Father yearns for us to share His heart by spending time in His presence."[64] In this way, the women seek to nurture God, protecting him from those who curse or ignore him and bring him pain. This maternal dimension to the relationship completes the circle of intimacy, as each party fulfills the role of nurturant protector to one in need.

While emphasizing God's pure love for them and the impossibility of ever repaying God for the grace bestowed upon them, the women also speak of wanting to be good for God, to please God, to give back to God some of what he has given to them. This desire is particularly explicit in Jane's story: "I wanted desperately to give Jesus a gift. Something really special. But what did I have that I could give to the King? I thought of how many times I had heard since childhood, 'All He wants is you.' 'I have already given You myself, Lord, and what else do I have? I have nothing . . . no talent . . . no personality . . . no money . . . what can I give to You? What would be a real expression of my love to You?'" In prayer, Jane writes, God directed her thoughts to her family and friends, showing her how "possessive" she has been of them, thinking that she owned them and could manipulate them at will. Asking God's forgiveness, Jane turned these people over to God "in total surrender" and notes, "A beautiful refreshing feeling spread within me. I rejoiced that I had, at last, found something to give to Jesus."[65]

Jane's desire to "give Jesus a gift," repeated in other narratives, stems from a professed feeling of gratitude for all that God has given his children, gifts of unconditional love that their receivers want to reciprocate. If one does not feel grateful, however, one can even request the gift of gratitude. Jo Anne tells of "suffering from a prolonged drought of ingratitude" some time ago, eventually becoming so "disgusted" with herself that she prayed, "Lord, do what you have to do to give me a grateful heart." God answered the prayer, she writes, by enabling her to appreciate all that she had, all that he had given her, so that she learned to praise God gratefully for his largess. The complicated and cyclical nature of this exchange is like that of the "spiritual gifts": God's allotment of blessings enables the women to give in reciprocation, showering God with prayers of praise, worship, and surrender.[66]

This cyclical theme of gift and gratitude suffuses all of evangelical culture and characterizes evangelical women's sense of divine intimacy. According to this formula, God has given his children untold gifts deserving of gratitude, which will then be rewarded with various other gifts, and on and on. Like the processes of exchange that occur within the social world of Aglow members, this exchange between the individual and God is based on the assumption that all gifts are free and are also therefore sincere, honest, and genuine. Rather than comprising an equal transaction, however, the interchange binds the women into a hierarchical relationship based on their utter powerlessness ever to repay or fully compensate God for his gifts. Intimacy with God, then, requires ceaseless recognition of all that he has bestowed upon them, constant praise and gratitude for such generosity, and the perpetual desire to obey God's will in all circumstances.

In Aglow narratives this divine relationship requires both total surrender of the will and an unending struggle to "know" God and please him. Whereas she once felt entirely isolated and lost within a world of uncaring, neglectful people, particularly family members, the spirit-filled woman now experiences a kind of boundless and unconditional love from her "daddy" that makes her feel she can never be lonely again. Moreover, her sense of self is apparently expanded by believing that her love, both in its nurturing aspects and in its more childlike dimensions, can prevent God himself from experiencing loneliness. As in the title of the book cited earlier, intimacy with God is a "mystery" for those who have not experienced it; for women who have, however, it is always said to feel utterly simple and natural, as though one has finally discovered oneself and come home. By framing this event as natural—the rhetorical marker used to prove God's part in the experience—the women both critique their previous lack of intimacy with God and blame that distance on the individualism and selfishness cultivated by modern American culture.

In narratives such as these, complex social relations—parent-child ties, marriage, friendship, and so on—are crystallized into mysteries about intimacy for which God holds the key. Even as they presume and dictate a universal human need for distinctive forms of love, such narratives interpret intimacy in terms of freedom rather than compulsion, a divine gift that, when properly utilized, yields emotional fulfillment and personal transformation. Because they believe God cares even about "the nitpicking problems" in their lives, spirit-filled women are able to experience closeness with him, as father, husband, lover, and friend, and they search for this same familiarity and affection with other people in their lives. Longing to share their most shameful secrets as well as their most seemingly mundane desires, these women strive to surrender themselves, dissolving their walls of protection, in order to find full acceptance of who they are. This dissolution takes place most tangibly through prayer, in which they reveal themselves to God—and he reveals himself to them. When they open themselves to God this way in public, they also expose their secret failings, disappointments, and sufferings to other female sympathizers. It also appears likely, for a variety of reasons, that the kinds of hierarchical arrangements that characterize their intimacy with God may also characterize their close social relationships, including alliances with the evangelical women to whom they have divulged their inner shame. Next, then, we return to the social context of Aglow to examine the ways in which self-disclosure and intimacy refashion relationships of power and reconstitute notions of obedience and authority.

5

Free to Submit

Discipline, Authority, and Sacrifice

Margaret has always had what she calls a "weight problem." As a teenager, having long attributed her weight to having "big bones," Margaret finally "had to face the fact that [she] was FAT." As "a good Catholic," she assumed then that she would simply join a convent and wear a black habit to hide her "flabbiness." Only when she fell in love with Dick, the finest athlete at the parochial high school they both attended, did Margaret manage—through water pills, diet pills, and self-starvation—to lose eighty pounds.

When Dick broke up with her soon afterward, Margaret gained back those eighty pounds "almost overnight," then added to her problems by drinking too much alcohol and smoking too many cigarettes. She writes: "I began to pop one pill after another and spent most of my waking hours in a bar, drinking twelve to fourteen drinks, one after another. I felt that someday at the right bar the right man would come in. We would fall in love, and I would once more be happy. I couldn't admit I was kidding myself." Wearing too much makeup and a size 24 1/2 dress, she led a wild party life that soon resulted in petty theft, as she developed a penchant for shoplifting and leaving restaurants without paying the bill. "I would have loved to have been [different] and looked and acted differently," she later recalled, "but I couldn't control whatever it was that was leading me on to destruction." Juxtaposing the thrills of this life with its repercussions, Margaret remembers, "Life was very exciting, adventurous, wild and very, very lonely."

When her brother Larry became a "religious fanatic," Margaret was acutely irritated. For nine months, she had to listen to him announce that he was praying for her, until one day he invited her to a church-sponsored picnic. Always eager for a free meal, she agreed to go with him but nervously warned him on the way there, "Now, remember, I'll stay there one hour. Not one minute longer! One hour!" Once at the dinner, she found to her great surprise and relief that people "were so friendly" and even seemed to like her. At their urging, she accepted an invitation to attend a Christian music concert the next evening, and as she listened to songs of Jesus' love, Margaret was moved. When, near the end of the program, the leader summoned anyone who was "lonely, despairing, unhappy or just experiencing a void in your lives" to raise his or her hand, Margaret abruptly realized, "It was me he was talking about," and her arm shot into the air.

Walking slowly to the front of the room in response to the evangelist's invitation, an agitated Margaret knelt at the stage. The evangelist approached her there and bent down to ask what was troubling her, but her lips quivered so uncontrollably she couldn't answer. The man urged her to let go of the heavy burden she was needlessly bearing by letting Christ enter her heart and set her free. Feeling Margaret's responsiveness, he led her in a simple prayer: "Jesus . . . I'm sorry for my sins. I need You, Jesus Christ, and I need You right now. Please help me. . . . I accept You as my Lord and Savior. Come into my life and make me the kind of person You want me to be." After twenty minutes of strenuous weeping, Margaret began to feel "inexpressibly clean" and instantly realized that she was loved, that "big and fat Margaret ———— was loved by Jesus." Years of self-hatred, marked by excessive overeating, alcohol and drug abuse, and crime, had ended, replaced with a new life of joy.

After being saved, Margaret told her parents, relatives, and friends about the events of that dramatic night. Soon, longing for increased power to witness, she began praying to receive the baptism in the Holy Spirit. Lifting her hands in praise at a prayer meeting, she later remembered, she thankfully received her "new language," an experience apparently more wonderful than she had even dreamed. "Now I knew what they meant when they called people Spirit-filled, born-again, Pentecostal, charismatic Catholics!"

Years later, Margaret reflects, "I am a new person. I changed. My lifestyle changed. My terrible habits changed. Jesus and I worked together to get my life cleaned up. I took back all that I had stolen,

flushed all my pills away and asked forgiveness of all whom I'd hurt."
Having lost fifty-five pounds, still her weight troubles her and those
around her, and she recalls her brother saying to her on occasion, "Slim
down, Sweetie." Perceptibly ashamed by her continued weight problem, she struggles to end her story with assurance: "As Jesus and I work
together, I will lose the rest . . . and without diet pills, shots or tran-
quilizers. . . . I can do all things through Christ who strengthens me."[1]

In one of the earliest published Aglow stories to deal explicitly and
at length with anxiety relating to bodily control—or lack of control—
and fat, this author writes loathingly of her gluttony for food, dispar-
ages her corpulence and, employing a familiar therapeutic idiom, attributes these and related troubles to a lack of love in her life.
Accentuating the degradation of a fat, unruly existence along with the
overwhelming domination of greedy appetites over her life, Margaret
frames her story as an internal battle for self-mastery, a fight that she
could not win alone but only by surrendering wholly to Jesus. Her story
at once highlights both the misery of being out of control and the immeasurable relief of finally unshouldering her burdens and letting another take control over her life. While her account centers on the dynamic of female surrender to male authority—here represented by
Margaret's brother Larry, the male evangelist who led her in prayer, and
Jesus—it also proclaims the empowerment, maturity, and strength that
such surrender reportedly bestows. Margaret's story is a useful point of
entry into the themes of authority and discipline within conservative
evangelical culture and the visible tension between such themes and the
persistent avowals of freedom and power that recur in spirit-filled
women's narratives.

Slim for Him

From the organization's founding to the present, a prominent
theme in Aglow has been concern over weight loss and bodily control,
for the sake of beauty perhaps even more than health. Bolstered by di-
etary obsessions in contemporary American culture, this dread of fat,
spanning the range from pudginess to obesity, has been exacerbated by
distinct moral and spiritual meanings within evangelical culture that
make eating and dieting deeply religious issues for Aglow participants
and other religious women as well. As recently as 1995, local Aglow
fellowships have sponsored sessions on such topics as "spiritual weight
loss."[2] While striving to reject the narcissism of contemporary society's

"worldly" emphasis on female beauty and thinness, such teachings nonetheless reproduce in only slightly modified form the standards promoted in the wider culture by investing them with the will of God. These themes of diet, weight, and body bear examination for the role they have played in conservative Christian women's lives and the ways in which they signal a shift of external authority into internal modes of discipline and control.

Anxiety over food and fat emerges in Aglow narratives in a variety of forms. Like Margaret, sensing Jesus' assistance in her weight-loss program, another writer tells a story of "dieting with Jesus." Melba describes her "victory in dieting" after years of unsuccessful attempts at controlling her appetite—at times, she says, she weighed up to 230 pounds—and offers "a doing my best for Jesus diet." Codified as a nine-step process, generally echoing the twelve steps of Alcoholics Anonymous, Melba's plan urges the discouraged dieter to "admit you are overweight" and "determine in your heart that whatever it takes, you will deny yourself, pick up your cross and follow Jesus." Attributing the temptation to overeat to Satan's attacks, she cautions readers to surrender their own attempts to control their eating behavior and simply to take hold of the strength offered by God. Her own "victory," after years of constant fluctuation, came only when she realized she "did not have to diet by myself" but rather, as the title of her story indicates, could diet with Jesus. Through a combination of surrender and self-denial, Melba has managed to maintain a "regular weight of 125 pounds" for more than two years.[3]

This theme of self-denial also guides the story of Fran, who struggled unsuccessfully for years to lose weight. Even prayer didn't seem to help, she later wrote, until one day she began to realize the root cause of her desire to overeat. "Even though [the Lord] was number one in my life, I unknowingly was rebelling against Him by complaining about my circumstances and rewarding myself with food. My over-eating was a form of rebellion." Attempts to "let go and let God" remained unsuccessful, however, until Fran realized that God "was trying to teach me to really let go of diets and let Him be everything to me, including my appetite. He told me, 'It's not will power but My power.' "[4]

Some five years later Fran published a second article on overeating in *Aglow* magazine, once again attributing her continuing desire to overeat to rebellion—here, defiance against her husband, with whom she had become irritated after he criticized her. "If I had walked in the Spirit by allowing the Lord to win victory over the criticism, I would not have created a need and would not have desired two bowls of ice cream. I had to fulfill the lust of my flesh through ice cream, as a result of not walking in the Spirit." Had she allowed God to "supply forgiveness and love" through her to her husband, she writes, she would not have experienced the "emptiness" or loneliness that caused her to overeat in order to try to fill that void. She invites her readers to join her in "commit[ting] our eating to Jesus" and submitting their wills completely to God.[5]

Margaret, Melba, and Fran all assume that to "overeat" and to be "overweight" is to be living in sin; in their stories, God appears to want them to diet as a sign of their commitment to and trust in him. In a similar vein, another woman writes of "losing pounds for [God's] glory" and describes hearing God speaking to her "heart": "You know you are in My will losing pounds."[6] As Margaret says her brother Larry remarked to her, God appears to be telling these Aglow women, "Slim down, Sweetie," teaching his daughters to turn to him for fulfillment of their hunger rather than to ordinary food. Overeating is both sin and sickness, construed as gluttony and as rebellion against authority.

In 1975 overeating received even greater prominence in Aglow circles with the publication of an Aglow Bible study entitled *God's Answer to Overeating: A Study of Scriptural Attitudes*. Calling for women to increase their will power and resistance to the temptation of gluttony, the author gives a dramatic description of its way of dishonoring God: "Overindulgence of the senses or the attempt to satisfy spiritual hunger by physical means has no place in a Christian's life. The Lord Jesus Christ did not die to give those who believe in Him as Savior liberty to cater to their sensual appetites. He died to give Christians the power to keep their own desires in control in order to serve Him and other people. He set men free from the domination of physical appetites in order to enjoy full satisfaction of the spirit, soul and body—in that order." Here again, both the selfishness of physical desires and their ability to take control over a woman are central; as the author later notes, "Overeating is one of the most self-centered occupations there is. Your mind and desires are focused on what you like, your hands and eyes are busy with the food you know is going into your mouth, and you are trying to fill empty places in yourself that probably cannot be filled with food." Urging her readers to bring their eating under the "lordship" of Jesus, she suggests ministering to needy people, "devaluating physical food," and "eating lots of spiritual food" as methods for taking one's mind off physical food.[7]

That women especially are inclined to overeat or "overindulge" is a firmly held assumption throughout most of this literature, in part because women are perceived as the primary preparers and givers of food but also because women are characterized as helpless to resist such alluring pleasures. Writers in this genre uphold this stereotype, emphasizing that although some might consider these indulgences innocent or trivial, they are in fact serious matters of intemperance. "The Holy Spirit seems to be universally moving upon the hearts of women to honestly face their weight problems," solemnly writes *Aglow* magazine's editor.[8] Indeed, numerous authors stress the point that godly women ought to realize the critical nature of dieting, including the two women who co-wrote the inspirational cookbook *Aglow in the Kitchen:* "We, as Christian women, should be disciplined enough to stop before we open the refrigerator door for another snack, to resist reaching for another cookie."[9] While ordinary women, those who have not committed themselves to God, may be expected to live gluttonously, those who claim to be witnesses for Christ must be willing to give up their obsession with food; thinness, cultivated through discipline, is deeply linked to holiness.

Besides Aglow's own published literature, a wide array of other diet books are popular among evangelical women. One that I purchased at a local Aglow meeting is Patricia B. Kreml's *Slim For Him,* published in 1978. Kreml's rhetoric is unequaled in its skillful portrayal of Satan luring well-intentioned Christians into debauched eating patterns, and she deftly importunes readers to shun demonic temptations in order to "keep your mind and heart facing the Promised Land of weight-loss."[10] In the format of a daily devotional, complete with recommended prayers of repentance and assistance for weight loss, Kreml distributes advice on various subjects related to weight control, connecting overeating to Eve's consumption of the forbidden fruit in the Garden of Eden. That losing weight is the will of God is made explicit, first in the highly suggestive title—where the pursuit of slimness is reassuringly shifted from a matter of vain conceit to one of divine male preference, "Slim" not for oneself but rather "for Him"—and with impressive detail throughout the book. Kreml is optimistic: "The Lord is doing a mighty work, in the area of diet and eating habits, to set His people free by teaching them who they are in Him and what their rights and *responsibilities* are as His children" (italics in original).[11]

Those not yet "set free" are those whom Kreml aims to edify, for, by remaining fettered to Satan's false promises, they reveal a serious lack of trust in God's faithfulness to fulfill their needs. "Think about your favorite foods," she urges. "Did you ever hide that last piece of cake so you could have it later? Do you ever find yourself hoping there will be leftovers from your favorite dish so you can eat it all by yourself the next day? Do you stuff yourself with your favorite foods when you have them because you're afraid you won't be able to have them again (especially if you're about to go on a diet)? All these are similar breaches of trust in God. . . . Hoarding food and stuffing it in because you enjoy it isn't really depending on God and glorifying Him."[12] Emphasizing gluttony as a "sin" connected to selfishness (and soberly reminding readers that the biblical punishment for it was death by stoning), Kreml argues that such excesses not only spawn physical and spiritual sickness but obliterate freedom as well.

On the positive side, according to Kreml, dieting yields copious benefits, including the priceless advantage of becoming a tool for evangelism: "Your body will slim down and that will prove to others you have been keeping God's Word."[13] Melba too notes this benefit of weight loss, writing: "While you don't need to indiscriminately broadcast your success, when friends ask, 'What has happened to you?' tell them. Blessings from Jesus are to be shared with others."[14] The clear implication here is that while fat people may be poor witnesses for God, thin Christians radiate their own dutiful righteousness as well as God's loving grace. Kreml particularly underscores the rewards and benefits that will accrue to those who diet successfully, noting, "Whatever you do (within God's will, of course) will prosper."[15] Victory, prosperity, and the sublime blessings of slimness await the obedient dieter.

She who abstains must be careful, however, to keep her eyes on the holy reasons for losing weight, rather than those sanctioned by the secular world. Kreml cautions her readers against egotism even while assuring them that they will become more beautiful by controlling their eating: "We don't diet, lose weight, and firm our bodies just so we can look nice and get compliments. This will be a result of our efforts but not the main reason for them. Our first reason has to be keeping our bodies under subjection that we might live the temperate, Christ-like life we are called to live."[16] The body is God's temple, Kreml and other authors remind their readers, and the aim of keeping it "under subjection"—thin, firm, disciplined—is not self-gratification but deference and gratitude to God. Like the innumerable Aglow stories in which "outward beauty" is seen as reflecting "the inner glow that shines from

a dedicated, Spirit-filled woman," these teachings affirm that the primary effect of slimness is to glorify God.[17]

In more recently published narratives, since the 1980s, overeating
has been explicated somewhat differently, viewed less as weakness or
rebellion and more as a possible symptom of early abuse or neglect.
While not abolishing entirely the focus on excess weight as a sign of
transgression, these later writers often focus less on the sinful dimensions than on the root sufferings that purportedly cause women to
overeat. One instance of this modification is the story of Gwen, the
Aglow speaker described at the beginning of Chapter 2, who has written about her lifelong battle with weight and her obsession with food
in *Hyper to Holy: How Jesus Touched the Life of a Housewife.*
Attributing her compulsive overeating to her childhood desire to win
her father's attention and love, she tells of becoming "a fat little girl at
age ten or so. . . . Dad would kid that I could outeat any truck driver
he knew." Although she tried to joke about her appetite, she writes,
"inside, I felt like such a loser. . . . For many years it seemed someone
was always making fun of my size."

Recalling the cruel taunts of her high school peers, Gwen evokes the
fear implanted by her supposedly well-meaning mother: "It was at this
point Mother thought maybe she could get me to wake up and see that
I was ruining my life. She kept telling me to look at myself—that I was
becoming a fat slob and no man was ever going to love me. I know with
all my heart she didn't mean that and only said it to try to help me see
what I was doing to myself. But I did feel all those things already deep
within myself." In an exuberant account of her healing process, Gwen
tells of going to a local group for compulsive overeaters and realizing
that her problem was "an illness, a disease much like alcoholism."
Following the twelve steps, and praying continually for healing and
freedom from her food obsession, Gwen recalls her rapid "deliverance"
from her habit of overeating as well as from the shame at the root of it.
Gwen, like many other evangelical writers on this topic, stresses that
she was never able to succeed at diets and that her healing came only
after she saw that she had a disease and understood the need for love
at the root of her compulsion.[18]

The injunctions related to food and dieting in these texts reflect the
tension and ambivalence with which Aglow narratives generally approach surrender and control. As in other areas of Aglow theology and
practice, dieters are paradoxically advised both to "let go" of their own
efforts to control their desire for food and, simultaneously, to fight the

temptation to overeat. Surrender and discipline appear to harmonize as the will of God is internalized in the will of the individual, and all forms of excessive hunger are seen as self-destructive, alienating behavior. Like other diet writers, Kreml urges her readers to resist temptation by "simply say[ing] a firm no" and then trusting in God's power to deliver them from compulsive eating, suggesting this prayer: "I know that through your strength I can be victorious, so teach me to reach for you, not the lemon pie, because you are sweeter by far and can surely satisfy all my desires."[19] Ultimately, Aglow writers teach, these struggles will cease as the dieter's carnal hunger receives fulfillment in the "sweeter" delights of divine love.

This concern with weight and dieting is reflected much more widely in evangelical Christian literature, where male as well as female writers during the second half of the twentieth century have often dealt with the topic either as their primary focus or as a secondary one relating to beauty, discipline, and health. Owners of Christian bookstores, well aware of the popularity of diet books, keep their shelves well stocked with them, although they reportedly lament the superficiality, frivolity, and obsessiveness this genre encourages among women. One (male) shop owner noted that he can sell "five times as many diet books" as pro-life books. "This proves to me," he complained, "that we're more interested in our own bodies than in the bodies of the innocent unborn. We hate fat more than murder."[20] Despite such grumbling, of course, he and other religious booksellers continue to give their customers— predominantly middle-aged women—what they want, understanding and capitalizing on the market potential for diet books that offer religious solutions to the American female's battle against the body.[21]

Book titles of female-authored diet books attract readers with messages linking weight loss to liberation and control *(Free to Be Thin)*, affection and intimacy *(Loving More, Eating Less)*, selflessness and sacrificial devotion *(More of Jesus, Less of Me)*, success in other areas of life *(There's More to Being Thin Than Being Thin)*, and permanent independence and empowerment *(God Knows I Won't Be Fat Again)*.[22] Employing a confessional tone, writers like Shirley Cook, author of *Diary of a FAT Housewife*, attest to their own battles with food and their failure to maintain permanent weight loss on such nonreligious programs as Weight Watchers and Overeaters Anonymous.[23] They also demonstrate the intense emotion that issues of overeating generate among women, as well as the relief and euphoria that often accompany successful weight loss. Carol Showalter, founder of a Christian diet group called "Diet, Discipline, and Discipleship" and author of *3D*, recalls the moving testimony of one group member who realized that her extra weight was "nothing more than stored-up tears that finally had a chance to come out," to which a weeping Showalter responded, "Well, Mary, if shedding tears will take the pounds off, a lot of us are going to go home thinner tonight."[24]

Marie Chapian, a successful and prolific writer of evangelical books, and coauthor Neva Coyle, founder of what she advertises as the "phenomenally successful weight-loss program" of Overeaters Victorious, exemplify the conjunction of surrender, control, and freedom that prevails in Christian diet literature. In their first diet book, *Free to Be Thin,* Chapian and Coyle combine a therapeutic emphasis on overeating as a "compulsive act" and a sign of "psychoneurosis" with a theological emphasis on overeating as sin. In terms reminiscent of the Aglow study, *God's Answer to Overeating,* these authors assure readers that "Jesus went to the cross so that His people no longer need be the victims of compulsive acts." To lose weight successfully, Chapian and Coyle affirm, one must "enter into a covenant to lose weight His way," following God's commandments and receiving additional strength and self-control as a reward. A particularly rousing motivational passage suggests: "Think of your 'promised land' as a thin body. You can enter into your promised land and enjoy the fullness of life that God gives to those who are obedient, or you can forfeit it." Just as Kreml, in *Slim for Him,* transposes the biblical land of Canaan into "the Promised Land of weight-loss," Coyle and Chapian liken thinness to paradisaical bliss and redemption.[25]

In their 1984 sequel, *There's More to Being Thin Than Being Thin,* Coyle and Chapian further accentuate the parallel between weight loss and liberation, noting forcefully that "victory over every problem, including overeating, is rightfully yours as a Christian person." Yet, they remind readers, such victory is found only through complete obedience to God, including earnest avoidance of fatty foods. According to these authors, God will explicitly instruct his children about losing pounds, giving them their goal weight, daily caloric intake, and ability to choose among different foods. Again, in the "totally revised and updated" version of their first book, *The All-New Free to Be Thin* (1993), the authors illustrate a main point in the Christian diet literature—that the "key to dynamic living and power" is "obedience": "The Bible tells us in Galatians 5:23 that evidence of the Holy Spirit's working in our lives is self-control. Therefore, our goal in *The All-New Free to Be Thin* lifestyle plan is to help you learn how to hear the Lord and how to obey Him when He gently urges, 'Don't eat that.'" Acquiescence even to God's most tender urgings, then, is the key to freedom from the prison of the gluttonous body, liberation from food obsession, and renewed self-esteem. The body remains under subjection, but its sinful master of compulsion has, in the view of these authors, been replaced by a holy desire to conform to the loving will of God.[26]

All these discussions of food and fat—and there are untold others in evangelical literature—resonate with wider cultural concerns about women's bodies, so that, from a feminist perspective, they almost beg to be interpreted as a kind of internalized oppression, in which social prescriptions and taboos pertaining to weight are given divine sanction and even origin. Many religious diet authors apparently recognize this possibility, as attested by their evident (if ambivalent) disdain for the focus on beauty and sexuality that pervades the secular dieting literature and their insistence that thinness is intended primarily for God's glory. Coyle and Chapian seem particularly keen on rejecting social prescriptions for women, writing in feminist tones: "One woman in deep need of spiritual enlightenment told us, 'Thin is really what counts when you want to attract the opposite sex, right?' Then she added, 'A thin body and big breasts are all I need to get a man.' A sad commentary on the way women have come to think of their bodies, and the way advertising has exploited us!" Yet these writers, like others, tread this area carefully, rejecting the "shallowness" of appearance while admitting its value and appeal even for Christians. "There is nothing wrong with wanting to look attractive," they assure their readers. "In fact, when a person becomes a Christian, he or she usually gains a new attractiveness and vibrancy. The life within gives a radiance that wasn't there before."[27] Despite evangelical authors' attempts to resist current standards of female attractiveness, these standards crop up here as throughout American culture, their power hardly diminished but, indeed, reinforced by the assumption that they reflect divine will.

Even while defending the holiness of their message, then, evangelical diet writers appeal therapeutically to women's desire for beauty and male approval, marketing weight loss as freedom that procures happiness and coding fatness as a prison that engenders misery. Urging both discipline and surrender, these authors describe slimming down as a natural and simple process, the result of total submission to the will of God and to one's inward desire for self-control and freedom. That surrender leads to self-control and obedience to liberation is echoed again and again; as Coyle and Chapian affirm, "A life of prayer is a life of power."[28]

Yet, despite all the determined efforts to maintain this triumphal optimism, the oppressiveness of bodily disciplines may well prevail over the liberation they supposedly produce, as these evangelical formulas ultimately fail to free people from cultural prescriptions of beauty. Even while promoting her own fitness plan, evangelical diet guru Stormie Omartian recognizes the tyranny of such codes: "Most people carry on a battle with food and a struggle with exercise that is agonizing, exhausting, defeating, and a prelude to the most intense feelings of failure. I've seen convicted and confessed killers have less remorse than many people I know who beat themselves up emotionally because they've eaten too many cookies." Exploring the pathology behind anorexia and related eating disorders, Omartian deplores the pressure upon women in American society to be perfect and entreats her readers to remind themselves that success and happiness do not depend upon looks or weight but only on God. Encapsulating her point in another passage, she counsels readers to stop mistreating and criticizing their bodies and beseeches, "You must make up your mind to have respect, love, and appreciation for the body God gave you, no matter what shape it is in at this moment."[29] The success and rapid growth of the religious fitness industry attest that such a respectful, appreciative attitude is an aberration even, and perhaps especially, among the most disciplined evangelicals. For women, both in and out of Aglow, the battle apparently rages on.

Free to Submit

The paradox of surrender and control so deeply ingrained in evangelicalism also emerges in notions of individual authority within Aglow, notions that may, subtly or not, contradict or compete with one another. The group has always held explicitly egalitarian views about its membership, promoting it as a "network of caring women" wherein all are sinners equally called to repentance and equally qualified to learn about and receive God's love. At the same time, however, Aglow has long maintained a comprehensive edifice of hierarchical authority, including local, regional, national, and international officers—president, vice-president, treasurer, and various secretaries—and a similarly extended system of advisory boards. While working to preserve the evangelical emphasis on individual access to the scriptures and the Pentecostal emphasis on personal, experiential access to God, Aglow has simultaneously developed a corporate structure to guide, oversee, and, if necessary, contain these impulses.

Aglow's advisory boards were initially composed of male ministers from different Christian denominations, with the prominent Episcopal rector Dennis Bennett playing a key role. As Aglow expanded across the United States, lower-level advisory boards were established for all local chapters, with regional boards and finally international boards at the top. Advisors were selected largely through election, and the earliest board members were, like Bennett, well-known ministers in charismatic churches.[30] Until 1993 all advisors at the various levels were required by the Aglow constitution to be men; in that year, the constitution was amended so that two women could be added as international advisors, yet all-male advisory boards continued at the lower levels. By the mid-1990s, the board of International Advisors-at-Large included such well-known Pentecostal and charismatic leaders as David (formerly Paul) Yonggi Cho of Korea and John Dawson, C. Peter Wagner, and Rick Joyner of the United States.[31]

The role of these male advisors in an otherwise all-women's organization has always been somewhat vaguely defined. The *U.S. Area Handbook,* published by Women's Aglow Fellowship in 1982 and again in 1987, outlines the functions of area advisors as consultants on a variety of subjects, including approval of candidates for local office, endorsement of speakers at local Aglow meetings, and support for all non-Aglow literature for sale at Aglow functions. Additionally, advisors are responsible for counseling the Area Board on spiritual issues such as judging prophecy, helping to prevent unqualified people from gaining power over a meeting, handling potential disturbances at meetings, and generally determining what is "of the spirit," or truly divine, and what is "of the flesh,"and therefore unacceptable behavior, at meetings. While advisors are not to attend local board meetings "except for special circumstances," board members are to meet with advisors two to three times per year, send them reports of monthly meetings, and invite them to retreats. The authority of advisors appears here to be largely symbolic—the handbook notes that advisors "should be willing to give advice to the Area Board without being dictatorial."[32] Similarly, the 1995 General Bylaws of Aglow International states that advisors, appointed by the (all-female) national, area, and local boards, "may be called upon to provide spiritual, legal, business, or other advice as they are qualified *and as such advice is deemed necessary*" (emphasis mine).[33]

The original justification for having only men as advisors pertained to the scripturally based belief that women require a protective "covering" from men, a doctrine closely aligned with the emphasis on female submission to male "headship." As one Aglow author wrote in 1974: "A study of history and culture shows us that woman is so constructed as to be more physically vulnerable to attack than man. This vulnerability is also evidenced in the realm of the emotions and the spirit (II Timothy 3:6–7); therefore, God places her under the headship of man for her protection."[34] In like terms one of Aglow's most influential early leaders told me that while women are "more spiritually attuned" than men, they are "also more easily deceived" and so need the protective covering provided by men.[35]

More recent leaders have moderated the emphasis on headship, however, exchanging it for an accent on gender symmetry. As the 1995 General Bylaws assert, "Aglow International believes that male advisors bring an important balance to Aglow as a women's ministry." Having shifted from "headship" to "balance," Aglow leaders have managed to retain the organization's traditional advisory structure while lightening its potential burdens and opening the way for female advisors. As these Bylaws state, "Aglow International also believes valuable input may be gained from qualified female leaders in the Body of Christ who would serve in an advisory capacity to The Board of Directors." At the highest level, then, Aglow no longer imagines itself under an exclusively all-male "headship" of authority or "covering" of protection.

So far, local Aglow chapters retain the all-male advisory structure, yet participants (both leaders and members) vary somewhat in their sense of the advisors' official purpose and capacity. Some accounts describe the role of advisors as minor, with the men simply meeting once a year with the female leadership to give Aglow officers financial or legal advice. At times, however, it seems the men have intervened more vigorously, as in 1980, when they helped some of the women officers oust Aglow president Margaret Moody from office in an episode that threatened to rupture the whole body of the organization. Justifying the advisory system as a useful mechanism for helping solve such internal conflicts, a Nebraska woman reported in a newspaper interview, "They [the pastors] provide accountability. . . . And they have a lot of wisdom. They have been through some of these problems before."[36]

Today, the advisors tend to downplay their role, insisting that the women are in charge and that the men keep a respectful distance unless specifically called upon for help.[37]

My interviews also show that Aglow women hold a broad range of interpretations concerning the role of male advisors. According to some, the men have little more than symbolic authority, while others view them as constantly overseeing the women and correcting theological mistakes. One of the charter members of the original Aglow fellowship in Seattle recounted that during the early organizational discussions, she felt afraid that an all-women's group would be prone to doctrinal errors and so suggested that the organization needed pastoral advisors to guide those leading meetings and those publishing the new magazine: "Since we were all women, we needed some ministers!"[38] Another early member agreed and also praised the early male advisors for taking care to see that some of the women who "were controlling and wanted to take over the fellowship" were kept in their place. Disclosing her suspicion of some of her evangelical sisters, she told me, "I appreciate so much the advisors. . . . Father Bennett knew what the score was with controlling women."[39]

Many of the women today differ in the way they interpret the male advisory role. Helen, longtime president of a local chapter in New England, remarked in 1993 that the men "play a very minor role in Aglow," usually acting only to "help in dealing with problems on the Area Board or whatever, problems the women can't handle." On the other hand, Erma, an Aglow leader in Tennessee, observed: "We need the men so that we [women] don't stray too far from the true meaning of the scriptures." When I informed Helen of Erma's remark, she expressed dismay and staunchly denied that male advisors play such a restrictive theological role, insisting, "We have *tremendous* freedom in Aglow, tremendous freedom in the Word. If we stick to the principles of Aglow, we're all right."[40] In asserting that the primary authority is the Bible, equally accessible to all, Helen seemed eager to relegate the male advisors to mere figurehead positions within Aglow, mediating conflicts without intruding in the day-to-day running of the organization.

These mixed responses suggest that the women of Aglow are ambivalent as to the amount of power they want their male advisors to possess and how much intervention they think is necessary. Advisors are encouraged to attend monthly meetings and are welcomed with apparent enthusiasm when they come; but their attendance at local meetings appears infrequent, if not rare. Local differences likely also contribute to these interpretive variations, since one former Aglow officer told me that the degree of participation or interference of male advisors varies widely and appears to depend on the wishes of the individual chapter.[41] Chapters that are well established (like Helen's), where the leadership is stable and conflicts minimal, may view the male advisory role as rather less weighty than those that are young and headed by inexperienced leaders or those that are marked by friction.

Another acknowledged reason for these variations is Aglow's changing sense of male-female relations, a change explored more thoroughly in Chapter 6. A current high-ranking national officer indicated in an interview that through the years Aglow has moved into a more healthy understanding of the male "covering" and "headship" than before, so that now advisors serve "a very loose role" with "no real oversight." Rather than occupying the highest positions of leadership, as they were once thought to do, the men now act in "a supportive role," giving "input" on "spiritual . . . or even legal matters."[42] As Erma's comment indicates, however, this evolving perception of Aglow's male advisors does not necessarily trickle through all sectors of the organization.

Whatever other functions the men may perform, the presence of male advisory boards has guarded Aglow against charges of being doctrinally unsound, a service that has undoubtedly aided the organization's growth and bolstered its prestige in charismatic and Pentecostal circles. The explicit approval such boards lend to an all-women's organization has perhaps also prevented Aglow from being denounced for fostering feminism, which so many conservative churchmen have damned. In this way, the male boards can provide freedom for the women to pursue their own agendas, confident that they are acting in accordance with authoritative doctrine and the support of church leaders. Since the men play little active role in the day-to-day running of the organization, the women are, unofficially at least, able to experience Aglow as fully their own and thereby manage to benefit from the doctrine of the male covering.

Despite their apparent nonintrusiveness, however, the male advisors may well exert informal constraints on the organization. Their ministerial status requires a kind of professional deference, and the women are apt to give them that at all times, at least when they are being observed. The presence of an advisor would be expected to change the dynamics of the otherwise all-female meeting, perhaps substantially, although such alterations in the rhythms of the meetings are difficult to measure.

Perhaps the most significant and lasting impact the men make on the organization is to uphold and reinforce for the women the sense that they cannot expect to run their own organization but require protection, counsel, and supervision from male authorities. That is a forceful message indeed.

In light of this instruction, it is interesting that an ample part of the discussion among the women at Aglow meetings (before, during, and after the main service) involves jokes about male behavior, including generalizations about men's "nature" that can have a rather sharp edge to them. These stories and jokes often lampoon men, including "good" husbands who are seen to be well-intentioned but essentially helpless and perplexed when it comes to understanding women. Such wryly humorous accounts, which seem to provide a kind of catharsis through shared acknowledgment of painful or maddening situations, suggest that many Aglow women may experience high levels of tension over gender relations in their everyday lives; moreover, these accounts include generalizations about maleness broad enough in scope to include even their ministers and members of the Aglow advisory boards. Ruptures within gender relations in the women's personal lives, then, extend into Aglow as well, where they may be managed carefully without challenging the traditional stress on female submission to male authority.

Clearly, the role of men in the Aglow organizational structure has changed somewhat over time, partly because charismatic Christians have increasingly accepted women as ministers and appropriated certain feminist ideas.[43] The 1993 constitutional change that allowed the first female advisors to be appointed to the international board was not widely advertised at first, apparently to avoid controversy among Aglow participants and supporters. The initial secrecy of this major change, a change explained to me in 1993 as if confidentially by an officer at the national Aglow headquarters, hints that Aglow leaders may have suspected that such a move would not be popular among certain supporters of Aglow or even some constituents. In a 1996 interview a second Aglow leader denied that this was ever a concern, pointing out that by 1994 the female advisors-at-large, along with the male advisors-at-large, were named on the masthead of Aglow's newsletter. Whatever the case, the change in policy toward female advisors is significant, reflecting what both leaders described as a "healthy" move toward a more thoroughly woman-oriented ministry, and, from the evidence I have been able to gather, the change seems to have generated neither controversy nor acclaim.[44] The apparent indifference toward this change may well indicate, not apathy, but growing acceptance of female leadership roles in the broader religious and social worlds of Aglow women.

At any rate, the change in advisorial policy at the top levels is hardly felt in local fellowships, where advisors remain all-male. Here, Aglow women continue to profess support of and satisfaction with the hierarchical structures of their organization, however they view the role of their advisors. Yet local participants also attest that advisorial guidance is more loose than tight and the hierarchy is rarely visible in any but the faintest way. In that sense, the male advisory structure exerts, at most, a kind of token authority with little directly perceived impact on ordinary women who participate in these fellowships. Even if men attend occasional officers' meetings and a few monthly meetings per year, they do not go to smaller meetings such as home Bible studies and weekly prayer groups. In those settings, unobserved by the men purporting to "cover" or protect them, the women are on their own.

On the other hand, token or not, symbolic authority is a powerful force indeed, and its continuing maintenance at the local levels of the organization may prove to be far more important than the appointment of two women to the highest advisory board. Certainly, the women whom I have observed and interviewed consistently uphold and praise the men's roles in their organization, even if their language for describing these roles has undergone significant mutations. Further modifications bear watching, as American evangelical culture—indeed, American culture at large—continues to revise its ideals and standards of gender into the twenty-first century.

Because the role of men in the Aglow organization has tended to remain obscure, other modes of authority have had far more visible impact on the running of local chapters. At all levels of the Aglow hierarchy—international, national, regional, and local—various women have held highly influential leadership positions. The most prominent has undoubtedly been Jane Hansen, International President of Women's Aglow since 1980. Blonde, attractive, and younger looking than her years (she was born in the mid 1930s), Hansen has long been seen by Aglow members as a model of the ideal Christian woman. Her husband Howard, who accompanies her on most of her speaking engagements and sits on the stage with her at national and international conferences, and her three children and six grandchildren, provide the model Christian family for the thousands of women who look up to her as their leader. Her photograph decorates nearly all Aglow published material, and she is commonly described with reverence (and sometimes faint envy) by Aglow members.

Hansen's dynamic mien has influenced the lower levels of the organization, where local leaders may unabashedly admit that they "want to be like Jane."[45] By imitating her style of dress, hair, and exuberant smile, they hope to appear similarly successful, spiritually as well as financially. Jane herself, though invariably attired in expensive clothes during public appearances, maintains an image of humility by describing herself as "an ordinary woman," one who struggles with the same kinds of difficulties that other women have, from housekeeping to deep insecurities about her own worth. In her autobiography, entitled *Inside a Woman: Revealing Her Longings, Pain, and the Journey to Love,* Hansen emphasizes her own weaknesses and the joy to be found in realizing that God accepted and valued her, "just as I was."[46]

Hansen's claim to humility and her apparent plea for empathy are not universally successful, however. At least one current member whom I have interviewed has expressed palpable uneasiness toward Hansen, feeling somewhat disquieted by her heavy-handed style of leadership, her expensive taste in clothes, and the barrage of monetary solicitations she sends out to members on a regular basis.[47] Various former Aglow officers and staff members, several of whom resigned shortly after Hansen assumed the presidency, have also expressed concern about her methods of running the organization, some even suggesting that under her leadership Aglow will eventually fold. Others at Aglow headquarters, when questioned about such complaints, demonstrated unqualified loyalty to Hansen and blamed the snipings both on "sour grapes" and on the financial troubles of Aglow in the early 1990s that resulted in controversial staff layoffs.[48] It may also be that some of this opposition results from the very conformism evident in the desire to be "like" Jane—evident also in the wider evangelical culture among women who have seemingly modeled themselves after famous figures from Marabel Morgan to Anita Bryant, Dale Evans Rogers, Daisy Osborn, Jan Crouch, Kathie Lee Gifford, Beverly LaHaye, and the oft-caricatured Tammy Faye Bakker—for such conformism readily metamorphoses into anger and envy.

As this discussion suggests, social relations among the women of Aglow are highly structured, even when they are meant to seem flexible and equality is held up as the norm. Although participants clearly differ in economic and educational status, they claim not to recognize such differences, as "all are one in Christ." Yet some distinctions remain evident, both between members of apparently different social classes and between leaders and members. For example, leaders not only must meet certain theological and spiritual standards to be installed as officers but are customarily attractive and well dressed, reflecting an oft-repeated notion in popular evangelicalism that a neat, comely appearance makes one a better witness for the Christian way of life.[49] International and national leaders are models of this teaching, while ordinary members emulate their style in various ways, adopting the buoyant style of deportment, speech, and gesture intended to communicate the inner radiance of a close relationship with Jesus. In this way, aspects of physical appearance, including weight, hairstyle, makeup, clothing, and so forth, work as indicators not simply of social status but of moral righteousness as well and so further uphold distinctive hierarchies within the organization at large.

One of the most important ways that members may attain some kind of spiritual authority, of course, is through public prophecy. Interpreters of Pentecostalism and other spirit-oriented religious movements have long noted the power that believers attribute to prophetic words believed to originate from God.[50] Prophecies given in native languages or in tongues are a potent source of power, marking one's specialness as vessel for the spirit's witness to the community.[51] These gifts are especially significant for women: where "feminine qualities" are upheld as the norm, female prophets and mediums are able to embody passive femininity while departing in some sense from the religious silence traditionally maintained by women in church settings. For Aglow women, likewise, prophetic utterances enable ordinary members to feel reassured that they, like their more authoritative leaders, are loved and utilized by God.

Among the women themselves, leaders as well as members, the language of intimacy analyzed in the previous chapter works as a kind of counterdiscourse to the hierarchical relationships discussed here, undercutting and ameliorating possible tensions arising from any perceived pecking order within the organization. Involving as it does an exchange of secrets between equals and resulting in mutually satisfying friendships, the cultivation of intimacy would seem to flatten the differences among women and to uphold an ideal of mutuality and equality. Creating their own "female world of love and ritual," to use historian Carroll Smith-Rosenberg's evocative phrase, Aglow women seem to have found among themselves the mutuality of affection and caring that many apparently do not possess with their husbands.[52] Having access to such a world may well work to help such women cope with the sometimes grim necessities of living as a submissive wife or female church member, as well as oppose the burdensome pressure to fulfill the feminine ideals of Aglow itself.

On the other hand, the strict rules of self-disclosure, the ever-present danger of hypocrisy, and above all the insistence upon certitude of meaning and belief may cause this type of intimacy to reinforce power relations among the women themselves, as they encourage one another to reveal their deepest secrets and then become interpreters and translators of one another's experiences. Because leaders or "adepts" are so easily distinguishable from ordinary members or "baby Christians" (as the newly initiated are called), mutuality becomes a self-contradictory ideal. As the adept interpret stories recounted by the less adept and identify what they claim to be the God-given lessons, possibilities arise for disagreement, conflict, and construals of "rebellion" in need of correction. By means of what French sociologist Danièle Hervieu-Léger, describing charismatic prayer meetings, calls a "dialectic between spontaneity and regulation," the free emotional expression cultivated in Aglow and like groups works to organize hierarchy and routinize control by religious authorities.[53] Because both intimacy and truth may only be attainable here in terms of hierarchical authority, participants may well possess far less freedom in this woman-centered context than they imagine.

The story of Nora, told to me in private conversations, provides one example of what may occur when a woman shares a secret with others who then interpret it differently than she expected.[54] Nora joined Aglow a short time after discovering that she was a childhood victim of incest. Raped repeatedly by her maternal grandfather, she had also, more horribly in her view, been the victim of sexual abuse from her own mother for many years. Devastated by emerging memories of these events, Nora sought help from psychiatrists and ministers before finding consolation in Aglow. Along the way, Nora's emotional problems had become manifested physically, causing parts of her body to twitch uncontrollably. Her Aglow friends prayed for her for several years, assuring her that she would eventually be healed not only from the emotional trauma but from her physical problems as well.

Almost five years later, after Nora's spasms had diminished only slightly, Marge, the local and much beloved Aglow leader, invited Nora to come to her home for intensive healing prayer. According to Nora's account, Marge took her into the bedroom and had her lie down on the floor. Along with three other Aglow women, all leaders in some way or another, Marge prayed over Nora for several hours, performing spiritual warfare in an attempt to get rid of the anger and condemnation believed to be at the root of Nora's physical difficulties.

During these prayers, as the spasms apparently worsened, one of the women suddenly exclaimed that she believed Nora was afflicted with a demon, telling the others that she had received this piece of information directly from the Holy Spirit. Agreeing with this interpretation, the other women joined in strategic maneuvers meant to send the devil out of Nora's body. Rather than addressing Nora's continuing feelings of hurt and betrayal at the hands of her family, Marge and the others focused on the role played by Satan and tried to heal Nora by performing a kind of exorcism. However, Nora's body was not healed during the grueling session, leaving all the women, including Nora, perplexed about the efficacy of their actions and about God's will in this situation.

When Nora informed me of these events, several months after the fact, she expressed grave ambivalence toward the interpretation that the women had given her problem, questioning their certainty as to its demonic roots. While feeling appreciative to her friends for their effort and time, Nora was also convinced that their methods were hasty and misguided. She was particularly upset that Marge and the other women had prayed for her in a bedroom, a site Nora found highly inappropriate because of her associations with sex and incest. However, Nora continued to call on these women frequently for emotional support and to participate actively in that same Aglow chapter. Despite her ambivalence (if not resistance) toward these women's interpretation of her physical and emotional problems, she continued to accept their authority and to chastise herself for her "rebellion," never feeling able to confront them openly about her mixed feelings and seek resolution of her inner conflict. Her story suggests the strength of the need for intimacy at any cost, even if one does not fully trust those with whom one is intimate.

Nora's story also indicates the tensions inherent in self-disclosure within a context of belief in direct revelations from God. So-called prophetic words, ostensibly divine in origin, have the power to reveal a hidden secret about someone that she herself has not revealed and may not even know, as when the one woman professed to have learned from the Holy Spirit that Nora was possessed.[55] Nora's immediate response to this revelation is unclear, though it seems that she said nothing to confirm or deny it. Later, however, she came to resent the interpretation, denying it even as she perhaps felt threatened by the possibility of its truth. In her accounts of the story, she frequently asserted the need for "discernment" between true prophecy and false pretenses.

In talking to me, Nora felt a constant need to absolve herself of any guilt for inappropriate behavior on her part, frequently assuring me that she did not wish to "gossip" about these women and reiterating her continued love for them. The more I listened to her, the bolder Nora became about challenging the view of her Aglow authorities, and the more indignant her response; still, she tempered her words with pleas such as "God, forgive me" and insisted that the women, though at times "controlling," truly meant well in their efforts and were good servants of God. The evident conflicts arising from this kind of situation, then, not only involve the "truth" of a story—was Nora afflicted by a demon or did she simply need help overcoming her shame?—but also how stories are to be told and to whom, that is, how resistance to authority is allowed and where it must be restrained.

The search for certitude of belief is fulfilled in part by the commitment to the group and to the relationships the women form as a result; yet such a commitment is fragile and fraught with strain. Even as certain power relations among the women are contested and revamped, others are buttressed and vindicated. Many Aglow women are undoubtedly like Nora: even their tendencies to partial resistance are crushed by their desire for authoritative guidance and acceptance within the group. Others may find it easier to discount or directly challenge interpretations they think are false, without fearing loss of affection and friendship. Still others, perhaps, simply leave Aglow and go elsewhere or begin attending another local chapter, as Nora eventually did. Even when a woman fails to find decisive truth in the authorities to which she has submitted herself, she can always return to God in prayer and seek immediate experience of divine reality, for prayer represents the ultimate "safe place" where trust is always upheld and one's secrets are never made fodder for gossip. Moreover, prayer helps heal even the bad feelings that emerge from the questioning of authority; as one prays again with those by whom one has felt betrayed, as Nora has done many times, such feelings may diminish and eventually be forgotten.

The two modes of authority discussed here—that of the male advisors and that of the female leaders—work together to inculcate a kind of internalized discipline similar to that already observed in evangelical diet literature. Systems that sustain particular ideas about gender roles and social distinctions exert pressures that are not always tangibly felt by participants but that help secure conformity by seeming to attain the status of religious truth. In this way, standards of behavior and appearance are reinforced at multiple levels, with little resistance, beyond jokes, to what may be seen as rigid prescriptions for ideal Christian womanhood. A third area in which such authority is deployed pertains to money, whose symbolic and practical value invests Aglow financial matters with peculiarly intense meanings of discipline and sacrifice.

Sacrificial Money Management

Like all religious organizations, Aglow heavily relies on the financial support of members and participants to keep going. Such support is necessary at all levels, to cover everything from building rental fees to the salaries paid at the higher—national and international—echelons of the organization. Because Aglow sponsors mission work throughout the world, moreover, those at the helm need large sums of money in order to keep programs running. Not surprisingly, then, Aglow leaders have developed a wide array of fund-raising strategies, modeled in part on those used by churches but also directed explicitly toward their own constituencies of Christian women. Fortunately for them, the Bible contains many passages on the importance of generous giving, passages that make the task of requesting money much easier for Bible-believing Christians. Of course, the Bible also offers multitudinous critiques of avarice, cupidity, and hyperacquisitiveness, excerpts that can be brought to bear against the very strategies invoked to raise funds. At any rate, Aglow's survival depends upon the proficiency of leaders in exhorting women to dig into their pocketbooks once more, as a form of spiritual discipline and Christian sacrifice.[56]

Naturally, the best chances for raising money are the powerful, emotional meetings in which Aglow women gather to worship God and enjoy fellowship with one another. Offering baskets are passed at all monthly meetings and at every service during retreats and conferences. Local chapter treasurers frequently act out skits to convey their message that "The Lord loves a cheerful giver," leaving participants with a vivid image of all the good local works their money can accomplish—feeding the poor, saving the lost, bringing hope to the inner cities as to the suburbs—if given the chance to leave their billfolds. Volunteers who work with prison ministries often tell equally vivid stories of the prostitutes and criminals to whom they have witnessed in jail and of the varied mission programs and inspirational literature that extra money could help provide for such women in need.[57] Most often, those in charge of taking up offerings cite innumerable instances of the global events taking place by means of contributions at the local, national, and international levels, reciting colorful statistics of the women spanning the nations from Australia, Korea, and China, to Africa, the Middle East, Europe, and Latin America who have recently been saved, baptized, and rejuvenated under the influence of Aglow missionaries and recently birthed fellowships. In all cases the underlying message resounds over and over: Such glorious events occur only when Christians fulfill their call to overcome human covetousness and to offer monetary sacrifices for the welfare of God's lost children.

That such cash-based sacrifices can feel arduous even to the most willing believers is repeatedly acknowledged by the leaders who enjoin their listeners to give. American society is depicted as compelling its citizens to hoard their assets and ignore the call of Jesus to look for their treasure in the things of heaven rather than of the world. Often in the regular speeches requesting money, sacrificial giving is contrasted with the practice, so long associated with women, of recreational shopping. Women are asked to forgo the pleasure they might take from a new sweater, for instance, in order to give the money they would have spent to Aglow. "Just cut down on some of your shopping," one Aglow president urged potential members during a membership drive. As a reward for making the financial commitment to join Aglow, this impeccably dressed leader displayed the new and "beautiful" name-tag badges available for new members, tokens to set apart insiders and outsiders.[58] What you renounce when you choose to follow God, her words implied, will reap generous dividends, as God approvingly repays your willingness with the special benefits of communal reception.

Aglow leaders know that participants may hesitate to give money for a variety of reasons: perhaps they think they have made enough of a sacrifice by tithing and giving offerings to their churches, or maybe they are wary of writing checks without the approval of their husbands. Possibly they do not think they should have to put money in the basket for a fourth or fifth time during a weekend-long conference; the pressure to give simply begins to make them weary, and they may wonder where all the money is going. Those in charge of raising funds are ready to deal with such challenges, stressing that, "Every penny [given for offerings and membership] goes to outreach projects."[59] At one international Aglow conference a woman framed her discussion of Aglow's pledge campaign around the theme of foreign mission work, playing on her listeners' consciences by lamenting that while numerous new nations were now "open" to Aglow, there was no money in the budget to send Aglow missionaries to them.[60]

These words rightly suggest that the theme of sacrifice often works through the strategy of guilt: How many women might die unsaved or unbaptized if the money isn't there to witness to them? How many women in prison for theft, prostitution, or murder, will not hear the gospel because of scarce resources? How many Chinese, Indian, or Moroccan women will persist in believing "false doctrines" rather than following Christ because they have never had access to a Bible? We cannot do it all, the leaders imply; we are doing all we can; you must give more, more, more to God through us. Twice, I have heard local leaders complain that their chapters were "in the red" or "in arrears" and that officers and board representatives had been forced to delve into their own bank accounts to save the fellowship from crumbling altogether.[61] Desperate times call for desperate measures.

A different yet related strategy for collecting funds is to persuade listeners that giving is a privilege rather than a burden.[62] Aglow leaders repeatedly invoke all the ways in which giving brings joy and peace to the giver: Now those poor sinners in Ecuador or Belgium or Nepal may hear the gospel and receive eternal salvation. Now your sacrifice has brought honor to God and furthered his wondrous heavenly Kingdom. A similar metaphor for encouraging contributions uses terms of barter and exchange, as when women describe Aglow as "an investment for the highest return," harvesting "dividends" far greater than any other.[63] One international leader, speaking in front of thousands of Aglow women from around the world, noted that when a woman gives money to Aglow, she can expect a miracle from the Lord in return. Here, in tones reminiscent of the strands of positive thinking that have long suffused American Christianity, was a promise that could not fail to garner support: Don't think in the depressing terms of sacrifice but anticipate the rewards you will ultimately reap! Using the same tactic to a somewhat different end, this same leader tried to lighten the burden of more immediate sacrifices by remarking, "Don't you think this conference has enriched us? It's more than money can buy!"[64]

Prophetic words may also provide dramatic justification for asking for money. At one session of an international conference, a board representative in charge of the morning's offering lectured her listeners about "a spirit of sacrifice," calling out, "Many of you, I feel, need to sacrifice today! Maybe you need to sacrifice that blouse you were going to buy!" But she went further. Her voice rising in volume and in tempo, she called out, "The Lord told me some of you can pledge $10,000, some can pledge $20,000. Some of you can pledge only $1, and you need to give that today!"[65] At another conference the following year, a speaker urging women to give money to the Aglow Capital Campaign called out that she believed someone was in the room who could donate the enormous sum of $150,000 to fix "the computer debt" at Aglow headquarters.[66] While her words exemplify the very specific requests that Aglow leaders sometimes make to participants, more often such pleas for money simply urge participants to think in terms of giving the money directly to God. Once again, this notion implies that God will give money back directly as well: a New Zealand attendee at an international conference informed me that she has been able to attend several Aglow International conferences but has never had to pay for anything because, "The Lord has provided for me."[67]

In the same way that God is said to be handling the money, Satan is often said to be attacking and even stealing money away from Christian ministries. Techniques of spiritual warfare are often applied in such cases, as the women come together in warfare prayer, shouting, "Satan, we bind you from the finances of . . . Aglow!"[68] Similarly, the offering speaker at an international conference informed her audience that it is "the Enemy" that keeps people from giving enough money, keeping Aglow from ministering throughout the world.[69] Placing the blame on Satan and performing corporate spiritual warfare against his evil works relocates the source of the problem away from possible financial mismanagement on the part of organizational leaders, an idea that could undoubtedly arise among women who hear the same drastic call for money year after year, at every meeting they attend. Such activity also takes some of the guilt and pressure off participants, who can for the moment feel that their prayers do as much good as their money would.

Yet the blame is just as often placed on the women themselves, and leaders sometimes move beyond ordinary guilt to reprimand participants for poor money management when it comes to sacrificial giving. At the national conference in Nashville in 1994 a top Aglow leader directly chided her female audience for spending so much money on frivolous purchases during conferences, when Aglow could put that money to much holier use. She noted that at the international conference in Phoenix the year before, a man selling watches (at $10 apiece) in the conference hotel netted $120,000 from Aglow women alone, and that the malls near that hotel actually wrote to Aglow to thank them for breaking all previous shopping records. Having successfully generated palpable chagrin throughout the audience, this leader declared that she did not want her words to be "scolding," but rather wanted simply to "share the grief in my heart."[70] Later that evening, a second woman (also a leader) spoke to the audience about how she was "convicted" by the earlier message and was now seeking repentance. Deploring the "strongholds of greed" that she proclaimed were continuing to bind the women present from giving all they could to Aglow, this leader beseeched everyone in the auditorium to stand, grasp the hands of those next to them, and pray aloud to break those strongholds, after which she adjured them to open their purses and give as much as they could to the offering baskets passing down the aisles.[71]

The degree to which money matters dominate these large national and international conferences seems rather astonishing to an outsider, yet, as one staff member informed me, such conferences are Aglow's biggest moneymaker, providing the bulk of the funds the organization needs to keep going. Organizational records confirm the importance of conferences to the operating budget of the organization. Financial statements show that during 1993 Aglow's gross profit from publication sales was $275,298 and membership dues totaled $457,023. Conference fees, meanwhile, garnered the organization $648,068, a figure topped by contributions totaling $1,159,456. With the addition of "other income" ($149,817), the total support and revenue for that year was $2,689,662.[72] Without the high income generated by conferences, which garner much of the publication sales and contributions as well, Aglow's budget would be cut by at least half.

Fund-raising is complicated by the repeated evangelical refrain against materialism and greed, sins with which religious leaders in the broader culture are often charged. Yet Aglow leaders seemingly manage to avoid such charges themselves, even though the costly apparel that some national and international leaders often wear at conference meetings might raise a few eyebrows. Indeed, the organization's fundraising strategies work extremely well, cultivating the sense of giving as simultaneously responsibility, privilege, and miracle-maker. Yet the internalization of discipline is somewhat less visible here than in the instances discussed earlier. Clearly, if leaders must scold about excessive shopping at the potential expense of the ministry, it must be occurring on a significant scale. Of course the most elementary form of resistance is simply not to put additional money in every collection basket; as one woman whispered to me at a conference during yet another pressurized offering speech, "I pay enough just to get here; I never give at these things."[73]

This admission of mild dissent provides a striking contrast to participants' open assent to the authority of their leaders in other realms, suggesting that some women may feel that money is more a matter of private choice than, say, theology or body standards. Such opposition, particularly as manifested in indefatigable shopping, also hints at these women's comfort with certain "worldly" themes from the broader culture and Aglow's inability to curb that comfort significantly. Indeed, many Aglow leaders' own attraction to fashion speaks louder than any words berating the women who follow that example. These contradictory messages—sacrifice all you have to Jesus *and* dress yourself well—can never be fully reconciled, even for the most affluent members, and some kind of compromise is inevitable. If the discipline of truly sacrificial giving is in some ways challenged by such a compromise, the clothes consciousness of Aglow's well-dressed leaders becomes rather easier to swallow.

To make this point is neither to condemn those leaders or participants who enjoy shopping and cultivating their appearance nor to denounce outright the ways in which religious leaders are impelled to ask continually for financial contributions to their organization. Rather, it is to distinguish an important sphere in which conflicting cultural ideals create a quandary regarding authority and obedience. This dilemma is undoubtedly exacerbated for many women by the reality that their husbands, not all of whom are Christians or Aglow supporters, may call them to account for whatever they spend. Yet even those who do not have this added concern must make perplexing choices about where to put their cash, deciding how much will go to pleasure and how much to duty while adjudicating the sometimes blurry line between the two. While the elegance and finery of many national and international leaders may buttress their legitimacy as being visibly blessed by God, it may also retard some audience members' enthusiasm to dispense additional funds in their direction.

In this chapter I have tried to present several interrelated dimensions of authority and discipline within Aglow, articulated in the themes of eating and dieting, modes of authority within the organizational structure, and financial sacrifices. Through such themes, the organization is able to tighten certain boundaries around proper belief and behavior and to cultivate interior discipline relating to subjection of the body, obedience to religious hierarchy, and sacrificial offerings of money. This disciplinary framework may differ depending on the local setting, and women who come to Aglow meetings must make choices about whether to accept or reject what they encounter there. These Aglow hierarchies are not so rigid as to prevent innovation or even reversal; in fact, there is a high degree of plasticity on every level of the organization. Just as the women manifest theological creativity in their ways of imagining God, so too they are able to creatively rework their own positions within the organizational structures and to move around within the social network in perhaps unexpected ways. As this description suggests, certain rules and scripts upholding discipline and hierarchy are embedded in the Aglow framework of beliefs and practices and are also variously resisted, softened, and qualified within that framework. Let us now examine more explicitly the gender ideals of female submission and surrender within Aglow and the challenges, mutations, and modifications that may work to ameliorate them.

Submissive Wives, Wounded Daughters, and Female Soldiers

Reinventing Christian Womanhood

Dorothy was a young wife and the mother of two preschool boys in 1965, when she found herself wishing that her husband Elmer "could be someone different." "Overnight, by some quirk in my mental osmosis," she later wrote, "I became obsessed with the thought that my healthy, happy, needed-to-be-changed-in-my-sight husband was going to die." Believing her vision represented "a revelation from God," Dorothy began spending most of her time alone, brooding over her husband's imminent death. She "withdrew" from all social activities, "making excuses against participating in any endeavor that would take me from the house." She closed the drapes in her home to avoid visits from neighbors and was in bed by nine every night "to dwell undisturbed in my other world." She went so far in her preoccupation as to plan the details of Elmer's funeral service, "even to the hymns that would be sung." Yet she concealed her thoughts so well that Elmer "had no idea anything was wrong with me." Later describing this time as one of great illness in which she "subconsciously" wished for her husband to die, Dorothy noted emphatically, "Oh, God, how sick I was!"

Eventually, Dorothy broke her long isolation by confiding in a friend, who told her that her thoughts represented a delusion from Satan. Realizing that she "had been deceived" and that "God would [n]ever work in this way," Dorothy prayed. "As I prayed," Dorothy explained, "I realized the depth of that deception. The truth was, I wanted my husband more than I wanted anything else, whether he changed or not." She "gladly . . . renounced Satan and his lies and his hold on my life," then confessed everything to Elmer. Elmer's response to Dorothy's confession affirmed the rightness of her decision, for he became "a man I had never seen before. He had every right to slap me in the face but instead he took me in his arms. With tears streaming down his face he whispered, 'Honey, all I care about is that you get well.'" Dorothy began to recuperate from what she later called her "mental illness" by returning to the Bible and praying regularly for healing from her fear and guilt. After a few weeks she felt Jesus speak to her the words of Luke 8:48: "Daughter, be of good comfort: thy faith hath made thee whole; go in peace." Surrendering herself to those words, she experienced release from the guilt and pain that had plagued her for so long.

Ten years later Dorothy testified in print to the changes that occurred in her life following her confession and surrender: "My life has been so utterly transformed that I can't find words to express it. My husband, who showed me his real strength the night he forgave me, became the man I had always longed for when I began to appreciate him. I had longed for a husband who would be my spiritual head; I have him. I had longed for a man who would counsel me spiritually rather than I, him; I've been blessed with one. I had longed for a husband who could pray down the power of God with believing prayer; I stand amazed now when I see Elmer's faith." Finally in total submission both to God and to her husband, Dorothy felt herself to be healed from her terrible sickness and to be living a new life of joyous certainty and peace. In 1975, when her story was published in *Aglow* magazine, Dorothy was praying "constantly," thanking God for her "wonderful man" and for the friend who was "bold enough" to confront her with the fact of her delusion.[1]

Jerry grew up with an alcoholic, emotionally distant father. According to her account, printed in *Aglow* in 1974, she felt hostile toward him from a very young age and continued to resent him throughout much of her adult life, as his drinking worsened. In 1971, when Jerry learned her father had cancer, she and her husband postponed their long-awaited vacation to visit him, just prior to his major surgery; as she later testified, however, "I went to him, not from love, but because he was old, alone, and it was my duty." Seeing the care he would need following surgery, Jerry reluctantly moved her father close to her home and resigned as youth director at her church. Throughout his radiation therapy, he continued to drink every day, while Jerry bitterly contemplated the sacrifices she had made in her life for this man she did not love.

As her unhappiness increased, Jerry discussed the situation with her doctor and then her pastor, who told her she must rid herself of the hostilities in her life so that she "could be the effective Christian God wanted [her] to be." The minister prayed with her but she still felt despondent and burdened, not knowing "where to leave those hostilities." She began to pray daily that God would remove her bitterness toward her father and give her "a clean heart." She asked forgiveness for her disgust with her father's drunkenness and pleaded with God to help her love him as he was. On the fifth day of praying these forlorn prayers, she began to feel "totally immersed in God's love from the head to toe"; suddenly, "cleansing tears" flowed down her cheeks, as she "began to laugh and praise the Lord." Surrendering herself to this unexpected, consoling experience of "such peace and love," she felt freed from her anger, "able to love freely and reach out for love."

From that time on, Jerry wrote, her obligation to her father became "a joy." As he lost strength, she "grew to love him so much." Shortly before he died, her father took her hand and for the first time said to her the words she had longed for all her life: "Jerry, honey, I love you." She told him she loved him too and, released from her anger and the suffering it had brought her, Jerry continued to feel the joyous inner peace that came to her during prayer. Jerry concluded her story: "It was a gift from God that I will always treasure, but a gift He could only give after He had taken away the hostilities in my heart."[2]

Dorothy and Jerry crafted their narratives for *Aglow* magazine in the early 1970s, a time when religious presses in America were rapidly churning out literature crusading to save the traditional Christian family. Both had experienced crises within their families and were struggling to love in the face of intense disappointment, frustration, and anger. In each case the woman was challenged by other Christians to pray for release. Through prayer she experienced a change—first in her attitude and second in her circumstances—that eradicated the suffering. Surrendering to God, these stories tell us, leads to freedom from depression, guilt, and hostility; submission brings victory.

Such stories provide a useful lens for examining the complex meanings that "home" and "family" have held for spirit-filled women and the varied ways in which notions of surrender and submission, enacted through prayer, have been used to alleviate the conflicts and contradictions arising within women's family lives. Incorporating powerful themes from evangelical culture, narratives like those of Dorothy and Jerry explicitly counsel their female audience to surrender their wills to God and to submit themselves to God's hierarchy of earthly representatives, particularly clergymen and husbands. According to narrative conventions, domestic unhappiness stems largely from stubborn willfulness, so that healing can occur only when the wife pliantly consents to obey her husband and allows him to reign as the leader of the home. While further analysis of the stories reveals multiple possibilities for reinterpreting and even subverting the doctrine of submission, most stories in this genre prescribe an exceptionally conservative model of traditional gender roles.

These stories also offer a medium for perceiving significant shifts over time in Aglow's teachings about women, submission, and power. Stories like Dorothy's recall other stories from Aglow texts printed in the 1970s, yet they differ from many stories printed from the mid-1980s onward, when women faced a wider range of options involving submission and power. This chapter unfolds these shifting notions of Christian womanhood by exploring the range of meanings that Aglow women attach to female submission and surrender, historical changes in these meanings and challenges to former attitudes, and the effects of these meanings upon family roles and relationships. Prayer, the turning point in Aglow stories, marks the moment when a woman abandons all attempts to assert control over the conditions in her family life in favor of sacrificial obedience, acceptance, and gratitude. In this way, prayer plays a crucial role in the fashioning of practical Christian womanhood, aiming to reform domestic life even as it transforms the ordinary, sinful self into an extraordinary woman of God.

The Man I'd Always Longed For

Many Aglow stories invoke the theme of marital disappointment, describing in detail the authors' frustrations as wives. Like the women interviewed in studies conducted by sociologists Mirra Komarovsky and Lillian Rubin, and the survey respondents in the Kelly Longitudinal Study analyzed by historian Elaine Tyler May, women in Aglow often express dissatisfaction with their husbands and spend much time and effort sharing advice for dealing with difficult home lives.[3] *Aglow* magazines are filled with stories of domestic pain, described variously in terms of abuse, neglect, lack of love, or simply boredom. Fantasies of suicide and divorce abound and are richly elaborated, as the authors tell of falling into bleak despair and of longing to escape through death. Only at this final point of grim desperation is the path to healing revealed, a path that begins with a prayer of surrender and ends with a joyful commitment to wifely submission.[4]

While few evangelical women express fantasies about their husbands' deaths in terms as explicit as Dorothy's, her story is typical in the meanings she draws from her situation and in the messages she conveys about coping with an unhappy home life. Aglow testimonies from the 1970s frequently depict women who say they were once miserable in their marriages because of their refusal to submit to the will of God and husband. Only when they learned to yield their own desires to these male wills were they able to become happy. Like Dorothy, writers typically describe their misery in terms of both sickness and sin, construing their despair as caused by Satan but deepened by their own acquiescence to it. Their lives seem isolated and they fail at their wifely roles because they wish for their husbands to be, in Dorothy's words, "someone different." To be healed, they must repent of their error and realize the "deception" behind it, taking full responsibility for their unhappiness and accepting their husbands without expecting them to change. Giving up all hopes or expectations of marital satisfaction and simply accepting the duties bestowed by their supposedly God-given role of wife as helpmeet, these women describe the pleasant surprise of discovering the greater happiness that is the reward for this sacrificial obedience, some finding their husbands to be "the man I had always longed for." Two more stories will help illustrate this process as it is typically described in Aglow literature.

Mary, deeply disappointed in her marriage, was planning a divorce from her unappreciative husband Cal, who frequently snapped at her with such cutting remarks as "Can't you ever be happy?" and "Just once I'd like to have a meal on time." Miserable and near despair, Mary asked Jesus to come into her heart, forgive her sins, and be the master of her life. Grimly, she prayed: "If you don't do it there's no point in going on with life. You aren't getting any bargain, but if you can use me, here I am." Shortly afterward she was baptized in the Holy Spirit and miraculous changes appeared to occur in all areas of her life, most significantly in her marriage:

> A few weeks later when again Cal said, "Where's lunch?" I began screaming and then stopped midway and prayed, "Jesus, I'm losing my temper, I'm sorry. Forgive me and help me."

> Once again Cal came in at noon and said, "Where's lunch?" I felt
> the old anger starting to rise in my body. I clenched my jaws shut so I
> wouldn't cry out. I prayed, "I'm losing it again, Jesus. Forgive me and
> help me." No bitter words came out and the anger backed down and
> disappeared. I was able to say later, "Cal, I've irritated you by not having
> your lunch ready. I'm sorry." He was amazed. From that time on we
> began to grow in love for each other and for Jesus until now, five years
> later, we are able to minister to others.

As Mary learned to surrender her anger to Jesus and submit lovingly to
her husband, she writes, her misery dissolved and, without any apparent changes in Cal, her bleak marriage was transformed. As she felt herself filled to overflowing with the loving warmth and comfort of the
Holy Spirit, the domestic tasks that once made her life feel like drudgery
became "a joy."[5]

Donna, who once felt lost and disconsolate in her marriage, later recalled that period as her own "state of rebellion." Her bitter conclusion
at the time, however, was that she "had married the wrong man. At
least that was a good excuse for my being in such a mess." Resentful of
her husband's constant changes in career plans, she began criticizing
Doug and telling him what to do. "I felt my ministry was to constantly
let my husband know how backslidden he was, how unspiritually-
minded he was, and that I was doing all I could to hang on in the hope
that some day he would wake up and see the light." From Doug's point
of view, she later realized, she was not being "a help-meet for his
needs": "Unaware of my position as a wife I thought God had made me
a leader and that my husband was not making a very good follower."

Finally, after God spoke to her rather sternly, Donna says she realized that she needed to surrender to Jesus. When she did, she later
wrote, "it seemed a lot of the blame I had put on my husband for things
just disappeared. God completed the healing he had begun in our marriage." Her lesson for her readers is to follow her example in submitting themselves to God and husband: "You may never be able to change
your circumstances. If you have five children, you have five children. If
your husband is a doctor, your husband is a doctor. If your husband
works as a plumber, that is his job. Quit saying, 'If my circumstances
were only different, then I know God could use me.' But begin to pray,
'Jesus, help me to allow You to use me in the circumstances in which
you have seen fit to place me.'" Accepting the circumstances of one's
life, even the aspects that seem least appealing, and then fulfilling one's
God-given roles within those circumstances, provide the recipe for a

happy life, the means for achieving contentment in the midst of daily struggles.[6]

The stories of Mary and Donna, like that of Dorothy, assure their readers that good results will follow a wife's willing acquiescence: once women's attitudes are transformed and they accept their submissive role, their husbands also become happier and more benevolent, reflecting the benevolence of God. Such stories show how personal power may be encoded in the doctrine of submission, as the women center their narratives on their own capacity to initiate personal healing and cultivate domestic harmony. While not viewed as essential to the woman's healing, changes in a husband's behavior furnish added confirmation that such healing has taken place. For instance, the fact that Dorothy's husband actually wept when she told him of her illness is highly significant to her story. Rather than slapping her in the face, as she says he had "every right" to do, Elmer embraced her lovingly and expressed his concern that she be healed. Likewise, Mary's husband, Cal, responded to her newfound submission with love and appreciation, and Donna's husband, Doug, was transformed even as she was. Such changes, these writers assert, occurred in large part as the result of the decisive actions of the wives.

These narratives are meant to convince *Aglow* readers of the sincerity of the husbands' love for their wives and the assurance of their manly protection; as Dorothy writes of Elmer, he "showed me his real strength the night he forgave me." Such husbands represent the ideal Christian man, upholding the image of a loving Father God: strong yet gentle, a dynamic leader who is unafraid to express tender feeling, stern and rugged in his righteousness yet willing to forgive and to respond in benevolence. Dorothy, Mary, and Donna submit to their husbands' authority, which, like that of Jesus, is depicted as compassionate and wise, never dominating or cruelly oppressive. Submit to your husband, the authors instruct their readers, and you too will discover the man you've always longed for, his seeming harshness softened by your willing obedience to his demands.

This message may reassure women whose husbands are spirit-filled Christian men, holding a similarly benevolent perspective on male authority, but for women whose husbands are "unsaved" or "backslidden," as is often the case, exhortations to wifely submission may be received more ambivalently. Aglow literature has repeatedly addressed this common dilemma. In 1974 an anonymous writer, her own "heart ach[ing]" as the wife of an "unbeliever," offered this somewhat gloomy advice: "Sometimes a Christian wife is under bondage in her home. It is not her own to do with as she pleases. In God's divine order, the wife is placed under the authority and direction of the husband whether he is saved or not. If he does not wish her to accept visits from her minister or have church meetings there, then according to Scripture, she should abide by his wishes. . . . At times you may feel that you can't bear another week, another month—and you will be right; you can't. However, you can live for today and this is all that you are asked to do." Urging her readers to do all they can to love and serve their husbands, she concludes with great hopefulness that "The Christian wife, by her trust, her prayers, her life and her love, can loose the Holy Spirit and the grace of God to do a special work in her husband's life.'"[7]

This lesson of submitting to a non-Christian husband in hopes that he will eventually be saved through the good example of his wife is frequently extended in Aglow literature into a lesson on surrendering more fully to God. The anonymous wife of an unsaved husband articulated this dynamic in poignant terms: "Each time Ralph has failed me, I have grown closer to the Lord and have learned to love my husband more." Over the years, she says, she has learned to be patient and to await God's plan for her husband, who—she is certain—will someday be saved. "At first I prayed for my husband's salvation; now I simply and gratefully thank God for it. . . . Often I get specific in my prayers concerning events I want my husband to attend, things I'd like him to read, facts I want him to hear. But I have learned not to be disappointed if these prayers are not answered the way I want them to be. God knows more about it than I do."[8] The only option for dealing with an unsaved husband in these Aglow stories is cheerful submission to his will in mundane things, construed as an act of surrender to the will of God. When the will of God and the will of the husband conflict, as they inevitably do, the wife must simply trust that her necessary obedience to her husband enables God to deal directly and swiftly with him. In other words, as a male fundamentalist minister put it, "Submission is the wife learning to duck, so God can hit the husband."[9]

Informing these doctrines of male authority and female submission, as Dorothy and other Aglow women describe them, are meanings attached to the ideals of home and family, meanings formed out of desire for the pleasure and security that these ideals promise. The significance of the family in American evangelical culture, long analyzed by historians of American religion, has been helpfully illuminated by anthropologist Carol Greenhouse, who describes how one community understands the family as representing not simply "a set of relationships (as anthropologists might see the family, for example)" but rather "a set of interlocking roles, or identities."[10] Thus, Greenhouse notes, the individuals who hold this view of family life strive to perfect the roles expected of them—wife, mother, daughter, sister, husband, father, son, brother—and then to feel those roles as authentic and natural. She concludes that "family life, while all-important as a model for society itself, is also crucial to the cultural formation of individuals by isolating them within relationships over which they believe they have no control."[11]

According to this conceptualization, as Greenhouse observes, family harmony hinges upon the expectation that each member will perform his or her God-ordained role properly, accepting and following its prescriptions. When conflict arises, the solution is seen to lie in the restoration of proper rule-governed behavior. Like other groups rooted historically and socially in Pentecostal, fundamentalist, and/or evangelical culture, Women's Aglow has always idealized the family and, like Greenhouse's community, has taught that the solution to family disharmony lies in the restoration of proper familial roles.[12] Thus, even as Aglow stories and prayers have been filled with references to the pain of marriage, motherhood, and domestic life generally, they emphasize how such pain may be healed through a submissive and disciplined commitment to what is perceived as true Christian womanhood. The stories recounted here suggest a context in which women describe neglectful parents, distant husbands, and delinquent children, but whose relationships are eventually transformed and made whole because of a woman's submissive behavior. Yet it is evident from these accounts that the family continues to be a source of great suffering; no family manages fully to live up to the expectations and ideals promoted by the popular idealization of the "Christian home."

In her important study of evangelical family life, sociologist Judith Stacey examines the complexities and often unacknowledged contradictions within the "widespread nostalgia for eroding family forms" prominent in many varieties of political and religious conservatism. Her research, which uncovers the ordinariness and frequency of divorce behind the rhetoric upholding the "traditional family," demonstrates the negotiations made by those who find their own family patterns clashing with their religious ideals.[13] As with Stacey's families, Aglow women and their sisters dream of creating a perfect family, but their hopes inevitably remain at least in part unrealized. In cases where even moderate domestic happiness seems impossible, an alternative family may be constructed, taking the place of the disappointingly real family at home. Where no loving father is present, there is a protective, nurturing Father in Heaven; in place of uncommunicative and generally inadequate husbands, God or Jesus may act as the romantic lover-husband, ever faithful and solicitous of his beloved's needs. In addition to the alternative marriage provided by a relationship with God, the Aglow community, as "a network of caring women," ideally becomes a surrogate family. Members frequently refer to each other as "my sisters," a common enough appellation in evangelical circles but one with distinctive meanings in Aglow. For women who have experienced painful estrangement from their families, and who have perhaps failed to find fulfillment in recovery groups, a local Aglow fellowship may provide a satisfying form of intimacy, although, as observed in Chapter 5 such closeness may carry with it a loss of privacy or the undesired reinterpretation of one's story. Still, the organization allows for the reinvention of personal identity in a collective process of narrative construction.

Praying together helps Aglow women create alternative families and ease the conflicts that may occur when such alternatives supplant the earthly family at home. Praying aloud before an audience that includes many others dealing with similarly conflicted situations allows the women both to articulate their crises—and perhaps gain sympathy and support from the other women who hear their stories—and to begin resolving them by surrendering their own will and asking God to take control. Perhaps the most important role of prayer is to help Aglow women accept the limitations of the family and the need to work unceasingly at improving their capacities as wives and homemakers. Through an intricate and highly ritualized process, guilt and anger are to be transformed into surrender and acceptance, so that possibilities for redemptive healing can emerge.[14]

The Power of Submission

Surrendering one's will to an authority is a vital meaning of submission, but this is not its sole meaning for evangelical women; in fact, submission is in no way a transparent, unidimensional, or static concept but is rather a doctrine with a fluid history, even in the relatively short time period examined here. Far from being a fixed entity churning out traditional teachings on gender roles, evangelical ideology has always been varied, so that even a group as apparently conservative as Aglow contains a broad repertoire of choices and mutable scripts dealing with such ideals as female submission to male authority. While many outsiders might assume that the conservative Christian women in Aglow are merely participating in their own victimization, internalizing patriarchal ideas about female submission that confirm and increase their sense of personal inferiority, the women themselves claim the doctrine of submission leads both to freedom and to transformation, as God rewards His obedient daughters by healing their sorrows and easing their pain. Thus interpreted, the doctrine of submission becomes a means of asserting power over bad situations, including circumstances over which one may otherwise have no control. As both oral and written narratives suggest, the ideology of submission contains a rich variety of meanings that, in practice, prove more intricate and subtle than they initially seem.

One text that illuminates these intricacies is a kind of evangelical self-help book for women, written by Darien B. Cooper, entitled *You Can Be the Wife of a Happy Husband*. First published in 1974, this book remains in print and is still used and revered by Aglow women. While teaching submission as "God's role for you as a woman and a wife," Cooper assures her female readers that in becoming submissive wives they will also see changes in their husbands, and that they will find the greatest happiness possible fulfilling their role: "I believe the role of the wife in the marital relationship is the choice role. . . . Submission never means that your personality, abilities, talents, or individuality are buried, but that they will be channeled to operate to the maximum. . . . Submission never imprisons you. It liberates you, giving you the freedom to be creative under the protection of divinely appointed authority."[15] Cooper supports this perspective by insisting upon women's need for protection in a dangerous world, claiming that within their protected sphere women may enjoy the flourishing of their God-given creativity.

According to Cooper, a woman's marital dissatisfaction stems from "preconceived ideas of how her husband should act." She writes, "When he fails to live up to your expectations, you may be hurt, irritated, and disappointed. You and your husband will only be contented and free when you quit setting goals and stop expecting him to be who he is not." Cooper tells women to display pride in their husbands rather than shame, to accept them as they are rather than "ridiculing" or "belittling" them. Instead of trying to manipulate a husband, she advises,

"Respond to his leadership in a relaxed manner, and you will find that your husband usually wants to please you." She recounts story after story of women whose wifely submission improved their marriages by bringing their husbands closer to Jesus. The husband will respond lovingly to a submissive attitude, Cooper asserts: "As God's Word fills and controls your heart, you will gain the praise of your man. Wait for it; do not demand it." Throughout her book Cooper enjoins women to "Accept him as he is!"[16]

In Cooper's view, then, submission brings benefits not only to the husband, but also and equally to the wife. Submission is not about grimly resigning oneself to a subordinate position; rather, it is about freedom. Cooper addresses women's concerns about submission: "Many women are afraid that they will lose their individuality if they subject themselves to their husbands. . . . Paradoxically, only when you submit to God—in any area—do you know the fullest freedom and power."[17] Submission may be about dependency and compliance, but it is not about helplessness, according to Cooper. Of course, the fact that she feels compelled to make submission seem more palatable for women reveals a conflict over the notion, a point to which I will return.

Cooper's book, as I have noted, is widely used among Aglow women, and she speaks to Aglow groups around the country on how to have "happy husbands." Her claim—that the doctrine of submission is ultimately beneficial to women—gets added energy from the belief that men's natural passions need to be domesticated and contained; left unchecked, these passions will rage out of control and may cause injury to women. According to Cooper, men's sexual appetites must be satisfied lest they revert to savagery or adultery. She advises her readers to satisfy their husbands sexually and warns, "If you do not fulfill your husband's sexual needs, you may be a stumbling block in his life and cause him to be led away from spiritual truths instead of toward God." She concludes: "Your husband will be the happy man you want him to be when he feels that you accept him as he is, admire him for his masculinity, and put him first and foremost (after God) in your life. He will feel needed at home because he knows he is respected as the family leader, provider, and protector."[18] The wife's influence is also her responsibility; it is up to her to see that her man is kept satisfied as well as contained, assuring him of his worth by admiring his virility.[19]

Such advice has long been articulated by antifeminist women, among others, to diverse ends. In *The Power of the Positive Woman,* for instance, antifeminist activist Phyllis Schlafly writes: "A wife must appre-

ciate and admire her husband," observing that the marriage will fail unless "she is willing to give him the appreciation and admiration his
manhood craves." Feminist writer Barbara Ehrenreich rightly notes
that Schlafly's analysis, here and throughout her spoken and written
pronouncements on similar matters, betrays a deeply distrustful and
contemptuous image of men as weak or monstrous (or both), in contrast to a view of women as active and loving.[20] From this perspective
wifely submission is good for wives as well as husbands because it
works as a strategy of containment. It is what men need to bolster their
fragile egos, and women should comply in order to maintain domestic
harmony as well as their own security. If this is done properly, all parties benefit. Thus the author of a 1976 Aglow booklet, *Quiz for
Christian Wives,* tells of the healing that took place in her unhappy marriage when she realized the importance of openly admiring the "good
qualities" in her husband Arthur: that is, the qualities for which *he*
wanted to be admired, such as his "broad shoulders" and his "big strong
hands." "Such a simple little thing," she remarks, was the turning point
in their relationship and the beginning of her new life of love and joy.[21]

Nancy, a local Aglow leader whom I asked about wifely submission,
repeatedly declared that she was a "former feminist" who had finally
learned "to move beyond all that" into God's true purpose for her life.
Having realized that feminism was "bad for [her] marriage," Nancy
gave up trying to "compete" against her husband and learned to follow
the "marriage principles" of wifely submission to male authority. When
I pressed her to explain, Nancy brought up the Hollywood movie *War
of the Roses* as an example of what happens when men and women do
not obey God's prescribed roles and persist in doing things their own
way: they destroy each other. Nancy's own marriage, in contrast, was
professedly saved when she pledged herself to wifely submission, a
pledge which, she admitted with a chuckle, she did not always manage
to keep. In any case, Nancy averred that her husband had stopped
drinking and now made her very happy, a transformation that she attributed in great part to her obedience to the marriage principles.[22]

Related to this tactical notion of submission as a means for turning
men into happy husbands who then want to please their wives is the
notion of what may be termed "sacred housework," wherein surrendering to one's ordained tasks is seen as an act of worship that also
leads to greater happiness within the home. This idea is frequently articulated in Aglow literature, as in *Aglow in the Kitchen,* a cookbook
for Christian wives. The author of that book writes of being "stunned"

when her husband taught her that "cooking and homemaking are ministries *to the Lord*." Recalling the kinds of "homey tasks" that Jesus had performed during his time on earth, she tells of getting the lettuce from the refrigerator, tearing it up for salad, and "talk[ing] to the Lord": "Jesus, thank You for showing me that housework is sacred. Help me to realize while I am cooking and cleaning that I am doing them for You because You are living here and my husband is Your representative." In this way, what was once drudgery can apparently be transformed into worship, service, and domestic happiness.[23]

When housework is perceived as sacred, it may also become an important source of self-esteem. As a young housewife and mother whose husband was a traveling evangelist, Betty found herself "very dissatisfied" and "depressed." Finally, she was healed from her misery when Jesus gave her a "vision" of her "role in the home as a happy wife and mother." She began to see that if she were happy, her husband and her children would also be happy, a notion that allowed her to begin to see herself as "the 'hub' of the wheel," around which "everything revolves." She notes, "I began to see myself as VERY IMPORTANT to the members of my family." Her concluding words suggest the continuing ambivalence she feels toward this state, along with her hopeful determination to feel good about herself as a housewife: "I know from experience that I will not always be staying at home, but I also know that with God's help I can have that real contentment WHEREVER I AM."[24]

Here again the lesson is that surrendering to the roles of housewife and mother brings joy to everyone in the home, most significantly to the submissive woman herself. As Betty tells her readers, women find joy and learn that they are "VERY IMPORTANT" when they simply yield to God's expectation of them, transforming housework from a source of boredom and depression into a wellspring of joy and self-esteem. The frequent admissions by Aglow authors that they find such work as cooking and cleaning and running errands mind-numbingly dull show that such a transformation is anything but easy. Still, in their description of submission and surrender as "natural" and in the reminder that other members of the family could not get along without them, the women of Aglow formulate what they perceive as a workable solution to a persistent dilemma, achieving a kind of pride and self-respect in the most mundane and ordinary of tasks.

Once again, for these evangelical women the meanings of submission and surrender represent far more than simple passivity. They are central notions around which the women of Aglow rework their identities, creatively balancing compliance with strength as they transform themselves into ideal Christian women. At the same time submission works as a valuable tool for containing husbands and thereby regulating the home, and may be subtly modified or subverted, so that the women retain a kind of mediated agency through their reliance on the omnipotent God. Out of a doctrine that would seem to leave them helpless, evangelical women have generated a variety of substantial yet flexible meanings through which they experience some degree of control, however limited it may often appear.

The story does not end here, however. Since the mid-1980s, discussions of the doctrine of wifely submission have significantly, and more or less quietly, dropped off in Aglow literature. While wifely submission continues to receive scattered mention, the general message has perceptibly shifted toward a notion of modified or "mutual submission." Writers often emphasize that while the Bible clearly dictates female submission to male authority, earthly men have not infrequently abused that doctrine to their own selfish ends, rather than accepting their own authority as the Christ-like responsibility intended by God. The chronological shift in the meaning of wifely submission is most clearly seen in the popular Aglow Bible study, *God's Daughter*. Written by Aglow staff member Eadie Goodboy and first published in 1974, this booklet has been widely used by Aglow participants; by 1991 it had gone through fourteen printings. The tenth chapter offers the most comprehensive and sustained examination in Aglow literature of the biblical doctrine of submission, and the important changes that have taken place in this chapter over time indicate shifting notions of Christian womanhood in Aglow, as in American evangelicalism at large.[25]

In 1974 this chapter began by emphasizing the difficulty women face in accepting the doctrine of submission: "The area of submission in the Christian walk has been widely neglected and ignored. To many women it may carry threatening overtones. We visualize Jesus as our Shepherd and ourselves as sheep under His loving care, and we find it easier to yield to His Lordship spiritually than physically to people in authority over us." The passage goes on to observe that "our natural tendency is to confuse submission with servitude, and picture one who is submissive as downtrodden and abused, a 'doormat.'" Yet, the writer suggests, the opposite is the case. Just as the sacrifice made by Jesus on the cross was a "willing" one for the benefit of others, so too should the marriage relationship reflect that same willing self-sacrifice. Thus, "Submissiveness is not an outward form or a role of foolish servitude, but an attitude of the heart."

In this view, woman's particular vulnerability requires protection from man, which is why God places her under the headship of her husband (or, in the case of an unmarried woman, her father). The result is not imprisonment but just the opposite: "Since everything which comes to us from God is meant for our good, we find that coming into an attitude of submission produces freedom. A train is created to run on a track. As long as the train stays on its track, it is free to fulfill that for which it was made. When it jumps the track, chaos results." Rather than participating in the "role-reversal so common in society today," the author concludes, women are to find "service and creativity in our God-ordained roles" as wives, mothers, and homemakers.

In 1985 this chapter was substantially altered. Now, rather than suggesting that teaching submission is like giving medicine to an unwilling child, the author places the idea of submission in the context of previous lessons about the joy of following God's will. She writes: "The emphasis of these lessons has been on the subject of yieldedness: letting or allowing the Lordship of Jesus to have total expression through our lives. We have been renewing our minds, unlearning old behavior patterns, tuning in to hear what the Father is saying, studying what He desires, becoming sensitive to sin and to the joy of obedience." She invites readers to "look again at this area of ministry of submission," which, though "often misunderstood or questioned," is the "root of all things spiritual, because it alone takes the proper attitude before God and others." Now, in place of the Biblical passages emphasized in the earlier edition, the author cites verses in which Jesus spoke of his own total submission to God; rather than turning this immediately into a lesson about wifely submission, moreover, the author points to Jesus' relationship with God as "the pattern for *us* to follow in our personal relationship with God." The chapter then moves into a detailed discussion of humility and of the choice entailed in making this commitment to God, a choice that seemingly has nothing to do with gender but is required of all people, men and women, as children of God.

Finally, the last third of the chapter turns to Ephesians 5:22, the passage about wifely submission that was the centerpiece for the earlier edition of this booklet. The author notes, "This may seem to be a difficult position for some of us who are married women to joyfully agree with, especially in an age when misunderstanding of this verse may have caused some abuse. We need to understand, however, what God desires and how He perceives it." Placing this verse in the context of the larger passage from which it is taken, the author notes that there are various scriptural "counterbalance(s)" to the notion of wifely submission and argues: "Submission to our husbands does *not* make us "second-class citizens" or those who are ranked "lower on the totem pole" as lesser beings than the husband. As viewed by God, we have a side-by-side relationship. He looks at us as equally important, but each is designed to function for His glory, in his or her role." Urging a far more limited version of wifely submission to male authority than earlier affirmed, the chapter ends by asserting that, "The entire Christian life is to be a submitted life." Though still affirming gender role differences, this passage has excised the stress on female vulnerability, rebellion, and rigidly defined female roles so central to the original study.

What these different versions suggest is a range of notions pertaining to power and thus also to surrender, a range confirmed in the larger literature of Aglow. Surrender to God may be seen, first, as a way of releasing divine power, enacted in (and only in) prayer; second, as complete submission to the husband as God's representative and leader of the home; third, as a more carefully nuanced form of the latter, which accepts the husband *as he is* while retaining some room for private critique of his behavior; and fourth, as what I have termed "containment," that is, a submission more of word than of deed that celebrates the power to influence—or, in less flattering terms, manipulate—one's husband to one's own ends.[26] Although Aglow writers often conflate these assorted meanings, they imply very different techniques for dealing with familial relationships, and for understanding one's own capabilities in the larger world. As teachings on proper gender roles have fluctuated over time, the strictest interpretation has gradually given way to more lenient, flexible interpretations centered on women's capacity to release divine power and effect change.

Both submission and surrender, then, are far more slippery concepts than they first appear. Out of the hodgepodge of meanings embedded within them may emerge diverse and even contradictory attitudes toward the obligations and freedoms bestowed upon women by an omnipotent God. While these concepts contain an unmistakable potential for subjugation, they may also offer what feminist theologian Sarah Coakley has approvingly termed "power in vulnerability," that is, "the willed effacement to a gentle omnipotence which, far from 'complementing' masculinism, acts as its undoing."[27] Between these two options is the more commonly stated objective, that submission is most valuable for wives, that by willing and joyous submission, a man may be domesticated, his will to power contained and transformed into loving protection of his wife. In the latter case, submission provides women a strategy for getting what they want, which in these cases appears to be the taming of men's naturally monstrous urges into gentleness, appreciation, and affection and the creation of ideal Christian families. In this sense, submission may tactically help the relatively powerless recover their power and create a space within which they can feel both fulfilled and free.[28]

Unable to Like, Yet Compelled to Love

The disillusionment and disappointment Aglow women have felt toward their families is repeatedly apparent in Aglow narratives from the 1970s to the 1990s, as is the desire to replace disappointment with happiness and bring greater harmony into their homes. The homes women increasingly seek to correct are, however, not only the ones they find themselves in at the moment but also the ones they recall experiencing as children. An examination of Aglow literature shows that growing numbers of women since the 1970s have described the families they grew up in as debilitating for them when they later tried to form families of their own. Stories are filled with accounts of abusive, alcoholic parents who did not attend lovingly to their children and whose violent methods of coping with their own misery wounded those around them. Like Jerry, whose story I recounted at the beginning of this chapter, countless women tell about wretchedly unhappy childhoods in which they were bereft of nurturing and grew up unaware or mistrustful of parental love.[29]

Becky, writing in 1985, told of her parents' divorce when she was two years old. Between that time and her senior year in high school, she had seen her father only once. "It was obvious he didn't care about pursuing a relationship with me or my younger sister. I tried not to dwell on it, but whenever I found myself in an uncomfortable situation . . . I would fall to pieces."[30] Jessica, writing her testimony for *Aglow* magazine in 1990, recounted her pain at being the daughter of a severely alcoholic mother and her longing for a "shared-love relationship with Mom" that was not to be. When her rage, "a too-long-dormant volcano," finally erupted at her mother, Jessica was tormented by guilt and fear until she begged God to help her heal and understand her mother's pain. Even now, she writes, "the tears begin to fall again. But now tears of release mix with those of pain; release for what might have been, but is not; for the devastation alcoholism has caused; and for my mom— the woman I am unable to like and yet compelled to love."[31]

Accounts such as these have spawned an outpouring of self-help books published by Aglow since the mid-1980s, all centered on healing from the childhood traumas of neglect and abuse. In *Daddy, Where Were You?: Healing for the Father-Deprived Daughter,* the author writes vividly of her own pain when her father deserted her at a young age, and of the healing she received from learning that God is her true father.[32] Another, *When Love Is Not Perfect: Discover God's Re-Parenting Process*, discusses issues of child abuse—emotional, physical, and sexual—and provides "a biblical framework to help victims experience God's re-parenting."[33] Others, such as *Healing the Angry Heart: A Strategy for Confident Mothering*, further describe the "tragic cycle" of child abuse and low self-esteem, offering help for those who have been caught in this cycle as children and, later, as mothers.[34] All authors advocate prayer for healing and counsel their readers to ask God to help them forgive and love their abusive parents, as difficult as such an act may seem. In practicing this kind of forgiveness, readers are told, victims of abuse will in turn be free to love their own children more fully. It is not a forgiveness easily achieved, writers agree, but rather one that must be sought with determination and, once attained, carefully guarded. As one Aglow author urges, "Pledge to pray for your parents every day."[35]

Childhood shame, rooted in emotional, physical, and/or sexual abuse, continues to be of great concern to Aglow women today, as I indicated in Chapter 4. Glenda, a local Aglow officer, angrily recounted during our interview the ways in which her mother constantly made her feel like a "bad girl" as a child by incessantly criticizing her behavior, mocking her blemished complexion and frizzy hair, and ridiculing her awkwardness in front of other people. Glenda observed that her main problem throughout her life had been low self-esteem, noting, "I felt like I never measured up." Only when a woman prayed with her at an Aglow meeting did she begin to realize, in her words, "the idiocy of everything I had pointed out [about myself]. *None* of us are worthy. That's why Jesus died on the cross!" After a long and painful process, Glenda says her relationship with her mother has been healed, yet throughout our conversations she constantly lambasted herself for being "a terrible mother" and always spoke in self-deprecating terms about herself. The persistent effects of Glenda's childhood shame were all too evident.[36]

This theme of looking at one's childhood for the causes of adult frustrations and unhappiness, then learning to forgive one's parents as the first step in healing, is repeatedly echoed by popular speakers at Aglow events. Gwen, whose public descriptions of childhood incest were recounted in chapters two and four, is one example. Another is Quin Sherrer, a long-time member of Aglow's international board, prolific writer of books and articles on prayer, and popular speaker at Aglow conferences, who publicly speaks about being deserted by her father at the age of twelve. At the time her father left, she says, she "closed off" her heart to him and vowed silently, "I'll never forgive him." Years of bitterness and "stuffing" her feelings of anger and hurt down inside herself changed after she was told by a minister to repent of her anger against her father and to forgive him. She was then able to go to her father and experience the restoration of their relationship. Quin's story has become paradigmatic for many women in Aglow dealing with similar feelings of hatred, as they struggle to follow her example and hope for similarly miraculous results.[37]

The long-term consequences of childhood abuse and neglect have been studied by numerous researchers, including those who are particularly interested in the role of religion in these situations. In a study comparing evangelical Christian adult children of alcoholics with evangelical Christian adult children of nonalcoholics, clinical psychologist Sandra D. Wilson found the former to be "significantly more depressed, self-blaming, and distrustful" than the latter. Finding her study group to resemble adult children of alcoholics in the general population, Wilson noted that the evangelical adult children displayed "an impaired capacity to trust," based on childhood experiences of parental unavailability, that could have a profound effect on all other interpersonal and intimate relationships. Her findings suggest that these evangelicals, far more than evangelicals from nonalcoholic homes, had difficulty feeling God's love and forgiveness, trusting God as a father, and forgiving other people, problems that Wilson connects to neglect from their own earthly fathers. Yet she also found that these evangelicals practiced devotional practices such as prayer and Bible study as often as their peers, concluding, "It appears that although evangelicals raised in alcoholic families often strive in vain to experience God's love and to believe he cares for them, they continue to strive."[38]

While Wilson does not, unfortunately, mention gender differentials in her study, her findings are clearly relevant to understanding contemporary evangelical women. An important question raised in her work, one that Wilson notes but does not attempt to answer, is whether adult children of alcoholics may be particularly drawn to evangelical churches or groups such as Aglow that stress a personal relationship with a loving, dependable, powerful father God. The increasingly numerous descriptions of alcoholic and abusive families in Aglow narratives, along with the emphasis on fatherly images, certainly suggest this possibility, though there is no conclusive evidence either way. A second (and, to Wilson, more disturbing) question pertains to the apparently similar levels of "depression, self-blaming, and distrust" between evangelical adult children of alcoholics and the general population adult children of alcoholics. Wilson asks, "Why does the faith of evangelicals from alcoholic families apparently fail to make a practical difference in these problem areas?" Perhaps further exploration should be devoted to *where* evangelicals practice their faith: Aglow women, sharing their stories in communities of praying women, would undoubtedly affirm that their faith makes all the difference in the world. On the other hand, Glenda's example suggests that some patterns are simply too deep for religious faith to erase.

As common as accounts of neglect and abuse are in Aglow narratives, it would be incorrect to identify Aglow as composed only of women who were seriously abused as children or whose primary concern is healing from the failures of their parents. Many narratives do not directly address such issues, while some women praise their parents as models of love and virtue. Still, vast energy among Aglow women is given to teaching each other to pray for and forgive parents for their shortcomings and to work through the anger caused by their mistakes. The introduction of Aglow support groups in 1989 and their explosion since that time give evidence of this theme, illustrated in the following passage describing women in pain: "They live next door, they jog past you in the park, brush against you in the express elevator of the downtown office building, and hand you your prescription from the pharmacy. The cumulative effects of dysfunctional homes, divorces, abuse, addictions, compulsions, financial stress, and multiple role expectations have gripped the lives of countless millions of women, imprisoning them in hopelessness, isolation, shame, depression, and fear."[39] Whatever the extent of actual abuse in these women's lives, it is evident that one function of the narratives recounted in *Aglow* magazines and at their meetings, and of the prayers described in these narratives, is to bring about healing from the pain and anger of perceived mistreatment at the hands of parents and husbands.

Two points bear emphasis. First, Aglow narratives have from the beginning contained various permutations on the common theme outlined here: the pain of family life. While there has apparently been a shift in emphasis from marital problems to childhood traumas—and thus from the sin of wifely disobedience to the pain of daughterly victimization—that shift should not obscure the fact that both narrative patterns have been present from the beginning and continue to be articulated today, as women struggle to cope with various forms of domestic unhappiness. Second, within the Aglow organization, there is a certain cachet (as well as pathos) to having a bad family life. Expressions of sorrow are not simply allowed but encouraged and take on scripted forms within the narrative context. Like the recovery movement to which it is so closely connected, Aglow fosters a kind of victimology that attributes women's suffering to the family—often construed today as "dysfunctional"—yet makes that suffering meaningful for Aglow women when domestic crises are identified as opportunities for personal atonement and growth. In this way the meaning of "bad parents" or a "bad husband" changes when women leave their homes and enter Aglow: while living in an unhappy home might well be a terrible experience, Aglow offers women the chance to reinterpret family crises in ways that replace the burden of guilt and shame with redemption and hope for healing.

Although the notion of victimization and the conviction that one's "sickness" is one's own burden of sin apparently contradict one another, these beliefs are held together through an avowal of the need for prayer and surrender. In all the narratives the key to restoration of the family is a prayer confessing total impotence and begging God for help. Relinquishing her desire to control the circumstances of her life, the woman surrenders her will to God's and may submit to her husband or begin to work through her anger at her parents. The result, which can occur only after the woman accepts responsibility for her situation, expresses repentance, and forgives her husband and any others toward whom she has felt anger, is a presumably transformed home life. Her surrender enables the woman to believe her sins have been forgiven, but it also works to rid her of her earlier sense of injustice and victimhood, bringing her out of bitter disappointment and depression into a sense of her own responsible agency. She is, according to the narrative formula, no longer victim but victor.

The "Beautiful Boldness" of Spiritual Warfare

In 1980 Aglow president Jane Hansen heard a message from God, saying, "Aglow will be a network of praying, warring, interceding women, covering the face of the earth."[40] Since that time, spiritual warfare has occupied an increasingly important role in Aglow, as leaders and members have intensified their engagement in the putative battle being waged between God and Satan, as interpreted within the "third-wave" movement of the spirit to which Aglow is intimately connected.[41] Hansen herself is an active member of the Spiritual Warfare Network, a group "specializing in intercession specifically directed to weaken the territorial spirits or principalities and powers which obstruct the spread of the Gospel."[42] Most of Aglow's international advisors and advisors-at-large are also members of the Spiritual Warfare Network, including David (formerly Paul) Yonggi Cho, leader of the world's largest church; George Otis, Jr., author of several books on spiritual warfare and "spiritual mapping" and a leader in the A.D. 2000 and Beyond Movement; John Dawson, director of Youth With a Mission and author of *Taking Our Cities for God*; Dick Eastman, author of *Hour That Changes the World*; Cindy Jacobs, president of Generals of Intercession and member of the executive council of the National Prayer Embassy; and C. Peter Wagner, professor of Church Growth at Fuller Theological Seminary and coordinator of the Spiritual Warfare Network. All are active participants in the "third wave of the Holy Spirit," a term Wagner describes in his 1983 book by the same name. Having already sent the "first wave" as Pentecostalism and the "second wave" in the form of the charismatic movement, Wagner writes, God has now sent an even more powerful "third wave" of spiritual work, distinguished by a new emphasis on healing, spiritual warfare, and what John Wimber has termed "power evangelism," as well as a premillennial or apocalyptic theology.[43]

Under Jane Hansen's leadership, Aglow has increasingly moved in this direction, and so heightened participants' ongoing belief that they are living in the "end times" or "last days" and that Christ's return to earth to usher in the Kingdom of God is imminent. From its leaders Aglow has also adopted some rather controversial spiritual warfare strategies in the form of "spiritual mapping," in which warfare prayers are made over geographical diagrams—particularly the "10/40 Window," a rectangle between 10° and 40° latitude in which over 90 percent of the world's non-Christian population is supposedly located—of areas across the Earth where evil spirits and "strongholds" are believed to exert force against the gospel. Throughout these spiritual warfare networks, and particularly in Aglow, women are seen as having a crucial role, called by God not only to evangelize in traditional ways but also to "do battle" against the evil forces thought to be at work in the world. Even as they insist that they are merely "ordinary women," then, they have claimed a role with extraordinary implications.[44] Shifting notions of womanhood in Aglow are sharply illumined by these and other practices of spiritual warfare, for at the same time that the language of daughterly neglect has partly displaced that of wifely guilt and repentance, talk of spiritual warfare now occupies far greater space in Aglow women's narratives than do worries about usurping a husband's authority.

Notions pertaining to spiritual warfare have a long history in millennial theology and evangelicalism and are rooted in scriptural passages such as the following: "Put on the full armor of God so that you can take your stand against the devil's schemes. For our struggle is not against flesh and blood, but against the rulers, against the authorities, against the powers of this dark world and against the spiritual forces of evil in the heavenly realms" (Ephesians 6:11–12, NIV).[45] Aglow's emphasis on women's important roles in this battle, a seemingly sharp contrast to their stress on submissive femininity and loving nurture, requires some explanation. Here, unlike actual military war, men are not perceived as the primary combat soldiers, with women at the sidelines cheering them on. Nor are men and women envisioned as precisely equal in either responsibility or power. Rather, Aglow teaches that women must be at the front lines of the war, with a role that sometimes appears more central than that of Christian men.[46]

In *A Woman's Guide to Spiritual Warfare,* published in 1991, co-authors Quin Sherrer and Ruthanne Garlock, both affiliated with Aglow, describe the battle against "discouragement, fear, harassment, and other ploys of the evil one," and defend women's role in the spiritual war: "Sure, men are also called to duty, but women have a special interest in this battle." Admonishing their female readers who perceive themselves as weak and helpless, the authors note, "Why is it that we are so influential? Perhaps because women often feel things deeply. We are readily moved with compassion." Moreover: "Quin's theory is that because women were created to give birth in the natural realm, we know more about travailing to give birth in the spiritual realm. We have a high tolerance for pain. We have the tenacity to stick it out until the birthing is done and our loved ones are brought from darkness into the light of Jesus." The lesson resounds: Christian women, not despite but actually because of their "feminine" emotionalism and biologic fortitude, are called to a position of great responsibility, in which they must fight against evil by enlisting as loyal and vigorous soldiers in God's army.[47]

As Aglow women describe and practice it, spiritual warfare involves "intercession," mediating between God and the person one is praying for as well as standing between that person and Satan to "restrict satanic forces." This is a process of "binding" Satan by forbidding him, in the name of Jesus, to tempt or destroy human beings who rightfully belong to God. As performed in Aglow groups, spiritual warfare is a loud and vigorous process, involving shouting—in tongues and in English—and dramatic bodily gestures that indicate combat with unseen yet powerful forces. By fighting against Satan and constantly praying to God for assistance, the women believe that Satan's evil power can be blocked and ultimately conquered: "The enemy's attempt to draw us into sin causes our inner conflict. But if we choose to obey God, he gives us success in these skirmishes. Then we are empowered to battle outwardly, dispelling the powers of darkness and setting other captives free."[48] This passage reveals once again the implications of power within the doctrine of surrender. In choosing to obey God's will rather than give in to Satan's temptations, women are rewarded with the God-given authority to banish Satan and to render him virtually powerless.

Satan's attacks on women include destroying their marriages and bringing misery into their homes, and Aglow literature contains frequent illustrations explaining how spiritual warfare may be waged against the sinful actions of children and husbands. Alicia, whose husband Carl appeared to be having an extramarital affair, sought advice from her Aglow friend Ruthanne, who recounted the story in print: "I told Alicia that I felt Satan was using this woman's attention as a snare to ruin her husband's testimony and his marriage. I advised her to renounce her hurt and anger, then forgive both of them. Alicia prayed and forgave Carl and the woman involved. Then we bound the spirits of deception, pride, and lust in both of them. We declared in the name of Jesus that all ties of sexual attraction between Carl and this woman, or any other woman he had lusted after, were broken. We asked the

Holy Spirit to reveal truth to him, to expose the enemy's snare, and to bring Carl to repentance." Afterward, Ruthanne told Alicia that she should no longer argue with her husband about the situation; instead, she advised, "Just ask the Lord to help you express love to him." That very night Ruthanne saw a "radiant" Alicia, who exclaimed, "I can't believe the change in Carl! . . . The Lord must have dealt with him . . . , because he . . . apologized to me for his involvement with that woman and for hurting me. I told him I forgave him. His whole attitude has changed, and I know the Lord will help us work everything out."[49]

While not directly challenging the doctrine of wifely submission, Alicia subverts it through a legitimate means; rather than confronting Carl with her pain and anger at his infidelity, she went straight to the authority of God, who, in her view, took control of the situation and transformed Carl's heart. The story of Alicia represents a rather different alternative from that taken by Dorothy; whereas Dorothy took responsibility for her marital unhappiness upon herself, Alicia perceives the problem as her husband's acquiescence to the power of Satan. This difference in the two stories, printed sixteen years apart, represents again a growing willingness to articulate the sins of the husbands (and parents) rather than taking the full burden of blame upon oneself.

Also intriguing are the ways that the language of spiritual warfare may work to undercut the claim to have surrendered fully to the will of God. Certainly God is believed to be the source of women's power, and yet it sometimes appears as if God takes a back seat while the women do battle against the demonic forces in the world. While prayers of assistance are incorporated into the practice of warring against Satan, for instance, the women take matters into their own hands by fighting him themselves as they "command" him to yield to their will. In their surrender, they do not limit their actions to praying for God to take charge of the situation but rather "come against" the enemy as soldiers waging war. Although the battle is always fought "in Jesus' name," the women's insistence on their own agency is apparent. As I heard one Aglow leader exclaim at a spiritual warfare workshop in 1993, "I just want to be a prayer warrior, and I'm going to pray until I win! Because our God is a winning God, and we are winning women!"[50]

Besides forces tearing apart families, there are various other "strongholds" or "spirits" that Aglow women attack by means of spiritual warfare. These include witchcraft, Freemasonry, and "occult" phenomena that are believed to lurk menacingly in the world and to induce people to act immorally. Such forces are believed to seep into one's life and home even without one's knowing it, as when one woman recounted discovering a book she had purchased second-hand was tainted by witchcraft because of the sins of its previous owner.[51] By fighting these spirits through practices of spiritual warfare, Aglow women believe that they play not only a significant role but a truly necessary one in the lives of their families, their neighborhoods, and the nation as a whole, protecting the safety of innocent people who may well be unaware that such spirits exist. More visible targets of spiritual warfare may include illegal drugs, homosexuality, and abortion, all of which are believed to be forces of Satan that are contributing to a precipitous moral decay in American society. Sending prayers to God about these issues is considered at least as important as doing actual political work against them, for the women believe that their prayers may help to change people's hearts and cleanse society from even the most threatening forms of evil.

At the spiritual warfare workshop mentioned previously, I observed one of the ways in which spiritual warfare has political ramifications. During the meeting, several active Aglow participants stood and spoke to the rest of the group about particular areas they felt needed immediate warfare prayer. One woman, Renee, started with a testimony, informing her audience that the Lord had woken her up a few nights before at 3:00 a.m. and told her that she and other Aglow women needed to pray for repentance for their lack of support and love for President Bill Clinton. After emphasizing how hard it was to hear God correct her in this way, Renee began to pray feelingly for Clinton before her rapt (and visibly astonished) Aglow audience, observing aloud that "we need to be thankful for a President who truly loves this nation and whose heart is sensitive." At the end of this prayer Renee spoke again to the women, this time relaying God's message to her about four demonic strongholds binding President Clinton: witchcraft, the occult, Masonry, and rebellion. Upon hearing Renee's words, the women raised their arms and began shouting both in tongues and in English, sending out warfare prayers to cast out all these spirits "in the name of Jesus." During a lull, Renee read 1 Chronicles 22:11–13 "to Bill," then the spiritual warfare began again, as Renee shouted, "Father, we declare that our country *shall* serve God! Jesus Christ is *Lord* over the United States of America . . . and over Bill and Hillary . . . and Tipper and Al Gore!"[52] Here and elsewhere, Aglow women believe that their prayers are powerful religious, social, and even political weapons and that they as Christian women have a tremendous responsibility to make warfare prayers and be loyal soldiers of the cross.

The discourse of spiritual warfare prayer is distinct from that of submission, emphasizing female power and authority rather than meek surrender and extending women's realm of activism beyond home and church into the broader society. Like evangelical members of the Woman's Christian Temperance Union at the end of the nineteenth century, whose commitment to "Home Protection" impelled them to broaden the female sphere and revise the ideal of the True Woman, many evangelical women at the end of the twentieth century have seemingly undergone what historian Carolyn DeSwarte Gifford has termed "reconversion," a renewed conviction of God's great expectations for women to be prayer warriors in the public sphere. Called to be Deborahs and Esthers, both groups of women gradually came to believe that Christian womanhood involves the God-given authority to fight the principalities and powers of the world. As Aglow women frequently declare, they aspire to the "beautiful boldness" to which they avow God has summoned them.[53]

Reinventing Christian Womanhood

For the women of Aglow there is power in prayer, and its reach is not confined to the home but spread outward into "the world." Through acts of surrender as well as through the tactics of spiritual warfare, the women of Aglow believe that they may contain enemy forces—the lust of a husband, perhaps, or even social and political policies affecting the traditional family. These warfare strategies also help to subvert female submission and transform it into a tool of authority. Understanding how this process works may lead to greater understanding of the meanings of healing, transformation, and liberation that are so deeply a part of their faith and piety and may also challenge the flat interpretation made by some observers (including many feminists) that female submission is no more than "a delicately balanced commingling of resourcefulness and lack of self-respect."[54] What Aglow women feel (or say they feel) to be liberation or even empowerment may, of course, look like something very different to those whose experiences of power bear little resemblance to those of the women I have described here. The task is to bring these perspectives together—hearing the women's narratives on many levels or, in literary theorist Janice Radway's terms, viewing them through multiple lenses—to create a richer account of religion as it is lived by the women of Aglow and their evangelical sisters elsewhere.

This discussion of the family, prayer, and notions of submission and surrender in Aglow indicates the complex and varied meanings of Christian womanhood for evangelical women. Being a Christian woman involves compliance with male authority, but it also demands the strength and stamina to do battle against Satan. To be a Christian wife is to be privileged with God's choicest role, in the words of Darien Cooper: the role of holding the family together as a stable, happy unit. The ideal of Christian womanhood that charismatic women create and maintain is carefully positioned between the poles of timid passivity and defiant assertiveness. This ideal is articulated by president Jane Hansen, who warns against a facile interpretation of total submission to an authoritarian husband even as she rejects "the banner of women's lib, ERA and NOW": "I love being a housewife, a mother and all that goes with that. . . . That's part of who God created me to be. But he also created me to be more than that."[55] Repeatedly criticizing "the women's movement" for rejecting the notion that men should be heads of the household, Aglow participants continue to emphasize women's power to do great things in the world and, in very recent years, seem perceptibly to be be moving toward egalitarianism.[56] Admitting that the emphasis on female submission has changed greatly within Aglow, many women, including Hansen, now speak of "mutual submission" between husbands and wives as the ideal, an ideal long distorted, in their view, by church leaders but presently coming into its own.[57]

Historian Margaret Bendroth's observation about fundamentalism, that its "continuing attraction for women ensured that gender questions would arise over and over," remains true in the modern world, and not only for fundamentalism but for other forms of conservative or traditional religion as well. In the case of Aglow, older ideals have gradually mixed with modern realities to produce distinctive understandings of Christian womanhood.[58] By the mid-1990s, Aglow publications not only recognized that a high percentage of their readership comprised women who worked at jobs outside the home, but authors actually provided models for career women, in that few of them described themselves as full-time homemakers (as earlier writers almost inevitably had). As previously noted, for instance, a passage from the Aglow Bible study *God's Daughter* that originally read, "Because we, as women, are the homemakers, we have the blessing of opening our homes to God's people," was revised in 1985 to read more simply, "We, women, have the blessing of opening our homes to God's people."[59] Evangelical ideals of Christian womanhood, then, while always containing multiple possibilities for revision and even subversion, perceptibly shifted after the mid-1980s, as notions of submission were modified by other notions of female occupation as well as female power.

As increasing numbers of charismatic women have become divorced, single mothers, the older ideal of the happy, submissive wife has given way to newer models of women warriors battling the forces of Satan and helping each other surmount the ordinary obstacles of their lives. Admissions of childhood abuse and alcohol-drenched marriages have tempered the older idealism about squeaky clean and happy families, yet the tone of victory still resounds, as the women create alternative family relationships with God and with their evangelical sisters. Unlike most of the earliest stories published in *Aglow* magazines, written by women who assumed their audience to be mostly, like them, housewives with children, the Aglow literature produced in the 1990s assumes little about their readers' domestic status except that their lives are probably full of heartache or at least confusion over their roles as Christian women, a condition presumably connected to women's enduring quest for self-esteem. Changing ideals of Christian womanhood in Aglow literature are thus intricately connected to changing social patterns in American marriage and family life since the 1960s, and the variegation of such ideals reflects choice as well as uncertainty about dissolving gender role boundaries.[60]

Religious practices provide further insight into the processes of negotiation that occur as Aglow participants reshape and refine their identities as Christian women. Such practices create moments of active engagement with beliefs and assumptions that may conflict in unseen ways. Prayer is a particularly illuminating practice in the case of Aglow because of its dual function, serving simultaneously as a means of articulating the pain and frustration felt in daily life and as a tool for solving crises. As a means of both direct and indirect communication, prayer brings to light conflicts and contradictions that could otherwise remain hidden in Aglow women's lives and shows how very difficult submission, surrender, and forgiveness can be. Yet the women persevere, struggling to practice these ideals and hoping that in this case, practice can make perfect.

Conclusion

> I am searching for a language—one that breaks us out of our engendered prisons—a language in and through which we could all, men and women, see that dependence and independence, powerlessness and power, are deeply related and that not all forms of human vulnerability, can or should be rationalized out of our theories and our ways of being in the world.
>
> *Jean Bethke Elshtain*[1]

Conservative evangelical women who believe that their true liberation is found in voluntary submission to divine authority consider this a bold surrender, an act of assuming the crucial role God has called women to play in the making of history, especially in these critical "last days." Affirming this dialectic of female submission and empowerment, for instance, a local Aglow leader explained to me that throughout much of the world, women "are the downtrodden ones," and emphasized the potency that emerges from such a vulnerable state. "You know, it's the *women* who change their kids . . . [and] so often it's *women* who have a heart for the Lord! We are *powerful,* because [our work is] birthing in the spirit!"[2] Though despised and humiliated in myriad ways, according to Helen, women hold the unsurpassable advantage of being chosen by God to beget new forms of existence, to give birth to the Kingdom of God by means of a spiritual labor that is at once the most humble yet also the most glorious labor imaginable. Conservative evangelical women in late twentieth-century America, from Beverly LaHaye and Jane Hansen to Helen and other women who participate in Aglow and similar groups around the country, agree: God calls his daughters to perform mighty acts and inaugurate prodigious transformations through their prayers, rendering Christian women vital instruments of regeneration and healing to a broken and dying world. Believing that power issues from vulnerability—or, paradoxically, that vulnerability recreates itself as power—these women avow their capacity to remake all creation.

In examining charismatic evangelical women's devotional narratives over the past three decades, I have analyzed that paradox, focusing attention upon the shifting nature of gender identities and power relations in a religious world that tries to uphold the fixity of both. For instance, while Aglow participants recognize the benefits that women, not to mention Aglow as a whole, have gained from recent changes in American religious and social life—such as growing support for women in ministry and other careers—most have continued to emphasize traditional and "God-ordained" roles for women as wives and mothers. By expanding those roles from the domestic sphere to encompass a more general nurturing role in society, Aglow women have accounted for the fact that marriage and motherhood are not the primary or singular occupation of most current constituents or their leaders; yet they continue to validate and prize, as a rich source of female self-esteem, conventional notions of women as more supportive, loving, and spiritual than men. Amidst increasing acceptance of public female roles in religious and secular spheres of modern life, the concerns that charismatic women commonly express about modern female irreligiousness and dissatisfaction display a persistent ambivalence toward the potential effects of these role shifts. Out of this ambivalence emerges the determination to guard conservative gender hierarchies in a world where the traditional boundaries of sex and sexuality have substantially eroded.

Traditional gender ideals are vindicated and bolstered by scripts that echo throughout the culture of American evangelicalism; yet the kaleidoscopic patterns that emerge in devotional prayers reflect less the fixity of gender than its enduring fluidity. Careful analysis of these prayers and related practices affirms the suppleness of narrative itself in organizing identity but displays in turn the limits of this narrative flexibility within a tightly spun web of devotion. The evangelical tradition, claiming to present eternal truths in simple and direct terms, sustains what has been called a "centripetal tendency" in narratives that restricts the range of interpretation, legitimating particular readings of stories while discouraging alternative ones through highly elaborate rhetorical methods of persuasion, reinforcement, and discipline.[3] By transmitting in urgent terms the desolation of the outside world and the countless lives savaged by drug and alcohol addiction, sexual abuse, violence, or other evils, groups like Aglow cultivate participants' desire for deliverance and wholeness and help them experience spiritual rebirth into new identities as, in this case, Christian women. That rebirth will be challenged again and again, through trials and tribulations sent by a resentful Satan; but the "new person" that emerges will be nurtured and her pain given meaning by the community of women who say they have been where she is, understand that kind of suffering, and know where relief can be found. In such a community, as with the fundamentalist Christians described by anthropologist Susan Harding, belief involves a "willingness to join a narrative tradition, a way of knowing and being through storytelling, through giving and taking stories."[4] Those who accept the content of these narratives begin to tell their own lives in very precisely defined terms of transformation and healing, marking those who reject or question these scripts as rebellious, sinful, and miserable.

Those outsiders so marked may well dispute the aspersions heaped upon them, implicitly or explicitly, by such depictions. Many nonevangelicals will suppose that the fabricators of these labels are intolerant bigots and, lobbing some choice insults back in their direction, doubtless presume the matter settled then and there. Careful analysis of the people living out these scripts, however, demands a more judicious approach, at the very least a conscientious effort to grasp the meaning and subtlety of practices and symbols not one's own (or only partially one's own). Feminists who desire respectful treatment toward women in all spheres of life ought especially to employ such respect when journeying into the religious worlds of nonfeminist women. In the words of Adrienne Rich: "It is pointless to write off the antifeminist woman as brainwashed, or self-hating, or the like. I believe that feminism must imply an imaginative identification with all women . . . and that the feminist must, because she can, extend this act of the imagination as far as possible."[5] That most feminists, including Rich, find it far easier to be generous with women who adopt feminist ideals or who earn favor as prototypical victims of injustice reminds us that cultivating empathy for a presumed opponent is no easy task. Yet, as Nelle Morton insisted, "It is killing women not to be heard."[6]

In attempting to treat my subjects empathically and listen carefully to their stories, I have refused to interpret with undue haste the discourse of female submission as flatly or irrevocably oppressive. Such a depiction would disregard the complexities of evangelical faith and, worse, render these women's devotional lives unrecognizable to themselves. Instead, I have taken pains to credit their piety as a meaningful source of religious and social power, laden with copious practical strategies for

inverting conventional hierarchies and enabling women to influence husbands—perhaps even change or save them—and alter their family lives,
as well as to create newly whole and joyful selves. As women teach it to
each other, Christian submission is a flexible doctrine intricately attached to control—of self and other—and freedom, rather than a rigid
blueprint of silent and demoralizing subjugation. Likewise, the practice
of prayer is perceived as gloriously liberating, creating possibilities for
loving intimacy, healing of body and soul, renewed courage in the face
of sorrow, emotional maturity, and perpetual self-transformation.
Throughout assorted oral and written representations, devotional practices of surrender are affirmed as the key to women's fullest spiritual and
emotional fulfillment.

To be sure, no narrative is a pure reflection of the life it depicts; beyond simply recounting real experiences, narratives *create* experience
itself, reshuffling memories with each new telling and arranging them
according to the new context. For this reason my analysis has not
stopped with the accounts themselves but has scrutinized the social
fashioning of these accounts and their role in forging particular identities, identities that are variously ascribed, resisted, and embraced by
women in and through narrative. I have also paid close attention to visible gaps, that is, norms that seem to work against liberation and healing as authority and discipline are reinscribed and internalized. In particular, the bodies of the women themselves, clothed and groomed in
conformity with standards intended to set insiders apart from outsiders
and distinguish the spiritually correct from the spiritually suspect, expose the sharp limits of group identity and indicate some of the many
ways in which that most revered of charismatic values, spontaneity, is
regulated and controlled. The arenas described in Chapter 6—the diet
and grooming literature, the attitudes toward money, and the internal
hierarchies of the organization—represent intense and all but in-
escapable disciplinary codes. Even if female submission to male authority is not as rigid a doctrine as it sounds to many modern feminist
ears and even if it is possible to find expansive uses for it, one does not
have to look far to uncover idioms of control lurking within. Freedom
and discipline, as the Christian tradition has long taught, depend upon
one another for existence.

Evangelical women accept and even celebrate these disciplines, not
because they believe they have been manipulated by power-hungry men
but because such disciplines and the boundaries they engender make
them feel like true women: feminine, valuable, mighty women with a

unique and crucial role to play in the sacred drama of redemption. Their resistance to the notion that their own ideals of womanhood are culturally rather than divinely constructed derives from their faith in a God-ordained, hierarchically ordered universe and is further fueled by an abiding distrust of feminists, who seem from this perspective to have abandoned female identity for something closer to maleness.[7] The bitter irony of this distrust, fully reciprocated by feminists toward evangelical women, is that the disappointments and anxieties toward American life and culture that have long motivated each side have so much in common. Both groups of women have developed strategies for dealing with sundry issues facing modern Americans that are as similar in origin as they are distinctive in practice, strategies for coping with the pressures, sorrows, and fractures of intimate relationships as well as the larger social worlds that invariably frame these relationships. Once these correspondences are brought to light, a more nuanced historical perspective can begin to unfold: one that accentuates the common cultural roots of these divergent strategies and, by elucidating what is shared among players in the so-called gender wars, may work to deter the slanderous distortions and caricatures currently deployed by all sides.

Women, Modernity, and American Culture

Amidst the explosion of feminist scholarship during the past twenty-five years, the accuracy of certain key assumptions has remained largely unquestioned by historians of twentieth-century American women. The standard paradigm for women's history extols the liberation presumably wrought by second-wave feminism, in stark contrast to what is assumed to be women's near-universal oppression in American life prior to that time. Religion, particularly in its more traditional forms, is viewed as a tool for preserving patriarchy, suppressing women's energies and talents, and imbuing them with "false consciousness" in which hope for a better life is deferred toward expectations of heaven. Promoted in part by social historians, among others, variations of this narrative have also been explicated and augmented by numerous influential historians of women and religion, who have developed a powerful (and widely accepted) analytical framework celebrating women's liberation from traditional religious and social forms and lamenting whatever conservative remnants remain. Like its secular counterpart, this religious narrative is partially legitimate, grounded in the changing social dynamics of American religion as well as the experiences of those who have helped compose this theologically tinged framework. The problem, however, is that this narrative purports to tell the whole story—or *the* true story—of women in American religion, a presumptive fallacy that, as well-meaning as its defenders may be, calls for redress.[8]

The certain losers in that schema are religiously conservative women, those who have retained old religious ties or perhaps forged new ones instead of abandoning them for secular or spiritual feminism. More often than not, such women are perceived as either deluded—that is, brainwashed by the patriarchal structures of traditional religion—or simply repugnant, and at the very least participating outright in their own oppression. In the words of Andrea Dworkin: "The Right in the United States today is a social and political movement controlled almost totally by men but built largely on the fear and ignorance of women. The quality of this fear and the pervasiveness of this ignorance are consequences of male sexual domination over women. Every accommodation that women make to this domination, however apparently stupid, self-defeating, or dangerous, is rooted in the urgent need to survive somehow on male terms."[9] While Dworkin tries to temper her obvious distaste for conservative women and pay them a modicum of respect—these women are not stupid, just fearful and ignorant, she tells us—her supercilious view exemplifies the rigid victimization theory that continues to dominate most feminist analyses of nonfeminist women: No matter how much they claim to find liberation and fulfillment in prayer and Jesus, according to this perspective, evangelical women defeat themselves at every turn and ultimately buttress men's power at their own expense.

The persistence of this uncompromising outlook bespeaks more than a sensible wariness toward conservative attempts to maintain women's subordinate status. It betrays a rude gap in what I take to be a central feminist task: focusing with thorough mindfulness on women previously ignored or hidden from view, including—perhaps especially—those who challenge prior assumptions within feminist thought or who patently reject feminist tenets altogether. Since the beginning of feminism as both a women's political movement and a set of influential cultural meanings, internal challenges and debates over whom feminism can claim to speak for have perpetually tested the limits of feminist solidarity and inclusion. While feminists have deftly expanded their boundaries to include women previously left out of the mostly white, middle-class, educated elite who initially constituted both the authors and the subjects of feminism, they have responded less well to substantive critiques of the contradictions and problems within that program itself, including reform efforts by avowed feminists.[10] Yet surely there is adequate space within a feminist agenda for careful, empathic reconsideration of what might actually be at stake for those women who, for religious reasons and perhaps other reasons as well, persistently repudiate what they take to be established feminism.

These reasons are overwhelmingly tied to social divisions and the persistently derogatory stereotypes these divisions reinforce. Feminist ire against conservative women has ringing undertones of class and antireligious prejudice—attitudes that would be roundly condemned (or suppressed) if directed explicitly toward African American, Hispanic, or Native American women—as numerous investigations of the so-called culture wars make abundantly clear. Christopher Lasch's portrayal of this conflict as a battle between "the enlightened ethic of competitive achievement" on the one side versus "the petty-bourgeois or working-class ethic of limits" on the other crystallizes much of what is at stake in the current gender wars; and although I feel far deeper affinities with modern feminism than did Lasch, I share his revulsion for liberal, elite contempt for these traditional disciplines and the people who try to live them.[11] Feminist impatience with conservative religion does have sources apparently unrelated to social distinctions, such as the well-grounded suspicion that conservatives want to legislate narrow moral codes for all American citizens, yet the point remains that their general hostility toward religious and cultural "backwardness" is fueled by interests that are profoundly class-based. The continuing efforts—made, I am convinced, in good faith—by feminists to transcend class insularity and appeal more broadly to women in diverse social locations cannot succeed without reexamination of this deeper intolerance to religion and the limits imposed by faith on believers.

To be sure, conservative women vilify feminism with equal zeal and sometimes to unconscionable heights. Beverly LaHaye's tactical "emergency" letters to the constituents of her organization, Concerned Women for America, include ever more ominous warnings about the ways in which "radical feminists" are working to destroy families, schools, morals, and communities across the nation. A typical example of this conspiratorial thinking, a 1993 brief on the proposed congressional

Gender Equity in Education Act, is suffused with a sense of impending doom: "Not satisfied with indoctrinating just the students, this legislation would ensure the mandatory instruction of teachers to use the classroom as a bully pulpit for feminism. . . . Programs would encourage sexual promiscuity among students, sexual experimentation with "alternative lifestyles" such as homosexuality, challenge all traditional morals and values children learn in the home, and minimize the role of mothers and fathers in raising their children. . . . The feminists would try to persuade students to challenge all forms of parental authority. . . . The feminists would define many areas of traditional parenting as possible forms of child abuse."[12] In LaHaye's view, feminists are part of a concerted effort to wrest the responsibility for rearing children away from parents and place them under the control of the state, a plot with distinctly totalitarian overtones and made more repulsive by images of sexual excess and corruption. In promoting this extravagant message, LaHaye intends to incite the deepest fears of her family-oriented constituents, exactly as Dworkin, Barbara Ehrenreich, and other feminist critics charge.

Just as the feminist reproach of female accommodation to male authority is evidently accorded little merit among conservatives, the alarmist rhetoric of conservatives such as LaHaye fails to generate feminist introspection, a failing that is at once both understandable and distressing. To put it another way, what may be appropriate feminist antipathy toward the immoderate tocsins of Beverly LaHaye, Phyllis Schlafly, and other political types regularly extends into a lamentable intolerance toward the hundreds of thousands of other women who feel deeper affinities with religious answers to their lives than with feminist ones. If Adrienne Rich is correct that feminism entails trying to appreciate the differences among women, including those women whose vision of the good life one does not wholly share, then such petty attitudes toward conservative Christian women are conspicuously unwarranted. If Rich is mistaken, then it is difficult to see how either feminism or feminists can be of much benefit to any woman who does not already agree with their ideals. If the feminist concept of "experience"—a category increasingly understood as problematic yet indispensable—does not include conservative women's accounts, if it turns out that experience is only useful to announce a protracted "click" of feminist enlightenment, then countless numbers of women will continue to be swept aside in a contemptuously dismissive gesture that would cheer the staunchest defenders of male power.

From one perspective, conservative evangelical women are committed to a wholly antifeminist program, upholding doctrines of male privilege and female subservience that not only feminists but also liberal Christians and most secular Americans in general have long forsaken. As we have seen, however, those subservient women are supremely woman-centered in their communal spirituality, encouraging their spiritual sisters to achieve greater self-esteem and to love themselves whether or not they experience the love of men. While they are preoccupied with pleasing an undeniably male God, the very contrast in their vision between God and most earthly men slides into an expedient critique of the gender ideals preserving the status quo. Their faith in the mightiness of God, moreover, encompasses the conviction that God can transform men into tender creatures more closely resembling the gentle Jesus whom they adore. Arguing against the kind of twentieth-century feminism that from an evangelical perspective conceptualizes gender equality in worldly terms—promoting women's equal right to money and status and so pushing women to join the economic scramble of the market—religious women like those in Aglow claim to have found the true path to liberation and this-worldly fulfillment in a committed relationship with a Jesus who is at once father figure and lover, a relationship sustained and nurtured by communicative prayer.

In no way am I insinuating that conservative Christian women such as those who belong to either Aglow or Concerned Women for America are feminists. Such a claim would offend all parties and unnecessarily muddle this territory by denying vital differences. Yet it seems to me equally unhelpful to exaggerate the effects of so-called antifeminism embedded in their particular form of evangelical religion and to construct inflexible distinctions between feminist and antifeminist impulses.[13] As historian David Watt observes, even so noted an evangelical traditionalist as Marabel Morgan has promoted views strikingly close to the feminist agenda of critiquing the standard lot of most homemaker wives and mothers—Morgan saw their situation as like that of a bound and gagged prisoner of war—and helping women have better, more "adventuresome," and fulfilling lives.[14] Likewise, the desire among evangelical women to attain "the freedom to do what women [have] always done, but to see it valued differently" echoes one of the strongest impulses within the feminist spirituality movement in contemporary America.[15] The varied media through which evangelical women have communicated their stories to one another, prayed together, and felt transformed by these activities of sharing is not completely dissimilar—

is, in fact, quite similar—to what feminists have called consciousness-raising and interpreted as "a ritual in which stories are shared and sisterhood is affirmed."[16]

For evangelical women, sisterhood signifies both recognition of their common status as women and commitment to celebrating and defending that status against those who would denigrate it. While not using the term "patriarchy" to describe the source of their problems, such women explicitly denounce the irresponsibility shown by many husbands toward their families and express intense distrust of men in general. For them, moreover, feminism is not the answer but part of the problem: as Ruth Graham, wife of evangelist Billy Graham, has commented, the movement for women's liberation is "turning into men's lib because we [women] are freeing them from their responsibilities. I think we are being taken for a ride."[17] This skepticism toward men has obvious affinities with feminist critiques of male irresponsibility and exploitation of women, even if the responses and solutions offered seem almost diametrically opposed: Barbara Ehrenreich's portrayal of these disparities—that feminists have kindled women's anger while antifeminists have played on their fear of male abandonment—holds no small measure of truth.[18] Yet in her rush to paint such bald oppositions, Ehrenreich searches only the crudest polemics and so fails to do justice to the everyday lives of women, feminist and otherwise, where such antitheses dissipate and blur into other, less ideologically fixed, patterns of action. Again, the point is not to turn evangelical women into feminists (or feminists into anonymous or crypto-Christians) but rather to realize what is shared by these distinctive yet overlapping female cultures.[19]

One shared premise is that the social and cultural tasks, traits, and affinities traditionally coded as "female" or "feminine" ought to be accorded greater respect and value than they have been. Feminism, from the evangelical angle of vision, has erred by striving to eradicate the differences between women and men and setting women's sights upon achieving access to realms of power that men have most often occupied. Such a goal is viewed as both stifling and corrosive, in that feminists are ostensibly forced to reject those very qualities and desires that make them fully women, and so its "successes"—in promoting women's social and political power, for instance—are won at far too great a cost. From the feminist viewpoint, however, conservative evangelical women diminish the potential of women by restricting female influence to the realms of home and family—the power behind the throne—rather than expanding them into the world. Both conservative evangelical women and feminists, then, want to see women's cultural and social labor revalued, celebrated, and elevated in status; the basic difference between their images is that they ascribe contrary meanings to the substance of womanhood.[20]

It is hardly any wonder that these contrary meanings issue from the disparate vocabularies currently associated with the American "culture wars" even as they help reproduce and sustain such vocabularies. Nonetheless, the idea that these must be altogether different languages leaps across evidence to the contrary, ignoring the lexical and practical blending that occurs at the most basic levels of human action. Once this blending begins to be recognized, once the ways in which these vocabularies and cultures overlap begin to be illuminated, the historical context for understanding women's lives in twentieth-century America can be reframed. The focus of the study can then shift away from a story of social liberation versus oppression—or of a starkly oversimplified notion of culture wars—toward a more nuanced, complex, and less polarizing account that stresses cultural borrowing, decision-making, and self-refashioning in a world resplendent with possibilities yet fettered by disappointment, grief, and shattered dreams. Rather than evading the bitter struggles between opposing constituencies—whether feminist versus antifeminist or wider liberal/conservative and left/right configurations—this approach resituates those struggles in their broader cultural patterns, placing the development of these positions and the people who hold them in vivid relief. Obviously, the significant differences among women must not be ignored or erased, lest the naive conclusion be drawn (again) that sameness of sex confers upon one person unfailing insight into the passions of another.[21] The task of "doing justice to our differences," as I interpret it, requires neither bland acquiescence to variety nor fanciful insistence upon similarity but an effort at fair and forthright inquiry into the narratives, private as well as public, of so-called adversaries as well as presumed allies. [22]

This is one way in which cultural analysis of seemingly opposed constituencies might be fruitfully utilized: not so much as a bridge between people on opposite sides of cultural debates (who may not want to cross such a bridge in any case) but rather as a tool for more deeply understanding the processes by which particular identities are constructed and then made to seem unique, different, and even opposite to other kinds of culturally formed identities. Without reaching hopelessly for consensus and continuity where none exist, we may yet seek hidden commonalities of premise and experience with which women in real or imagined opposition to one another actually operate, creating ground for tentative dialogue preferable to current acrimonious and overwrought squabbles. If this is too much to ask, then such analyses ought at least to help us better understand the overlapping, powerful scripts shaping women's lives and identities in late twentieth-century America.

Resistance, Vulnerability, and the Paradox of Prayer

Central to this study of conservative Christian women are questions about how religious practices operate for those who enact them, how they relate to broader social matrices and how they affect everyday life. I have attempted to address these questions by examining the workings of social and spiritual power in the Aglow organization to discern whether practices such as prayer and storytelling about prayer more effectively oppose or conserve norms of discipline and authority, whether they foster resistance or perpetuate female subordination. More to the point, I have sought a way of transposing this bifurcation, so deeply embedded in American thought, between resistance and subordination: a way of supplanting that prosaic "either/or" option so as to evoke more subtle arrangements and orchestrations.

Nonetheless, assuming such a way could be determined, it would have little value if it could not help us understand the specific eventual affects of religious devotion upon particular women, including both its liberatory *and* its repressive dimensions. And there's the rub. It is, of course, a knotty problem to gauge resistance, especially among persons living within hierarchical orderings of power that they themselves avidly extol. In the case of evangelical women like those who belong to Aglow, celebrations of the male-dominated status quo are surely not without accompanying critique, yet the robust note of final triumph may well disarm whatever challenges reside there. If, in certain ways, prayer and testimony seem to create possibilities for the liberation and transformation worshipers claim to experience, they may just as readily work to opposite ends, further institutionalizing the roles and boundaries that constrict women's space. From that angle, one consequence of a fervently charismatic, biblically oriented piety for women may be blindness to their own sociopolitical, religious, and domestic disempowerment, the hazardous result of seeing the world only through Jesus-colored glasses.

Yet Aglow and like-minded women defy this characterization, perceiving themselves not as blind victims but as clear-sighted dissidents opposing basic elements of the wider culture: its materialism and greed, for instance, along with its apathy, self-indulgence, and ubiquitous violence. Rejecting that realm, these women deliberately construct an enclave of opposition, impugning the so-called forces of evil and disputing the power of those forces to control, manipulate, or beat down any who side with God against them. When we perceive this very form of devotion as a kind of cultural resistance, we may begin to see beyond simple antitheses of liberation versus repression in Aglow women's lives, better understanding how these women utilize prayer and submission to flourish in the midst of an unstable, corrupt, and formidable world. If the ideology of submission to authority is in any sense subversive, it is so primarily within the context of the wider American society where (according to evangelical women's worldview) savagery and moral breakdown are increasingly the norm. The disciplines of prayer, of marriage, of conformity to Aglow rules and scripts, mean safety, integrity, and accountability to these women; and within such a realm they may well feel not simply virtuous but free.

That these disciplines will not appeal to everyone is patently obvious, yet the cultural indictment that drives these disciplines into high gear echoes similar charges long made by divers cultural critics such as Christopher Lasch, Wendell Berry, Stephen L. Carter, and Jean Bethke Elshtain. The notion that a pervasive narcissism, embodied in modern forms of individual and corporate greed, resentment, complacency, irresponsibility, and deceit, is unraveling the American social fabric with devastating and perhaps irreversible speed resonates far beyond the conservative religious world of women elaborated here. Linking these critical social hazards to what they believe to be the sinful quest for personal power and gain, conservative religious women are not the only ones to recognize that unyielding commitment to power at the expense of vulnerability, restraint, and attachment may well suffocate rather than liberate the seeker and will surely wreak havoc elsewhere as well. Perhaps the evangelical landscape even offers resources for a language by which to represent what Elshtain characterizes as the intertwining of "dependence and independence, powerlessness and power" and to affirm a human vulnerability framed in terms other than victimology. If one desires and believes in the possibilities of such a language as an alternative to current "gendered rigidities" and "cages . . . of gendered constructions," then, in Elshtain's words, "worlds of ambiguity, and sympathetic identity, and mutual vulnerability open up—and these, surely must be the starting point to a new politics of gender representation."[23]

This search for fresh ways to think about power and resistance may also offer a method for considering the practical effects of activities such as prayer: one that would avoid the either/or perspective, by which practices are viewed as *either* opposing *or* conserving certain meanings and values, but rather understand them as doing both, upholding power arrangements even while exposing them to unexpected challenges. One way of articulating such a method might be to think in terms of "making room," that is, expanding one's sense of place, creating more out of less or less out of more, taking part in the opening of new worlds. To make room is to defy the constraints of vision and action that have been promulgated by cynics, to give voice to imagined longings and forge new ways of being real without ever losing sight of life's tragedies. Although it may create new impediments, unexpected burdens, or chances for failure, this hopeful act of augmentation is meant to provide increased latitude in which to breathe, to move, to be.

From this perspective, prayer, telling stories about prayer, and related forms of expression have the potential to unlock or amplify domains that would ordinarily seem tightly bounded or compressed. By making room for new ways of imagining a situation, such practices push at the walls of those boundaries, set them into motion, and stretch the range of options within that world. Dorothy opens up the drapes in her living room and imagines her world expanding. Alicia, doing battle against the "powers of darkness" that have attacked her adulterous husband, receives assurance that her marriage has been saved and her husband transformed. Mothers discover fruitful ways for dealing with sick or troubled children, balancing a sense of responsibility with awareness that sometimes the best they can do is "turn it over to the Lord." Although difficulties may well persist and other hardships are sure to transpire, there is always room for hope, setting up new occasions for effective, even courageous, action and fresh chances for responding to defeat with faith rather than despair. What emerge are not simply glib or superficial solutions to life's trials but spaces of calm assurance, expectation, and possibility.

Lest this notion of opened space appear quixotic, however, it should be remembered that old boundaries are not erased but rather shift, tightening in spots that are not always immediately evident. Dorothy, Alicia, and others may find reconciliation with their husbands and forge newly rapturous connections with God, but these hierarchical relationships may also come at a high price, in some cases requiring women to renounce whatever desires and aspirations conflict with more authoritative wills. The capacity for active protest and dissent shrinks drastically, and while it may not wither away altogether, the sanctions against "rebellion"—including rebellion against conventions strictly upheld within devotional communities—are great. Dissatisfaction and unhappiness with one's life may rise to the surface only to illuminate personal weaknesses, while one recognizes the responsibility to surrender again and accept whatever comes, as in the case of Nora. The potential for abdicating personal will and desire in this worldview seems not only individually stifling but also, and perhaps more ominously, politically immobilizing. Female surrender in this context all too often seems to include abdicating independent reflection and forfeiting self-protection, capacities which these women cannot afford to sacrifice.

In the end, then, the room these women make for themselves may be countered by the room they lose, however many prayers they pray and however much they support and love one another. Yet, paradoxically, the hope created within that context may well have greater significance than any outsider can fathom; so the women themselves have told me, again and again. Notions of submission and surrender, of secrecy, openness, and intimacy, and of healing and transformation—all of which are enacted through prayer, through stories, and through changed behavior in everyday life—provide these women with means of reinventing themselves, of "making room" for new selves within a social context that is also believed to be made new. The larger political implications of this process may be unforeseeable, but at the very least it would seem that the determination these women manifest in reworking their lives holds potential for more changes in the future. Aglow prayer narratives hinge on moments when the possibilities for a new identity are conceived, and it is in surrendering to such possibilities that new selves may be born.

Notes

Introduction

1. Here and throughout the text I have invented pseudonyms for Aglow participants and other sources to disguise their identities. When quoting from *Aglow* magazines, I use writers' actual first names but omit surnames altogether. Authors of pamphlets or books published by Aglow and publicly distributed are cited in full.

2. Schlafly, best known for helping defeat the Equal Rights Amendment in 1982, is an author, a lawyer, the ultraconservative founder of the Eagle Forum, and former chair of the Republican National Coalition for Life. LaHaye, a popular speaker on Christian radio and wife of the fundamentalist minister Tim LaHaye, is founder and president of Conservative Women for America.

3. Nelle Morton traced this expression to 1971 and first presented it in "The Rising Woman Consciousness in a Male Language Structure," *Andover Newton Quarterly* 12, no. 4 (March 1972): 177–190. "Hearing to speech," by which she meant to suggest a liberatory practice of feminist consciousness-raising, is further elaborated in Morton, *The Journey Is Home* (Boston: Beacon Press, 1985). Describing women's consciousness-raising as a recent phenomenon, she explains: 'A new kind of seeing and hearing was beginning to be experienced by one group of women after the other. Once they recognized in themselves a common oppression, they could hear from one another that which many, more astute and intellectual than they, could not hear. . . . Women came to new speech simply because they were being heard. Hearing became an act of receiving the woman as well as the words she was speaking" (*Journey,* 17).

4. Exceptions to this blind spot regarding conservative Christian women often come from ethnographers, who may be surprised to find forms of "protofeminism" or, in Judith Stacey's terms, "postfeminism," among such

women. See Stacey, *Brave New Families: Stories of Domestic Upheaval in Late Twentieth Century America* (New York: Basic Books, 1991); Stacey and Susan Elizabeth Gerard, " 'We Are Not Doormats': The Influence of Feminism on Contemporary Evangelicals in the United States," in *Uncertain Terms: Negotiating Gender in American Culture,* ed. Faye Ginsburg and Anna Lowenhaupt Tsing (Boston: Beacon Press, 1990), 98–117. A finely nuanced account of fundamentalist women and men is Stephen Bates, *Battleground: One Mother's Crusade, the Religious Right, and the Struggle for Control of Our Classrooms* (New York: Poseidon Press, 1993). Other useful analyses of traditional religious women and power in the twentieth century include Elaine J. Lawless, *Handmaidens of the Lord: Pentecostal Women Preachers and Traditional Religion* (Philadelphia: University of Pennsylvania Press, 1988); Robert Anthony Orsi, *The Madonna of 115th Street: Faith and Community in Italian Harlem, 1880–1950* (New Haven: Yale University Press, 1985), esp. 129–149; Kristin Luker, *Abortion and the Politics of Motherhood* (Berkeley: University of California Press, 1984); and Mary McClintock Fulkerson, *Changing the Subject: Women's Discourses and Feminist Theology* (Minneapolis: Fortress Press, 1994), esp. 239–298.

5. The only published study of Aglow is Susan M. Setta, "Healing in Suburbia: The Women's Aglow Fellowship," *Journal of Religious Studies* 12, no. 2 (1986): 46–56. Even scholars of pentecostal and charismatic movements have essentially ignored Aglow. Several recent studies of contemporary American religion and culture have mentioned Aglow in passing; see, for instance, Meredith B. McGuire, with the assistance of Debra Kantor, *Ritual Healing in Suburban America* (New Brunswick, NJ: Rutgers University Press, 1988), 19–21; Faye D. Ginsburg, *Contested Lives: The Abortion Debate in an American Community* (Berkeley: University of California Press, 1989), 85; and Charles H. Lippy, *Being Religious, American Style: A History of Popular Religiosity in the United States* (Westport, CT: Greenwood Press, 1994), 231, 232.

6. Various female ethnographers have similarly described being cast in the role of daughter, reflecting on the kinds of information denied one in this role as well as the intimacy that can develop and carry new kinds of information unavailable to more distant observers. See Lila Abu-Lughod, *Veiled Sentiments: Honor and Poetry in a Bedouin Society* (Berkeley: University of California Press, 1986), 1–35; Dorinne Kondo, *Crafting Selves: Power, Gender, and Discourses of Identity in a Japanese Workplace* (Chicago: University of Chicago Press, 1990), 9–17; and Jean L. Briggs, *Never in Anger: Portrait of an Eskimo Family* (Cambridge: Harvard University Press, 1970), 225–299.

7. Lila Abu-Lughod describes this problem as the "sense of inauthenticity" that resulted from having felt compelled at times to lie to her Bedouin informants about her life in order that they not shun her as a modern American woman (*Veiled Sentiments,* 18–19).

8. Brown, *Mama Lola: A Vodou Priestess in Brooklyn* (Berkeley: University of California Press, 1991), 12.

9. See Catherine A. Lutz, *Unnatural Emotions: Everyday Sentiments on a Micronesian Atoll and Their Challenge to Western Theory* (Chicago: University of Chicago Press, 1988), 46.

10. See Joan W. Scott, "Experience," in *Feminists Theorize the Political,* ed. Judith Butler and Joan W. Scott (New York: Routledge, 1992), 22–40; also Rosemary Hennessy, *Materialist Feminism and the Politics of Discourse* (New York: Routledge, 1993), 67–99.

11. The most influential critique of this kind is the series of essays edited by James Clifford and George E. Marcus, *Writing Culture: The Poetics and Politics of Ethnography* (Berkeley: University of California Press, 1986). Feminist ethnographers have raised objections to the slighting of feminist contributions to this enterprise (discussed by Clifford in his introduction to the volume) and have continued to address the issue of ethnographic reflexivity. A feminist critique was first formulated in Deborah A. Gordon, "Writing Culture, Writing Feminism: The Poetics and Politics of Experimental Ethnography," *Inscriptions* 3/4 (1988); numerous other responses followed. Ruth Behar recounts and expands these feminist readings of *Writing Culture* in "Introduction: Out of Exile," *Women Writing Culture,* ed. Ruth Behar and Deborah A. Gordon (Berkeley: University of California Press, 1995), 1–29. See also Margery Wolf, *A Thrice-Told Tale: Feminism, Postmodernism, and Ethnographic Responsibility* (Stanford, CA: Stanford University Press, 1992).

For better or worse, however, these critiques of "self-erasure" perfomed in the name of objectivity have, in various ways, called into question virtually all attempts at cultural description, resulting in a climate recently characterized by anthropologist Clifford Geertz as "a pervasive nervousness about the whole business of claiming to explain enigmatical others on the grounds that you have gone about with them in their native habitat or combed the writings of those who have." Indeed, in the present postcolonial context, writes Geertz, "the very right to write—to write ethnography—seems at risk (Geertz, *Works and Lives: The Anthropologist as Author* (Stanford, CA: Stanford University Press, 1988), 130–31, 133). One of the more questionable responses to this dilemma is a style of thinking and writing that is the very opposite of self-erasure, resulting in solipsistic analyses of ethnographers themselves rather than their subjects. Sharp critiques of this "reflexive self-absorption" have been leveled, for instance, at *Women Writing Culture* (see Kate Gilbert, "Fastening the Bonds of Womanhood," in the *Women's Review of Books* 8 no. 9 (June 1996), 21–22). Self-reflection can surely go too far.

12. Gramsci, *Prison Notebooks* (New York: Columbia University Press, 1991); Williams, *Marxism and Literature* (Oxford: Oxford University Press, 1977); Michel de Certeau, *The Practice of Everyday Life,* trans. Steven Rendall (Berkeley: University of California Press, 1984); Bourdieu, *Outline of a Theory of Practice,* trans. Richard Nice (Cambridge, England: Cambridge University Press, 1977; orig. 1972); Giddens, *The Constitution of Society: Outline of the Theory of Structuration* (Berkeley: University of California Press, 1984).

13. Lila Abu-Lughod, "The Romance of Resistance: Tracing Transformations of Power through Bedouin Women," *American Ethnologist* 17:1 (February 1990): 41–55.

14. Ortner, "Theory in Anthropology Since the Sixties," *Comparative Studies in Society and History* 26, no. 1 (January 1984): 126–166. Further elaboration of practice theory is given in Rosemary J. Coombe, "Room for

Manoeuver: Toward a Theory of Practice in Critical Legal Studies," *Law and Social Inquiry* 14, no. 1 (Winter 1989): 69–121.

15. See, for instance, Davis, "City Women and Religious Change" in *Society and Culture in Early Modern France: Eight Essays by Natalie Zemon Davis* (Stanford, CA Stanford University Press, 1975), 65–95; and "Women on Top" in *ibid*, 124–151; and Bynum, *Holy Feast and Holy Fast: The Religious Significance of Food to Medieval Women* (Berkeley: University of California Press, 1987); and *Fragmentation and Redemption: Essays on Gender and the Human Body in Medieval Religion* (New York: Zone Books, 1991).

16. Stacey, *Brave New Families*; Elizabeth E. Brusco, *The Reformation of Machismo: Evangelical Conversion and Gender in Colombia* (Austin: University of Texas Press, 1995), 137.

17. Michel de Certeau, *The Practice of Everyday Life,* esp. 29–42; see also James C. Scott, *Weapons of the Weak: Everyday Forms of Peasant Resistance* (New Haven: Yale University Press, 1985). The wider literature theorizing power relationships is obviously too vast to summarize here; besides de Certeau and Scott, works that I have found particularly useful include Michel Foucault, *Discipline and Punish: The Birth of the Prison,* trans. Alan Sheridan (New York: Vintage Books, 1977); Pierre Bourdieu, *Outline of a Theory of Practice;* and Janice A. Radway, *Reading the Romance: Women, Patriarchy, and Popular Literature* (Chapel Hill: University of North Carolina Press, 1991 [1984]).

18. For critiques of romanticizing resistance, see Lila Abu-Lughod, "Romance of Resistance," 42; and Scott, *Weapons of the Weak,* 29. I am grateful to Robert Orsi for persistently urging me to grapple with this issue.

19. Lawless, "Rescripting Their Lives and Narratives: Spiritual Life Stories of Pentecostal Women Preachers," *Journal of Feminist Studies in Religion* 7, no. 1 (Spring 1991): 60.

20. See Carol Goldman, "Creating Sacred Emotional Space," in *Sacred Dimensions of Women's Experience,* ed. Elizabeth Dodson Gray (Wellesley, MA: Roundtable Press, 1988), 17–22; and Jo Ann Cooney Cripe, "Integrative Relationality: Themes of Transition of Women's Faith Development," *Journal of Women and Religion* 8 (1989): 4–20. Both are cited in Jody Shapiro Davie, *Women in the Presence: Constructing Community and Seeking Spirituality in Mainline Protestantism* (Philadelphia: University of Pennsylvania Press, 1995), 9. From a different angle, Davie's own study of Presbyterian women's spirituality highlights the workings of silence and various "internal speech barriers" in preventing such narrative sharing from taking over identity formation.

See also Miriam Therese Winter, Adair Lummis, and Allison Stokes, *Defecting in Place: Women Claiming Responsibility for Their Own Spiritual Lives* (New York: Crossroad, 1994).

21. Some of these findings are briefly and coherently summarized in Peggy J. Miller et al., "Narrative Practices and the Social Construction of Self in Childhood," *American Ethnologist* 17:2 (May 1990): 292–311.

22. Lawless, "Rescripting," 53–71. See also Ginsburg, *Contested Lives,* 133–145.

23. Lawless, "Rescripting," esp. 62–63.

24. 18 May 1993.

25. 19 May 1993; 13 August 1993; 2 August 1993.

26. 21 April 1993.

27. 20 January 1994.

28. Wuthnow, *Sharing the Journey: Support Groups and America's New Quest for Community* (New York: The Free Press, 1994).

29. Brief but informative articles about these newly emerging Christian women's groups include Gustav Niebuhr, "Conference About God for Women With Faith," *New York Times* 27 January 1997: A10; Karen Testa, "Women Put God First: Praise Keepers Hopes to Emulate Success of Men's Christian Groups," *Chattanooga Times* 4 January 1997: C2 (reprinted from the Associated Press); and John Dart, "New Women's Organizations Emerge," *Los Angeles Times* 1 February 1997: B5.

Analysis of the devotional lives of men within evangelical and charismatic culture—participants in all-male parachurch organizations such as the Full Gospel Businessmen's Fellowship International and Promise Keepers, for instance—will help determine more substantially the dynamics of gender within that broader culture. Fruitful work has been done on the Vineyard Christian Fellowship by Paul W. Kennedy, "Socializing Secularization: A Sociological Analysis of the Vineyard Christian Fellowship" (Ph.D. diss., University of Southern California, 1993). Kennedy is part of a team of researchers under sociologist Donald E. Miller, whose study of Calvary Chapel, the Vineyard, and Hope Chapel is soon to be published as *Reinventing American Protestantism: Christianity in the New Millennium* (Berkeley: University of California Press, 1997).

30. Scholarly debates about defining these labels are ongoing and complicated, and any brief description of them necessarily entails a loss of subtlety. In essence, "fundamentalist" emerged in Christian circles as a theological term, suggesting one who believes in the inerrancy of the Bible, the virgin birth of Jesus and the truth of his miracles, forgiveness for sin through his death, the reality of his bodily resurrection, and his eventual return to Earth. "Pentecostal" implies a piety of affective emotion combined with a Biblical theology centered on the scriptural descriptions of Pentecost (Acts 2) and the spiritual gifts (1 Corinthians 12); the term refers historically to those Christians who, since the beginning of the twentieth century, have focused on experiential knowledge of God, through the Baptism in the Holy Spirit with the evidence of glossolalia or speaking in tongues, and who withdrew from the historic Protestant churches to form their own institutions and denominations such as the Assemblies of God and the Church of God in Christ. "Charismatics" are those who adopted a similar experiential piety later in the twentieth century but who have, at least until recently, largely remained in the historic Protestant and Catholic churches. "Evangelical" is an umbrella term that may include all those who believe in the necessity of a "born again" experience, in which one confesses one's sins and accepts Christ in order to receive eternal salvation. Such distinctions, like all labels, mask the permeability of these boundaries.

31. Randall Balmer, *Mine Eyes Have Seen the Glory: A Journey into the Evangelical Subculture in America* (New York: Oxford University Press, 1989), xii. Donald W. Dayton and Robert K. Johnston have made some

suggestions for resolving this terminological problem; see the final two chap-
ters of *The Variety of American Evangelicalism,* ed. Dayton and Johnson
(Downers Grove, IL: Intervarsity Press; Knoxville: University of Tennessee
Press, 1991), 245–272.

32. See also McGuire's discussion of this issue in *Pentecostal Catholics:
Power, Charisma, and Order in a Religious Movement* (Philadelphia: Temple
University Press, 1982), 20–21.

33. 18 May 1993.

34. Wolf, *A Thrice-Told Tale,* 126.

Chapter 1

1. February 1994.

2. May 1994.

3. "Reflections on Aglow's Twenty-Year Ministry to Women around the
World," brochure (Lynnwood, WA: Aglow Publications, 1987), 4.

4. "When the day of Pentecost had come, they were all together in one place.
And suddenly from heaven there came a sound like the rush of a violent wind,
and it filled the entire house where they were sitting. Divided tongues, as of fire,
appeared among them, and a tongue rested on each of them. All of them were
filled with the Holy Spirit and began to speak in other languages, as the Spirit
gave them ability" (Acts 2:1–4, NRSV).

5. The recent literature on Pentecostalism is quite large; on the early history of
the movement, see Donald W. Dayton, *Theological Roots of Pentecostalism*
(Grand Rapids: Francis Asbury Press, 1987); Robert Mapes Anderson, *Vision of
the Disinherited: The Making of American Pentecostalism* (New York: Oxford
University Press, 1979); Nils Bloch-Hoell, *The Pentecostal Movement: Its Origin,
Development and Distinctive Character* (New York: Humanities Press, 1964); and
John Thomas Nichol, *Pentecostalism* (Plainfield, NJ: Logos International, rev. ed.
1971). The classic study is still Walter James Hollenweger, *The Pentecostals: The
Charismatic Movement in the Churches* (Minneapolis: Augsburg Publishing
House, 1972). See also Edith L. Blumhofer, *Restoring the Faith: The Assemblies of
God, Pentecostalism, and American Culture* (Urbana: University of Illinois Press,
1993). For further sources on Pentecostalism, see Charles Edwin Jones, *A Guide
to the Study of the Pentecostal Movement,* 2 vols. (Metuchen, NJ: Scarecrow Press
and the American Theological Library Association, 1983).

6. David Edwin Harrell, Jr., *All Things Are Possible: The Healing and
Charismatic Revivals in Modern America* (Bloomington: Indiana University
Press, 1975).

7. Blumhofer, *Restoring the Faith,* 216.

8. These denominational periodicals include the *Church of God Evangel,* the
Christian Evangel, the *Pentecostal Herald,* and the *Pentecostal Holiness
Advocate;* larger, nondenominational organs such as the *Voice of Healing* were
also important in spreading the Pentecostal message of healing.

9. R. Marie Griffith, "'Joy Unspeakable and Full of Glory': The Vocabulary
of Pious Emotion Among American Pentecostal Women, 1910–1945," in Peter

N. Stearns and Jan Lewis, eds., *An Emotional History of the United States* (New York: NYU Press, in press).

10. The best study of the charismatic movement is still Harrell, *All Things Are Possible*. Two works that trace the development of the charismatic movement among non-Pentecostal groups are Richard Quebedeaux, *The New Charismatics: The Origins, Development, and Significance of Neo-Pentecostalism* (New York: Doubleday, 1976), completely revised and published as *The New Charismatics II: How a Christian Renewal Movement Became Part of the American Religious Mainstream* (San Francisco: Harper & Row, 1983); and Vinson Synan, *The Twentieth-Century Pentecostal Explosion: The Exciting Growth of Pentecostal Churches and Charismatic Renewal Movements* (Altamonte Springs, FL: Creation House, 1987). Scc also Margaret M. Poloma, *The Charismatic Movement: Is There a New Pentecost?* (Boston: Twayne, 1982). Studies of the charismatic movement among American Catholics abound; they include McGuire, *Pentecostal Catholics;* Richard J. Bord and Joseph E. Faulkner, *The Catholic Charismatics: The Anatomy of a Modern Religious Movement* (University Park: Pennsylvania State University Press, 1983); and Mary Jo Neitz, *Charisma and Community: A Study of Religious Commitment within the Catholic Charismatic Renewal* (New Brunswick: Transaction Books, 1986). For a comprehensive guide to the literature on the charismatic movement, see Charles Edwin Jones, *The Charismatic Movement: A Guide to the Study of Neo-Pentecostalism with Emphasis on Anglo-American Sources* (Metuchen, NJ: The American Theological Library Association and Scarecrow Press, 1995).

11. Historian David Harrell explains, "Local chapter meetings in leading hotels put on display charismatic fervor in a dignified setting before a much broader and more sophisticated audience than the revivalists ever reached." (David Edwin Harrell, Jr., *All Things Are Possible,* 148.) The history of the FGBMFI is recounted in Vinson Synan, *Under His Banner: History of Full Gospel Business Men's Fellowship* (Costa Mesa, CA: Gift Publications, 1992).

12. Harrell, *All Things Are Possible,* 147. Vinson Synan reports that the *Full Gospel Voice* reached a readership of 700,000 by 1989 (*Under His Banner,* 81).

13. Harrell, 148. Of Oral Roberts' continuing ties to the FGBMFI, Harrell writes: "For many years, Roberts remained the most powerful supporter of the new group and probably benefited most from its growth" (147). Roberts' own move from Pentecostal to "neo-Pentecostal" was completed when, in March of 1968, he joined the wealthy Boston Avenue Methodist Church in Tulsa.

14. Wuthnow, *The Restructuring of American Religion: Society and Faith Since World War II* (Princeton: Princeton University Press, 1988). While Wuthnow's model has been challenged as having too neatly separated religious groups into distinctly bounded camps, it helpfully illuminates the general trajectory of charismatic Christians since the late 1970s.

15. For a historical analysis of the religious right, see George M. Marsden, "Preachers of Paradox: The Religious New Right in Historical Perspective," in *Religion and America: Spirituality in a Secular Age,* ed. Mary Douglas and Steven M. Tipton (Boston: Beacon Press, 1983), 150–168. An excellent study that uses the term "New Christian Right" is Clyde Wilcox, *God's Warriors: The*

Christian Right in Twentieth-Century America (Baltimore: Johns Hopkins University Press, 1992). See also Robert C. Liebman and Robert Wuthnow, eds., *The New Christian Right: Mobilization and Legitimation* (New York: Aldine, 1983). The term "cultural fundamentalism" was early used in Joseph R. Gusfield, *Symbolic Crusade: Status Politics and the Temperance Movement* (Urbana: University of Illinois Press, 1963), and was taken up in Richard Hofstadter, "Pseudo-Conservatism Revisited—1965," in Hofstadter, *The Paranoid Style in American Politics and Other Essays* (Chicago: University of Chicago Press, 1965), 66–92. It has been used with greater precision and insight by Joseph Tamney and Stephen Johnson, "The Moral Majority in Middletown," *Journal for the Scientific Study of Religion* 22 (June 1983): 145–157; Donald G. Mathews and Jane Sherron De Hart, *Sex, Gender, and the Politics of ERA: A State and the Nation* (New York: Oxford University Press, 1990), esp. 175–180; and David Snowball, *Continuity and Change in the Rhetoric of the Moral Majority* (New York: Praeger, 1991), 32. Thinking in terms of cultural (as opposed to biblical) fundamentalism allows observers to focus on the particular cultural issues—especially the family and domestic life—that have most successfully mobilized these groups and individuals into political conservatism and upheld a form of civil religion.

16. Mathews and De Hart, *Sex, Gender, and the Politics of ERA,* 178. See also Jane J. Mansbridge, *Why We Lost the ERA* (Chicago: University of Chicago Press, 1986).

17. Sociologist Rebecca E. Klatch has rightly observed that "no consensus exists on the exact boundaries of the New Right." She notes: "Generally, when people use the term 'New Right' they refer to a network of people and organizations that came into prominence in the mid-1970s, including conservative politicians such as Jesse Helms, Orrin Hatch, and Jack Kemp, conservative think-tanks such as the Heritage Foundation, general-purpose organizations such as the Conservative Caucus, the National Conservative Political Action Committee, and the Committee for the Survival of a Free Congress, as well as the religious sector, including prime-time preachers, the Moral Majority, and groups working against such issues as abortion, gay rights, and pornography" (*Women of the New Right* [Philadelphia: Temple University Press, 1987], 13).

18. Much of the literature on conservative evangelism comes from the fields of political science and sociology. One of the more influential studies is James Davison Hunter, *Evangelicalism: The Coming Generation* (Chicago: University of Chicago Press, 1987); see also Hunter, *Culture Wars: The Struggle to Define America* (New York: Basic Books, 1991). A more sensationalist but still useful account is Sara Diamond, *Spiritual Warfare: The Politics of the Christian Right* (Boston: South End Press, 1989).

19. Undated, obtained from Aglow headquarters in June, 1993.

20. Personal correspondence with Aglow headquarters, 3 May 1996; and interview, 15 August 1996.

21. "Bill's Story," in *Alcoholics Anonymous: The Story of How Many Thousands of Men and Women Have Recovered from Alcoholism,* 3rd edition (New York: Alcoholics Anonymous World Services, Inc., 1976) [42nd printing, 1991], 14.

22. The group's own version of its history is recounted in *Alcoholics Anonymous*. For information on AA's roots in the Oxford Group, see John F. Woolverton, "Evangelical Protestantism and Alcoholism 1933–1962: Episcopalian Samuel Shoemaker, the Oxford Group and Alcoholics Anonymous," *Historical Magazine of the Protestant Episcopal Church* 52:1 (March 1983): 53–65; and Ernest Kurtz, *Not-God: A History of Alcoholics Anonymous* (Center City, MN: Hazelden Educational Services, 1979). On the origins of the Oxford Group, see Daniel Edward Sack, "Disastrous Disturbances: Buchmanism and Student Religious Life at Princeton, 1919–1935" (Ph.D. thesis: Princeton University, 1995).

23. The twelve steps are:

1. We admitted we were powerless over alcohol—that our lives had become unmanageable.

2. Came to believe that a Power greater than ourselves could restore us to sanity.

3. Made a decision to turn our will and our lives over to the care of God *as we understood Him.*

4. Made a searching and fearless moral inventory of ourselves.

5. Admitted to God, to ourselves, and to another human being the exact nature of our wrongs.

6. Were entirely ready to have God remove all these defects of character.

7. Humbly asked Him to remove our shortcomings.

8. Made a list of all persons we had harmed, and became willing to make amends to them all.

9. Made direct amends to such people wherever possible, except when to do so would injure them or others.

10. Continued to take personal inventory and when we were wrong promptly admitted it.

11. Sought through prayer and meditation to improve our conscious contact with God *as we understood Him,* praying only for knowledge of His will for us and the power to carry that out.

12. Having had a spiritual awakening as a result of these steps, we tried to carry this message to alcoholics, and to practice these principles in all our affairs.

[Cited in *Alcoholics Anonymous,* 59–60.]

24. Statistics obtained from the public information office of Alcoholics Anonymous World Services Incorporated: February 9, 1995.

25. On the growth of the recovery movement in America, see Wendy Kaminer, *I'm Dysfunctional, You're Dysfunctional: The Recovery Movement and Other Self-Help Fashions* (New York: Vintage Books, 1993).

26. Rieff, *The Triumph of the Therapeutic: Uses of Faith after Freud* (New York: Harper & Row, 1966), 24–25. Rieff also described attributes of the therapeutic in *Freud: The Mind of the Moralist,* 3rd edition (Chicago, 1979), 329–357. See also Christopher Lasch, *The Culture of Narcissism: American Life in an Age of Diminishing Expectations* (New York: Basic Books, 1978).

27. Rieff, *Triumph of the Therapeutic,* 251.

28. On Protestant liberal reactions to modern science, see William R. Hutchison, *The Modernist Impulse in American Protestantism* (Cambridge: Havard University Press, 1976); see also his "Introduction" in *American*

Protestant Thought in the Liberal Era, ed. Hutchison (Lanham, MD: University Press of America, 1968), 1–16.

29. A. Z. Conrad, "Modern Psychology the Foe of Truth," *Moody Bible Institute Monthly,* November 1929, 116. Cited in David Harrington Watt, *A Transforming Faith: Explorations of Twentieth-Century American Evangelicalism* (New Brunswick, NJ: Rutgers University Press, 1991), 139. Chapter 7, "Modern Psychology," provides a helpful discussion of the relationship between evangelicalism and therapeutic culture.

30. Watt, *Transforming Faith,* 141.

31. For an evangelical assessment of these developments, see Tim Stafford, "The Therapeutic Revolution: How Christian Counseling is Changing the Church," *Christianity Today* 37, no. 6 (May 17, 1993): 24–32.

32. Watt, *Transforming Faith,* 139.

33. See, for instance, Charles L. Allen, *In Quest of God's Power* (Westwood, NJ: 1952), 83; cited in Watt, 144.

34. Watt, *Transforming Faith,* 145.

35. Meyer, *The Positive Thinkers: A Study of the American Quest for Health, Wealth and Personal Power from Mary Baker Eddy to Norman Vincent Peale* (New York: Doubleday, 1965); republished as *The Positive Thinkers: Religion as Pop Psychology from Mary Baker Eddy to Oral Roberts,* 2nd edition (New York: Pantheon Books, 1980).

36. Meyer, *Positive Thinkers,* 358.

37. E. Brooks Holifield, *A History of Pastoral Care in America: From Salvation to Self-Realization* (Nashville: Abingdon Press, 1983); T. J. Jackson Lears, "From Salvation to Self-Realization: Advertising and the Therapeutic Roots of the Consumer Culture, 1880–1930," in *The Culture of Consumption: Critical Essays in American History, 1880–1980,* ed. Richard Wightman Fox and T. J. Jackson Lears (New York: Pantheon Books, 1983), 1–38. Both Holifield and Lears see a shift from Victorian Protestant preoccupations with morality and restraint in hopes of receiving an abundant afterlife to later emphases on pleasure, self-fulfillment, and general well-being in this life.

38. Lears, "From Salvation to Self-Realization," esp. 16–17; see also Lears, *No Place of Grace: Antimodernism and the Transformation of American Culture, 1880–1920* (New York: Pantheon Books, 1981).

39. Wuthnow, *Sharing the Journey,* 3–4. See also the companion volume to this study, *"I Come Away Stronger": How Small Groups Are Shaping American Religion,* ed. Robert Wuthnow (Grand Rapids, MI: Eerdmans, 1994).

40. Wuthnow, *Sharing the Journey,* 45, 65, 52; *"I Come Away Stronger,"* 344–349. While Wuthnow's definition of "small groups" is rather broad, including virtually any group (of approximately twenty-five members) that "meets regularly and provides caring and support for those who participate in it," he documents a real rise in religious and therapeutic groups (*Sharing the Journey,* 45).

41. Kaminer, *I'm Dysfunctional, You're Dysfunctional,* 27.

42. See McGuire, *Ritual Healing in Suburban America.* McGuire, following Arthur Kleinman, distinguishes *disease* ("a biological disorder") from *illness* ("the way the ill person experiences his or her disease, in a given social and

cultural context") and notes that "alternative" healing systems generally address illness more than disease (6). See also Kleinman, "The Failure of Western Medicine," *Human Nature* 1 (1978): 63–88, and *The Illness Narratives: Suffering, Healing, and the Human Condition* (New York: Basic Books, 1988); and Robert A. Orsi, *Thank You, St. Jude: Women's Devotion to the Patron Saint of Hopeless Causes* (New Haven: Yale University Press, 1996), 150–173.

43. In 1992, the last year when gender ratios were estimated, Alcoholics Anonymous' total membership was 35 percent female and 65 percent male. For participants under the age of thirty, however, the ratios were 43 percent female to 57 percent male. (Statistics obtained from AA World Services in New York, February 1995.)

44. See Kaminer, *I'm Dysfunctional*, 73. Kaminer particularly emphasizes codependency's construction as a "feminine disease," noting that most books on it are written for women; she cites one publisher's claim that the codependency market is 85 percent female (*I'm Dysfunctional*, 14–15). A feminist analysis of women who read these self-help books is Wendy Simonds, *Women and Self-Help Culture: Reading between the Lines* (New Brunswick, NJ: Rutgers University Press, 1992).

45. Wuthnow, *Sharing the Journey*, 47.

46. Unpublished essay received during a personal interview with the author, September 1993.

47. *Aglow's Connection* 12, no. 1 (Winter 1995):3. Newbrough, with Carol Greenwood, *Support Group Leaders' Guide* (Lynnwood, WA: Women's Aglow Fellowship, 1993).

48. February 1993.

49. Lears notes that while descriptions of neurasthenia were varied, "they were united by their emphases on the neurasthenic's paralysis of will, his sense that he was no longer able to plunge into 'the vital currents of life,' his feeling that life had become somehow unreal" ("From Salvation to Self-Realization," 7).

50. George Beard, *American Nervousness* (New York: G. P. Putnam's Sons, 1881), 5, 10; quoted in Meyer, *The Positive Thinkers*, 23, 24. See also Elaine Showalter, *The Female Malady: Women, Madness, and English Culture, 1830–1980* (New York: Pantheon Books, 1985), esp. 121–164; and Gail Bederman, *Manliness and Civilization: A Cultural History of Gender and Race in the United States, 1880–1917* (Chicago: University of Chicago Press, 1995), 84–88 and 124–134.

51. Havelock Ellis, *The Psychology of Sex: A Manual for Students* (New York, 1960); cited in Mary P. Ryan, *Womanhood in America from Colonial Times to the Present*, 2nd. ed. (New York: New Viewpoints, 1979), 158–59.

52. In Nathan G. Hale, *Freud and the Americans* (New York, 1971), 338; cited in Ryan, *Womanhood in America*, 159.

53. Ryan, *Womanhood in America*, 159.

54. H. W. Frink, *Morbid Fears and Compulsions* (New York, 1918), 136; quoted in Ryan, *Womanhood in America*, 163–164.

55. Studies authored or coauthored by women include Marie Robinson, *The Power of Sexual Surrender* (Garden City, NY: Doubleday, 1959); Helene Deutsch, *The Psychology of Women* (New York: Grune and Stratton, 1945);

and Ferdinand Lundberg and Marynia F. Farnham, M.D., *Modern Woman: The Lost Sex* (New York: Grosset and Dunlap, 1947); all are cited in Ryan, *Womanhood in America,* 168. On anxiety over women and labor during World War II, see William H. Chafe, *The Paradox of Change: American Women in the 20th Century* (New York: Oxford University Press, 1991), esp. 154–172.

56. Elaine Tyler May, *Homeward Bound: American Families in the Cold War Era* (New York: Basic Books, 1988), 89; Leila J. Rupp and Verta Taylor, *Survival in the Doldrums: The American Women's Rights Movement, 1945 to the 1960s* (New York: Oxford University Press, 1987), 14. See also Peter G. Filene, *Him/Her/Self: Sex Roles in Modern America,* 2nd ed. (Baltimore, MD: Johns Hopkins University Press, 1986 [1974]), 148–176.

57. Wylie, *Generation of Vipers* (New York: Farrar and Rinehart, 1942); Strecker, *Their Mothers' Sons: The Psychiatrist Examines an American Problem* (Philadelphia: Lippincott, 1946).

58. Arnold W. Green and Eleanor Melnick, "What Has Happened to the Feminist Movement?" in *Studies in Leadership,* ed. Alvin W. Gouldner (New York: Russell and Russell, 1950), 183; cited in Rupp and Taylor, *Survival in the Doldrums,* 19.

59. Lundberg and Farnham, *Modern Woman,* 11; 356.

60. "The Girls," *Life* 27 (Aug. 15, 1949), 39–40; "An Introduction by Mrs. Peter Marshall," *Life* 41 (Dec. 24, 1956), 2–3; cited in Rupp and Taylor, *Survival in the Doldrums,* 17.

61. Komarovsky with the collaboration of Jane H. Philips, *Blue-Collar Marriage* (New Haven: Yale University Press, 1987; first published by Random House in 1962), 331.

62. *Ibid.,* 26; 331–332.

63. *Ibid.,* 334; 335.

64. Betty Friedan, *The Feminine Mystique* (New York: Laurel, 1984; first published by Norton in 1963), 11.

65. *Ibid.,* 15.

66. *Ibid.,* 339.

67. Typical examples from this vast literature include Anita Bryant, *Mine Eyes Have Seen the Glory* (Old Tappan, NJ: Revell, 1970) and (with Bob Green) *Raising God's Children* (Old Tappan, NJ: Revell, 1977); Beverly LaHaye, *The Spirit-Controlled Woman* (Irvine, CA: Harvest House, 1976) and *I Am a Woman by God's Design* (Old Tappan, NJ: Revell, 1980); Marabel Morgan, *The Total Woman* (New York: Pocket Books, 1973) and *Total Joy* (Old Tappan, NJ: Revell, 1976); Lynn Thibodeau, ed., *The Happy Housewife* (St. Paul, MN: Carillon, 1977); Elisabeth Elliot, *Let Me Be a Woman* (Wheaton, IL: Tyndale, 1976); Roger Elwood, ed., *Christian Mothers Reveal Their Joys and Sorrows* (Cincinnati, OH: Standard, 1979); Sandie Chandler, *Lovingly Liberated: A Christian Woman's Response to the Liberation Movement* (Old Tappan, NJ: Revell, 1975); Marilee Horton, *Free to Stay at Home: A Woman's Alternative* (Waco, TX: Word, 1982); Pat Brooks, *Daughters of the King* (Carol Stream, IL: Creation House, 1975); Elaine Stedman, *A Woman's Worth* (Waco, TX: Word, 1975); and Shirley Boone, *One Woman's Liberation* (Carol Stream, IL: Creation House, 1972).

68. Mrs. Norman Vincent Peale, *The Adventure of Being a Wife* (Englewood Cliffs, NJ: Prentice-Hall, Inc., 1971); quote from book jacket.

69. See Elliot, *Let Me Be a Woman,* 142–147.

70. Jane Hansen, Women's Aglow Fellowship 1995 International conference, November 1995; interview with Hansen, 15 August 1996.

71. "How It All Began," *Aglow* 1, no. 1 (November 1969): 1. The description of Jesus as "Savior, Baptizer, Healer, and Deliverer" is the foundation of the "full gospel," a term with historical resonances that go back to early Pentecostalism.

72. "How It All Began," *Aglow* 1, no. 1 (November 1969): 8.

73. Ruth Gothenquist, unpublished essay about Aglow's founding, received during interview, September 1993; personal correspondence with Gothenquist, June 1994.

74. Gothenquist essay.

75. Interview with Fortune, September 1993.

76. Romans 12:11 (Amplified Version).

77. Interview, September 1993. See also "Reflections on Aglow's Twenty-year Ministry to Women around the World" (1987) and Pat King, "AGLOW" *Logos Journal* (May–June 1974), 34–35.

78. The 1983 change is explained in the opening editorial of the "new" *Aglow* magazine, no. 60 (September/October 1982), 2, 12.

79. The "doctrinal statement" followed the form of the Nicene Creed, adding points about the inerrancy of scripture and the spiritual gifts. The "purpose" focused on evangelism of the unsaved into the "full gospel" and including working for "spiritual unity among Christian believers," "foster[ing] fellowship among women," and "assist[ing] in activities approved, promoted, or sponsored" by full gospel churches. See *Aglow* (Summer/Fall 1970), 2.

80. "History Summary of Women's Aglow Fellowship," December 1992 (obtained from Aglow International archives).

81. Pat King, "AGLOW," 35.

82. Hansen is on the board of such large prayer organizations as Intercessors International, the Spiritual Warfare Network, and A.D. 2000. Hansen, a Pentecostal, may also have been the brunt of one former member's complaint that Aglow has been "taken over by the Pentecostals" in recent years. (Interview, September 1993).

83. Emendation first printed in *Aglow* 19, no. 4 (July/August 1988): 4. Wimber, "Power Healing—It's for Today," *Aglow* 19, no. 4, 6–7 and 16–17; Hayford, "Women in Ministry," *Aglow* 19, no. 5 (September/October 1988): 4–6 and 30–31; Christenson, "The Theology of the Cross," *Aglow* 22, no. 3 (March/April 1991): 6–8; Jepson, "Women of Influence," *Aglow* 20, no. 4 (July/August 1989): 7–8 and 13–14; Sherrill, "Helene's Story," *Aglow* 22, no. 3 (March/April 1991): 16–19; Sontag, "Can Christians Love Too Much?" *Aglow* 20, no. 4 (July/August 1989): 10–12; Miller, "The Art of Contentment," *Aglow* 21, no. 1 (January/February 1990): 6–8.

84. See *Aglow,* no. 60 (September/October 1982), 2; no. 70 (May/June 1984), 2; 18, no. 1 (January/February 1987), 4.

85. In one magazine article that same year the organization gave an obviously overblown estimate of its international membership, claiming to serve

"more than 500,000 women" at monthly meetings; see Quin Sherrer and Steve Galloway, "Jane Hansen: Waking Up from the American Dream," *Charisma & Christian Life* (November 1987): 19.

86. The address of the Web site is [http://www.aglow.org/].

87. Data received in interviews with Aglow administrators in Lynnwood, Washington, September 1993. The woman who gave me the statistic on current membership added spontaneously that this number was "just ten less than last year." In 1993 alone, she added, Aglow added fellowships in at least eleven countries that previously were without Aglow.

88. Information received from Aglow headquarters, August 1996. International fellowships at that time totaled more than 1,400 in 123 nations outside the United States.

89. 10–11 November 1994.

90. 12 November 1994.

91. *Aglow's Connection* 12, no. 1 (Winter 1995): 4.

92. These predominantly white Christian organizations have recently apologized for racism and articulated their commitment to eradicating its continuing legacy. See Gustav Niebuhr, "Baptist Group Votes to Repent Stand on Slaves," *New York Times,* 21 June 1995: A2; Marianne Kyriakos, "Racial Barriers Tumble Down at Gathering of Christian Men," *Washington Post,* 26 May 1996: BO2; Kevin Sack, "A Penitent Christian Coalition Offers Aid to Burned Churches," *New York Times,* 19 June 1996: A19: and Jason DeParle, "The Christian Right Confesses Sins of Racism," *New York Times,* 4 August 1996: E5.

93. For instance, Hansen was a featured speaker at a National Affairs Briefing in January of 1996, an event sponsored by The Roundtable and various religious forums and described as a "Who's Who" gathering of mainstream conservative Christian leadership in the United States. Hansen was apparently asked to "answer Beijing" (in reference to the 1995 International Conference on Women held there); according to Aglow's publication, *Connection,* her talk was entitled, "The Fatherheart of God and His Eternal Plan for Women" (13, no. 1 [March 1996], 2).

Chapter 2

1. February 1993.

2. As Catherine A. Lutz argues, an emotion concept is "an index of a world of cultural premises and of scenarios for social interaction; each is a system of meaning or cluster of ideas which include both verbal, accessible, reflective ideas and implicit practical ones" (Lutz, *Unnatural Emotions: Everyday Sentiments on a Micronesian Atoll and Their Challenge to Western Theory* [Chicago: University of Chicago Press, 1988], 210–11). The term "emotion rules" is from Arlie R. Hochschild, "Emotion Work, Feeling Rules, and Social Structure," *American Journal of Sociology* 85(1979): 551–575.

3. "Results of the 1992 'We Are Hearing You' Survey" (unpublished, obtained at Aglow headquarters), 11.

4. "My Spiritual Hunger Was Fulfilled in Him," *Aglow* no. 10 (Spring/Summer 1972): 20–21.

5. "A New Sisterhood," *Aglow* no. 2 (Spring 1970): 10.

6. "Loving an Old Friend," *Aglow* no. 70 (May/June 1984): 21.

7. 14 September 1993.

8. 8 October 1993. Additionally, charismatic (and evangelical) churches have increasingly promoted the growth of small groups within their congregations, a strategy recommended by church growth experts. California's Calvary Chapel has numerous such groups, many of them apparently similar to Aglow groups—the Women's Intercessory Prayer Group, Women's Joyful Life Bible Study, and the Women's Prayer Meeting, for instance. However, I have not investigated the impact of these groups upon Aglow's membership. (Randall Balmer and Jesse T. Todd, Jr., "Calvary Chapel, Costa Mesa, California," in *American Congregations.* Vol. I, *Portraits of Twelve Religious Communities,* ed. James P. Wind and James W. Lewis [Chicago: University of Chicago Press, 1994]: 663–698.)

9. 26 February 1994.

10. "Letters," *Aglow* 19, no. 6 (November/December 1988): 15–16. Original story: "The Summer We Were Almost Too Busy for Catalina," *Aglow* 19, no. 4 (July/August 1988): 8–10.

11. Sociologist Meredith McGuire's finding that the "key analytical concept" relevant for understanding the Catholic Pentecostal movement is "power" holds true more broadly for such charismatic women as Aglow members. McGuire describes the dynamics of power in four primary qualities of the movement: "(1) a belief that the power of God is given directly to ordinary humans (through the 'gifts of the Holy Spirit'), (2) that, as a result, members have the power to see the relevance of religion in their everyday lives, and prayer groups experience a power which serves as the basis for meaning and moral norms, (3) this power has a strong experiential component, and (4) all these beliefs and experiences compel members to seek out a community of fellow believers—a community which both produces and is the product of power" (*Pentecostal Catholics,* 7–8).

12. See 1 Cor. 12:8–10.

13. Classical Pentecostals differ from charismatic Christians in their understandings of tongues. For Pentecostals, glossolalia is always of divine origin and, in order to be considered valid, must be accompanied by interpretation. The notion of glossolalia as a private "prayer language" emerged from the charismatic renewal movement of the 1960s.

14. Goodboy, *God's Daughter: A Study of Practical Christian Living for Women.* Aglow Bible Study No. 2 (Edmonds, WA: Aglow Publications, 1974), 49.

15. Charles Lloyd Cohen, *God's Caress: The Psychology of Puritan Religious Experience* (New York: Oxford University Press, 1986), 239–40.

16. From *Turning Point,* 4th ed. (Lynnwood, WA: Aglow Publications, 1991), 30.

17. "He Restoreth My Soul," *Aglow* 15 (Winter 1974): 21.

18. "A Gift From God," *Aglow* no. 69B (March/April 1984): 18.

19. The first codified doctrinal statement was printed in *Aglow* magazine in the Summer/Fall 1970 issue (p. 2) as:

1. We believe in one God, maker of all things and being in trinity of Father, Son and Holy Spirit.

2. We believe that the Son of God, Jesus Christ, became incarnate, was begotten by the Holy Spirit, born of the Virgin Mary and is true God and true man.

3. We believe the Bible in its entirety to be the inspired Word of God and the only infallible rule of faith and conduct.

4. We believe in the resurrection of the dead, the eternal happiness of the saved and the eternal punishment of the lost.

5. We believe in personal salvation of believers through the shed blood of Christ.

6. We believe in sanctification by the blood of Christ, in personal holiness of heart and life, and in separation from the world.

7. We believe in divine healing, through faith in the name of Jesus Christ, and that healing is included in the atonement.

8. We believe in the baptism in the Holy Spirit, accompanied by the initial physical sign of speaking with other tongues as the Spirit of God gives utterance, as distinct from the new birth; and we believe in the nine gifts of the Spirit as available to believers.

9. We believe in the Christian's hope—the soon-coming, personal return of the Lord Jesus Christ.

10. We believe in evangelization and missionary work in accordance with the Christian commission.

20. See, for instance, brochure advertising Women's Aglow membership for 1993, "Weaving a Ribbon of Hope."

21. See masthead in *Aglow* 22, no. 3 (March/April 1991): 4.

22. For a critique of this shift from an insider's perspective, see David F. Wells, *No Place For Truth, or Whatever Happened to Evangelical Theology?* (Grand Rapids, MI: Eerdmans, 1993). A contrasting view is Richard J. Mouw, *Consulting the Faithful: What Christian Intellectuals Can Learn from Popular Religion* (Grand Rapids, MI: Eerdmans, 1994).

23. This apocalyptic emphasis extends beyond contemporary charismatic movements into neoevangelical and fundamentalist groups as well, captured in such bestselling eschatological accounts as Hal Lindsay, *The Late Great Planet Earth* (Grand Rapids, MI: Zondervan, 1970); and Tim LaHaye, *The Beginning of the End* (Wheaton, IL: Tyndale House, 1972). A solid study of modern apocalypticism is Paul Boyer, *When Time Shall Be No More: Prophecy Belief in Modern American Culture* (Cambridge, MA: Harvard University Press, 1992); see also Charles B. Strozier, *Apocalypse: On the Psychology of Fundamentalism in America* (Boston: Beacon Press, 1994).

24. Balmer and Todd, "Calvary Chapel." By "soft Pentecostalism," Balmer and Todd refer both to Calvary Chapel's "accommodation to mainstream, middle-class sensibilities" and the de-emphasis on public manifestations of glossolalia.

25. Marsha G. Witten, *All Is Forgiven: The Secular Message in American Protestantism* (Princeton, NJ: Princeton University Press, 1993), 53.

26. Russell P. Spittler, "Are Pentecostals and Charismatics Fundamentalists?: A Review of American Uses of These Categories," in *Charismatic Christianity*

as a Global Culture, ed. Karla Poewe (Columbia, SC: University of South Carolina Press, 1994), 113–114.

27. See "Just To Be Free," *Aglow* no. 36 (September/October 1978): 27–28.

28. For injunctions to pray in these mundane spaces, see "Pray As You Go," *Aglow* no. 30 (Summer 1977): 22–24; "When You Pray," *Aglow* no. 41 (July/August 1979): 14; "Failure Doesn't Need to Be a Dead End," *Aglow* no. 33 (March/April 1978): 9; "Amazing Grace," *Aglow* no. 4 (Winter 1970): 12.

29. Durkheim, *The Elementary Forms of the Religious Life* (New York: Free Press, 1967; George Allen and Unwin Ltd., 1915).

30. Smith, *To Take Place: Toward Theory in Ritual* (Chicago: University of Chicago Press, 1987).

31. See Gaston Bachelard, *The Poetics of Space,* trans. Maria Jolas (Boston: Beacon Press, 1964 [1958]).

32. For a historical analysis of the ways in which Protestant worship spaces were transformed by the model of the theatre in the late nineteenth century, see Jeanne Halgren Kilde, "Spiritual Armories: A Social and Architectural History of Neo-Medieval Auditorium Churches in the U.S., 1869–1910" (Ph.D. thesis: University of Minnesota, 1991).

33. Financial estimates available from the Christian Booksellers Association, Colorado Springs, Colorado; cited in Colleen McDannell, *Material Christianity: Religion and Popular Culture in America* (New Haven: Yale University Press, 1995), 222. See also R. Laurence Moore's treatment of this theme in *Selling God: American Religion in the Marketplace of Culture* (New York: Oxford University Press, 1993). On the commercial appropriation of religious holidays in America, see Leigh Eric Schmidt, *Consumer Rites: The Buying and Selling of American Holidays* (Princeton, NJ: Princeton University Press, 1995).

34. McDannell, "Creating the Christian Home: Home Schooling in Contemporary America," in *American Sacred Space,* ed. David Chidester and Edward T. Linenthal (Bloomington: Indiana University Press, 1995), 187–219. See also McDannell, *The Christian Home in Victorian America, 1840–1900* (Bloomington: Indiana University Press, 1986).

35. Goodboy, *God's Daughter,* 27. The quoted passage is from a chapter entitled, "God's Daughter: Ministering Hospitality." This study underwent its fourteenth printing in 1991. The theme of hospitality as ministry is evident in the wider evangelical culture as well; see, for instance, Karen Burton Mains, *Open Heart, Open Home: How to Find Joy through Sharing Your Home with Others* (Elgin, IL: David C. Cook Publishing Co., 1976).

36. 19 May 1993; 21 April 1993.

37. 26 April 1993.

38. Meredith McGuire notes that testimony is "a fundamental—if not *the* fundamental—aspect of the induction process" into charismatic prayer meetings and notes their centrality as "a commitment and resocialization mechanism" (*Pentecostal Catholics,* 64).

39. I am grateful to Robert Orsi for this insight (personal correspondence, July 1995).

40. Catherine Bell, *Ritual Theory, Ritual Practice,* (New York: Oxford University Press, 1992), esp. 197–223. Using Foucault's analytics of power, Bell

argues that ritualization both recreates hegemonic structures and opens up spaces for creative resistance. "It is in ritual—as practices that act upon the actions of others, as the mute interplay of complex strategies within a field structured by engagements of power, as the arena for prescribed sequences of repetitive movements of the body that simultaneously constitute the body, the person, and the macro- and micronetworks of power—that we can see a fundamental strategy of power. In ritualization, power is not external to its workings; it exists only insofar as it is constituted with and through the lived body, which is both the body of society and the social body. Ritualization is a strategic play of power, of domination and resistance, within the arena of the social body" (204).

41. Carol J. Greenhouse, *Praying for Justice: Faith, Order, and Community in an American Town* (Ithaca: Cornell University Press, 1986), 87. Another interesting analysis of prayer—in the form of vernacular religious songs performed in medieval Italian confraternities—is Jennifer Fisk Rondeau, "Prayer and Gender in the *Laude* of Early Italian Confraternities," in Richard C. Trexler, ed., *Gender Rhetorics: Postures of Dominance and Submission in History* (Binghamton: State University of New York, 1994): 219–233.

42. Greenhouse, *Praying for Justice*, 90.

43. 27 February 1993.

Chapter 3

1. "Into Light and Life," *Aglow* no. 30 (Summer 1977): 18–20.

2. 21 April 1993.

3. McGuire, *Ritual Healing in Suburban America*. I am following McGuire's definition of "alternative healing" as referring to "a wide range of beliefs and practices that adherents expect to affect health but that are not promulgated by medical personnel in the dominant biomedical system" (3). Examples cited by McGuire include "naturopathy, faith healing, Christian Science, psychic healing, Transcendental Meditation (TM) and other meditational systems, occult and New Age therapies, human potential therapeutic methods (such as Arica, est, and psychosynthesis), reflexology, iridology, and Native American healing methods" (4).

4. "My God's Not Dead," *Aglow* no. 10 (Spring/Summer 1972): 23.

5. "With Healing in His Wings," *Aglow* no. 37 (November/December 1978): 22–24.

6. "God Wrapped Me in His Love," *Aglow* no. 54 (September/October 1981): 18, 26.

7. "The Lord Has a Sense of Humor," *Aglow* no. 29 (Spring 1977): 12.

8. "Conformed to His Image" *Aglow* no. 42 (September/October 1979): 5–9.

9. "Into Light and Life," 19.

10. "God Used My Deformity to Demonstrate His Divinity," *Aglow* no. 50 (January/February 1981): 23.

11. The note read, "This is to certify that I substantiate the account of Mrs. Diane — — —, in relation to the accident her daughter had on June 30, 1982.

Truly, God, through His Holy Spirit gave us peace and confidence that He worked out all things for His glory" ("Emergency," *Aglow* no. 65 [July/August 1983]: 7). Other stories include these: a woman so sick she could no longer walk was healed at an Oral Roberts meeting; as she tells it, she told her doctor and "tears came to his eyes" as he marveled, "You're a miracle" ("Arise and Walk," *Aglow* no. 18 [Summer 1974]: 10). Another woman, whose son's freak soccer accident left doctors predicting he'd be a cripple, recalls one physician's astonishment when Tony was healed: "Well, I'll be. . . . A year ago, I wouldn't have given a plugged nickel for his chances. But, look at him now!" ("The Mountain Climber," *Aglow* no. 52 [May/June 1981]: 24).

12. "Into His Arms," *Aglow* no. 38 (January/February 1979): 10.

13. "Child of Joy and Pain," *Aglow* no. 54 (September/October 1981): 2–6.

14. 21 April 1993.

15. "God Unveiled the Game Plan," *Aglow* no. 48 (September/October 1980), 16.

16. "Into His Arms," 9.

17. "Remember Me When You Laugh," *Aglow* no. 74 (January/February 1985): 3–5.

18. An editorial note beneath this story tells that Joyce died ("went to be with the Lord") four months before publication.

19. "Tiny Corners of the Kingdom," *Aglow* 20, no. 4 (July/August 1989): 37.

20. See, for example, "Cry for the Lonely," *Aglow* 18, no. 1 (January/February 1987): 17.

21. "Face to Face," *Aglow* no. 71 (July/August 1984): 15.

22. "I Failed . . . But God Didn't," *Aglow* no. 48 (September/October 1980): 23–24.

23. "Fools on Assignment," *Aglow* no. 74 (January/February 1985): 21–23.

24. "Fools on Assignment," 23; "Remember Me When You Laugh," 5.

25. "Jesus Healed Me," *Aglow* no. 33 (March/April 1978), 14 [italics in the original].

26. "No Love in My Life," *Aglow* no. 41 (July/August 1979): 9–13.

27. "Get Me Out of Here!" *Aglow* no. 37 (November/December 1978): 9–10.

28. "Forgiveness: As Natural as Breathing," *Aglow* no. 29 (Spring 1977): 2–5.

29. JoAnne Sekowsky, *Praise the Lord, I'm under Construction* (Lynnwood, WA: Aglow Women's Fellowship, 1978): 34.

30. Miller, *Healing the Angry Heart: A Strategy for Confident Mothering* (Lynnwood: Aglow, 1984) chap. 1 passim.

31. "Out of Control," *Aglow* no. 76 (May/June 1985): 6.

32. "Tiny Corners of the Kingdom," *Aglow* 20, no. 4 (July/August 1989): 35.

33. 12 November 1994.

34. Frank and Ida Mae Hammond, Pentecostal practitioners of spirit deliverance, compiled a demonological chart listing fifty-three "root or master spirits" and scores of other "subordinate spirits"; these are analogous to the spirits described by the charismatic women in my study. See Hammond and Hammond, *Pigs in the Parlor: A Practical Guide to Deliverance* (Kirkwood,

MO: Impact Books, 1973), 113–115; reprinted in Thomas J. Csordas, *The Sacred Self: A Cultural Phenomenology of Charismatic Healing* (Berkeley: University of California Press, 1994), 182–184.

35. 27 February 1993.

36. 10 May 1993.

37. "A Family at Last," *Aglow* no. 32 (Winter 1978): 12.

38. "Failure . . . ," *Aglow* no. 33 (March/April 1978): 9.

39. "I Choose to Forgive," *Aglow* no. 29 (Spring 1977): 11.

40. "The Song That Changed: A Story of Forgiveness," *Aglow* no. 76 (May/June 1985): 19.

41. "I Choose to Forgive," 10.

42. Dorothea DeGrandis Sudol, *I Am a Woman; I Am Catholic; I Am Charismatic; I Am Divorced; What Next?* (nd, np), 52. Rita Bennett, *Making Peace with Your Inner Child* (Old Tappan, NJ: Revell, 1987).

43. See Kaminer, *I'm Dysfunctional, You're Dysfunctional*, 119–150; Watt, *Transforming Faith*, 137–154.

44. On this theme, see Csordas, *The Sacred Self*, 18.

45. "Behold, I'll Show You a Mystery," *Aglow* no. 6 (Spring 1971): 6.

46. "Delivered from Fear," *Aglow* no. 47 (July/August 1980): 6.

47. "Pieces of the Puzzle," *Aglow* no. 11 (Fall 1972): 27.

48. Anne Ortlund, *Disciplines of the Beautiful Woman* (Waco, TX: Word Books, 1977), 44.

49. "Creative Outreaches Draw Thousands in Need," *Aglow's Connection* 10, no. 2 (Summer/Fall 1993): 1, 3.

50. Ortlund, *Disciplines*, 82.

51. "A Family at Last," 11–12.

52. "Delivered from Fear," 6.

53. "Free Indeed!," *Aglow* no. 46 (May/June 1980): 26.

54. "Twice Healed by a Miracle of Love," *Aglow* 19, no. 5 (September/October 1988): 27.

55. "Happiness Is Jesus!" *Aglow* no. 13 (Spring 1973): 25.

56. "The Supposed Impostor Became My Messiah," *Aglow* no. 11 (Fall 1972): 18.

57. Sandra D. Wilson, "Evangelical Christian Adult Children of Alcoholics: A Preliminary Study," *Journal of Psychology and Theology* 17, no. 3 (Fall 1989): 271; Lawrence J. Crabb, *Understanding People* (Grand Rapids, MI: Zondervan, 1987), 69.

58. 27 February 1993.

Chapter 4

1. "What Do You Do When Your Husband Says . . . I Don't Love You Any More," *Aglow* no. 29 (Spring 1977): 27–30.

2. The theme of the "hiddenness" of pain and women's silence as a means of coping with that pain in a male-dominated society has been widely analyzed by feminists. See, for instance, Robin Morgan, "The Politics of Silence," in *The Word*

of a Woman: Feminist Dispatches 1968–1991 (New York: Norton, 1992); Tillie Olsen, *Silences* (New York: Delacorte, 1978); Deborah Tannen and Muriel Saville-Troike, eds., *Perspectives on Silence* (Norwood, NJ: Ablex, 1990); Adrienne Rich, *On Lies, Secrets, and Silence: Selected Prose 1966–1978* (New York: Norton, 1979); and Harriet G. Lerner, *The Dance of Deception: Pretending and Truth-Telling in Women's Lives* (New York: HarperCollins, 1993).

3. Newbrough, *Support Group Leader's Guide,* 26–27, 101.

4. "Fran Lance: Minister to the Sexually Abused," *Aglow* 19, no. 5 (September/October 1988): 22.

5. February 1993.

6. "Fran Lance," 20–22, 29.

7. See Lerner, *Dance of Deception,* 62. Lerner cites psychiatrist Judith Lewis Herman: "In the protected environment of the consulting room, women had dared to speak of rape, but the learned men of science had not believed them. In the protected environment of consciousness-raising groups, women spoke of rape and other women believed them" (Herman, *Trauma and Recovery* [New York: Basic Books, 1992], 29).

8. Miller, *Healing the Angry Heart,* 32; 46.

9. "What Do You Do," 27; 28.

10. 12 November 1994.

11. Accounts of Luchsinger's story were printed in several newspapers and magazines, beginning with *USA Weekend,* 27–29 October 1995, 8.

12. A fascinating account of the intertwining of piety and wife abuse is Ann Taves, ed., *Religion and Domestic Violence in Early New England: The Memoirs of Abigail Abbot Bailey* (Bloomington: Indiana University Press, 1989). In her introduction Taves notes the role of religion in facilitating Abigail's eventual separation from her husband but also observes the ways in which it had long kept her dependent on him (see esp. 24–35).

13. "Miracle of Love," *Aglow* no. 23 (Fall 1975): 3–9.

14. "Make Jesus the Lord of Your Day," *Aglow* no. 22 (Summer 1975): 24–26.

15. May, *Homeward Bound,* 199; 197. See Komarovsky, *Blue-Collar Marriage.* A useful psychological analysis of women's depression is Dana Crowley Jack, *Silencing the Self: Women and Depression* (Cambridge: Harvard University Press, 1991).

16. "Too Busy," *Aglow* no. 26 (Summer 1976): 25.

17. "Discipline and the Power of Prayer," *Aglow* no. 70 (May/June 1984): 13.

18. "Out of Control," 3–6.

19. "How I Came to Love My Son," *Aglow* no. 27 (Fall 1976): 21.

20. "The Battle for Love," *Aglow* no. 34 (May/June 1978): 8.

21. 8 June 1993.

22. "By His Spirit," *Aglow* no. 2 (Spring 1970): 3.

23. 10 November 1994.

24. "Although I Had Gone My Own Way God Gave Me a Second Chance," *Aglow* no. 11 (Fall 1972): 10–11.

25. Nineteenth-century Protestant anxieties over sincerity have been analyzed in Karen Halttunen, *Confidence Men and Painted Women: A Study of*

Middle-Class Culture in America, 1830–1870 (New Haven: Yale University Press, 1982). See also Lionel Trilling, *Sincerity and Authenticity* (London: Oxford University Press, 1972); and Arlie Russell Hochschild, *The Managed Heart: Commercialization of Human Feeling* (Berkeley: University of California Press, 1983).

26. S. R. R., "Female Charms," *Godey's Lady's Book* 33 (1846), quoted in Halttunen, *Confidence Men,* 57; Leigh Eric Schmidt, *Holy Fairs: Scottish Communions and American Revivals in the Early Modern Period* (Princeton, NJ: Princeton University Press, 1989), 79.

27. Lerner, *Dance of Deception,* 151.

28. "God Stripped My Masks Away," *Aglow* no. 44 (January/February 1980): 24–28.

29. Ranelda Mack Hunsicker, *Secrets: Unlocking the Mystery of Intimacy with God* (Lynnwood, WA: Aglow Publications, 1991), 66.

30. Marilyn Mason, *Intimacy* (Center City, MN: Hazelden Foundation, 1986), 16–17.

31. "There Must Be an Answer Somewhere," *Aglow* no. 24 (Winter 1976): 12–15. Another article about women healed from lesbianism is "We Can't Hold God's Love Captive: South Carolina Prisoners Respond to Ministry," *Aglow* no. 63 (March/April 1983): 14–15.

32. "God Stripped My Masks Away," 25.

33. "He Restoreth My Soul," *Aglow* no. 15 (Winter 1974): 21.

34. Quin Sherrer, *How to Pray for Your Children* (Lynnwood, WA: Aglow Publications, 1986), 38, 39.

35. Or, as described in Chapter 1, Aglow leaders may urge listeners to stay home from church and "lie in bed" with their husbands on occasional Sunday mornings, making sure the latter feel cared for and loved (February 1994).

36. "A Full Life & Empty Heart," *Aglow* no. 6 (Spring 1971): 21.

37. "Happiness is Jesus!" *Aglow* no. 13 (Spring 1973): 25.

38. "Jesus Saves, Fills, Heals & Delivers," *Aglow* no. 2 (Spring 1970): 11.

39. Marie Sontag, *When Love Is Not Perfect: Discover God's Re-Parenting Process* (Lynnwood, WA: Aglow Publications, 1991), 78.

40. See, for instance, Newbrough, *Support Group Leader's Guide,* 36.

41. November 1994.

42. "My Wonderful Father," *Aglow* no. 27 (Fall 1976): 17.

43. Heather Harpham, *Daddy, Where Were You?: Healing for the Father-Deprived Daughter* (Lynnwood, WA: Aglow Publications, 1991), 139; 144.

44. Isaiah 54:5, NIV.

45. "A Christian Road Map for Women Traveling Alone," *Aglow* no. 20 (Winter 1975): 8; 9.

46. "'I Shall Not Fear'," *Aglow* no. 31 (Fall 1977): 16.

47. "Testimony: A Story of God's Care," *Aglow* no. 33 (March/April 1978): 23.

48. Sociologist Susan D. Rose also observed notions of God as husband among the charismatic women in her study. She quotes one divorced mother as saying, "Christ serves all my needs. He is my bridegroom—literally. If it's God's will and the right man comes along, I would like to get married again. If that happens, then Christ will step aside and that man can fulfill the role of bridegroom. But until that

time, I am content." See Rose, "Women Warriors: The Negotiation of Gender in a Charismatic Community," *Sociological Analysis* 48, no. 3 (1987), 252.

49. Stapleton, *The Gift of Inner Healing* (Waco, TX: Word Books, 1976), 32; 33–34.

50. Janice A. Radway, *Reading the Romance: Women, Patriarchy, and Popular Literature* (Chapel Hill: University of North Carolina Press, 1991), 81; "A Christian Road Map," 10. I am aware, from conversations with Aglow leaders, that evangelical and charismatic women may resent this comparison. In making it, I do not in any way mean to sound condescending or scornful but only to point out these analogous male images.

51. Hunsicker, *Secrets,* 69.

52. Hunsicker, *Secrets,* 107; 120.

53. "From Applesauce to Peace of Heart," *Aglow* no. 25 (Spring 1976): 26–28.

54. "My Friend and I," *Aglow* no. 26 (Summer 1976): 11.

55. February 1993.

56. "'Arise and Walk,'" *Aglow* no. 18 (Summer 1974): 9.

57. "Adventure Unlimited," *Aglow* no. 16 (Winter 1974): 11.

58. "Where Two or Three," *Aglow* no. 7 (Summer 1971): 12–13.

59. Gendered speech patterns are analyzed in Carol Gilligan, *In a Different Voice: Psychological Theory and Women's Development* (Cambridge: Harvard University Press, 1982); and Deborah Tannen, *You Just Don't Understand: Women and Men in Conversation* (New York: Ballantine Books, 1990).

60. "When Poppy Blooms," *Aglow* no. 19 (Fall 1974): 20–21.

61. "The Best Beauty Shop in Town," *Aglow* no. 18 (Summer 1974): 3. See also "Even Little Things," *Aglow* no. 30 (Summer 1977): 17.

62. For a more thorough examination of Bible reading in a charismatic prayer group, see Daniele Hervieu-Léger, "'What Scripture Tells Me': Spontaneity and Regulation within the Catholic Charismatic Renewal," in *Lived Religion in America: Toward a History of Practice,* ed. David D. Hall (Princeton, NJ: Princeton University Press, in press).

63. "Lost: One Bible," *Aglow* no. 31 (Fall 1977): 8–9.

64. Bobbye Byerly, "How to Receive a Burden from God," in *Women of Prayer Released to the Nations* (Lynnwood: WA: Aglow Publications, 1993), 29. See also *Knowing the Heart of God* (Lynnwood, WA: Aglow Publications, 1994); Newbrough, *Support Group Leader's Guide,* 16–18.

65. "The Gift," *Aglow* no. 34 (May/June 1978): 9–10.

66. "A Grateful Heart," *Aglow* no. 73 (November/December 1984): 10–11.

Chapter 5

1. "Slim Down, Sweetie," *Aglow* no. 18 (Summer 1974): 13–15.

2. "Meetings," *Indianapolis Star,* 10 April 1995: B05.

3. "Dieting with Jesus," *Aglow* no. 23 (Fall 1975): 27.

4. "Diet-Free in Jesus," *Aglow* no. 12 (Winter 1972–73): 29–31.

5. "Two Dishes of Ice Cream," *Aglow* no. 30 (Summer 1977): 28.

6. Agnes Lawless and Ann Thomas, eds., *Aglow in the Kitchen: A Collection of Nutritious Recipes, Creative Homemaking Hints, and Inspiration* (Lynnwood, WA: Aglow Publications, 1976), 125.

7. Ann Thomas, *God's Answer to Overeating: A Study of Scriptural Attitudes,* Aglow Bible Study no. 7 (Edmonds, WA: Aglow Publications, 1975), 5, 46. By 1981 this booklet had gone through its seventh printing.

8. "Diet-Free in Jesus," 29.

9. Lawless and Thomas, *Aglow in the Kitchen,* 129.

10. Patricia B. Kreml, *Slim for Him* (Plainfield, NJ: Logos International, 1978), back cover.

11. *Ibid.,* Introduction (ix).

12. *Ibid.,* 9.

13. *Ibid.,* 41.

14. "Dieting with Jesus," 27.

15. Kreml, *Slim for Him,* 41.

16. *Ibid.,* 126.

17. "Nuggets from the Word," *Aglow* no. 38 (January/February 1979): 15. See also "I Am a Princess," *Aglow* no. 37 (November/December 1978): 21; and "Lasting Inner Beauty," *Aglow* no. 15 (Winter 1973): 4.

18. Gwen Mouliert, *Hyper to Holy: How Jesus Touched the Life of a Housewife* (Columbus, GA: Brentwood Christian Press, 1990), 9; 10–11; 89.

19. Kreml, *Slim for Him,* 4.

20. "Open Forum," *Bookstore Journal* (August 1991): 10. Cited in McDannell, *Material Christianity,* 260.

21. On middle-aged women as the primary consumers of Christian merchandise, see Thomas W. Gruen et al., *1992 CBA Christian Bookstore Customer Profile Expanded Statistics* (Colorado Springs: Christian Booksellers Association Center for Research and Information, 1991); cited in McDannell, *Material Christianity,* 256. This survey found that three quarters of these customers were between the ages of twenty-five and fifty-four and were female; 90 percent were white and only 4 percent African-American. Roughly equivalent numbers of female shoppers were homemakers (23 percent) and white-collar working women (21 percent).

22. Marie Chapian and Neva Coyle, *Free to Be Thin* (Minneapolis: Bethany House Publishers, 1979); Neva Coyle and Marie Chapian, *There's More to Being Thin than Being Thin* (Minneapolis: Bethany House, 1984); Evelyn McDaniels, *Loving More, Eating Less* (Laramie, WY: Jelm Mountain Press, 1988); Joan Cavanaugh, with Pat Forseth, *More of Jesus, Less of Me* (Plainfield, NJ: Logos International, 1976); Karen Wise, *God Knows I Won't Be Fat Again* (Nashville, TN: Thomas Nelson, 1978). Titles of books authored solely by men tend to have less to do with love and more to do with health, such as: Salem Kirban, *How to Eat Your Way Back to Vibrant Health* (Irvine, CA: Harvest House, 1977); Charlie W. Shedd, *The FAT is in Your Head* (Waco, TX: Word Books, 1972); and Nathan M. Ware, *The B.I.B.L.E. Diet: Believing In Becoming Lighter Eaters* (Madison, IN: Mark Art Productions, 1990).

23. Shirley Cook, *Diary of a FAT Housewife* (Denver, CO: Acent Books, 1977).

24. Carol Showalter, *3D* (Orleans, MA: Rock Harbor Press), 1977), 119–120.

25. Chapian and Coyle, *Free to be Thin,* 14, 16, 17–18.

26. Coye and Chapian, *There's More to Being Thin,* 28; Coyle and Chapian, *The All-New Free to Be Thin* (Minneapolis: Bethany House, 1993), 12. The biblical passage mentioned reads, "By contrast, the fruit of the Spirit is love, joy, peace, patience, kindness, generosity, faithfulness, gentleness, and self-control" (Galatians 5:22–23, NRSV).

27. *The All-New Free to Be Thin,* 25–26.

28. *The All-New Free to Be Thin,* 17.

29. Omartian, *Better Body Management* (Nashville: Sparrow Press, 1993), 9; Omartian, *Greater Health God's Way: Seven Steps to Health, Youthfulness, and Vitality* (Chatsworth, CA: Sparrow Press, 1984), 19.

30. Rita Bennett, Dennis's widow, told me in an interview that the idea of Aglow having male advisors was originally her husband's. Other early leaders claim that the Aglow women themselves came up with this idea, after praying for guidance for their budding organization (September 1993).

31. See, for instance, *Connection* (U.S. edition) (May 1996): 2. The two women on the international board, both long active as Aglow leaders and speakers, were Marfa Cabrera and Cindy Jacobs.

32. *U.S. Area Handbook* (Lynnwood, WA: Women's Aglow Fellowship, Intl., 1987), 7–9.

33. *Constitution and Bylaws,* Article VIII, Section 1 (September 1995), 7.

34. Goodboy, *God's Daughter,* 47–48.

35. Personal interview, September 1993.

36. Julia McCord, "Fellowship Burns Bright: An Overview," *Omaha World Herald,* 13 May 1995: 59.

37. Conversations with Gary Clark, March 1994, and Mark Pearson, May 1993.

38. Telephone interview, 16 September 1993.

39. Telephone interview, 16 September 1993.

40. Personal interviews, March 1993.

41. Telephone interview, February 1995.

42. Interview at Aglow headquarters, September 1993.

43. See Judith Stacey and Susan Elizabeth Gerard's helpful essay, " 'We Are Not Doormats': The Influence of Feminism on Contemporary Evangelicals in the United States," in *Uncertain Terms: Negotiating Gender in American Culture,* ed. Faye Ginsburg and Anna Lowenhaupt Tsing (Boston: Beacon Press, 1990), 98–117. Stacey has expanded this analysis in her ethnographic study *Brave New Families.*

44. Interview at Aglow headquarters, September 1993; personal correspondence from Aglow headquarters, May 1996.

45. Personal interview, July 1993. The woman interviewed was herself somewhat indifferent toward Hansen but suggested that many other women try to look and dress like her.

46. Hansen with Carol Greenwood, *Inside a Woman: Revealing Her Longings, Pain, and the Journey to Love* (Lynnwood, WA: Aglow Publications, 1992), 126.

47. Various phone conversations and personal interviews, including April 1993; October 1993; May 1994; and February 1995.

48. Interview at Aglow headquarters, 16 August 1996.

49. To be installed as an officer, a woman needs letters of recommendation from three pastors. In the past, a married woman was also required to obtain the written permission of her husband to assume leadership; now, the requirement is the husband's "approval."

50. This point is invariably made in historical, anthropological, and sociological analyses of Pentecostalism. For a charismatic Christian insider's discussion of prophecy, see Paul Anderson, "Your Sons and Daughters Shall Prophesy," in *Charisma* (June 1985): 36–43.

51. Research has shown that in traditions where authority derives from direct spirit communication, women are more likely to hold power and positions of authority. See, for instance, Rosemary R. Ruether and Eleanor McLaughlin, introduction to *Women of Spirit: Female Leadership in the Jewish and Christian Traditions,* ed. Rosemary R. Ruether and Eleanor McLaughlin (New York: Simon & Schuster, 1979), 16–28. On women as prophets, see Phyllis Mack, *Visionary Women: Ecstatic Prophecy in Seventeenth-Century England* (Berkeley: University of California Press, 1992); on women as mediums, see Ann Braude, *Radical Spirits: Spiritualism and Women's Rights in Nineteenth-Century America* (Boston: Beacon Press, 1989), esp. 82–116.

52. Carroll Smith-Rosenberg, "The Female World of Love and Ritual: Relations between Women in Nineteenth-Century America," in *Disorderly Conduct: Visions of Gender in Victorian America* (New York: Oxford University Press, 1985), 53–76.

53. Hervieu-Léger, "What Scripture Tells Me." This notion of dialectic has obvious affinities with Meredith McGuire's observation of the "controlled spontaneity" within Catholic charismatic prayer meetings (*Pentecostal Catholics,* esp. 75–106).

54. Nora first told me this story in August of 1994 and discussed it with me several times after that.

55. An experience of this kind occurred in my fieldwork when, after I had assured a local Aglow leader of my benign reasons for doing this study, she responded, "Oh yes. God told me why you're here. He brought you here; He's in charge. We know." She evidently meant that my project was divinely inspired and guided, whether I realized and accepted that or not.

56. The *U.S. Area Handbook* offers a series of instructions on offering procedures for local leaders; see 28–30. On the subject of sacrificial giving in American Christianity, see Susan Harding's analysis of Jerry Falwell's fundraising techniques: "The Gospel of Giving: The Narrative Construction of a Sacrificial Economy," in *Vocabularies of Public Life: Empirical Essays in Symbolic Structure,* ed. Robert Wuthnow (London: Routledge, 1992): 39–56.

57. Aglow headquarters has also produced a videotape on prison ministries, "Casting a Net of Evangelism" (1994).

58. 21 April 1993.

59. 13 May 1993; 21 April 1993.

60. 12 November 1994.

61. 21 May 1993; 13 May 1993.

62. 8 October 1993.

63. 8 October 1993.

64. 9 October 1993.

65. 9 October 1993.

66. 12 November 1994.

67. 8 October 1993.

68. 12 May 1993. This kind of prayer is made at virtually all Aglow meetings.

69. 12 November 1994.

70. 11 November 1994.

71. 11 November 1994.

72. *Women's Aglow Fellowship International Financial Statements* (Year ended December 31, 1994, with Comparative Totals for the Year ended December 31, 1993, and Independent Auditor's Report).

73. 9 October 1993.

Chapter 6

1. "My Husband's Going to Die," *Aglow* no. 22 (Summer 1975): 9–11.

2. "Daddy Never Said, 'I Love You!'" *Aglow* no. 16 (Winter 1974): 24–26.

3. Komarovsky, *Blue-Collar Marriage*; Lillian Breslow Rubin, *Worlds of Pain: Life in the Working-Class Family* (New York: Basic Books, 1976); May, *Homeward Bound*. See also Brett Harvey, *The Fifties: A Woman's Oral History* (New York: Harper Collins, 1993); William Henry Chafe, *The American Woman: Her Changing Social, Economic and Political Role, 1920–1970* (New York: Oxford University Press, 1972); Carl Degler, *At Odds: Women and the Family in America from the Revolution to the Present* (New York: Oxford University Press, 1980); Benita Eisler, *Private Lives: Men and Women of the Fifties* (New York: Franklin Watts, 1986); Eugenia Kaledin, *Mothers and More: American Women in the 1950s* (Boston: Twayne Publishers, 1984); and Rupp and Taylor, *Survival in the Doldrums*.

4. Sociologist Susan D. Rose, writing about similar narrative scripts among charismatic women, observes that whereas feminists would interpret the illnesses of these women as signifying both surrender to and rebellion against their prescribed female roles, the women themselves perceive such illnesses as warning signs that they stepped out of their proper place. See Rose, "Women Warriors," 245–258.

5. "Master of My Life," *Aglow* no. 13 (Spring 1973): 20–23.

6. "Pieces of the Puzzle," *Aglow* no. 11 (Fall 1972): 20–23, 27.

7. "The Wife of the Unbeliever," *Aglow* no. 19 (Fall 1974): 29–31.

8. "My Non-Christian Husband," *Aglow* no. 29 (Spring 1977): 20–23. See also "Glad You Asked That," *Aglow* no. 15 (Winter 1974), 16–17. For success stories of converting a previously unsaved husband, see "He Gave Me Love," *Aglow* no. 28 (Winter 1977): 3–6; and "We've Made It," *Aglow* no. 35 (July/August 1978): 12–14.

9. Ed Hindson, "The Total Family," *Faith Aflame* 4:1 (January–February 1979), 12; cited in Joan Jacobs Brumberg, *Mission for Life: The Story of the Family of Adoniram Judson, the Dramatic Events of the First American Foreign Mission, and the Course of Evangelical Religion in the Nineteenth Century* (New York: Free Press, 1980), 222.

10. Greenhouse, *Praying for Justice*, 48.

11. Greenhouse, *Praying for Justice,* 49.

12. Particularly since World War II, this religious concern for family life has taken on an increasingly anxious tone among conservative evangelicals and fundamentalists. David Harrington Watt and Margaret Lamberts Bendroth have separately argued that there was a shift after the war from the earlier fundamentalist preoccupation with apocalyptic speculation to increased attention toward "practical issues of moral conduct." In particular, the new emphasis turned, often quite fiercely, to the issue of the Christian home. Bendroth describes this shift as initiated by "a desire within fundamentalism for more uniform standards of feminine conduct and a movement toward greater structure in gender relationships." The new emphasis on female submission to masculine headship reshaped notions of hierarchy and had a significant impact on evangelical ideals of family life. See Bendroth, *Fundamentalism and Gender, 1875 to the Present* (New Haven, CT: Yale University Press, 1993), 98–99; Watt, *A Transforming Faith,* 84–91. An important work that focuses on the pre-war years (more precisely, 1880 to 1930) is Betty A. DeBerg, *Ungodly Women: Gender and the First Wave of American Fundamentalism* (Minneapolis: Fortress Press, 1990).

13. Stacey, *Brave New Families.*

14. Nancy Tatom Ammerman has discussed this process in *Bible Believers: Fundamentalists in the Modern World* (New Brunswick, NJ: Rutgers University Press, 1987), esp. 134–146. See also Stacey, *Brave New Families,* 113–146.

15. Cooper, *You Can Be the Wife of a Happy Husband* (Wheaton, IL: Victor Books, 1974), 17.

16. Ibid., 30; 78; 119; 138.

17. Ibid., 139.

18. Ibid., 153.

19. This image of men as naturally out of control and so needing constraint is common in contemporary evangelical teachings on the family, as in the following passage from Christian family guru James Dobson: "The single male is often a threat to society. His aggressive tendencies are largely unbridled and potentially destructive. . . . When a man falls in love with a woman, dedicating himself to care for her, protect her, and support her, he suddenly becomes the mainstay of the social order. Instead of using his energies to pursue his own lusts and desires, he sweats to build a home, save for the future, and seek the best job available. His selfish impulses are inhibited. His sexual passions are channeled. He discovers a sense of pride—yes, masculine pride—because he is needed by his wife and children. Everyone benefits from the relationship." From Dobson, "A New Look at Masculinity and Femininity," *Moody Monthly* 82 (June 1982): 54.

20. Schlafly, *The Power of the Positive Woman* (New Rochelle, NY: Arlington House, Inc., 1977), 54–55; cited in Ehrenreich, *The Hearts of Men:*

American Dreams and the Flight from Commitment (Garden City, NY: Anchor Press/Doubleday, 1983), 163.

21. Mae Erickson, *Quiz for Christian Wives* (Lynnwood, WA: Aglow Publications, 1976), 6–8.

22. 27 January 1994.

23. *Aglow in the Kitchen*, 7. Another author, in a prayer printed for "my son's partner," writes: "If housework ever seems to be a monotonous chore to her, help her realize that whatever she does in word or deed, she should do it with all her heart as working for You" (Sherrer, *How to Pray for Your Children*, 34).

24. "My Home: My Ministry," *Aglow* no. 11 (Fall 1972), 25; 26.

25. For this discussion, I compared three versions of this booklet by Eadie V. Goodboy: the original (*God's Daughter: A Study of Practical Christian Living for Women*, 1974), a version revised in 1976 (*God's Daughter: Practical Aspects of a Christian Woman's Life*); and a version revised in 1985 and reprinted through 1991 that retained the latter title.

26. I am indebted to theologian Sarah Coakley for helping me distinguish between these forms of power and surrender.

27. Coakley, "*Kenōsis* and Subversion: On the Repression of 'Vulnerability' in Christian Feminist Writing," in *Swallowing a Fishbone?: Feminist Theologians Debate Christianity*, ed. Daphne Hampson (London: SPCK, 1996), 110.

28. See Michel de Certeau, *The Practice of Everyday Life*, esp. xviii–xx; 24–28; 29–42.

29. Shirley Dobson, wife of well-known evangelical psychologist James C. Dobson, has described her own childhood in an alcoholic home and its after-effects. See, for instance, "Shirley Dobson: From Shaky Childhood to Secure Womanhood," in Helen Hoosier Kooiman, *Living Cameos* (Old Tappan, NJ: Fleming H. Revell Co., 1971), 30–38.

30. "The Best Choice," *Aglow* no. 76 (May/June 1985), 7.

31. "Mom's an Alcoholic!" *Aglow* 21, no. 1 (January/February 1990), 1–12.

32. Heather Harpham, *Daddy, Where Were You?: Healing for the Father-Deprived Daughter* (Lynnwood, WA: Aglow Publications, 1991).

33. Marie Sontag, *When Love Is Not Perfect: Discover God's Re-Parenting Process* (Lynnwood, WA: Aglow Publications, 1991). Sontag writes that "as many as one out of four adults" are victims of some form of child abuse (14).

34. Miller, *Healing the Angry Heart*, esp. 39–46; quote on p. 39.

35. Miller, *Healing the Angry Heart*, 46. Another example of this genre published by Aglow Publications is Stanley C. Baldwin, *If I'm Created in God's Image Why Does It Hurt to Look in the Mirror?: A True View of You* (1989); see also Ann Lunde, "When You Hurt: A Study of God's Comfort" (Aglow Encourager Bible Study Series, 1987).

36. 18 May 1993.

37. Quin Sherrer first published her narrative in "The Song That Changed: A Story of Forgiveness," *Aglow* no. 76 (May/June 1985), 18–20; quotes from p. 19; she also told this story in a workshop at the U.S. Women's Aglow Conference in November 1994.

38. Wilson, "Evangelical Christian Adult Children of Alcoholics: A Preliminary Study," 268; 271.

39. Newbrough, *Support Group Leader's Guide,* 26.

40. This prophecy has been recounted in numerous places, including the Women's Aglow Prayer Map, and *Women of Prayer Released to the Nations,* 9.

41. Metaphors of warfare have been utilized by a wide variety of cultural fundamentalists. See David Snowball, *Continuity and Change in the Rhetoric of the Moral Majority,* (New York: Praeger, 1991), esp. 123–149. As Snowball notes, the effectiveness of prowar rhetoric requires optimism that the war can indeed be won (135).

42. Brochure of the Spiritual Warfare Network, coordinated by C. Peter Wagner. This network is part of the United Prayer Track of the A.D. 2000 and Beyond Movement and is supported by Global Harvest Ministries, Pasadena, California.

43. C. Peter Wagner, *The Third Wave of the Holy Spirit: Encountering the Power of Signs and Wonders* (Ann Arbor, MI: Servant Publications, 1988); John Wimber (with Kevin Springer), *Power Evangelism* (San Francisco: Harper & Row, 1986). See also Wimber and Springer, *Power Healing* (San Francisco: Harper Collins, 1987). An evangelical critique of this movement is Michael G. Moriarty, *The New Charismatics: A Concerned Voice Responds to Dangerous New Trends* (Grand Rapids, MI: Zondervan, 1992).

44. For recent elaborations of this view by international Aglow leaders, see the essays in *Women of Prayer Released to the Nations.*

45. The passage continues: "Therefore put on the full armor of God, so that when the day of evil comes, you may be able to stand your ground, and after you have done everything, to stand. Stand firm then, with the belt of truth buckled around your waist, with the breastplate of righteousness in place, and with your feet fitted with the readiness that comes from the gospel of peace. In addition to all this, take up the shield of faith, with which you can extinguish all the flaming arrows of the evil one. Take the helmet of salvation and the sword of the Spirit, which is the word of God. And pray in the Spirit on all occasions with all kinds of prayers and requests. With this in mind, be alert and always keep on praying for all the saints" (Ephesians 6:13–18, NIV).

46. Other evangelical groups who utilize military imagery have emphasized women as warriors, notably the Salvation Army; see Diane H. Winston, "Boozers, Brass Bands, and Hallelujah Lassies: The Salvation Army and Commercial Culture in New York City, 1880–1918" (Ph.D. thesis, Princeton University, 1996), esp. 117–129. Women have been dramatized as warriors in other cultural and historical settings as well; a particularly interesting study is Dianne Dugaw, *Warrior Women and Popular Balladry, 1650–1850* (Chicago: University of Chicago Press, 1996; orig. pub. by Cambridge University Press, 1989).

47. Quin Sherrer and Ruthanne Garlock, *A Woman's Guide to Spiritual Warfare: A Woman's Guide for Battle* (Ann Arbor, MI: Servant Publications, 1991), 12, 58.

48. Ibid., 41.

49. Ibid., 164–65.

50. February 1993.

51. 21 April 1993.

52. 27 February 1994. The biblical passage reads: "Now, my son, the Lord be with you, and may you have success and build the house of the Lord your God, as he said you would. May the Lord give you discretion and understanding when he puts you in command over Israel, so that you may keep the law of the Lord your God. Then you will have success if you are careful to observe the decrees and laws that the Lord gave Moses for Israel. Be strong and courageous. Do not be afraid or discouraged" (NIV).

53. Gifford, "Home Protection: The WCTU's Conversion to Woman Suffrage," in *Gender, Ideology, and Action: Historical Perspectives on Women's Public Lives,* ed. Janet Sharistanian (Westport, CT: Greenwood Press, 1986): 95–120.

54. Andrea Dworkin, *Right-Wing Women* (New York: G.P. Putnam's Sons, 1983), 26.

55. Quin Sherrer and Steve Galloway, "Jane Hansen: Waking up from the American Dream," *Charisma & Christian Life* (November 1987): 23.

56. As Helen, a local Aglow leader, explained to me: "Within those bounds [of female restraint], we [women] are given great freedom to minister and to grow," citing various women's ministries as evidence (March 1993).

57. Interviews 14 September 1993; 18 May 1993; 14 May 1993. In contrast, some elderly women who were early members of Aglow but are no longer affiliated with the organization emphasized the doctrine of female submission in much stronger terms. Phone interviews 16 September 1993.

58. Bendroth, *Fundamentalism and Gender,* 7.

59. Goodboy, *God's Daughter,* 27 (in original version) and 29 (in 1991 version).

60. For related writings by women on contemporary evangelical ideals of Christian womanhood, see Helen Kooiman Hosier, *Living Cameos.* A 1995 international Gallup poll found that the majority of Americans continue to uphold traditional gender roles ("Americans Attached to Traditional Roles for Sexes, Poll Finds," *New York Times,* 27 March 1996: A15).

Conclusion

1. Jean Bethke Elshtain, "Cultural Conundrums and Gender: America's Present Past," in *Cultural Politics in Contemporary America,* ed. Ian Angus and Sut Jhally (New York: Routledge, 1989), 131.

2. 23 March 1993.

3. Marsha Witten, "The Restriction of Meaning in Religious Discourse: Centripetal Devices in a Fundamentalist Christian Sermon," in Robert Wuthnow, ed., *Vocabularies of Public Life: Empirical Essays in Symbolic Structure* (London: Routledge, 1992), 19–38 passim.

4. Harding, "Convicted by the Holy Spirit: The Rhetoric of Fundamental Baptist Conversion," *American Ethnologist* 14 (February 1987): 167–181; cited in Virginia Lieson Brereton, *From Sin to Salvation: Stories of Women's Conversions, 1800 to the Present* (Bloomington: Indiana University Press, 1991), 41.

5. Rich, "The Antifeminist Woman," in *On Lies, Secrets, and Silence: Selected Prose 1966–1978* (New York: W. W. Norton & Co., 1979), 71. I have omitted from this quote Rich's parenthetical addition, "(and with the ghostly woman in all men)," an odd phrase which Rich herself disputed in 1978 (see "The Antifeminist Woman," 69).

6. Morton, "The Rising Woman Consciousness in a Male Language Structure," in *The Journey Is Home*, 30. A good discussion of methodological empathy, including its potential problems, is McGuire, *Pentecostal Catholics*, 19–22. McGuire's use of "empathy" is taken from Jack D. Douglas, *Research on Deviance* (New York: Random House, 1972), 28. Similarly, James Scott warns against replacing descriptions made by human beings of their lives with an interpreter's ostensibly superior theory (Scott, *Weapons of the Weak*, 46–47).

7. See Mathews and De Hart, *Sex, Gender, and the Politics of ERA*, esp. 152–180. Feminists have long been accused of rejecting femininity and appropriating masculine values, an accusation recently fueled by associations between the ERA and support for women in combat; see Mansbridge, *Why We Lost the ERA*, 67–89.

8. Examples abound; perhaps the most influential advocates of this perspective are Rosemary Radford Ruether and Rosemary Skinner Keller, coeditors of the three-volume *Women and Religion in America* (San Francisco: Harper & Row, 1981–1986) and the more recent *In Our Own Voices: Four Centuries of American Women's Religious Writing* (San Francisco: Harper San Francisco, 1995). Each has also authored many influential books and articles. Both are distinguished scholars whose combined efforts have played a crucial role in launching the field of American women's religious history. Yet their primary interest in historical women who serve as role models of liberationist activity has contributed to a view that, whether implicitly or explicitly, censures conservative religious women who renounce, adjust, or amend feminist ideals. While this standpoint is challenged by several monographic studies (see introduction), it remains a dominant paradigm in studies of twentieth-century women and religion.

The following essays are very useful for understanding the range of current scholarly perspectives on this and related issues pertaining to the study of women and American religion: Virginia Lieson Brereton and Margaret Lamberts Bendroth, "Recent Work on Women in Twentieth-Century Protestantism," in *Women and Twentieth-Century Protestantism* 1 (Fall/Winter 1997): 4–9; Ann Braude, "Women's History *Is* American Religious History," in Thomas A. Tweed, ed., *Retelling U.S. Religious History* (Berkeley: University of California Press, 1997): 87–107; Elizabeth Fox-Genovese, "Two Steps Forward, One Step Back: New Questions and Old Models in the Religious History of American Women," *Journal of the American Academy of Religion* 53, no. 3 (1985): 465–471; Catherine A. Brekus, "Studying Women and Religion: Problems and Possibilities," *Criterion* 32 (Autumn 1993): 24–28; Ann Taves, "Women and Gender in American Religion(s)," *Religious Studies Review* 18 (October 1992): 263–270; and "Forum: Female Experience in American Religion," *Religion and American Culture* 5 (Winter 1995): 1–21. See also R. Marie Griffith, "American

Religious History and Women's History: Old Divides and Recent Developments," *Reviews in American History* 25, no. 2 (June 1997).

9. Dworkin, *Right-Wing Women,* 34. Dworkin's view is echoed in Ehrenreich, *The Hearts of Men,* 144–168.

10. I am thinking here of the vitriolic and sometimes very personal attacks upon scholars and writers such as Christina Hoff Sommers, a self-described "feminist who does not like what feminism has become" and the author of *Who Stole Feminism? How Women Have Betrayed Women* (New York: Simon & Schuster, 1994). See reviews by Nina Auerbach (*New York Times Book Review,* 12 June 1994, 13); Barbara Ehrenreich (*Time, 1* August 1994, 61); and Susan Faludi, "'I'm Not a Feminist But I Play One on TV'," *Ms.* 5, no. 5 (March/April 1995): 31–39. While Sommers' excessive claims and her penchant for blaming feminism for problems endemic to the broader culture invite vigorous debate, the author hardly deserves the scathing treatment she has received from other feminists, who have scorned and bashed her without addressing the issues she raises. A fairer and more trenchant review of Sommers is Jean Bethke Elshtain, "Sic Transit Gloria," *The New Republic,* 11 July 1994, 32–36.

11. Christopher Lasch, *The True and Only Heaven: Progress and its Critics* (New York: Norton, 1991).

12. "Legislative Analysis Report: The Gender Equity in Education Act," mailing sent to Concerned Women for America members, September 1993. These and other warnings are reminiscent of Pat Robertson's famous 1992 fund-raising letter reporting that feminism "encourages women to leave their husbands, kill their children, practice witchcraft, destroy capitalism and become lesbians" (see "Robertson Letter Attacks Feminists," *New York Times,* 26 August 1992: A16).

13. Making a similar point, Mary McClintock Fulkerson notes that typical studies of Pentecostal women "tend either to grant the ostensible egalitarianism in early Pentecostal practice an idealized status, or to emphasize the unliberated character of their situation given the obeisance to male authority that characterizes their posture toward the limitations on their ordination status" (*Changing the Subject,* 285).

14. Watt, *Transforming Faith,* 131–136; see also Bendroth, *Fundamentalism and Gender,* 118–127.

15. Cynthia Eller, *Living in the Lap of the Goddess: The Feminist Spirituality Movement in America* (New York: Crossroad, 1993), 45.

16. Carol P. Christ, *Diving Deep and Surfacing: Women Writers on Spiritual Quest* (Boston: Beacon Press, 1980), 127; cited in Eller, *Living,* 44.

17. Quoted in Phyllis Schlafly, *The Power of the Positive Woman* (New York: Jove Publications, 1977), 72–73; cited in Rebecca E. Klatch, *Women of the New Right* (Philadelphia: Temple University Press, 1987), 137.

18. Ehrenreich, *The Hearts of Men,* 148–149.

19. Susan Rose makes a similar point, though unfortunately relying on a reductionist deprivation theory of religion: "It may not be that the needs and desires of some of these evangelical women are so different from many of their more feminist or mainstream counterparts, but rather that their means for

achieving a satisfying, or at least reasonable, life differ. The balance rests in favor of accommodation rather than resistance. And secular means having failed them, they turned to religious resolutions" ("Women Warriors," 252).

20. See Klatch, *Women of the New Right,* 139. Andrea Dworkin has from a somewhat different angle pointed to the similar circumstances of so-called right-wing women and their feminist counterparts. She writes: "Not wanting to die, and knowing the sadism of men, knowing what men can do in the name of sex, . . . for the sake of pleasure, for the sake of power, knowing torture, having been able to predict all the prisons from her place in the bedroom and the brothel, knowing how callous men are to those less than themselves, . . . seeing the indifference of men to human freedom, seeing the enthusiasm of men for diminishing others through physical domination, seeing the invisibility of women to men, seeing the absolute disregard of humanity in women by men, seeing the disdain of men for women's lives, and not wanting to die—*and not wanting to die*—women propose two very different solutions for themselves in relation to men and this man's world" (*Right-Wing Women,* 189; emphasis in original).

21. This point has long been made by feminists; a recent argument is Sylvia Yanagisako and Carol Delaney, eds., *Naturalizing Power: Essays in Feminist Cultural Analysis* (New York: Routledge, 1995), 16. Elizabeth Fox-Genovese has also forcefully stated this point: "The ideological claims of feminism are, at one level, universal. Therein lies their strength. . . . But to the extent that those claims abstract from the specific lives of many women, to the extent that they are enunciated on the basis of the needs of a specific group of women, they make a mockery of their own universality" (*Feminism without Illusions: A Critique of Individualism* [Chapel Hill: University of North Carolina Press, 1991], 19).

22. The phrase is from political theorist Michael Brint, who writes: "To do justice to our differences, we must first learn to see our cultural topography as a complex, multifaceted conjunction and disjunction of different vocabularies, traditions, activities, and practices. We must then learn to challenge the monopolization of our culture by any single value, dominant vocabulary, or privileged philosophical position. . . . Such a respect for difference urges us to seek an understanding of our distinct discursive and ethical practices" (Michael Brint, *Tragedy and Denial: The Politics of Difference in Western Political Thought* [Boulder, CO: Westview Press, 1991], 164–165).

23. Elshtain, "Cultural Conundrums and Gender," 133. A feminist theological version of this argument is Coakley, "Kenōsis and Subversion," esp. 106–111.

Selected Bibliography

Primary Sources

Aglow. Aglow Publications, 1969–1991.

Aglow's Connection. Aglow Publications, 1991–1996.

Baldwin, Stanley C. *If I'm Created in God's Image, Why Does It Hurt to Look in the Mirror? A True View of You*. Lynnwood, WA: Aglow Publications, 1989.

Bennett, Dennis J. *Nine O'Clock in the Morning*. South Plainfield, NJ: Bridge Publishing, 1970.

———, and Rita Bennett. *The Holy Spirit and You: A Study-Guide to the Spirit-Filled Life*. Plainfield, NJ: Logos International, 1971.

Bennett, Rita. *Making Peace with Your Inner Child*. Old Tappan, NJ: Revell, 1987.

Bigliardi, Patricia A. *Beyond the Hidden Pain of Abortion*. Lynnwood, WA: Aglow Publications, 1994.

Boone, Shirley. *One Woman's Liberation*. Carol Stream, IL: Creation House, 1972.

Brooks, Pat. *Daughters of the King: A Startling Proclamation for All Women Who Wish to Be Truly Free*. Carol Stream, IL: Creation House, 1975.

Bryant, Anita. *Mine Eyes Have Seen the Glory*. Old Tappan, NJ: Revell, 1970.

———, and Bob Green. *Raising God's Children*. Old Tappan, NJ: Revell, 1977.

Bush, Barbara. *Mastering Motherhood*. Grand Rapids, MI: Zondervan, 1981.

Casting a Net of Evangelism. Video produced by Aglow International, 1994.

Cavanaugh, Joan, with Pat Forseth. *More of Jesus, Less of Me*. Plainfield, NJ: Logos International, 1976.

Chandler, Sandie. *Lovingly Liberated: A Christian Woman's Response to the Liberation Movement*. Old Tappan, NJ: Revell, 1975.

Chapian, Marie, and Neva Coyle. *Free to Be Thin*. Minneapolis: Bethany House Publishers, 1979.

Cook, Barbara. *Ordinary Women, Extraordinary Strength: A Biblical Perspective of Feminine Potential*. Lynnwood, WA: Aglow Publications, 1988.

Cook, Shirley. *Diary of a FAT Housewife*. Denver, CO: Accent Books, 1977.

Cooper, Darien B. *You Can Be the Wife of a Happy Husband*. Wheaton, IL: Victor Books, 1974.

Cooper, Mildred, and Martha Fanning. *What Every Woman Still Knows: A Celebration of the Christian Liberated Woman*. New York: M. Evans and Co., 1978.

Coyle, Neva, and Marie Chapian. *The All-New Free to Be Thin*. Minneapolis: Bethany House Publishers, 1993.

———. *There's More to Being Thin than Being Thin*. Minneapolis: Bethany House Publishers, 1984.

Cresse, Michelle. *Jigsaw Families: Solving the Puzzle of Remarriage*. Lynnwood, WA: Aglow Publications, 1989.

Dobson, James, Dr. *What Wives Wish Their Husbands Knew about Women*. Wheaton, IL: Tyndale House, 1975.

Dull, Elaine, and JoAnne Sekowsky. *Teach Us to Pray*. Lynnwood, WA: Aglow Publications, 1980.

Elliot, Elisabeth. *Let Me Be a Woman*. Wheaton, IL: Tyndale House Publishers, 1976.

Elwood, Roger. *Christian Mothers Reveal Their Joys and Sorrows: Interviews by Roger Elwood*. Cincinnati, OH: Standard, 1979.

Erickson, Mae. *Quiz for Christian Wives*. Lynnwood, WA: Women's Aglow Fellowship, 1976.

Fortune, Katie. *Receive All God Has to Give*. Lynnwood, WA: Women's Aglow Fellowship, 1987 (1971).

Friedan, Betty. *The Feminine Mystique*. New York: Dell Publishing, 1983 (1963).

George, Denise. *God's Gentle Whisper*. Lynnwood, WA: Aglow Publications, 1993.

Goodboy, Eadie. *God's Daughter: A Study of Practical Christian Living for Women*. Aglow Bible Study 2. Edmonds, WA: Aglow Publications, 1974.

———. *God's Daughter: Practical Aspects of a Christian Woman's Life*. rev. ed. Edmonds, WA: Aglow Publications, 1976.

———. *God's Daughter: Practical Aspects of a Christian Woman's Life*. 2nd rev. ed. Lynwood, WA: Aglow Publications, 1986.

Graham, Ruth Bell. *It's My Turn*. Old Tappan, NJ: Revell-Spire, 1982.

Hammond, Mary. "I Am a Charismatic Feminist." *Daughters of Sarah* 16, no. 6 (Nov/Dec 1990): 8–9.

Hansen, Jane, with Carol Greenwood. *Inside a Woman: Revealing Her Longings, Pain, and the Journey to Love*. Lynnwood, WA: Aglow Publications, 1992.

Harpham, Heather. *Daddy, Where Were You?: Healing for the Father-Deprived Daughter*. Lynnwood, WA: Aglow Publications, 1991.

Hill, Harold, with Irene Burk Harrell and Gretchen Black. *How to Flip Your Flab—Forever*. Plainfield, NJ: Logos International, 1979.

Holmes, Marjorie. *Who Am I, God?: The Doubts, the Fears, the Joys of Being a Woman*. Garden City, NY: Doubleday, 1971.

Horton, Marilee. *Free to Stay at Home: A Woman's Alternative*. Waco, TX: Word Books, 1982.

Howard, Linda. *The Secret Life of a Housewife*. Plainfield, NJ: Logos International, 1978.

Hunsicker, Ranelda Mack. *Secrets: Unlocking the Mystery of Intimacy with God*. Lynnwood, WA: Aglow Publications, 1991.

Jacobs, Cindy. *Possessing the Gates of the Enemy: A Training Manual for Militant Intercession*. Grand Rapids, MI: Chosen Books, 1991.

Joyner, Rick. *The Harvest*. Pineville, NC: Morningstar Publications, Inc., 1989.

King, Pat. "Aglow." *Logos Journal* 4 (May–June 1974): 34–35.

Kooiman, Helen Hoosier. *Living Cameos*. Old Tappan, NJ: Revell, 1971.

Kreml, Patricia B. *Slim for Him*. Plainfield, NJ: Logos International, 1978.

Kruger, Diana. *Who Says Winners Never Lose? Profiting from Life's Painful Detours*. Lynnwood, WA: Aglow Publications, 1990.

LaHaye, Beverly. *I Am a Woman by God's Design*. Old Tappan, NJ: Revell, 1980.

———. *The Restless Woman*. Grand Rapids, MI: Zondervan, 1984.

———. *The Spirit-Controlled Woman*. Irvine, CA: Harvest House Publishers, 1976.

———. *Who But a Woman?: Concerned Women Can Make a Difference*. Nashville, TN: Thomas Nelson Publishers, 1984.

Lawless, Agnes, and Ann Thomas, eds. *Aglow in the Kitchen*. Lynnwood, WA: Women's Aglow Fellowship, 1976.

Mains, Karen Burton. *Open Heart, Open Home: How to Find Joy through Sharing Your Home with Others*. Elgin, IL: David C. Cook Publishing Co., 1976.

Malcolm, Kari Torjesen. *Women at the Crossroads: A Path beyond Feminism and Traditionalism*. Downers Grove, IL: InterVarsity Press, 1982.

Mason, Marilyn. *Intimacy*. Center City, MN: Hazelden Foundation, 1986.

Mattox, Beverly. *Help! I'm a Woman*. Schaumburg, IL: Regular Baptist Press, 1977.

McDaniels, Evelyn. *Loving More, Eating Less*. Laramie, WY: Jelm Mountain Press, 1988.

Mech, Doris. *Joy with Honey*. Lynnwood, WA: Women's Aglow Fellowship, 1979.

Miller, Kathy Collard. *Healing the Angry Heart: A Strategy for Confident Mothering*. Lynnwood, WA: Aglow Publications, 1984.

———. *Sure Footing in a Shaky World: A Woman's Guide to Security*. Lynnwood, WA: Aglow Publications, 1990.

Morgan, Marabel. *The Electric Woman: Hope for Tired Mothers, Lovers, and Others*. New York: Pocket Books, 1985.

———. *Total Joy*. Old Tappan, NJ: Revell, 1976.

———. *The Total Woman*. New York: Pocket Books, 1973.

Mouliert, Gwen. *Hyper to Holy: How Jesus Touched the Life of a Housewife.* Columbus, GA: Brentwood Christian Press, 1990.

Neff, Miriam. *Discover Your Worth: How to Improve Your Self-Esteem as Woman, Wife, and Mother.* Wheaton, IL: Victor Books, 1979.

Newbrough, Jennie, with Carol Greenwood. *Support Groups Leader's Guide.* Lynnwood, WA: Women's Aglow Fellowship, 1993.

Omartian, Stormie. *Better Body Management.* Nashville, TN: Sparrow Press, 1993.

———. *Greater Health God's Way: Seven Steps to Health, Youthfulness, and Vitality.* Chatsworth, CA: Sparrow Press, 1984.

Ortlund, Anne. *Disciplines of the Beautiful Woman.* Waco, TX: Word Books, 1984.

Osborn, Daisy. *New Life for Women.* Tulsa, OK: OSFO Publishers, 1991.

———. *The Woman Believer.* Tulsa, OK: OSFO Publishers, 1990.

———. *Women and Self-Esteem.* Tulsa, OK: OSFO Publishers, 1991.

Peale, Mrs. Norman Vincent. *The Adventure of Being a Wife.* Englewood Cliffs, NJ: Prentice-Hall, Inc., 1971.

Peretti, Frank E. *Prophet.* Wheaton, IL: Crossway Books, 1992.

Polston, Ruth Ann. *You Deserve to Be Happy: You Owe It to Yourself.* Irvine, CA: Harvest House, 1978.

Price, Eugenia. *The Burden Is Light!: The Autobiography of a Transformed Pagan Who Took God at His Word.* Westwood, NJ: Revell, 1955.

Ravan, Pam. *Sock Hunting and Other Pursuits of the Working Mother.* Lynnwood, WA: Aglow Publications, 1991.

Rogers, Dale Evans, with Carole C. Carlson. *Woman: Be All You Can Be.* Old Tappan, NJ: Revell, 1980.

Rushford, Patricia H. *Lost in the Money Maze? How to Find Your Way Through.* Lynnwood, WA: Aglow Publications, 1992.

Schaffer, James, and Colleen Todd. *Christian Wives: Women behind the Evangelists Reveal Their Faith in Modern Marriage.* Garden City, NY: Doubleday, 1987.

Schlafly, Phyllis. *The Power of the Positive Woman.* New York: Jove Publications, 1977.

Sekowsky, JoAnne. *Praise the Lord, I'm under Construction.* Lynnwood, WA: Women's Aglow Fellowship, 1978.

———. *Spiritual Warfare: Strategy for Winning.* Aglow Workshop Series. Lynnwood, WA: Women's Aglow Fellowship, 1983.

Sherrer, Quin. *How to Pray for Your Children.* Lynnwood, WA: Aglow Publications, 1986.

Sherrer, Quin, and Steve Galloway. "Jane Hansen: Waking up from the American Dream." *Charisma & Christian Life* (November 1987): 18–23.

Sherrer, Quin, and Ruthanne Garlock. *A Woman's Guide to Spiritual Warfare: A Woman's Guide for Battle.* Ann Arbor, MI: Servant Publications, 1991.

Showalter, Carol. *3D.* Orleans, MA: Rock Harbor Press, 1977.

Smith, Susy. *The Conversion of a Psychic.* Garden City, N.Y.: Doubleday, 1978.

Sontag, Marie. *When Love Is Not Perfect: Discover God's Re-parenting Process.* Lynnwood, WA: Aglow Publications, 1991.

Stapleton, Ruth Carter. *The Gift of Inner Healing.* Waco, TX: Word Books, 1976.

Stedman, Elaine. *A Woman's Worth.* Waco, TX: Word Books, 1975.

Sudol, Dorothea DeGrandis. *I Am Woman; I Am Catholic; I Am Charismatic; I Am Divorced; What Next?* USA: np, nd.

Thibodeau, Lynn, ed. *The Happy Housewife.* St. Paul, MN: Carillon Books, 1977.

Thomas, Ann. *God's Answer to Overeating: A Study of Scriptural Attitudes.* Aglow Bible Study 7. Edmonds, WA: Women's Aglow Fellowship, 1975.

Turning Point, 4th ed. Lynnwood, WA: Aglow Publications, 1991.

U.S. Area Handbook. Lynnwood, WA: Women's Aglow Fellowship, 1987.

Wagner, C. Peter. *The Third Wave of the Holy Spirit: Encountering the Power of Signs and Wonders.* Ann Arbor, MI: Servant Publications, 1988.

Weising, Gwen. *Guidance: Knowing the Will of God.* Aglow Workbook Series. Lynnwood, WA: Women's Aglow Fellowship, 1985.

White, John. *When the Spirit Comes with Power: Signs & Wonders among God's People.* Downers Grove, IL: Intervarsity Press, 1988.

Williamson, Norma. *Please Get off the Seesaw Slowly: How One Woman Handles the Ups and Downs of Being a Christian Wife and Mother.* Old Tappan, NJ: Revell, 1975.

Wimber, John, and Kevin Springer. *Power Evangelism.* San Francisco: Harper & Row, 1986.

————. *Power Healing.* San Francisco: Harper Collins, 1987.

Women of Prayer Released to the Nations: Sixteen Prayer Leaders Around the Earth Reveal the Heart, Spirit, and Power of Prayer. Lynnwood: WA: Aglow Publications, 1993.

Women's Aglow Fellowship International Financial Statements: Year Ended December 31, 1994, with Comparative Totals for the Year Ended December 31, 1993, and Independent Auditor's Report. 1995.

Word Ministries, Inc. *Prayers That Avail Much: An Intercessor's Handbook of Scriptural Prayers,* vols. 1 & 2. Tulsa, OK: Harrison House, 1989.

Secondary Sources

Abu-Lughod, Lila. "The Romance of Resistance: Tracing Transformations of Power through Bedouin Women." *American Ethnologist* 17, no. 1 (February 1990): 41–55.

————. *Veiled Sentiments: Honor and Poetry in a Bedouin Society.* Berkeley: University of California Press, 1986.

————. *Writing Women's Worlds: Bedouin Stories.* Berkeley: University of California Press, 1993.

Aidala, Angela A. "Social Change, Gender Roles, and New Religious Movements." *Sociological Analysis* 46, no. 3 (1985): 287–314.

Alcoholics Anonymous: The Story of How Many Thousands of Men and Women Have Recovered from Alcoholism. 3rd rev. ed. New York: Alcoholics Anonymous World Services, 1976.

Alexander, Bobby C. "Pentecostal Ritual Reconsidered: Anti-Structural Dimensions of Possession." *Journal of Ritual Studies* 3, no. 1 (Winter 1989): 109–128.

Ammerman, Nancy Tatom. *Bible Believers: Fundamentalists in the Modern World*. New Brunswick, NJ: Rutgers University Press, 1987.

Anderson, Robert Mapes. *Vision of the Disinherited: The Making of American Pentecostalism*. New York: Oxford University Press, 1979.

Aptheker, Bettina. *Tapestries of Life: Women's Work, Women's Consciousness, and the Meaning of Daily Experience*. Amherst, MA: University of Massachusetts Press, 1989.

Asad, Talal. *Genealogies of Religion: Discipline and Reasons of Power in Christianity and Islam*. Baltimore, MD: Johns Hopkins University Press, 1993.

Austin, J. L. *How to Do Things with Words*. 2nd ed. Cambridge: Harvard University Press, 1975.

Bachelard, Gaston. *The Poetics of Space: The Classic Look at How We Experience Intimate Places*. Trans. Maria Jolas. Boston: Beacon Press, 1964 (1958).

Bal, Mieke. *Narratology: Introduction to the Theory of Narrative*. Trans. Christine van Boheemen. Toronto: University of Toronto Press, 1985.

Balmer, Randall. *Mine Eyes Have Seen the Glory: A Journey into the Evangelical Subculture in America*. New York: Oxford University Press, 1989.

Balmer, Randall, and Jesse T. Todd, Jr. "Calvary Chapel, Costa Mesa, California." In *American Congregations*. Vol. 1, *Portraits of Twelve Religious Communities*, ed. James P. Wind and James W. Lewis (Chicago: University of Chicago Press, 1994): 663–698.

Bates, Stephen. *Battleground: One Mother's Crusade, the Religious Right, and the Struggle for Control of Our Classrooms*. New York: Poseidon Press, 1993.

Bauman, Richard, and Joel Sherzer, eds. *Explorations in the Ethnography of Speaking*. London and New York: Cambridge University Press, 1974.

Bederman, Gail. *Manliness and Civilization: A Cultural History of Gender and Race in the United States, 1880–1917*. Chicago: University of Chicago Press, 1995.

Behar, Ruth, and Deborah A. Gordon, eds. *Women Writing Culture*. Berkeley: University of California Press, 1995.

Bell, Catherine. *Ritual Theory, Ritual Practice*. New York: Oxford University Press, 1992.

Bendroth, Margaret Lamberts. *Fundamentalism and Gender, 1875 to the Present*. New Haven, CT: Yale University Press, 1993.

———. "The Search for 'Women's Role' in American Evangelicalism, 1930–1980." In *Evangelicalism and Modern America*, ed. George Marsden. Grand Rapids, MI: Eerdmans, 1984.

Bernard, Jessie. *American Family Behavior*. New York: Harper and Bros., 1942.

———. "Homosociality and Female Depression." *Journal of Social Issues* 32 (1976): 213–235.

Blumberg, Leonard. "The Ideology of a Therapeutic Social Movement: Alcoholics Anonymous." *Journal of Studies on Alcohol* 38, no. 11 (1977): 2122–2143.

Blumhofer, Edith L. *Restoring the Faith: The Assemblies of God, Pentecostalism, and American Culture*. Urbana: University of Illinois Press, 1993.

Bord, Richard J., and Joseph E. Faulkner. *The Catholic Charismatics: The Anatomy of a Modern Religious Movement*. University Park: Pennsylvania State University Press, 1983.

Bourdieu, Pierre. *Outline of a Theory of Practice*. Trans. Richard Nice. Cambridge: Cambridge University Press, 1977.

Boyer, Paul. "Minister's Wife, Widow, Reluctant Feminist: Catherine Marshall in the 1950s." In *Women in American Religion*, ed. Janet Wilson James, 253–271. Philadelphia: University of Pennsylvania Press, 1980.

———. *When Time Shall Be No More: Prophecy Belief in Modern American Culture*. Cambridge, MA: Harvard University Press, 1992.

Braude, Ann. *Radical Spirits: Spiritualism and Women's Rights in Nineteenth Century America*. Boston: Beacon Press, 1989.

Brereton, Virginia Lieson. *From Sin to Salvation: Stories of Women's Conversions, 1800 to the Present*. Bloomington: Indiana University Press, 1991.

Briggs, Charles L. *Competence in Performance: The Creativity of Tradition in Mexicano Verbal Art*. Philadelphia: University of Pennsylvania Press, 1988.

———. *Learning How to Ask: A Sociolinguistic Appraisal of the Role of the Interview in Social Science Research*. Cambridge: Cambridge University Press, 1986.

Briggs, Jean L. *Never in Anger: Portrait of an Eskimo Family*. Cambridge, MA: Harvard University Press, 1970.

Brint, Michael. *Tragedy and Denial: The Politics of Difference in Western Political Thought*. Boulder, CO: Westview Press, 1991.

Brown, Karen McCarthy. *Mama Lola: A Vodou Priestess in Brooklyn*. Berkeley: University of California Press, 1991.

Brusco, Elizabeth E. *The Reformation of Machismo: Evangelical Conversion and Gender in Colombia*. Austin: University of Texas Press, 1995.

Butler, Judith. *Gender Trouble: Feminism and the Subversion of Identity*. New York: Routledge, 1990.

Bynum, Caroline Walker. *Holy Feast and Holy Fast: The Religious Significance of Food to Medieval Women*. Berkeley: University of California Press, 1987.

———. "Introduction: The Complexity of Symbols." In *Gender and Religion: On the Complexity of Symbols*, ed. Caroline Walker Bynum, Stevan Harrell, and Paula Richman, 1–20. Boston: Beacon Press, 1986.

Caffrey, Margaret M. "Women and Families." In *American Families: A Research Guide and Historical Handbook*, ed. Joseph M. Hawes and Eliabeth I. Nybakken. New York: Greenwood Press, 1991.

Cancian, Francesca M. "The Feminization of Love." *Signs* 11, no. 4 (1986): 692–709.

Chafe, William Henry. *The American Woman: Her Changing Social, Economic and Political Roles, 1920–1970.* New York: Oxford University Press, 1972.
———. *The Paradox of Change: American Women in the 20th Century.* New York: Oxford University Press, 1991.
Chase, Elise. *Healing Faith: An Annotated Bibliography of Christian Self-Help Books.* Westport, CT: Greenwood Press, 1985.
Chi, S. Kenneth, and Sharon K. Houseknecht. "Protestant Fundamentalism and Marital Success: A Comparative Approach." *Sociology and Social Research* 69, no. 3 (April 1985): 351–375.
Clifford, James. *The Predicament of Culture: Twentieth-Century Ethnography, Literature, and Art.* Cambridge, MA: Harvard University Press, 1988.
Clifford, James, and George E. Marcus, eds. *Writing Culture: The Poetics and Politics of Ethnography.* Berkeley: University of California Press, 1986.
Coakley, Sarah. "*Kenōsis* and Subversion: On the Repression of 'Vulnerability' in Christian Feminist Writing." In *Swallowing a Fishbone?: Feminist Theologians Debate Christianity,* ed. Daphne Hampson, 82–111. London: SPCK, 1996.
Conover, Pamela Johnston, and Virginia Gray. *Feminism and the New Right: Conflict over the American Family.* New York: Praeger Publishers, 1983.
Coombe, Rosemary J. "Room for Manoeuver: Toward a Theory of Practice in Critical Legal Studies." *Law and Social Inquiry* 14, no. 1 (Winter 1989): 69–121.
Coontz, Stephanie. *The Way We Never Were: American Families and the Nostalgia Trap.* New York: Basic Books, 1992.
Cott, Nancy. *The Bonds of Womanhood: "Woman's Sphere" in New England, 1780–1835.* New Haven, CT: Yale University Press, 1977.
Cox, Harvey Gallagher. *Fire from Heaven: The Rise of Pentecostal Spirituality and the Reshaping of Religion in the Twenty-First Century.* Reading, MA: Addison-Wesley, 1995.
Crews, Mickey. *The Church of God: A Social History.* Knoxville: University of Tennessee Press, 1990.
Csordas, Thomas J. *The Sacred Self: A Cultural Phenomenology of Charismatic Healing.* Berkeley: University of California Press, 1994.
Cvetkovich, Ann. *Mixed Feelings: Feminism, Mass Culture, and Victorian Sensationalism.* New Brunswick, NJ: Rutgers University Press, 1992.
D'Antonio, Michael. *Fall from Grace: The Failed Crusade of the Christian Right.* New York: Farrar, Straus, Giroux, 1989.
Davidman, Lynn. *Tradition in a Rootless World: Women Turn to Orthodox Judaism.* Berkeley: University of California Press, 1991.
Davie, Jody Shapiro. *Women in the Presence: Constructing Community and Seeking Spirituality in Mainline Protestantism.* Philadelphia: University of Pennsylvania Press, 1995.
Davis, Natalie Zemon. *Society and Culture in Early Modern France: Eight Essays by Natalie Zemon Davis.* Stanford, CA: Stanford University Press, 1975.

Dayton, Donald W., and Robert K. Johnston, eds. *The Variety of American Evangelicalism*. Downers Grove, IL: Intervarsity Press; Knoxville: University of Tennessee Press, 1991.

DeBerg, Betty A. *Ungodly Women: Gender and the First Wave of American Fundamentalism*. Minneapolis, MN: Fortress Press, 1990.

De Certeau, Michel. *The Practice of Everyday Life*. Trans. Steven Rendall. Berkeley: University of California Press, 1984.

Degler, Carl. *At Odds: Women and the Family in America from the Revolution to the Present*. New York: Oxford University Press, 1980.

D'Emilio, John, and Estelle Freedman. *Intimate Matters: A History of Sexuality in America*. New York: Harper & Row, 1988.

Diamond, Sara. *Spiritual Warfare: The Politics of the Christian Right*. Boston, MA: South End Press, 1989.

di Leonardo, Micaela. "Introduction." In *Gender at the Crossroads of Knowledge: Feminist Anthropology in the Postmodern Era*, ed. Micaela di Leonardo, 1–48. Berkeley: University of California Press, 1991.

Douglas, Mary, *Natural Symbols: Explorations in Cosmology*. New York: Pantheon Books, 1973.

Ducey, Michael H. *Sunday Morning: Aspects of Urban Ritual*. New York: The Free Press, 1977.

Durkheim, Émile. *The Elementary Forms of the Religious Life*. Trans. Joseph Ward Swain. New York: Free Press, 1967; George Allen and Unwin Ltd., 1915.

Dworkin, Andrea. *Right-Wing Women*. New York: G. P. Putnam's Sons, 1983.

Ehrenreich, Barbara. *The Hearts of Men: American Dreams and the Flight from Commitment*. New York: Anchor Press/ Doubleday, 1983.

Eisler, Benita. *Private Lives: Men and Women of the Fifties*. New York: Franklin Watts, 1986.

Eller, Cynthia. *Living in the Lap of the Goddess: The Feminist Spirituality Movement in America*. New York: Crossroad, 1993.

Elsbree, Langdon, *The Rituals of Life: Patterns in Narratives*. Port Washington, NY: Kennikat Press, 1982.

Elshtain, Jean Bethke. "Cultural Conundrums and Gender: America's Present Past." In *Cultural Politics in Contemporary America*, ed. Ian Angus and Sut Jhally, 123–134. New York: Routledge, 1989.

Filene, Peter G. *Him/Her/Self: Sex Roles in Modern America*. 2nd ed. Baltimore, MD: Johns Hopkins University Press, 1986 (1974).

Fish, Stanley. *Is There a Text in This Class?: The Authority of Interpretive Communities*. Cambridge, MA: Harvard University Press, 1980.

Flake, Carol. *Redemptorama: Culture, Politics and the New Evangelicalism*. Garden City, NY: Doubleday-Anchor, 1984.

Forrest, John. *Lord I'm Coming Home: Everyday Aesthetics in Tidewater North Carolina*. Ithaca, NY: Cornell University Press, 1988.

Foster, Dennis A. *Confession and Complicity in Narrative*. Cambridge: Cambridge University Press, 1987.

Foucault, Michel. *Discipline and Punish: The Birth of the Prison*. Trans. Alan Sheridan. New York: Vintage Books, 1977.

Fox, Richard Wightman, and T. J. Jackson Lears, eds. *The Culture of Consumption: Critical Essays in American History, 1880–1980*. New York: Pantheon Books, 1983.

Fox-Genovese, Elizabeth. *"Feminism Is Not the Story of My Life": How Today's Feminist Elite Has Lost Touch with the Real Concerns of Women*. New York: Doubleday, 1996.

———. *Feminism without Illusions: A Critique of Individualism*. Chapel Hill: University of North Carolina Press, 1991.

Fulkerson, Mary McClintock. *Changing the Subject: Women's Discourses and Feminist Theology*. Minneapolis, MN: Fortress Press, 1994.

Garrett, Clarke. *Spirit Possession and Popular Religion: From the Camisards to the Shakers*. Baltimore, MD: Johns Hopkins University Press, 1987.

Geertz, Clifford. *Local Knowledge: Further Essays in Interpretive Anthropology*. New York: Basic Books, 1983.

———. *The Interpretation of Cultures*. New York: Basic Books, 1973.

———. *Works and Lives: The Anthropologist as Author*. Stanford, CA: Stanford University Press, 1988.

Gennep, Arthur van. *The Rites of Passage*. Trans. Monika B. Vizedom and Gabrielle L. Caffee. Chicago, IL: University of Chicago Press, 1960.

George, Carol V. R. *God's Salesman: Norman Vincent Peale and the Power of Positive Thinking*. New York: Oxford University Press, 1993.

Gesch, Lyn. "Responses to Changing Lifestyles: 'Feminists' and 'Traditionalists' in Mainstream Religion." In *Work, Family, and Religion in Contemporary Society*, ed. Nancy Tatom Ammerman and Wade Clark Roof. New York: Routledge, 1995.

Giddens, Anthony. *The Constitution of Society: Outline of the Theory of Structuration*. Berkeley: University of California Press, 1984.

Gifford, Carolyn DeSwarte. "Home Protection: The WCTU's Conversion to Woman Suffrage." In *Gender, Ideology, and Action: Historical Perspectives on Women's Public Lives*, ed. Janet Sharistanian, 95–120. Westport, CT: Greenwood Press, 1986.

Gilbert, Kate. "Fastening the Bonds of Womanhood," *Women's Review of Books* 8, no. 9 (June 1996): 21–22.

Gill, Sam D. *Sacred Words: A Study of Navajo Religion and Prayer*. Westport, CT: Greenwood Press, 1981.

Ginsburg, Faye D. *Contested Lives: The Abortion Debate in an American Community*. Berkeley: University of California Press, 1989.

Goldsmith, Peter. "A Woman's Place Is in the Church: Black Pentecostalism on the Georgia Coast." *Journal of Religious Thought* 46 (Winter/Spring 1989–90): 53–69.

Gordon, Deborah. "Writing Culture, Writing Feminism: The Poetics and Politics of Experimental Ethnography." *Inscriptions* nos. 3/4 (1988): 7–24.

Gordon, Michael, ed. *The American Family in Social-Historical Perspective*. 2nd ed. New York: St. Martin's Press, 1978.

Greenhouse, Carol J. *Praying for Justice: Faith, Order, and Community in an American Town*. Ithaca, NY: Cornell University Press, 1986.

Griffith, R. Marie. "A Network of Praying Women: The Formation of Religious Identity in Women's Aglow Fellowship." Ph.D. thesis: Harvard University, 1995.

Gritzmacher, Steven A., Brian Bolton, and Richard H. Dana. "Psychological Characteristics of Pentecostals: A Literature Review and Psychodynamic Synthesis." *Journal of Psychology and Theology* 16, no. 3 (1988): 233–245.

Groothuis, Rebecca Merrill. *Women Caught in the Conflict: The Culture War between Traditionalism and Feminism*. Grand Rapids, MI: Baker Books, 1994.

Gunstone, John. "Group Prayer." In *The Study of Spirituality*, ed. Cheslyn Jones, Geoffrey Wainwright, and Edward Yarnold, S.J. London: SPCK, 1986.

Haaken, Janice. "From Al-Anon to ACOA: Codependence and the Reconstruction of Caregiving." *Signs* 18, no. 2 (Winter 1993): 321–345.

Hall, Charles. "Entering the Labor Force: Ideals and Realities among Evangelical Women." In *Work, Family, and Religion in Contemporary Society*, ed. Nancy Tatom Ammerman and Wade Clark Roof. New York: Routledge, 1995.

Hall, David D. *Worlds of Wonder, Days of Judgment: Popular Religious Belief in Early New England*. Cambridge, MA: Harvard University Press, 1990.

———, ed. *Lived Religion in America: Toward a History of Practice*. Princeton, NJ: Princeton University Press, in press.

Halttunen, Karen. *Confidence Men and Painted Women: A Study of Middle-Class Culture in America, 1830–1870*. New Haven, CT: Yale University Press, 1982.

Hambrick-Stowe, Charles E. *The Practice of Piety: Puritan Devotional Disciplines in Seventeenth-Century New England*. Chapel Hill: University of North Carolina Press, 1982.

Hardesty, Nancy, Lucille Sider Dayton, and Donald W. Dayton, "Women in the Holiness Movement: Feminism in the Evangelical Tradition." In *Women of Spirit: Female Leadership in the Jewish and Christian Traditions*, ed. Rosemary Ruether and Eleanor McLaughlin. New York: Simon & Schuster, 1979.

Harding, Susan. "Convicted by the Holy Spirit: The Rhetoric of Fundamentalist Baptist Conversion." *American Ethnologist* 14, no. 1 (February 1987): 167–181.

———. "Family Reform Movements: Recent Feminism and Its Opposition." *Feminist Studies* 7, no. 1 (Spring 1981): 57–75.

———. "The Gospel of Giving: The Narrative Construction of a Sacrificial Economy." In *Vocabularies of Public Life: Empirical Essays in Symbolic Structure*, ed. Robert Wuthnow, 39–56. London: Routledge, 1992.

Harrell, David Edwin, Jr. *All Things Are Possible: The Healing and Charismatic Revivals in Modern America*. Bloomington: Indiana University Press, 1975.

———. *Oral Roberts: An American Life*. Bloomington: Indiana University Press, 1985.

Hartmann, Susan M. *The Home Front and Beyond: American Women in the 1940s*. Boston: Twayne Publishers, 1982.

Harvey, Brett. *The Fifties: A Women's Oral History*. New York: Harper Collins, 1993.

Hassey, Janette. *No Time for Silence: Evangelical Women in Public Ministry around the Turn of the Century*. Grand Rapids, MI: Academie Books, 1986.

Heiler, Friedrich. *Prayer: A Study in the History and Psychology of Religion*. Trans. Samuel McComb. New York: Oxford University Press, 1958.

Hennessy, Rosemary. *Materialist Feminism and the Politics of Discourse*. New York: Routledge, 1993.

Heriot, M. Jean. *Blessed Assurance: Beliefs, Actions, and the Experience of Salvation in a Carolina Baptist Church*. Knoxville: University of Tennessee Press, 1994.

Hervieu-Léger, Daniéle. "'What Scripture Tells Me': Spontaneity and Regulation within the Catholic Charismatic Renewal." In *Lived Religion in America: Toward a History of Practice*, ed. David D. Hall. Princeton, NJ: Princeton University Press, in press.

Hewitt, Nancy A. "The Perimeters of Women's Power in American Religion." In *The Evangelical Tradition in America*, ed. Leonard I. Sweet, 233–256. Macon, GA: Mercer University Press, 1984.

Hochschild, Arlie R. "Emotion Work, Feeling Rules, and Social Structure." *American Journal of Sociology* 85: 551–575.

Hoffman, Lawrence A. *Beyond the Text: A Holistic Approach to Liturgy*. Bloomington: Indiana University Press, 1987.

Hoffman, Leonore, and Margo Culley, eds. *Women's Personal Narratives: Essays in Criticism and Pedagogy*. New York: Modern Language Association of America, 1985.

Hoge, Dean R., Benton Johnson, and Donald A. Luidens. *Vanishing Boundaries: The Religion of Mainline Protestant Baby Boomers*. Louisville, KY: Westminster/John Knox Press, 1994.

Holifield, E. Brooks. *A History of Pastoral Care in America: From Salvation to Self-Realization*. Nashville, TN: Abingdon Press, 1983.

Hollenweger, Walter J. *The Pentecostals: The Charismatic Movement in the Churches*. Minneapolis: Augsburg Publishing House, 1972.

Homan, Roger. "Interpersonal Communication in Pentecostal Meetings." *Sociological Review* 26 (3): 499–518.

Hudnut-Beumler, James. *Looking for God in the Suburbs: The Religion of the American Dream and Its Critics, 1945–1965*. New Brunswick, NJ: Rutgers University Press, 1994.

Hunter, James Davison. *Culture Wars: The Struggle to Define America*. New York: Basic Books, 1991.

———. *Evangelicalism: The Coming Generation*. Chicago: University of Chicago Press, 1987.

Hutchison, William R., ed. *Between the Times: The Travail of the Protestant Establishment in America, 1900–1960*. Cambridge, UK: Cambridge University Press, 1989.

———. *The Modernist Impulse in American Protestantism*. Cambridge, MA: Harvard University Press, 1976.

Hymes, Dell. *Foundations in Sociolinguistics: An Ethnographic Approach.* Philadelphia: University of Pennsylvania Press, 1974.

Jack, Dana Crowley. *Silencing the Self: Women and Depression.* Cambridge, MA: Harvard University Press, 1991.

Jackson, Michael. *Paths toward a Clearing: Radical Empiricism and Ethnograpic Inquiry.* Bloomington: Indiana University Press, 1989.

Jameson, Fredric. *The Political Unconscious: Narrative as a Socially Symbolic Act.* Ithaca, NY: Cornell University Press, 1981.

Jelen, Ted G., ed. *Religion and Political Behavior in the United States.* New York: Praeger Publishers, 1989.

Johnson, Daymon A. "Reformed New-Traditionalists: Patriarchal Models of Womanhood and the Christian Right." *Fides et Historia* 25, no. 3 (Fall 1993): 77–101.

Johnson, Stephen D., and Joseph B. Tamney, eds. *The Political Role of Religion in the United States.* Boulder, CO: Westview Press, 1986.

Jones, Charles Edwin, *The Charismatic Movement: A Guide to the Study of Neo-Pentecostalism with Emphasis on Anglo-American Sources.* Metuchen, NJ: The American Theological Library Association and Scarecrow Press, 1995.

Kaledin, Eugenia. *Mothers and More: American Women in the 1950s.* Boston: Twayne Publishers, 1984.

Kaminer, Wendy. *I'm Dysfunctional, You're Dysfunctional: The Recovery Movement and Other Self-Help Fashions.* New York: Vintage Books, 1993.

Kaufman, Debra Renee. *Rachel's Daughters: Newly Orthodox Jewish Women.* New Brunswick, NJ: Rutgers University Press, 1991.

Kennedy, Paul W. "Socializing Secularization: A Sociological Analysis of the Vineyard Christian Fellowship." Ph.D. dissertation, University of Southern California, 1993.

Klatch, Rebecca E. "Coalition and Conflict among Women of the New Right." *Signs* 13, no. 4 (1988): 671–694.

———. *Women of the New Right.* Philadelphia: Temple University Press, 1987.

Komarovsky, Mirra. *Blue-Collar Marriage.* New Haven, CT: Yale University Press, 1987; first published by Random House in 1962.

Kondo, Dorinne K. *Crafting Selves: Power, Gender, and Discourses of Identity in a Japanese Workplace.* Chicago: University of Chicago Press, 1990.

Kurtz, Ernest. *Not-God: A History of Alcoholics Anonymous.* Center City, MN: Hazelden Educational Services, 1979.

Kwilecki, Susan. "Contemporary Pentecostal Clergywomen: Female Christian Leadership, Old Style." *Journal of Feminist Studies in Religion* 3 (Fall 1987): 57–75.

Land, Steven J. *Pentecostal Spirituality: A Passion for the Kingdom.* Sheffield, UK: Sheffield Academic Press, 1993.

Lasch, Christopher. *The Culture of Narcissism: American Life in an Age of Diminishing Expectations.* New York: Norton, 1978.

———. *The True and Only Heaven: Progress and its Critics.* New York: Norton, 1991.

Lawless, Elaine J. *God's Peculiar People: Women's Voices and Folk Tradition in a Pentecostal Church.* Lexington: University Press of Kentucky, 1988.
———. *Handmaidens of the Lord: Pentecostal Women Preachers and Traditional Religion.* Philadelphia: University of Pennsylvania Press, 1988.
———. "'I was afraid someone like you . . . an outsider . . . would misunderstand': Negotiating Interpretive Differences between Ethnographers and Subjects." *Journal of American Folklore* 105 (Summer 1992): 302–314.
———. "Rescripting Their Lives and Narratives: Spiritual Life Stories of Pentecostal Women Preachers." *Journal of Feminist Studies in Religion* 7, no. 1 (Spring 1991): 53–71.
———. "Shouting for the Lord: The Power of Women's Speech in the Pentecostal Religious Service." *Journal of American Folklore* 96 (1983): 434–459.
———. "Women's Life Stories and Reciprocal Ethnography as Feminist and Emergent." *Journal of Folklore Research* 28, no. 1 (1991): 35–60.
Lawson, Matthew P. "Free to Choose: Submission in the Lives of Catholic Charismatics." Princeton University Department of Sociology Working Paper III-94.
Lears, T. J. Jackson. "From Salvation to Self-Realization: Advertising and the Therapeutic Roots of the Consumer Culture, 1880–1930." In *The Culture of Consumption: Critical Essays in American History, 1880–1980,* ed. Richard Wightman Fox and T. J. Jackson Lears, 1–38. New York: Pantheon Books, 1983.
———. *No Place of Grace: Antimodernism and the Transformation of American Culture, 1880–1920.* New York: Pantheon Books, 1981.
Lerner, Harriet G. *The Dance of Deception: Pretending and Truth-Telling in Women's Lives.* New York: HarperCollins, 1993.
Liebman, Robert C., and Robert Wuthnow, eds. *The New Christian Right: Mobilization and Legitimation.* Hawthorne, NY: Aldine, 1983.
Lippy, Charles H. *Being Religious, American Style: A History of Popular Religiosity in the United States.* Westport, CT: Greenwood Press, 1994.
Luborsky, Mark R. "Analysis of Multiple Life History Narratives." *Ethos* 15, no. 4 (December 1987): 366–381.
Lundberg, Ferdinand, and Marynia F. Farnham, M.D. *Modern Woman: The Lost Sex.* New York: Grosset & Dunlap, 1947.
Luker, Kristin. *Abortion and the Politics of Motherhood.* Berkeley: University of California Press, 1984.
Lutz, Catherine. *Unnatural Emotions: Everyday Sentiments on a Micronesian Atoll and Their Challenge to Western Theory.* Chicago: University of Chicago Press, 1988.
Mack, Phyllis. *Visionary Women: Ecstatic Prophecy in Seventeenth-Century England.* Berkeley: University of California Press, 1992.
Maltz, Daniel N. "Joyful Noise and Reverent Silence: The Significance of Noise in Pentecostal Worship." In *Perspectives on Silence,* ed. Deborah Tannen and Muriel Saville-Troike, 113–137. Norwood, NJ: Ablex Publishing Corporation, 1985.

———. "The Bride of Christ Is Filled with His Spirit." In *Women in Ritual and Symbolic Roles*, ed. Judith Hoch-Smith and Anita Spring. New York: Plenum Press, 1978.

Mansbridge, Jane J. *Why We Lost the ERA*. Chicago: University of Chicago Press, 1986.

Marcus, George E., and Michael M. J. Fischer. *Anthropology as Cultural Critique: An Experimental Moment in the Human Sciences*. Chicago: University of Chicago Press, 1986.

Marsden, George M. "Preachers of Paradox: The Religious New Right in Historical Perspective." In *Religion and America: Spirituality in a Secular Age*, ed. Mary Douglas and Steven M. Tipton, 150–168. Boston: Beacon Press, 1983.

———. *Understanding Fundamentalism and Evangelicalism*. Grand Rapids, MI: William B. Eerdmans Publishing Company, 1991.

Martin, David. "The Political Oeconomy of the Holy Ghost." In *Strange Gifts: A Guide to Charismatic Renewal*, ed. David Martin and Peter Mullen, 54–71. Oxford: Basil Blackwell, 1984.

Mason, Karen Oppenheim, and Yu-Hsia Lu. "Attitudes toward Women's Familial Roles: Changes in the United States, 1977–1985." *Gender & Society* 2, no. 1 (March 1988), 39–57.

Mathews, Donald G., and Jane Sherron DeHart. *Sex, Gender, and the Politics of ERA: A State and the Nation*. New York: Oxford University Press, 1990.

Matthews, Glenna. *"Just a Housewife": The Rise and Fall of Domesticity in America*. New York: Oxford University Press, 1987.

May, Elaine Tyler. *Great Expectations: Marriage and Divorce in Post-Victorian America*. Chicago: University of Chicago Press, 1980.

———. *Homeward Bound: American Families in the Cold War Era*. New York: Basic Books, 1988.

McCord, Julia. "Fellowship Burns Bright: An Overview." *Omaha World Herald*, 13 May 1995.

McDannell, Colleen. *The Christian Home in Victorian America, 1840–1900*. Bloomington: Indiana University Press, 1986.

———. *Material Christianity: Religion and Popular Culture in America*. New Haven, CT: Yale University Press, 1995.

McGuire, Meredith B. "Gendered Spirituality and Quasi-Religious Ritual." In *Between Sacred and Secular: Research and Theory on Quasi-Religion*, 273–287. Religion and the Social Order series vol. 4, ed. Arthur L. Greil and Thomas Robbins. Greenwich, CT: JAI Press, 1994.

———. *Pentecostal Catholics: Power, Charisma and Order in a Religious Movement*. Philadelphia: Temple University Press, 1982.

———. "Religion and the Body: Rematerializing the Human Body in the Social Sciences of Religion." *Journal for the Scientific Study of Religion* 29 (1990): 283–296.

———. "Ritual, Symbolism, and Healing." *Social Compass* 34, no. 4 (1987), 365–379.

McGuire, Meredith B., with the assistance of Debra Kantor. *Ritual Healing in Suburban America*. New Brunswick, NJ: Rutgers University Press, 1988.

McNamara, Patrick H. "The New Christian Right's View of the Family and Its Social Science Critics: A Study in Differing Presuppositions." *Journal of Marriage and the Family* (May 1985), 449–458.

Meyer, Donald. *The Positive Thinkers: Religion as Pop Psychology from Mary Baker Eddy to Oral Roberts*. Rev. ed. New York: Pantheon Books, 1980.

Miller, Peggy J., et al. "Narrative Practices and the Social Construction of Self in Childhood." *American Ethnologist* 17, no. 1 (May 1990), 292–311.

Mills, Watson E. *Charismatic Religion in Modern Research: A Bibliography*. Macon, GA: Mercer University Press, 1985.

Mintz, Steven, and Susan Kellogg. *Domestic Revolutions: A Social History of American Family Life*. New York: The Free Press, 1988.

Moore, R. Laurence. *Selling God: American Religion in the Marketplace of Culture*. New York: Oxford University Press, 1994.

Moriarty, Michael G. *The New Charismatics: A Concerned Voice Responds to Dangerous New Trends*. Grand Rapids, MI: Zondervan Publishing House, 1992.

Morton, Nelle. *The Journey Is Home*. Boston: Beacon Press, 1985.

Myerhoff, Barbara. *Number Our Days*. New York: E. P. Dutton, 1978.

Nietz, Mary Jo. *Charisma and Community: A Study of Religious Commitment within the Charismatic Renewal*. New Brunswick,NJ: Transaction Books, 1987.

O'Connor, Edward D., C.S.C. *The Pentecostal Movement in the Catholic Church*. Notre Dame, IN: Ave Maria Press, 1971.

O'Neill, William. *Everyone Was Brave: A History of Feminism in America*. Chicago: Quadrangle, 1969.

Ong, Walter J. *Orality and Literacy: The Technologizing of the Word*. London: Routledge, 1991.

Orsi, Robert A. "'Have You Ever Prayed to St. Jude?': Reflections on Fieldwork in Catholic Chicago." In *Reimagining Denominationalism: Interpretive Essays*, ed. Robert Bruce Mullin and Russell E. Richey, 134–161. New York: Oxford University Press, 1994.

———. "'He Keeps Me Going': Women's Devotion to Saint Jude Thaddeus and the Dialectics of Gender in American Catholicism, 1929–1965." In *Belief in History: Innovative Approaches to European and American Religion*, ed. Thomas Kselman, 137–169. Notre Dame, IN: University of Notre Dame Press, 1991.

———. *The Madonna of 115th Street: Faith and Community in Italian Harlem, 1880–1950*. New Haven, CT: Yale University Press, 1985.

———. *Thank You, St. Jude: Women's Devotion to the Patron Saint of Hopeless Causes*. New Haven, CT: Yale University Press, 1996.

Ortner, Sherry B. *Making Gender: The Politics and Erotics of Culture*. Boston: Beacon Press, 1996.

———. "Theory in Anthropology since the Sixties." *Comparative Studies in Society and History* 26, no. 1 (January 1984): 126–166.

Paris, Arthur E. *Black Pentecostalism: Southern Religion in an Urban World.* Amherst: University of Massachusetts Press, 1982.

Pohli, Carol Virginia. "Church Closets and Back Doors: A Feminist View of Moral Majority Women." *Feminist Studies* 9, no. 3 (Fall 1983): 529–558.

Poloma, Margaret. *The Charismatic Movement: Is There a New Pentecost?* Boston: Twayne, 1982.

Poloma, Margaret M., and George H. Gallup, Jr. *Varieties of Prayer: A Survey Report.* Philadelphia: Trinity Press International, 1991.

Poloma, Margaret M., and Brian F. Pendleton. "The Effects of Prayer and Prayer Experiences on Measures of General Well-Being." *Journal of Psychology and Theology* 19, no. 1 (1991), 71–83.

———. "Exploring Types of Prayer and Quality of Life: A Research Note." *Review of Religious Research* 31, no. 1 (September 1989): 46–53.

Porterfield, Amanda. *Feminine Spirituality in America: From Sarah Edwards to Martha Graham.* Philadelphia: Temple University Press, 1980.

Prell, Riv-Ellen. *Prayer and Community: The Havurah in American Judaism.* Detroit: Wayne State University Press, 1989.

Quebedeaux, Richard. *The New Charismatics II: How a Christian Renewal Movement Became Part of the American Religious Mainstream.* Rev. ed. San Francisco: Harper & Row, 1983.

———. *The Worldly Evangelicals.* San Francisco: Harper & Row, 1978.

Rabinow, Paul. *Reflections on Fieldwork in Morocco.* Berkeley: University of California Press, 1977.

Rabinow, Paul, and William M. Sullivan, eds. *Interpretive Social Science: A Reader.* Berkeley: University of California Press, 1979.

Radner, Joan Newlon, ed. *Feminist Messages: Coding in Women's Folk Culture.* Urbana: University of Illinois Press, 1993.

Radway, Janice A. *Reading the Romance: Women, Patriarchy, and Popular Literature.* Chapel Hill: University of North Carolina Press, 1991 [1984].

Rieff, Philip. *The Triumph of the Therapeutic: Uses of Faith after Freud.* New York: Harper & Row, 1966.

Robbins, Thomas. "Cults, Converts and Charisma: The Sociology of New Religious Movements." *Current Sociology* 36, no. 1 (Spring 1988): 1–248.

Roebuck, David G. "Pentecostal Women in Ministry: A Review of Selected Documents." *Perspectives in Religious Studies* 16, no. 1 (Spring 1989): 29–44.

Rogers, Susan Carol. "Female Forms of Power and the Myth of Male Dominance: A Model of Female/Male Interaction in Peasant Society." *American Ethnologist* 2, no. 4 (November 1975): 727–756.

Rondeau, Jennifer Fisk. "Prayer and Gender in the *Laude* of Early Italian Confraternities." In *Gender Rhetorics: Postures of Dominance and Submission in History*, ed. Richard C. Trexler, 219–233. Binghamton, NY: State University of New York at Binghamton, 1994.

Roof, Wade Clark, and William McKinney. *American Mainline Religion: Its Changing Shape and Future.* New Brunswick, NJ: Rutgers University Press, 1987.

Rosaldo, Michelle Zimbalist, and Louise Lamphere, eds. *Woman, Culture, and Society*. Stanford, CA: Stanford University Press, 1974.

Rosaldo, Renato. *Culture and Truth: The Remaking of Social Analysis*. Boston: Beacon Press, 1993.

Rose, Susan D. "Women Warriors: The Negotiation of Gender in a Charismatic Community." *Sociological Analysis* 48, no. 3 (1987): 245–258.

Rosenberg, Rosalind. *Beyond Separate Spheres: Intellectual Roots of Modern Feminism*. New Haven, CT: Yale University Press, 1982.

Rothman, Sheila M. *Woman's Proper Place: A History of Changing Ideals and Practices, 1870 to the Present*. New York: Basic Books, 1978.

Rubin, Lillian Breslow. *Worlds of Pain: Life in the Working-Class Family*. New York: Basic Books, 1976.

Ruether, Rosemary Radford, and Rosemary Skinner Keller, eds. *In Our Own Voices: Four Centuries of American Women's Religious Writing*. San Francisco: Harper San Francisco, 1995.

———. *Women and Religion in America*. Three volumes. San Francisco: Harper & Row, 1981–1986.

Ruether, Rosemary, and Eleanor McLaughlin, eds. *Women of Spirit: Female Leadership in the Jewish and Christian Traditions*. New York: Simon and Schuster, 1979.

Rupp, Leila J., and Verta Taylor. *Survival in the Doldrums: The American Women's Rights Movement, 1945 to the 1960s*. New York: Oxford University Press, 1987.

Ryan, Mary P. "The Power of Women's Networks: A Case Study of Female Moral Reform in Antebellum America." *Feminist Studies* 5 (Spring 1979): 66–85.

———. *Womanhood in America: From Colonial Times to the Present*. 2nd ed. New York: New Viewpoints, 1979.

Samarin, William J. *Field Linguistics: A Guide to Field Work*. New York: Holt, Rinehart and Winston, 1967.

Saville-Troike, Muriel. *The Ethnography of Communication: An Introduction*. Baltimore, MD: University Park Press, 1982.

Scanzoni, Letha Dawson, and Susan Setta. "Women in Evangelical, Holiness, and Pentecostal Traditions." In *Women and Religion in America*, vol. 3, ed. Rosemary Radford Ruether and Rosemary Skinner Keller, 223–265. San Francisco: Harper & Row, 1986.

Schechner, Richard. *Between Theater and Anthropology*. Philadelphia: University of Pennsylvania Press, 1985.

Schmidt, Leigh Eric. *Consumer Rites: The Buying and Selling of American Holidays*. Princeton, NJ: Princeton University Press, 1995.

Schneider, Louis, and Sanford M. Dornbusch. *Popular Religion: Inspirational Books in America*. Chicago: University of Chicago Press, 1958.

Scott, Anne Firor. *Natural Allies: Women's Associations in American History*. Urbana: University of Illinois Press, 1991.

Scott, James C. *Weapons of the Weak: Everyday Forms of Peasant Resistance*. New Haven, CT: Yale University Press, 1985.

Scott, Joan W. "Experience." In *Feminists Theorize the Political*, ed. Judith Butler and Joan W. Scott, 22–40. New York: Routledge, 1992.

———. *Gender and the Politics of History*. New York: Columbia University Press, 1988.

Setta, Susan M. "Healing in Suburbia: The Women's Aglow Fellowship." *Journal of Religious Studies* 12, no. 2 (1986): 46–56.

Sheppard, Gerald T. "'Enemies' and the Politics of Prayer in the Book of Psalms." In *The Bible and the Politics of Exegesis: Essays in Honor of Norman K. Gottwald on His Sixty-Fifth Birthday*, ed. David Jobling, Peggy L. Day, and Gerald T. Sheppard. Cleveland: Pilgrim Press, 1991.

Shriver, Peggy L. *The Bible Vote: Religion and the New Right*. New York: Pilgrim Press, 1981.

Shuman, Amy. *Storytelling Rights: The Uses of Oral and Written Texts by Urban Adolescents*. Cambridge, UK: Cambridge University Press, 1986.

Shweder, Richard A., and Robert A. Levine, eds. *Culture Theory: Essays on Mind, Self, and Emotion*. Cambridge, UK: Cambridge University Press, 1984.

Silk, Mark. *Spiritual Politics: Religion and America since World War II*. New York: Simon and Schuster, 1988.

Simonds, Wendy. *Women and Self-Help Culture: Reading between the Lines*. New Brunswick, NJ: Rutgers University Press, 1992.

Smith, Jonathan Z. *To Take Place: Toward Theory in Ritual*. Chicago: University of Chicago Press, 1987.

Smith-Rosenberg, Carroll. "The Female World of Love and Ritual: Relations between Women in Nineteenth-Century America." In *Disorderly Conduct: Visions of Gender in Victorian America*, 53–76. New York: Oxford University Press, 1985.

———. "Women and Religious Revivals: Anti-Ritualism, Liminality, and the Emergence of the American Bourgeoisie." In *The Evangelical Tradition in America*, ed. Leonard I. Sweet, 199–231. Macon, GA: Mercer University Press, 1984.

Snowball, David. *Continuity and Change in the Rhetoric of the Moral Majority*. New York: Praeger Publishers, 1991.

Spence, Donald P. *Narrative Truth and Historical Truth: Meaning and Interpretation in Psychoanalysis*. New York: W.W. Norton & Co., 1982.

Spittler, Russell P. "Are Pentecostals and Charismatics Fundamentalists?: A Review of American Uses of These Categories." In *Charismatic Christianity as a Global Culture*, ed. Karla Poewe, 103–116. Columbia: University of South Carolina Press, 1994.

Stacey, Judith. *Brave New Families: Stories of Domestic Upheaval in Late Twentieth Century America*. New York: Basic Books, 1991.

———. "Can There Be a Feminist Ethnography?" *Women's Studies International Forum* 11, no. 1 (1988): 21–27.

Stacey, Judith, and Susan Elizabeth Gerard. "'We Are Not Doormats': The Influence of Feminism on Contemporary Evangelicals in the United States." In *Uncertain Terms: Negotiating Gender in American Culture*, ed. Faye

Ginsburg and Anna Lowenhaupt Tsing, 98–117. Boston: Beacon Press, 1990.

Strozier, Charles B. *Apocalypse: On the Psychology of Fundamentalism in America*. Boston: Beacon Press, 1994.

Sullivan, Lawrence E. "Body Works: Knowledge of the Body in the Study of Religion." *History of Religions* 30, no. 1 (August 1990): 86–99.

———. "Sound and Senses: Toward a Hermeneutics of Performance." *History of Religions* 26, no. 1 (August 1986): 1–33.

Susman, Warren I. *Culture as History: The Transformation of American Society in the Twentieth Century*. New York: Pantheon, 1984.

Synan, Vinson. *The Twentieth-Century Pentecostal Explosion*. Altamonte Springs, FL: Creation House, 1987.

———. *Under His Banner: History of Full Gospel Business Men's Fellowship International*. Costa Mesa, CA: Gift Publications, 1992.

Tambiah, Stanley Jeyaraja. "A Performative Approach to Ritual." In *Culture, Thought, and Social Action: An Anthropological Perspective*, 123–168. Cambridge, MA: Harvard University Press, 1985.

Tamney, Joseph, and Stephen Johnson. "The Moral Majority in Middletown." *Journal for the Scientific Study of Religion* 22 (June 1983): 145–157.

Tannen, Deborah. "The Oral/Literate Continuum in Discourse." In *Spoken and Written Language: Exploring Orality and Literacy*, ed. Deborah Tannen. Norwood, NJ: Ablex, 1982.

Taves, Ann, ed. *Religion and Domestic Violence in Early New England: The Memoirs of Abigail Abbot Bailey*. Bloomington: Indiana University Press, 1989.

Tipton, Steven M. *Getting Saved from the Sixties: Moral Meaning in Conversion and Cultural Change*. Berkeley: University of California Press, 1982.

Titon, Jeff Todd. "The Life Story." *American Folklore* 93 (1980): 276–292.

———. *Powerhouse for God: Speech, Chant, and Song in an Appalachian Baptist Church*. Austin: University of Texas Press, 1988.

Turner, Victor. *From Ritual to Theatre: The Human Seriousness of Play*. New York: Performing Arts Journal Publications, 1982.

———. *The Ritual Process: Structure and Anti-Structure*. Chicago: Aldine, 1969; reprinted by Cornell University Press, 1977.

Tyson, Ruel W. "Culture's 'Hum and Buzz' of Implication: The Practice of Ethnography and the Provocations of Clifford Geertz's 'Thick Description'." *Soundings* 71 (Spring 1988): 95–111.

Tyson, Ruel W., James L. Peacock, and Daniel W. Patterson, eds. *Diversities of Gifts: Field Studies in Southern Religion*. Urbana: University of Illinois Press, 1988.

Visweswaran, Kamala. *Fictions of Feminist Ethnography*. Minneapolis: University of Minnesota Press, 1994.

Wacker, Grant. "The Functions of Faith in Primitive Pentecostalism." *Harvard Theological Review* 77 nos. 3/4 (July–October 1984): 353–375.

———. "The Holy Spirit and the Spirit of the Age in American Protestantism, 1880–1910." *Journal of American History* 72, no. 1 (June 1985): 45–62.

Warner, R. Stephen. *New Wine in Old Wineskins: Evangelicals and Liberals in a Small-Town Church*. Berkeley: University of California Press, 1988.

Watt, David Harrington. "The Private Hopes of American Fundamentalists and Evangelicals, 1925–1975." *Religion and American Culture* 1, no. 2 (Summer 1991): 155–175.

———. *A Transforming Faith: Explorations of Twentieth-Century American Evangelicalism*. New Brunswick, NJ: Rutgers University Press, 1991.

Weaver, C. Douglas. *The Healer-Prophet, William Marrion Branham: A Study of the Prophetic in American Pentecostalism*. Macon, GA: Mercer University Press, 1987.

Wessinger, Catherine, ed. *Women's Leadership in Marginal Religions: Explorations Outside the Mainstream*. Urbana: University of Illinois Press, 1993.

Wilcox, Clyde. *God's Warriors: The Christian Right in Twentieth-Century America*. Baltimore, MD: Johns Hopkins University Press, 1992.

———. "Religious Attitudes and Anti-Feminism: An Analysis of the Ohio Moral Majority." *Women and Politics* 7, no. 2 (Summer 1987): 59–77.

Wilcox, Clyde, and Elizabeth Adell Cook. "Evangelical Women and Feminism: Some Additional Evidence." *Women and Politics* 9, no. 2 (1989): 27–49.

Williams, Melvin D. *Community in a Black Pentecostal Church: An Anthropological Study*. Pittsburgh, PA: University of Pittsburgh Press, 1974.

Wilson, Sandra D. "Evangelical Christian Adult Children of Alcoholics: A Preliminary Study." *Journal of Psychology and Theology* 17, no. 3 (Fall 1989): 263–273.

Winter, Miriam Therese, Adair Lummis, and Allison Stokes. *Defecting in Place: Women Claiming Responsibility for Their Own Spiritual Lives*. New York: Crossroad, 1994.

Witten, Marsha G. *All Is Forgiven: The Secular Message in American Protestantism*. Princeton, NJ: Princeton University Press, 1993.

———. "The Restriction of Meaning in Religious Discourse: Centripetal Devices in a Fundamentalist Christian Sermon." In *Vocabularies of Public Life: Empirical Essays in Symbolic Structure*, ed. Robert Wuthnow, 19–38. London: Routledge, 1992.

Wolf, Margery. *A Thrice-Told Tale: Feminism, Postmodernism, and Ethnographic Responsibility*. Stanford, CA: Stanford University Press, 1992.

Woolverton, John F. "Evangelical Protestantism and Alcoholism 1933–1962: Episcopalian Samuel Shoemaker, the Oxford Group and Alcoholics Anonymous." *Historical Magazine of the Protestant Episcopal Church* 52:1 (March 1983): 53–65.

Wuthnow, Robert, ed. *"I Come Away Stronger": How Small Groups Are Shaping American Religion*. Grand Rapids, MI: William B. Eerdmans Publishing Co., 1994.

———. *Producing the Sacred: An Essay on Public Religion*. Urbana: University of Illinois Press, 1994.

———. *The Restructuring of American Religion*. Princeton, NJ: Princeton University Press, 1988.

————. *Sharing the Journey: Support Groups and America's New Quest for Community.* New York: The Free Press, 1994.

Yanagisako, Sylvia, and Carol Delaney, eds. *Naturalizing Power: Essays in Feminist Cultural Analysis.* New York: Routledge, 1995.

Yocum, Margaret R. "Woman to Woman: Fieldwork in the Private Sphere." In *Women's Folklore, Women's Culture,* ed. Rosan A. Jordan and Susan J. Kalčik. Philadelphia: University of Pennsylvania Press, 45–53.

Index

abortion, 33, 64, 195

Abu-Lughod, Lila, 216n. 7

abuse, 25, 38, 56, 113, 172, 187, 189, 198; of children, 7, 96, 115, 116, 118, 119, 187, 188, 198; of doctrine of wifely submission, 185; from fathers, 129; from husbands, 97, 116, 172; of male power, 5; overeating as a symptom of, 146; sexual, 4, 95, 97, 113–115, 159, 200; see also rape; incest

Adult Children of Alcoholics, 34

advisors to Aglow, 14, 49, 50, 151–156; *see also* men

African-American women, 3, 52, 53, 205

Aglow: budget, 166; Capital Campaign, 165; history, 12, 46–54; members, denominational preferences of, 59; support groups, 39

Aglow (magazine), history of, 47–49, 50–51

AIDS, 7, 64, 88

Al-Anon, 34

Alcoholics Anonymous (AA), 33, 34, 38, 142

alcoholism, 26, 113, 187; vs. compulsive overeating, 146

Allen, Asa, 29

"Alone in the Pew," 24–25, 60

American evangelicalism, 5, 16, 21, 64, 65, 156, 200

anger, 25, 26, 56, 57, 92, 95–97, 98, 99, 113, 114, 117, 119, 120, 122, 157, 160, 171, 178, 189; ambivalence toward, 97; hidden, 111, 117–118, 121; healing from, 96, 99–100, 111, 190; resulting from low self-esteem, 96; as a sickness, 96; as a sin, 95–96

anorexia, 119, 150

antifeminism, 12, 40, 201, 207, 208, 209

apocalypticism, 32

Bakker, Tammy Faye, 157

Balmer, Randall, 21, 65

baptism in the Holy Spirit, 9, 28, 31, 47, 61, 72, 81, 102, 114, 121, 140, 173

Beard, George, 39

beauty, 42, 92, 141, 142, 145, 147, 149, 150; conflicted notions over, 105; as an emblem of transformation, 104–105

Bell, Catherine, 231–232n. 40

Bendroth, Margaret Lamberts, 197, 242n. 12

Bennett, Dennis, 31, 58, 151, 153

Bennett, Rita, 46, 239n. 30

Berry, Wendell, 211

Bible, 31, 35, 37, 39, 44, 51, 63, 66, 72, 93, 95, 104, 115, 130, 135, 148, 153, 162, 164, 170; as a means of seeking intimacy with God, 135

Billion Souls Crusade, 29

Blumhofer, Edith, 29

Bourdieu, Pierre, 13

Branham, William, 29

Brint, Michael, 248n. 22

Brown, Karen McCarthy, 8

Brusco, Elizabeth, 14

Bryant, Anita, 44, 45, 157

Bynum, Caroline Walker, 14

Compositor:	Publication Services
Text:	Sabon
Display:	Bernhard Modern
Printer:	Malloy Lithographing, Inc.
Binder:	Malloy Lithographing, Inc.